DISCOURSE AND PRACTICE

SUNY Series, Toward a Comparative Philosophy of Religions
Frank Reynolds and David Tracy, editors

DISCOURSE AND PRACTICE

Frank Reynolds
and
David Tracy, Editors

State University of New York Press

Published by
State University of New York Press, Albany

For information, address State University of New York Press,
State University Plaza, Albany, N.Y. 12246

Production by Marilyn P. Semerad
Marketing by Dana E. Yanulavich

Library of Congress Cataloging-in-Publication Data

Discourse and practice / edited by Frank Reynolds and David Tracy.
    p.   cm. — (SUNY series, toward a comparative philosophy of
religions)
    Includes bibliographical references and index.
    Contents: Wisdom in practice / Fitz John Porter Poole —
Samantabhadra and Rudra / Matthew Kapstein — Buddhist philosophy in the art of
fiction / Francisca Cho Bantly — On demythologizing evil/ Philip Quinn
— The myth of original equality / Robin Lovin — Philosophy as metapraxis
/ Thomas Kasulis — Xunzi and Durkheim as theorists of ritual practice /
Robert F. Campany — Embodying philosophy / Judith Berling — The
drama of interpretation and the philosophy of religions / William Schweiker
— Reconciliation and rupture / Richard Bernstein.
    ISBN 0-7914-1023-4. — ISBN 0-7914-1024-2 (pbk.)

    1. Religion—Philosophy.   2. Philosophy and religion. 3. Myth.
I. Reynolds, Frank, 1930– . II. Tracy, David. III. Series.
BL51.D54 1992
291'.01—dc20   91-18680
                                                                     CIP

10 9 8 7 6 5 4 3 2 1

CONTENTS

SECTION IV
Concluding Comparative Reflections

Introduction

Frank Reynolds

During the past five years the University of Chicago Divinity School has sponsored a series of seven conferences devoted to the philosophy of religions. These conferences have helped to constitute an interpretive community that is committed to the task of discovering and nurturing ways of doing the philosophy of religions that take account of new developments in the field of philosophy and in relevant comparatively oriented disciplines, such as the history and the anthropology of religions. The *Toward a Comparative Philosophy of Religions* Series provides one of the primary mechanisms through which the issues and insights that this community is generating are being brought into the public arena for discussions and critique.[1]

Our series was initiated through the publication of a volume of essays dealing with *Myth and Philosophy*.[2] This topic was chosen because David Tracy and I (the codirectors of the project) were convinced that one of the most important tasks that confronts any contemporary effort to develop a philosophy of religions that is truly comparative is to deconstruct the received stereotypes of myth and philosophy being two mutually exclusive and hierarchically ordered modes of human expression. We were also convinced that it is necessary to begin the process of reconstructing a notion of philosophy that encompasses elements that we have come to classify as mythic, as well as a notion of myth that encompasses elements that we have come to identify as philosophic. In the discussions that ensued, and in the volume of essays that emerged, we were able to explore some of the descriptive and normative possibilities which are available to philosophically oriented scholars who share the conviction that it is essential to take the philosophies of "others" seriously into account.

1

The discussions that led to the production of the *Myth and Philosophy* volume also led to the recognition that there is another kind of hierarchically ordered binary opposition in the received tradition of Western scholarship that needs to be challenged and rethought in order to make way for the new kind of comparative philosophy of religions we are seeking. This is the polarity that is presumed, often implicitly, between discourse (which includes myth and philosophy in their various modalities and combinations), on the one hand, and practice, on the other.

As in the case of our discussions of myth and philosophy, so too in our discussions of discourse and practice, the commonly affirmed recognition that a challenge to reigning assumptions is needed has not led to a consensus concerning an appropriate alternative. However, this discussion has, as in the myth and philosophy case, led to a number of creative proposals. These include fascinating analyses of particular ways in which discourse and practice can be distinguished and related in the interpretation of specific historical phenomena. These proposals also include intriguing suggestions regarding ways in which the two have been (and could be) distinguished and related by those who seek to articulate and promote normative religious positions.

The discussion out of which this volume has arisen have also generated a terminology that has facilitated the exploration of key issues. Though there has been no absolute consensus among the participants—or even, for that matter, among the authors who have contributed to the present volume—a reasonably high level of terminological consistency has been achieved. For example, an original lack of clarity in differentiating between "practice" and "praxis" has been largely resolved. Generally speaking, "practice" has come to serve as the more encompassing term, whereas "praxis" has been limited to contexts in which an emphasis is being placed on the way(s) in which a religious orientation is effectively embedded in a some form of practical activity. This kind of usage accounts for the decision to use the term "practice" in the title of the volume, and for the tendency to move, in several of the chapters, toward a rhetoric of "praxis."[3]

The exploration of key issues was also greatly advanced by the use of the term "metapractice" or "metapraxis." A fuller explication of this important notion is spelled out later in this volume by the participant who introduced it (see Thomas Kasulis's chapter on "Philosophy as Metapraxis"). However, it is important to note at the outset that "metapraxis" has emerged as a pervasive notion that informs many of the other chapters as well. Whenever the term "metapraxis" is used, it identifies and characterizes a mode of reflexivity and reflection that serves to legitimate, to integrate, to explain, or to analyze a pattern or patterns of religious practice.

Taking this terminology into account, it is possible to formulate a unifying "thesis" that pervades the present volume. Stated briefly, it is the notion that any truly adequate comparative philosophy of religions must include a continuing effort to understand philosophical and religious practices (including, but not limited to, discursive practices), to understand the implicit metapractical orientations that are embedded in seemingly nonphilosophical types of religious discourse, and to understand the explicit metapractical theories that come to the fore in more explicitly philosophical contexts.

One aspect of this basic contention is that any truly adequate comparative philosophy of religions must maintain a concerted effort to interpret the practices and the metapractical reflections of a wide variety of religious communities and individuals—ancient and modern, Western and Eastern, and so on. Another equally important aspect of this contention is that the effort must include, both as a necessary prerequisite and as a goal to be fostered, a serious and critical reflection on the practices and correlated metapractical discourses in which we ourselves are engaged.

With this unifying "thesis" in mind, the group of ten chapters that are included in our present volume have been divided into four sections.[4] The first section is entitled "Philosophy in Narrative and Practice" because it contains chapters that focus on narratives and practices which many Western interpreters would not immediately recognize as philosophical. However, in each of the three chapters, the author shows that the narratives and/or practices under investigation do, in fact, have implicitly embedded in them, elements of reflexivity and sophisticated articulation that are clearly philosophical in character.

Fitz John Porter Poole initiates the discussion with a fascinating chapter on "Wisdom and Practice: The Mythic Making of Sacred History among the Bimin-Kuskusmin in Papua New Guinea." Challenging the notion that the practice of philosophy is limited to highly literate civilizations, Poole spins out a multifaceted description of an indigenous wisdom tradition among a contemporary tribal people who live in a very mountainous and relatively isolated area. Drawing on several years of on-site field work, Poole vividly portrays the way in which this highly sophisticated Bimin-Kuskusmin tradition was formulated in a complex and malleable mythology and the way it was embedded in very rich and flexible patterns of ritual practice. He then describes the process through which the philosophically oriented elders who transmit this tradition utilized and extended their notions of wisdom, their mythology, and their ritual practices in order to encompass and interpret the traumatic events that marked the penetration of Western intruders into their homeland.[5]

The second essay, written by Matthew Kapstein, is entitled "Samantabhadra and Rudra: Innate Enlightenment and Radical Evil in Tibetan Rnying-ma-pa Thought." Kapstein introduces his study with an extended reflection on the necessity of correlating myth and philosophy, both in our investigations of "others" and in our own Western context. This introduction is followed by an exploration of various ways in which the two complementary Tibetan myths of Samantabhadra and Rudra convey profound philosophical messages concerning "eternity and temporality, enlightenment and bewilderment, understanding and the rebellion of the will" and how, in so doing, they present the contours of a religious world within which Tantric Buddhist practice is both necessary and possible.

Francisca Cho Bantly completes the section with a fascinating discussion on "Buddhist Philosophy and the Art of Fiction."[6] Bantly sets the stage for her own interpretive project by directly challenging Paul Griffiths's identification of philosophy with what he calls "denaturalized discourse" (see Chapter 3 in *Myth and Philosophy*). She argues that while highly abstract "denaturalized discourse" is, in fact, an appropriate philosophical mode, there are certain religious ontologies that are most effectively expressed in other quite different discursive styles. In order to validate her position, she then turns her attention to a Buddhist form of East Asian religious literature. Using a late seventeenth-century Korean novel as her primary text, she shows how its author brilliantly embodies the basic Mahayana Buddhist philosophical teachings concerning illusion and reality in a highly sophisticated fictional narrative. In the process, she demonstrates how this fictional account is constructed in order to engage the audience in a reading process that is, like the writing itself, an efficacious form of Buddhist praxis.[7]

The second set of chapters is entitled "Myth and Practice in Philosophy." This title was chosen because the essays that are included in the section deal with subjects that, unlike those discussed in Section I, are easily recognized as philosophical. Here, the authors are not concerned to identify implicit philosophical dimensions in traditions and texts that seem at first glance to present themselves as mythic, fictional, or practice-oriented. Quite the contrary, the authors of the chapters in this section are concerned about identifying implicit mythic and practice-oriented dimensions in traditions and texts whose philosophical character is self-evident.

The first of the two contributions that are included is Philip Quinn's essay "On Demythologizing Evil." In this discussion, Quinn spells out the way in which the classical Western philosophical analyses of the problem of evil that were generated during the Middle Ages are grounded in the biblical myth of the sin of Adam and how they are more immediately dependent on the exegetical interpretation of that myth as set forth in the letters of Saint Paul. He then goes on to describe the process of "demythologization" that has occurred during the modern period and to point out some fundamental problems that the loss of a mythic dimension in the notion of evil has created for contemporary philosophers concerned with the formulation and legitimation of social and individual ethics. Quinn concludes his thoughts with some suggestive reflections concerning ways in which these contemporary issues might be creatively addressed.

Robin Lovin, in an essay entitled "The Myth of Original Equality," focuses on a crucial aspect of the political philosophies associated with modern liberalism in the West. This myth of original equality, he contends, is basic to the philosophical positions developed by a series of thinkers that began with Thomas Hobbes in the sixteenth century and continues today, most notably in the person of John Rawls. Lovin's basic historical contention is that, although this myth of original equality has been presented and interpreted by liberal philosophers in ways that have promoted more democratic and egalitarian forms of political and social practice, it has also contributed to the legitimation of various unjust forms of hierarchy and repression. At the normative level, Lovin's basic argument is that if the myth of original equality is to continue to provide an effective support for the achievement of a more democratic, egalitarian political and social practice, postliberal philosophers must creatively coordinate it with a historically relevant myth of final equality as well.[8]

The third set of chapters is entitled "Metapractical Discourse: Comparative Studies." Unlike the preceding essays, the three papers included in this section explore aspects of particular traditions and texts that are obviously metapractical in character. These papers also differ from those that have gone before by virtue of the fact that they are centrally concerned with the comparison of materials drawn from at least two quite different traditions.

Thomas Kasulis takes the lead with an essay that presents a strong case for recognizing the existence and importance of "Philosophy as Metapraxis." Kasulis initiates his discussion with an account of the differing interpretations of a very problematic passage from the Gospel of John in the Eastern and Western Churches. Using these interpretations as a starting point, he argues that Christian philosophers and theologians in the East have tended to highlight the centrality of praxis and metapraxis, while those in the West have tended to give a privileged position to epistemology and metaphysics. In the main body of his article Kasulis presents the work of the Japanese Buddhist philosopher Kukai (early ninth century C.E.) as a classic example of a philosopher who—in contrast to most Western philosophers and theologians—seriously engages in metapractical discourse.[9] In his more normatively oriented conclusion, Kasulis argues that any fully adequate religious philosophy or theology (whether it be Eastern or Western, Buddhist or Christian) must include metapractical claims that mesh with correlated forms of religious praxis, on the one hand, and with correlated metaphysical affirmations, on the other.

Robert F. Campany takes a rather different tack in his paper on "Xunzi and Durkheim as Theorists of Ritual Practice." Like several other contributors to the volume, Campany is particularly concerned to highlight the correlation between the interpretations generated by those "others" who often constitute the subjects of our study and by the interpretive efforts mounted by modern philosophers and academics. In his analysis, Campany convincingly demonstrates the high level of sophistication that characterizes the very different metapractical theories developed by the third century B.C.E. Chinese philosopher on the one hand, and the renowned twentieth-century social scientist on the other. He then goes on to identify specific philosophical and interpretive insights that can be generated by recognizing the very great differences in context, and then—with these differences clearly in mind—taking the contributions of both thinkers seriously into account.[10]

Judith Berling brings this section to a close with a contribution entitled "Embodying Philosophy: Some Preliminary Reflections from a Chinese Perspective." Berling, like Campany, draws explicit comparisons between perspectives that have developed in the modern academy and perspectives that she has encountered in her study of Chinese philosophy. She initiates her discussion by taking note of recent developments in contemporary academic research in philosophy, the history of religions, and the social sciences—research that reflects a new concern with the fact that ways of thinking, including religious ways of thinking, are necessarily generated from, embedded in, and expressed by bodily forms and activities. She then goes on to demonstrate that in the Chinese neo-Confucian context, philosophical teachings (which have often been treated by outside interpreters as reflecting concerns that were more metaphysical than metapractical) have little relevance in the tradition itself apart from their actual embodiment in the persons and actions of its past heroes and present practitioners.

The final section of the volume is constituted by a set of two chapters that provide "Concluding Comparative Reflections." In both cases, the authors address theoretical and methodological issues that are relevant to the further development of the kind of comparative philosophy of religions that the volume seeks to foster.

William Schweiker's "The Drama of Interpretation and the Philosophy of Religions: An Essay on Understanding in Comparative Religious Ethics" uses the category of "mimesis" to generate a performance-oriented theory of interpretation.[11] Emphasising the ritual and dramatic origins of the term "mimesis," and its pre-Platonic meaning of "to make like" or "to bring to presentation," Schweiker highlights two extremely important and closely correlated theoretical points. The first is that the religious and ethical discourses in the traditions that we study are forms of mimetic, performative praxis that proceed through a dialogical, hermeneutical process to generate religio-ethical worlds, or ethoi, within which their practioners live. His second point is that comparatively oriented philosophers of religions are themselves engaged in a similar form of mimetic, performative praxis that proceeds (or at least should proceed) through a similar kind of dialogical, hermeneutic activity.

Building on this basis, Schweiker carves out an important middle ground between formalistic, universalizing approaches and the sociolinguistic approaches advocated by radical relativists. He affirms a requisite commonality across cultures by maintaining that all religious, ethical, and philosophical "worlds," including those we ourselves bring into being and maintain, are constructed and discovered through mimetic, performative praxes. At the same time, he places equal emphasis on the very great differences that characterize the various traditions that we study, and on the differences between the patterns of praxis that they utilize, on the one hand, and our own academically oriented patterns of praxis, on the other.

Richard Bernstein, in his essay on "Reconciliation and Rupture: The Challenge and Threat of Otherness," provides a concluding reflection that very adroitly combines historical perspective with guidelines for future work. In Bernstein's view, the most important philosophical background for the kind of comparative philosophy of religions that the preceding essays (and the project that produced them) are striving to generate are to be found in the work of Hans-Georg Gadamer and Jacques Derrida.

Both of these giants of twentieth-century philosophy have, he argues, worked to produce a philosophy in which the reality of otherness is taken seriously and responsibly into account. According to Bernstein, what is needed at the present moment is a dual approach that creatively coordinates "hermeneutical" moments (à la Gadamer) with "deconstructive" moments (à la Derrida). What is required, in other words, is a two-pronged approach to the study of self and Other that creatively combines moments that emphasize conversation and the fusion of horizons, with moments that employ a sensibility which celebrates difference and focuses on the gaps, the fissures, and the disjunctions that resist every kind of interpretive effort. Some progress in forging and employing this kind of theoretical and methodological synthesis has, he suggests, already been made. At the same time, he makes it very clear that the real work has just begun.

Those who are tempted or challenged to read the ten chapters included in this volume should be able to catch a glimpse of the process of enthusiastic discussion and argument within which they have been conceived and written. Happily, thanks to the support of the University of Chicago Divinity School and the continued financial backing provided by the Booth Ferris and Luce Foundations, this process of discussion and argument will go forward in the years ahead. An eighth conference has already been announced. In addition, a third collection of essays will be published in our Toward a Comparative Philosophy of Religions Series. Tentatively entitled *Religion and Practical Reason,* this volume is scheduled to appear in 1992.

Notes

1.   Those interested in the process of discussion and community formation should consult a fascinating volume edited by Francisca Cho Bantly entitled *Deconstructing/Reconstructing the Philosophy of Religions: Summary Reports from the Conferences on Religions in Culture and History, 1986–1989.* This volume was published by the Divinity School of the University of Chicago in 1989 and can be obtained by sending a check for $5 made out to the University of Chicago to the Office of the Dean at Swift Hall, 1025 East Fifty-Eighth Street, Chicago, IL 60637.

2.   This volume, also edited by Frank Reynolds and David Tracy, was published by State University of New York Press in 1990. In addition to two edited collections, the Series already includes one single-authored book, Lee Yearley's

Mencius and Aquinas: Theories of Virtue and Conceptions of Courage, published by State University of New York Press in 1990. One additional collection and four other single-authored books are presently in process.

3. For a short statement suggesting this kind of usage, see the comments made by Richard Bernstein in the preface to his *Praxis and Action: Contemporary Philosophies of Human Activity* (Philadelphia: University of Pennsylvania Press, 1971).

4. The way that I have formulated the thesis that unifies the volume, and the way that I have used that thesis to organize the essays into a coherent unit, was suggested by the comments of Richard Parmentier, who served as a SUNY Press reader for the original draft of the manuscript. Though I have retained most of my original terminology and most of the original content, the impact of his advice concerning the ordering of the essays and the conceptualizations of the connections between them is evident throughout. I am deeply grateful for his contribution.

5. For a very different kind of presentation that makes a similar point concerning the level of philosophical sophistication in a relatively small-scale community, see Gregory Schrempp's superb essay on "Kant among the Maori" in *Myth and Philosophy* (Albany, N.Y.: State University of New York Press, 1990), pp. 151–82.

6. In addition to contributing her own essay, Ms. Bantly has served as the project assistant during the period that the manuscript was being compiled and shepherded it through the publication process. The editors wish to express their profound appreciation for the superb contributions that she has made to the project as a whole and to the intellectual and technical quality of this volume in particular. She has very professionally assumed many of the most important and taxing editorial responsibilities, including the preparation of the index. She has also made very substantive suggestions that have improved the quality of this introduction.

7. For a study of the philosophical importance of a slightly earlier Chinese novel written in the same Buddhist tradition, see Bantly, "Buddhist Allegory in the *Journey to the West," Journal of Asian Studies,* 48 (3, 1989):512–525.

8. Several of the issues discussed by Lovin are also treated by Winston Davis in two articles entitled "Natural Law: A Study of Myth in a World Without Foundations" and "Natural Law and Natural Right: The Role of Myth in the Discourses of Exchange and Community." Both appear in *Myth and Philosophy* (Albany: State University of New York Press, 1990), pp. 317–48 and 349–80.

9. In other contexts Kasulis has presented a more extended interpretation of Kukai's philosophical system. See Chapter 5 entitled "Kukai: Philosophizing in

the Archaic" that appears in *Myth and Philosophy* (Albany, N.Y.: State University of New York Press), pp. 131–50.

10.   Campany has recently published another essay which similarly attempts to compare Chinese and Western religious "theories." See his article on "'Survivals' as Interpretive Strategy: A Sino-Western Comparative Case Study" in *Method and Theory in the Study of Religion,* 2 (1, 1990):2–26.

11.   For a more complete development of Schweiker's basic position, see his *Mimetic Reflections: A Study in Hermeneutics, Theology and Ethics* (New York: Fordham University Press, 1990).

Section I

Philosophy in
Narrative and Practice

Wisdom and Practice: The Mythic Making of Sacred History among the Bimin-Kuskusmin of Papua New Guinea

Fitz John Porter Poole

The notion of 'wisdom' (*agetnaam*) finds its source—its root, its path—in 'understanding' what lurks inside or beneath the myths of Afek. . . .[1] These sacred myths are the kernel of all those 'images encased in words,' those instances of 'condensed, congealed speech. . . .'[2] They enfold something that is unknown, secret, sacred or ritually powerful,. . . that is ambiguous. . . .But their meaning and their foundation are not altogether apparent in their narration. . . . On the surface there are only the coverings of speech—hard, opaque. . . .[3] Their 'sacred meanings' (*aiyem'khaa*) are blurred and matted or twisted together. . . . Their understanding depends on being integrated and given shape through insightfulness, . . . through the experience of sacred ritual,. . . through being embedded or located in the ebb and flow of the everyday experience of living.

> —*Bosuurok, paramount ritual elder of the*
> *Watiianmin patrician and Bimin ritual moiety.*

This chapter sketches some foci and contours of a local perspective on the "epistemology" and "metaphysics" of myth in a traditional Melanesian society. It delineates key features of a folk model of the nature of myth and of myth-in-use as a framework of interpretation. Consequently, it explores some facets of the concept of 'wisdom' (*agetnaam*) as it pertains to an esoteric, indigenous *mythologique,* to the manner in which such a *mythologique* becomes implicated in certain representational, interpretive, or explanatory practices and to a mythic classification of significant historical events among the Bimin-Kuskusmin of the West Sepik hinterland of Papua New Guinea.[4] The broader context of this effort—at once both theoretical and ethnographic in its agenda—entails a vision of a comparative anthropology. Indeed, the endeavor is part of a broader exploration of how the nexus of cultural schemata[5] and patterns of social action is fundamentally anchored to the complex concept of personhood[6] in understanding Bimin-Kuskusmin "forms of life," in general, and the realm of myth and ritual, in particular.[7]

The analysis is fundamentally an exploration of the ethnography both of the general character of *mythologique* and of a particular case of mythic interpretation among Bimin-Kuskusmin, with attention to the essential sociocultural context of both the general and the particular in Bimin-Kuskusmin understandings of such matters. As an ethnographic analysis, the comparative implications of the exploration remain more tacit than explicit, for the intention of this chapter is to illuminate something of the elaborate, self-conscious, and indeed *philosophical* character of local interpretive efforts in a genre of society often thought to be unreflective on matters of myth and history. Indeed, at least in their recent history, Bimin-Kuskusmin have developed an exegetical tradition significantly focused on mythic understandings of historical occurrences that is constituted as an interpretive undertaking of some intricacy. In turn, particular mythicohistorical interpretations deemed significant, however they may come to be recast subsequently, may be resurrected in remarkable detail in the context of later interpretations because they are elaborately structured in ways that contain the multiple, interconnected vehicles of their own mnemonic system. Thus, mythic interpretations often draw upon their own legacy in attempting to capture the enduring significance embedded in the ebb and flow of historical circumstances. This interpretive effort is one of a special genre of the 'imagination' (*gaangan'nuuriin*) associated with the 'wisdom' of Bimin-Kuskusmin ritual elders, from whom all accounts have been reconstructed.[8]

Indeed, this chapter is constituted as an exercise in cross-cultural "imagination" in at least four senses.[9] First, it is concerned with representing ways in which a particular, non-Western people construct images of the world in which they live—and of community, person, and self and of senses of the 'sacred' (*aiyem*) that enfold these images—and how such images are cast in cosmological forms that both shape a people's view of themselves and their surroundings and, in turn, present a portrait in terms of which they construe, assess, and reflect upon the reality of their experiences in a "culturally constituted behavioral environment" (in Hallowell's phrase).[10] Second, it also focuses upon the ways in which people depict "possible worlds" different from the one they actually inhabit and experience and, thereby, enlarge their vision of the possibilities of human existence and establish grounds for change and for skepticism, criticism, distortion, and subversion vis-à-vis the extant sociocultural order. Third, it seeks to explicate some significant facets of the Bimin-Kuskusmin notion of the 'imagination' in the context of mythicohistorical understanding. Fourth, it implicates the construction of an ethnographic portrait that captures something significant of the Bimin-Kuskusmin sense of *mythologique* and renders it more or less intelligible in a Western, English-speaking, academic milieu. In all four senses, the exercise is one of comparative analysis, although the comparative effort is largely implicit and embedded in the construction of a narrative (re)presentation of particular aspects of Bimin-Kuskusmin 'wisdom.'

This project is carried forward by attending to the nuances of metaphoric constructions for at least three reasons. First, as Fernandez demonstrates, tropes play a significant role in the human casting of sociocultural experiences and bounding of the milieux in which such experiences occur,[11] and I shall be attending to aspects of the manner in which Bimin-Kuskusmin constitute their rich sense of *mythologique* through metaphor and the cultural schemata underlying such metaphoric constructions.[12] Second, as Lakoff suggests, attention to the metaphoric maps of a conceptual domain may afford important clues to the underlying and often tacit cultural schemata that inform that domain.[13] Third, as I discuss elsewhere, analogy or metaphor may be seen to play a significant conceptual role in the very constitution of a comparative analysis.[14]

These several emphases on metaphor—and especially on the possibilities of analogic mapping from a known domain to a domain to be explored and interpreted[15]—are bound up with my view that some manner of productive cross-cultural understanding and comparison is possible.[16] In the first instance, analogic mapping across domains seems to be extremely common in a diversity of communities for making sense of phenomena, and local modes of interpretation that make use of some manner of analogic mapping necessarily rend to some extent the fabric of the contexts of the domains to be compared.[17] That is, the comparative loosening of the bonds of context in the service of the interpretive assessment of similarity and difference of phenomena across contexts seems to be a quite general human intellectual activity in making sense of the world. In fact, attention to this commonplace intellectual activity may also yield insight into how local canons of reasoning and modes of argumentation are articulated, defended, criticized, amended, overturned, and so on, in local patterns of rationality, about which we still know remarkably little. In the second instance, an exploration of the modes of such analogic mappings should yield clues to the nature of the underlying cultural schemata that inform them. In the third instance, the notion of analogic mapping permits an appreciation of the fact that any ethnographer constructs initial mappings from the perspective of his local sociocultural milieu, which cannot be neutralized or surmounted in its affect on matters of perception.

Nonetheless, as one's local understanding comes to be seen as a possible view of "reality" set into a different pattern of such possibilities and coupled to a different appreciation of the foci, contours, and limits of modes of understanding, the ever-present threat of ethnocentrism beyond conscious awareness may be weakened and some approximation of local understanding may begin to become sharpened and enriched. The matter is always difficult and tentative, for the conceptual placement of the most illuminating contrast requires a gradual recasting of the subtle structure of the comparison. Comparative approximations are subtly improved. Attention to *their* metaphors in relationship to *our* metaphors may provide an initial step toward a sensitivity to better placement, better configuration of the pattern both of difference and of similarity that is the structure of comparison. In this chapter, the character of comparison—fundamentally embedded in problems of translation—is shaped by and anchored to several interwoven threads of the analytic construction of analogies, for it explores how Bimin-Kuskusmin craft analogies between myth and history by examining the analogic structure of their *mythologiques* through a narrative construction of analogies between their interpretive discourse and our own. It is in the kaleidoscopic web of these ever-turning analogies—in the continuous realignment of their trajectories, interconnections, and relations to context—that illumination of their interpretive practice is sought. Finally, it is in this manner of intellectual struggle with the comparative decipherment of local meanings—with the limits of anamorphic deformation in the service of illumination—that more general theoretical insight is most likely to emerge.

Beyond the great traditions of West and East, it has long been the case that *philosophy*—not to mention *history*—has not been thought readily applicable to those putatively unreflective, timeless societies that have long been at the center of anthropological interests, and that *myth*—especially sacred, cosmogonic myth—contrasts starkly with both *philosophy* and *history,* albeit on rather different grounds.[18] With respect to the Bimin-Kuskusmin of Papua New Guinea, however, I shall claim otherwise in suggesting that what constitutes Bimin-Kuskusmin (ethno-)philosophy is itself significantly constituted within a framework of mythology, and that much of the work of this mythicophilosophy is to assess the 'meaning' (*miit maagamiin*) of (ethno-)historical events in terms of their "fit" with mythological schemes and, thus, their significance for the jural, moral, and ritual orders of Bimin-Kuskusmin society. The senses of myth and of history that are central to this exploration will unfold in the unraveling of Bimin-Kuskusmin concepts, but the exploration is nonetheless bracketed by the notions of "philosophy" and "praxis" ("practice").

To be both brief and somewhat provocative, I adopt the following quite general and deliberately vague orientations to the key ideas of "philosophy" and "praxis." By "philosophy," I refer to an exploration of processes governing human thought, emotion, motivation, and conduct and of the principles that regulate the universe and underlie all human knowledge and senses of reality, including a deliberatively skeptical scrutiny of the premises underlying and claims concerning that exploration, which is at once analytic and argumentative.[19] By "praxis," I refer both to the performance of an activity—in this instance, mythicophilosophical analysis and interpretation—and, in a somewhat more narrowly Aristotelian sense, to that form of human activity manifested in the life of the community (the *polis*).[20] *Philosophy* is inevitably wedded to the historical contexts of its *praxis* to some significant extent and thus is at once both naturalized and denaturalized in different respects. These orientations seem appropriate to the present task of illuminating the nature of Bimin-Kuskusmin *mythologique* as a philosophical enterprise implicating the analysis of historical events, for Bimin-Kuskusmin mythicophilosophy is an activity which invariably focuses on puzzles presented by historical events vis-à-vis understandings of the human condition—the character of personhood—as the latter is understood within the Bimin-Kuskusmin community.[21]

The comparative puzzle begins with explicating certain aspects of the concept of 'wisdom' among Bimin-Kuskusmin, for it is 'wisdom' that encapsulates the capacity for mythicophilosophical 'thinking/feeling.' Bimin-Kuskusmin do not distinguish unambiguously between matters of intellect and matters of emotion, and some seventeen verb forms refer to differing kinds of 'thinking/feeling,' each with its own more or less distinctive modes of insight and puzzle-solving capabilities. Yet, the kind of 'thinking/feeling' that is characteristic of 'wisdom' is unique and peculiar to male ritual elders who have endured the decade-long, ten-stage course of the male initiation cycle both as novices and as initiators, have entered the inner sanctum of the ritual commissions of their patricians, devote much of their lives to the exoterica of ritual performances and knowledge, are conversant with much of the large corpus of sacred myths, and hold the exclusive entitlements to narrate these myths or to make interpretive pronouncements with respect to them. Their 'thinking/feeling' capacity and jural-ritual authority in such matters is predicated on the presumed effects of their long experience of ritual on their *finiik*, 'spirit or life-force,' their accumulated knowledge from such ritual experience, and the fact that they have begun to assume ancestral status in their advanced years. It is the *finiik*, however, that is the locus of a ritual elder's special capacity to 'think/feel' in a manner characteristic of 'wisdom.'

The *finiik*—strengthened by male substance,[22] experience, ritual, and knowledge[23]—is a male procreative contribution to the formation of the mystical and bodily constitution of any fetus. It emanates from an ancestral clan corpus of spirit substance, which it reenters when it is transformed into an ancestral spirit at death. Thus, the *finiik* is the idiom of intergenerational continuity and of the social regeneration of lineage, clan, and ritual moiety. Ideally and under normal circumstances, it is located in the heart, which is the symbolically focal organ of the 'male anatomy' in any person and the complex site of myriad processes of 'thinking/feeling.' The heart, and the *finiik* embedded in it, are nourished by semen, bone marrow, bone, male *finiik*-bearing foods, and the experiences and substances of male ritual, and thus the *finiik* is normally stronger and more active in men than in women. In many respects, the *finiik* represents some of the more social dimensions of personhood—the ordered, moral, proper, restrained aspects of the person that are ideally learned in ordained ways and settings which are associated with the very foundations of Bimin-Kuskusmin tradition. Hence, it is the *finiik* that absorbs the vital experiences of a decade of male initiation and other ritual performances and that encompasses capacities of internal control and shame. The *finiik* is the valued intellect, judgmental capacity, and Durkheimian *conscience* of the person, and it is strengthened by all ritual enhancement of masculinity or male parts of the anatomy. It is the substantial link that connects a person to a sociomoral order, and it is the idiom in terms of which rights and obligations are phrased. Its dominance over its antithesis—the wily *khaapkhabuurien* 'spirit or life-force' that idiosyncratically takes the impress of all of life experinece—ensures the proper development of *la personne morale*, which is said to be most developed in male ritual elders.

As a consequence of the special development of *finiik* and, thus, of personhood among ritual elders, they are deemed capable of an especially powerful 'understanding' (*khaim'khraakkhaan*) of "sacred meanings' (*aiyem'khaa*) with respect to matters of myth and ritual. For ritual elders, the concept of *aiyem*—a sense of the numinous—denotes something special, bounded, set apart under most circumstances, having to do primarily with mythic and ritual matters and the realm of initiated men, invoking the ancestral underworld and the 'sacred time-place.' Insight into the *aiyem* gained through an interpretive unraveling of puzzles with reference to a framework of 'sacred myth' is the very essence of 'wisdom,' but it is the conceptual placement of what is initially deemed ordinary with respect to the *aiyem* that constitutes the sense of puzzle founded upon a profound sense of incongruity, of tension in the construction of a commonality of pattern, of feature, of essence that is recognized to be fictive—the tenuous, fragile 'work of men' (*kunum ogaak'khaa*), yet also provocative, worthy of contemplation, and potentially illuminating.

The term *aiyem* may be used as an adjective ('sacred' or 'taboo') or a noun ('sacred phenomenon,' 'sacrificial entity' [with reference to contexts of ritual], 'sacredness' [as a quality, attribute, capacity, or sign], or 'taboo'). It may also take the form of a stative verb describing a state (with or without the morphological marking of a nominalizing suffix of infix affixed to the root ['be sacred,' or 'be taboo']), and of a transitive verb ('to sacralize,' 'to sanctify,' or 'to make taboo').

It implicates a hidden dimension which may or may not be capable of revelation, but if revelation is possible, its manner and the audience to which it is applied are restricted by gender and by ritual rank and by descent group affiliation at the least. In this regard, its revelation—verbal and/or nonverbal—is always deemed partial and ambiguous, and it always implies more than the senses reveal whatever the form(s) of revelation may be. This recognition of the essential incompleteness and ambiguity of revelation of the 'sacred'—beyond a recognition of the social restrictions placed upon revelation—often brings in its wake considerable ambivalence about the *aiyem* and tentativeness about its interpretation.

It emphasizes a secret dimension, with reference to esoteric ritual knowledge that is learned or experienced primarily in, or with respect to, ritual contexts and mythological narrations. In this regard, it suggests a complex sociology of knowledge bound to understandings of ritual hierarchy and other, intertwined social categories, of socially restricted revelation hedged about by elaborate taboos, and of a concomitant distribution of social authority and power vis-à-vis knowledge and entitlements in its "domain."

It indicates a genre of 'power' or 'influence' or 'potency' or 'efficacy' that simultaneously is deemed both beneficial and threatening, although the relationship of these two inevitable aspects may vary. It is generally recognized that this power, influence, potency, or efficacy is only partially, if at all, under human control under most circumstances.

Thus, interpretation with respect to the *aiyem* must exhibit the qualities of divination and be accompanied by sacrifice in order to channel 'ancestral wisom' to unraveling a conceptual puzzle.

It suggests a mythologically primordial reference—either explicitly or implicitly—and, thus, a notion that the *aiyem* may expand in content, but may not contract. The mythologically framed interpretations of historical events as possibly being *aiyem* may add to the corpus of 'sacred myth.' The mythic reference that signals the relevance of the *aiyem* usually involves—directly or indirectly—the androgynous figures of the original ancestors Afek and Yomnok, represented as the cassowary and the echidna, respectively, and an omniscient quality of 'thinking/feeling'—now lost forever in its full force—that characterized the primordial ancestors, who could apprehend the *aiyem* in a manner and with a clarity now obscure.

It connotes a dangerous quality—one that marks the fragility of an object, person, or event being transformed either in positive or in negative ways, or both. Thus, it may provoke anxiety, ambivalence, fear, and avoidance. Interpretation of the *aiyem* may also provoke ancestral wrath if done improperly. Thus, contact of any kind with the *aiyem*—and especially of an interpretive kind which harbors the potential of altering fundamental understandings—requires a certain quality, kind, and degree of personhood—of *finiik*—and more or less elaborate ritual preparations.

It implicates an ancestral conferral of 'male knowledge,' 'power,' the inchoate and threat that must be acknowledged in some manner in the form of a certain genre of sacrifice. Such sacrifice should focus on certain kinds of marsupials, known in ritual language as *aiyem,* that have been brought within the bounded space of the mythic-ritual domain by being captured alive in ritual taro gardens. The class of marsupials known as *aiyem* includes the echidna monotreme, and all marsupials identified as having *totemic* significance, and, thus, is associated with ancestral 'wisdom' and 'power.'

Some phenomena are intrinsically *aiyem*—they have always been so and are permanently so. Their identity is already represented in ritual performances (including mythic narratives), and they are not usually believed to present a classificatory problem. They may be destroyed—leaving nonetheless a representation in the ancestral underworld, which must be anchored there through special sacrifices, and a dangerous residue in the world of the living, which must be exorcized through rites of purification. Yet, these phenomena may not be desacralized, for they are ultimately possessed by a corpus of ancestral spirits which invariably encompasses and protects them. Some phenomena are made *aiyem*—their *aiyem* character must be periodically renewed through ritual action—including the performative speech acts of ritual elders as when they are recast again and again in new mythic narrations that are being incorporated among 'sacred myths.' They cannot be used to make other phenomena *aiyem;* they can be desacralized. In turn, some phenomena become *aiyem* by entering into or being placed within a 'sacred time-place.' Their *aiyem* character is context-bound, although they must undergo some form of ritual cleansing when they are removed from such contexts. Otherwise, they would damage, and be damaged by, contact with ordinary contexts unless such contexts were themselves transformed into 'sacred time-place' contexts through some manner of contact with the *aiyem.*

Although the essential quality of *aiyem* admits of degrees of 'strength,' no *aiyem* phenomena may be partially *aiyem* or not subject to restrictions of some kind. Thus, when interpretations that seek to "fit" phenomena to the mythic pattern of *aiyem* are made, the interpretations should be treated as *aiyem* unless they are abandoned—in which case ritual purification accompanies the disassembly of the interpretation and of the ritual displays that represent in some way the puzzle to be unraveled. The primary referents of *aiyem* should be noted in ritual language— an archaic language of primordial ancestors characterized by complex figurative constructions, special lexical and syntactic conventions, and a marked sense of ambiguity and incongruity. Those performative speech acts of ritual elders that are said to have the 'power' to transform phenomena into an *aiyem* state (including mythic narrations)—and are, in themselves, *aiyem*—must be phrased in this ritual language, which lends an aura of ambiguity to the speech acts themselves.

The term *aiyem* has two paramount senses that are invariably implicated in its use: one in reference to the heart as the site of the *finiik,* which is the locus of states and processes of 'thinking/feeling' (especially the unique form of 'thinking/feeling' that is distinctive of 'wisdom'), and one in reference to those *nuuk* ('certain marsupials and the echidna monotreme') that are selected for certain genres of sacrifice that accompany important acts of interpretation vis-à-vis incorporation of phenomena into a corpus of 'sacred myth.'

The term *aiyem,* thus, has connotations of what might loosely be termed "altered states of consciousness" (vis-à-vis 'thinking/feeling' states and processes) and of ritually/mythically forged connections between the ancestral underworld and the world of the living (vis-à-vis certain types of sacrifice). These connotations provide the rationale for noting that one cannot come into contact with *aiyem* phenomena without ritual preparation, nor can one remove oneself from the *aiyem* without ritual purification. Transitions between contexts or states of *aiyem* and non-

aiyem are invariably hedged about with myriad taboos. Indeed, only ritual elders can properly initiate contact with the *aiyem*. Such contact strengthens the *finiik* in a variety of ways by promoting a state of ritual hotness, although it may also damage the *finiik* if the individual has undergone inadequate ritual preparations for initiating the contact. Yet, if the consequence of such contact is essentially positive, new cognitive-perceptual-emotional vistas are opened up through the elaboration and special fusion and blurring of ordinary states and process of 'thinking/ feeling' and through the activation of a new state or process of 'thinking/ feeling' that is peculiar to being in a state of *aiyem* and making an interpretation with respect to *aiyem*. In order to commence a formal interpretation framed in terms of 'sacred myth,' one must induce a state of 'ritual hotness' and, thus, of appropriate 'thinking/feeling' states and processes.

Initial contact with the *aiyem* may be made through any ordinary sensory modality—seeing, hearing, touching, tasting, smelling, inhaling, or ingesting. However, an interpretation framed in terms of 'sacred myth' requires a fusion and blurring of these senses and the activation of the sensory modality distinctive of 'wisdom'—the state or process of 'think-ing/feeling' known as *kuurkhaaraniin* ('being in the same time-place with'). In other words, one must 'locate oneself within the sacred myth' (*uum khraan aiyem sang mutuuk ker duuranginamiin*) and, therefore, its 'sacred time-place' through an interpretive act of 'imagination' (*gaangan'nuuriin*), and then 'look from within the sacred myth' (*kiinraakhaan tuur aiyem sang mutuuk*) at the puzzling phenomena to be seen in terms of it, in terms of 'sacred meaning.' The idioms used to describe this somewhat diffuse awareness of 'sacred meaning' are cast metaphorically in reference to crystals, rainbows, waterfalls, spirit paths, spider webs, and phosphorus—all of which are bound up, in turn, with images of shadows and reflections that are the focus of Bimin-Kuskusmin divinations.

Crystals are held to be animate and sentient, endowed with *finiik*. They are said to reflect light or images both outwardly and inwardly. They capture their own reflections and shadows in the images of other phenomena. In a sense they can reflect themselves to themselves in the Bimin-Kuskusmin view. In some obscure way, crystals are thought to fuse all reflections and shadows from the outside into a single image on the inside, which cannot be seen or otherwise detected from the outside by mortals except through divination. Crystals are also said to be the eyes of the early ancestors, who could (and can) see and understand more than living men. Because they can somehow detect and fuse im-pressions from everywhere, these ancestral eyes form images that are neither static nor defined only by limited dimensions of phenomena. These ancestors can grasp the 'kernel meaning' (*dop aiyem*) of things because their crystalline eyes can absorb the totality of all phenomena. This kind of perception and consequent understanding takes place within the hearts of the early ancestors: it cannot be translated into discursive language, nor has it ever been necessary for the ancestors to do this. In consequence, the ancestors have not been able to transmit many fundamental aspects of knowledge of the *aiyem* to their descendants, who lack crystalline eyes. Therefore, through ritual, living men must create the feeble, distorting lenses through which they glimpse distorted surface reflections and shadows of what the ancestors can 'bring to the eye within' (*kiin mutuuk daakhaaraan*) themselves. And they must accomplish these interpretive acts in a manner that ultimately rests on analytic powers that are deemed obscure, impoverished, and ambiguous. In the end, most ritual elders understand that interpretation in the mythic mode is a highly personal and creative act. This creativity is constrained, however, by their understandings of the character and structure of myth, by their recognition of certain ordained analogies between mythic interpretation and rites of divination,[24] and by their acknowledgments of the consensual appraisals of their efforts by their peers.

In turn, rainbows, associated with the ritually important phenomena of thunder and lightning, fuse shadows and reflections in the multihued arc that forms a bridge between the ancestral underworld and the realm of the living—a connection that is central to the forging of 'sacred meaning.' Waterfalls obscure their shadows and reflections between the mists of their spray and the torrent of rushing water, often hiding a cavern of sacred crystals beyond. Spirit paths lead through sacred sites as they interconnect the ritual sites of men and of ancestors, yet are enshrouded in the gloom and mists of forest glades. Spider webs encase phenomena in a manner that makes them unrecognizable within the reflective surface of the web, which nonetheless gives an 'illusion' (*kiin'kwanaak*) of clarity of perception and security of place. It is noted that the phenomena encased within the web cannot be examined without damaging the delicate integrity of the pattern of the web. Phosphorus emits a glow that illuminates in a manner that is dim and blurred and infused with shadows—a 'fire that casts no light' (*weng danaamiin baniim*). Once again, the metaphors utilized to characterize the distinctive process of 'thinking/feeling' that penetrates the 'sacred meaning' of phenomena in terms of sacred myth give the illusion of a tradition-bound set of prescriptions and of illumination, for each metaphor is drawn from the iconic imagery of the final and most elaborate stage of male initiation ritual—the locus of narrations of the Afek myths. Yet, as ritual elders tend to recognize in the privacy of their inner sanctums, much free rein is given to a somewhat open-ended creativity in which the prescriptions of interpretation are constrained largely by how one has seen such creativity exercised by one's predecessors and by the analogic recognition that these metaphors are also drawn from the more fluid process of the interpretations given in divinatory rites.[25]

The complex concepts of *aiyem* and of 'sacred meaning' reside at the very core of Bimin-Kuskusmin perceptions of what is fundamentally involved in interpretation vis-à-vis 'sacred myth.' They implicate both an elaborate cognitive-affective process linked to ritual experience and a kind and degree of personhood that are bound together through the complex cultural schemata underlying the notion of *finiik*. Indeed, 'sacred meaning' and 'sacred myth' invariably implicate one another, for 'sacred myth' is said to be the 'voice' (*weeng'kwaar*) of ritual. It is the intricate corpus of 'sacred myths' known as Afek myths, narrated in an almost eighty-hour cycle in the apical rite of the male initiation cycle which traces a prescribed 'path' connecting myriad sacred sites and events across the encircling mountains as its mnemonic frame, that is the exemplar *par excellence* of the broader body of 'sacred myths.'

The narration of these exemplary myths is an integral part of the performance of these initiatory rites, in which they are complexly cosmogonic in character and portrayed as intricately fixed both in structure and in content. In this regard, they may be seen to function as "charters" (in the Malinowskian sense) for the institution of the rite, to operate narratively as integral parts of the rite as performed, and to be iconically represented in the *sacrae* of the rite as well as enacted nonverbally within it.[26] Yet, in the tightly bounded context of male initiation ritual, the formal narration of these 'sacred myths'—faithful to the mnemonic structure of the course of a mountainous 'path' connecting sacred sites, but variable in what is portrayed of the prescribed mythic events—is coupled with unexplicated displays of ritual *sacrae* marked both by tight encircling frames and by the lack of a demarcated border. It is the ritual elders' memory of these performances, enhanced by recent dreams, hallucinogenic experiences, and exegetical discussions of real and ideal ritual performances encompassing these myths among their peers, that enter into interpretive endeavors, which occur beyond the boundary of the ritual performances in which the formal narrations occur. In these guarded but significantly extraritual contexts, the character of myth becomes more open-ended and more fluid as the framework of 'sacred myth' is brought to bear upon puzzles deemed worthy of interpretive effort with respect to sacred meaning. In this regard, there are several more or less distinct key folk models of the structure of these 'sacred myths' that illuminate certain aspects of their open-endedness and fluidity or flexibility in interpretive contexts—esoteric models that are discussed almost entirely within the circle of ritual elders.

First, the character of sacred myth is depicted in terms of the onion-like, layered structure of a nut, fruit, or seed. This model is said to represent the 'plant flesh' (*diin*) of the myth—a quality of mythic structure that portrays myth as being significantly flexible in how it can be brought to bear on the interpretation of events or situations.[27] The 'skin or husk' or the 'tail or stem' is the most obvious and generally least significant layer of meaning, although it may always gain added significance in its relationship to what is hidden within it or in its hidden relationship to what else is revealed. The 'soft, outer flesh' is considered to be more important, but it is less significant than the more central 'hard flesh-bone,' which remains firm when the outer layers have rotted or been peeled away. And the 'kernel' contains the most sacred, secret, and hidden significance of all. In Bimin-Kuskusmin reckoning, it is the kernel of the nut, fruit, or seed that is the germinant part. By explicit analogy, the 'kernel meaning' of myth is what has greatest significance in that it leads—by inference—to other 'sacred meanings'—as the germinant kernel produces new plants. That is, the 'kernel meaning' is what links proximal significance to a broader network of cultural ideas. But the 'kernel meaning' is also obscured by many protective outer layers, and the interpretive 'peeling' (*guurdaakiin*) of these encompassing layers may damage, distort, or destroy the kernel. Also, as one ritual elder put the matter, "One can only see the husk of sacred things. . . .Sometimes there is nothing. . . .The kernel has rotted away." Furthermore, not only may there be no center, no 'kernel meaning' that is apparent, but also the significances of each of the several layers may not be congruent and may lead along different and even contradictory interpretive 'paths.'

Second, in extending the above metaphor, ritual elders note that nuts, fruits, and seeds are often found in clusters that are interconnected by 'strings,' e.g., vines, twigs, and stems. By analogy, the different layers of significance of any single entity are intricately bound up with those of both like and different entities on the same or neighboring plants in a network of intertwined nuts, fruits, and seeds. These networks add to the complexity of modeling the significance of particular aspects of myth that may be connected to other aspects in a diversity of ways.

Third, in continuing the plant metaphor, even 'kernel meanings' are said to have 'roots' and a propagative 'base' that are their 'source.' The vital fluids that course through the 'veins' of a plant and nurture it originate 'somewhere below,' with the implication of some obscure connection with the ancestral underworld and with the capillary system of an-

cestral fluids that give the traditional 'center place' its mythically enshrined and ritually enhanced territorial integrity.[28] But if these 'veins' are
cut or damaged, the nuts, fruits, or seeds above will perish with the
kernel being destroyed first. These roots and fluids are said to originate
deep beneath the ground where they cannot be seen, but where they
may mysteriously interconnect different plants and other nonplant phenomena in unknown ways. It is noted that root systems may extend for
long distances underground, may become entangled, and may produce
many interlinked plants that grow far apart. By analogy, plant roots and
fluids become idioms that are often used metaphorically to express the
ritual elders' suspicions that there are always 'sacred meanings' and relations that are hidden beyond the pale of what they can know. But their
lifelong experience with an ever-expanding set of mythic contents, structures, contexts, exegeses, and narrative presentations adds to the breadth
and depth of their mythic knowledge, understanding, and 'imagination.'

Fourth, entangled or buttress roots may encompass a center that is
hidden and may exhibit a delicacy of structure that cannot easily be
teased apart without damage. As one ritual elder observed, "Kernel meanings have many roots. . . . Some go deep and long. They can never all be
pulled up for everyone to see. . . . The kernel would perish. Some roots
are very small and fragile. Some roots break away and stay beneath the
ground. One cannot know where they were or where they burrowed.
They break and the fluids seep into the ground. . . . The roots may show
scars where they break." The extent of what can be interpretively in-
ferred is always limited by circumstance, by knowledge of precedent in
interpretation, by mythic knowledge, and by the delicacy and subtlety of
the act of interpretation.

Fifth, in complementation to the plant metaphors, which focus upon
the metaphoric implications of layers, fluids, roots, and so on, and draw
upon an extensive pragmatic understanding of *materia botanica,* there
are two interconnected folk models that are said to portray the 'animal
flesh' (*diim*) and the 'bone' of mythic structure. In the first instance,
through hunting, warfare, mortuary cannibalism, curing, sacrifice, divination (including divinatory "autopsies"), and animal augury, Bimin-
Kuskusmin elaborate a very detailed anatomical map, and all bodily phenomena are classified as male or female in creatures of either sex and are
further categorized in terms of classes of bodily organs and organ systems. Most, but not all, bodily parts are unambiguous with respect to
these anatomical classifications, although some organs may be classifica-
torily transformed in a generally temporary way under certain circumstances. Segments of 'sacred myth' are categorized in terms of these
organs, classes of organs, organ systems, and gender divisions, and parts

of myths seen to be members of the same class are paradigmatically substitutable for one another in the interpretive selections that are made and in the interpretive linkages that are forged. Furthermore, discriminations of ventral and dorsal, left and right, head and hindquarters, and interior and exterior may enter into such mythic partitionings as another mode of the classification of mythic segments. The balance between male and female anatomical parts may intrude upon classification, and ambiguous aspects of the anatomy may become "wild cards" in the interpretive system. In the second instance, and in complementation to the paradigmatic potential of the anatomical map, the skeleton of an animal—along any of several axes—may become a syntagmatic map of the linear order of the classified parts of a myth, with an important qualification. Although the ordered vertebrae of the spine are the syntagmatic model *par excellence,* one can trace more circuitous pathways through the skeleton based upon the hierarchical classes of bones that are reckoned in divination.

These several models of the paradigmatic and syntagmatic structure of a myth, a set of myths, or a cycle of myths may be interrelated in complex ways that give a sense of consensual organization to the process of interpretation and yet permit considerable flexibility in the construction of a map of mythological structure that may be properly deployed in the constitution of a mythically framed interpretation. Finally, however, there is an important model of mythic structure as it enters into matters of the use of myth in interpretation that focuses upon 'boundaries' (*siikhaan*) and 'surfaces' (*bangep'khaan*). In any mythically framed interpretation, there is an attempt to encase some event within the structure of the myth by casting that event in an appropriate form of myth-like narrative and embedding that newly created tale in terms of its perceived "fit"—on any of the aforementioned structural grounds and with respect to classificatory matters of content—with surrounding elements of the 'sacred myth.' In the first instance, this interpretive endeavor requires the establishment of 'boundaries' to the event. These 'boundaries' are established to separate and to distinguish event entities from one another, but by the very same process, they link the delimited entities together. As a 'boundary' is traced, it defines the interpretive integrity of each entity in terms of and in contrast to others; it establishes where each begins and ends. In the event domain to be interpreted in terms of myth, the structuring process seems less fluid, for the constituted structure of the narratively cast event should not be ambiguous.

Thus, a 'boundary' is clearly marked with discursive signs in order to function as a momentarily stable boundary, which may ultimately be rejected with the consequence that the interpretive effort must begin again. When one interpretively crosses a 'boundary,' this crossing is typically noted in the interpretation; for the vital matter of mythic "fit" and the gaps or incongruities that are noted with respect to that sense of "fit" depends upon relatively clear event 'boundaries'—both internal in terms of elements within the event and external in terms of the bounding of the event itself. However, although once a mythically framed interpretation is launched, the event 'boundaries' (both internal and external) are deemed closed; successive interpretive framings of the "same" event suggest that the 'boundaries' have become open in order to permit new framings of the event in the service of exploring various kinds and degrees of "fit" within the mythological scheme, which may itself be recast.

Once the matter of event 'boundaries' has been established, the matter of 'surfaces' with respect to 'boundaries' emerges in discussion, although the two issues have often arisen together in dialectical fashion in the constitution of an interpretation. In Bimin-Kuskusmin mythically framed interpretation, 'surfaces' have two distinguishable aspects. In the first instance, 'surfaces' are established by 'boundaries' and are the most external and obvious classifications of events or elements of events. In this sense, 'surfaces' are the edges of bounded categories—their 'shell'; they refer to where one entity ends and another begins, but do not refer to how and why the entity was bounded in a particular way to produce a particular 'surface.' In the second instance, however, 'surfaces' refer to the character of the relationship between or among entities that have 'surfaces' in the first sense. The first type of 'surface' (*bangep'khaan magaang*) may be described in terms of the external appearance of an entity; the second type of 'surface' (*bangep'khaan sauk'khaan*) refers to the linkage between 'surfaces' in the first sense or to the relational position of bounded event entities in some classificatory scheme.

These several models for the structuring of both the mythic framework of interpretation and the historical event to be interpreted draw significantly and explicitly on patterns of divination, and the discovery of a "fit" of some order between a 'sacred myth' and a historical event not enshrined in myth—as well as inevitable perceptions of at least partial lack of "fit"—establishes the grounds for making claims about the 'sacred meaning' of the historical event and possibly incorporating it—albeit rather tentatively and in a marked fashion—within the corpus of accepted 'sacred myths.' The elements and the interrelationships of elements that come to constitute the mythic frame and the narrative structure of the historical event admit of considerable flexibility in how they are assembled for interpretive purposes, but the structures that are manifested in various interpretive efforts are a consequence of some manner of consensus among ritual elders or meet consequential challenge among ritual elders, who also reach agreement on the legitimacy of the historical event as a worthy puzzle for interpretation and on an evaluation of the kind and degree of success exhibited by the interpretation. The divinatory model is manifested in the varying ways in which mythic and historical elements and relationships among elements are both constrained and flexible, in the aspects of creativity (and manipulation) that enter into the constitution of an interpretive effort, and in the complex interaction that is revealed in the selection of mythic framework and historical event and in the context of interpretation and in the struggle to achieve or to deny consensual validation of an interpretation that takes place among ritual elders.[29]

Mythically framed interpretations invariably are focused on historical events that are deemed worthy of such interpretation. What then are historical events in the Bimin-Kuskusmin view of the matter, and how are they selected. In the first instance, 'historical events' (*khaa'tebemaam*) are occurrences located beyond the pale of the 'sacred time-place' that circumscribes ritual (including mythic narration), are not unambiguously related to the 'traditional foundations' (*miit kiitaar'takhiin*) of local cultural and social forms and forces as manifested in institutional designs, have no obvious reference to ancestral powers or designs, and have not been seen to influence the patterned ebb and flow of community life in any but a more or less transient way. As one ritual elder put the matter, "Leaves and branches fall regularly into rivers, but most are swept away— rotting into the river mud, disappearing on the current, not interrupting the flow of the current in any noticeable way. . . . Some *khaa'tebemaam* pass without notice or are simply a recognizable part of our path of life. . . . Sometimes, however, a leaf or branch will temporarily dam the river, dislodge a bolder, . . . or even cause the river to change course. . . . When a *khaa'tebemaam* has a great effect, it must be observed for signs of its importance." Thus, 'historical events' are punctuations of the ordinary pattern of community life that may or may not have significance, which is reckoned in terms of the kind and degree of traditional moorings the event is seen to have and the actual or potential disruption or change in community life—whether enduring or not—that it is seen to provoke. When a 'historical event' is selected for interpretive attention with respect to 'sacred meaning,' however, other criteria are involved; for issues of the kinds and effects of disruption and change— especially in regard to the domain of sacred things—are identified through consensus among ritual elders and are typically reinforced by attending to omens and conducting divinations of some artifactual residue of the event.[30]

Perhaps the most profound 'historical event' to have an impact on the course of Bimin-Kuskusmin community life and their sense of the stability of their ritual traditions was the coming of the 'European

(*tabaarasep*) in this century. Although early Malay bird-of-paradise hunt-
ers wandering far to the West before the turn of the century attracted
little concerted attention, the appearance of white-skinned, humanoid
creatures at the periphery of their region in the early nineteenth century
soon became a source of elaborate speculation, a search for omens, and
a cause for concern. A member of the Kaiserin-Augusta-Fluss Expedition
in 1911 traveled to nearby Feramin and left steel axes in trade, and
Bimin-Kuskusmin acquired one of these mysterious objects through elaborate transactions with Feramin exchange partners. After appropriate divinations of the implement, they bestowed a name upon it and installed it
in the cult house of one of the senior patriclans, but being uncertain of its
nature vis-à-vis their traditional classificatory systems, they surrounded it
with ritual barriers to prevent some untoward type of contamination of
the cult house. Thereafter, patrols of exploration journeyed through distant territories of their region for several decades but had little direct
impact upon the 'center place' until the famed Hagen-Sepik Patrol of the
mid-1930s—preceded by an aerial reconnaissance that left terror in its
wake—penetrated the perimeter of their northern river valley. The patrol, however, turned abruptly northward to enter the land of the
Oksapmin people, who are enemy to Bimin-Kuskusmin, where a number of people who resisted the patrol were shot. Bimin-Kuskusmin emis-
saries examined the bullet-ridden bodies and reported the terrible effects
of an unknown but thunderous weapon. From that moment onward, all
movements of patrols were carefully monitored, but for some considerable period of time, no patrol again ventured near the 'center place.'
Shortly after the appearance of this patrol, the Bimin-Kuskusmin received
pumpkin seeds in trade from groups to the south, and the seeds were
identified as having come from the land of the European. The pumpkin
seeds were experimentally planted in a few nonsacred women's sweet
potato gardens where they germinated quickly, and some were placed
with the growing stock of steel axes in 'sealed' areas of several clan cult
houses, where they were subjected to periodic but inconclusive divinations.

In 1957, however, a patrol from Telefomin to the West traveled
ominously eastward and entered the Bimin-Kuskusmin northern valley
where it set up camp. Although the patrol was carefully and anxiously
watched by large parties of carefully hidden armed men, only a single,
but extremely powerful, ritual elder ventured forth to meet the patrol.
Having undergone all manner of prophylactic rituals of war and wearing
an impressive array of protective amulets, this ritual elder, Bosuurok of
the introductory quotation, carefully examined the appearance of the
patrol leader and asked his mission through Telefolmin interpreters. Satisfied that the patrol posed no immediate military threat, Bosuurok pro-

ceeded to examine its equipment. To his delight, he soon identified steel axes and packets of pumpkin seeds, confirming their suspected origin. Nonetheless, Bosuurok sought to acquire certain new European artifacts from the camp's supplies, but the patrol officer refused his magnificently generous offer of exchange with a burst of laughter—a grievous insult vis-à-vis the traditional etiquette of exchange to a man of paramount ritual rank. The patrol did trade a few insignificant trinkets for food, and soon made its way northward and beyond the perimeter of the 'center place.'

Although the coming of the European was cause for military concern and divinatory interest, however, encounters with the European remained sporadic and of little immediate significance for almost a decade. Then, in the late 1960s, a patrol from the newly established Oksapmin patrol post to the immediate north came unexpectedly in search of the Bimin-Kuskusmin's secret source of sacred oil—the semen of the ancestors and the ritually protected network of underground capillaries that lends cosmological integrity to the territory of the 'center place.' Despite concerted Bimin-Kuskusmin efforts to mislead the patrol, it finally discovered the sacred oil seep and took a sample away before the oil could be deconsecrated as is the custom when oil is traded abroad as a medicinal salve.

To the European, the oil proved to be of no commercial value, and the matter was soon forgotten. To the Bimin-Kuskusmin, however, the loss of the sanctified oil was a matter of deep ritual concern, for its loss was seen to erode the ritual integrity of the 'center place' and, consequently, to provoke ancestral wrath. Divinations were conducted in and around the oil seep to assess the damage, and protective shrines were erected at its perimeter. Sacrifices were held in every clan cult house to reestablish the integrity of the broken capillary network of sacred oil upon which all manner of fertility depends. In time, nonetheless, an ominous omen of the injury wrought by the taking of the oil became evident. From the eastern flank of the Strickland Gorge came an invasion of grasses that depleted the fertility of gardens left to fallow and of strange bees that stung but produced no honey. As the grasses and bees advanced, the ritual integrity and fertility of the 'center place' was seen to erode on its eastern flank, and an upsurge in sacrificial activity and the erection of a barrier of shrines against the invasion was of no avail. This devastating omen provoked a flurry of elaborate divinations to assess the significance of the advance of the depleting grasslands and the ferocious bee, but their results were deemed inconclusive. Consequently, in 1971 during the time of my first field research, ritual elders of all of the traditional clans of the Bimin-Kuskusmin met to consider what remedy might be at hand. It was unanimously decided that a mythically framed interpretation of the coming of the European was essential, for the 'sacred meaning' of this coming and the devastation that it had wrought remained ambiguous.

The preparations for this interpretation were elaborate, for all the key ritual elders were involved. Each underwent extensive purificatory rites and conducted preliminary sacrifices in their clan cult houses. It was decided that the framework of interpretation under the circumstances should be the most powerful 'sacred myths' drawn from the elaborate cycle of Afek myths that crown the cycle of male initiation. At a prearranged time at dusk, when day is beginning in the ancestral underworld and the constitution of a 'sacred bridge' between the worlds of the living and the dead can be accomplished through mythological narration and a proper bounding of the interpretation by the creation of the timeless, spatially liminal 'sacred time-place' can be constituted, the elders met in the high mountain forest at a site of sacred importance in the Afek myth cycle, near where the 1957 patrol had entered their terrain. A ritual display was created on the ground at this site—a display consisting of concentric circles of cassowary feces, representing the fertility of Afek, and the obnoxious bees strung on stems of the intrusive grass, representing the presumed effects of the desecrated oil. A set of auspicious 'bone' segments of the Afek cycle—coordinated with the sacred site of the interpretation—were assembled to reflect the most sacred segments of the entire mythic corpus, but since the focal points of the narrative reconstruction of the coming of the European centered on the invasive grasses and bees, no apt analogies could be discovered that were deemed sufficiently significant to warrant a claim that some aspect of 'sacred meaning' had been discovered. Bosuurok tried to emphasize an analogy between the spine of the Afek corpus and the association of the capillary system of sacred oil with the 'marrow' of the 'spine' of the central mountains that bisect the 'center place,' but this analogy was generally said not to be represented in any clear way in the mythic constellation that had already been constructed for interpretation. The historical and mythic narrative assemblages were abandoned, and the display destroyed. The effort would have to begin anew.

A few days later, another attempt at constructing and "fitting" mythic and historical narratives was about to be attempted when it was realized that one of the ritual elders had been ill with a fever—a genre of sickness said to cause the *finiik* to be dislocated from the heart. In this instance, the attempt was postponed. Within a week, however, Bosuurok—the accepted voice of this collective interpretive endeavor—announced that he had had a dream in which he had been wandering in the deep forest in search of marsupials near his lineage shrine when he had heard the sound of a steel axe nearby. Walking in the direction from which the axe blows seemed to come, he glimpsed the fleeting shadow of a large cassowary. He maintained that this dream seemed auspicious for the launching of a new and different mythically framed interpretation, for the association of the European axe and the symbol par excellence of Afek suggested a more encompassing approach to the quest for 'sacred meaning.' Furthermore, dream reports containing mythic images are considered to be of the category of 'images encased in words' or 'condensed, congealed speech,' which includes 'sacred myths.'

A few days later, Bosuurok began the construction of a ritual display at the sacred site that included a pairing of taro and pumpkin and of a stone adze and steel axe surrounded by radiating lines of grass, bees, hawk feathers, broken bone tips of arrows, shell exchange valuables, bamboo tubes of sacred oil, and both cassowary plumes and echidna quills. These items, he insisted, must all be encompassed in the narratives, for they represented the 'path' of the European into 'the center place'—the domain of the founding ancestors Afek and Yomnok. Thus, the pumpkin, steel axe, hawk feathers (representing the reconnaissance airplane in the 1930s), and the broken bone tips of arrows (representing the bullets that felled the Oksapmin) were associated with the European. The taro and stone adze would represent the Bimin-Kuskusmin community. The shell exchange valuables and the tubes of sacred oil would be seen as items of exchange—offered to and taken by the Europeans, respectively—that had resulted either in no transactions or in negative transactions, and the bees and grass were believed to be the consequences of the latter. Finally, the cassowary plumes and the echidna quills were common representations of Afek and Yomnok, respectively— the founding ancestors who gave primordial shape to the 'center place' which was integrated through the capillary system of sacred oil.

One day later, Bosuurok, in the company of the ritual elders of all of the original Bimin-Kuskusmin clans, began to construct his constellation of 'sacred myth.' He prepared himself with care—undergoing a divination to ensure his health, preparing a double sacrifice in his clan cult house both to Afek and to Yomnok, enduring rather arduous rites of purification involving fasting and vomiting. These rites both strengthened his *finiik* for the exhausting demands of the concentrated 'being in the same time-place with' mode of 'thinking/feeling' peculiar to the exercise of 'wisdom' among ritual elders and enriched his memory of the ritual performance of the initiation cycle in which the entire Afek myth cycle is celebrated. The mythic ensemble that he constructed was long and elaborate and exhibited the following kinds of structural arrangements.

Much attention was focused on linkages, e.g., 'strings' and 'roots,' extending from 'kernel meanings,' and these linkages were given much and unusual elaboration. Bosuurok was a master of the art of mythically framed interpretation. He first attended to the core 'bone' segment associated with the sternum, which lies at the very center of the body in Bimin-Kuskusmin reckoning and more or less directly over the heart—the locus of *finiik* and all states and processes of 'thinking/feeling.' This central segment portrays Afek and Yomnok—both in human and in cassowary or echidna form—as the creators of 'the center place' and the founders of the ritual and mythic traditions of the Bimin-Kuskusmin. He told of the toil of 'planting' the capillary network of sacred oil so that it was anchored to all of the domains of Bimin-Kuskusmin land, depicting the lush fertility wrought in each and the origin of the rituals designed to ensure the unbroken flow of oil between the ancestral underworld and the land of the living. In this portrait, he underscored the character of the 'sacred time-place' before the advent of death and the decline of human 'thinking/feeling' capacities. His construction then radiated outward along the rib segments in a pattern notably similar to the ritual display that he had assembled on the sacred site and in reference to displays of similar design in the final initiation rite in which the Afek myths are narrated most completely.

First, he spoke of the origin of the male, *finiik*-bearing taro, its association with Yomnok's head and Afek's loins, and the establishment of the sacrificial 'taro hearth' in the initiation house of the final stage of the initiation cycle. He noted the animate, sentient qualities of taro as a ritual substance and the sole food of Afek and Yomnok while they remained in the form of the cassowary and the echidna, respectively. He stressed the fibrous solidity of taro—its weight and texture and the manner of its propagation by the planting of stalks. Then, he emphasized the mythic segment that portrayed the making of the first stone adze from Afek's bone in a taro garden and how it was used first to cut firewood for the sacrificial fires of the 'taro hearth.' He noted the care that must be taken to fashion, sharpen, and preserve a stone adze and the beauty of its variegated color and smooth texture. He acknowledged that the adze is at once an implement of taro gardening, hunting, and war and the associations of each male activity with ritual displays in the final initiation rite. He observed how the adze was used to harvest and to replant taro in ritual gardens sanctified by the crystals buried within them in primordial times—thus making reference to the special 'thinking/feeling' capacity of *kuurkhaaraniin.*

In reference to yet another rib segment, he depicted the way in which cassowary plumes and echidna quills were once used to weave the web that was the canopy over the 'center place' before the sky was formed and populated with celestial bodies. He noted how such plume and quill cloaks are used to cover taro plants that have been anointed with semen in the final stage of initiation ritual. In the next segment, he depicted the linkage between shell valuables and taro, both of which had originally come from Afek's vagina and appeared in the initial *waneng'kariik* prestations of bridewealth in recognition of human fertility. In another segment, he portrayed how Afek had forbade the nonritual hunting of the cassowary by breaking bone-tipped arrows and placing a contingent curse on taro. Finally, he noted a mythic segment in which the hawk soars over the 'center place' in long gyrations, ensuring that no intruders enter the domain of all Bimin-Kuskusmin.

By attending only to 'kernel meanings' and organizing the 'bone' structure of his construction of 'sacred myth' in the manner of a center (the sternum) and radiating 'paths' (the ribs), Bosuurok created an unbounded mythic framework that enabled an extraordinary number of linkages to be made. When he had completed this circular anatomical pattern, he then bisected it by attending to a series of vertebra segments, each of which he linked to the rib segments with respect to their common content. He then returned to the sternum segment to recast and to enrich his earlier narration of the founding exploits and creations of Afek and Yomnok, relinking all of the elements of his ritual display in one or more new ways. With respect to each and every segment, he indicated relevant ritual displays from the last rite of the initiation cycle—embellishing each with portraits of sacrifices, divinations, dreams, and spells that further complicated both the key elements of his display and the now myriad linkages among them. The narrative construction unfolded over the course of about five hours. Other ritual elders occasionally added insights of their own or elaborated certain mythic segments so that the web of interlinkages became more and more complex and dense. Finally, Bosuurok concluded with a mythic segment associated with the heart beneath the sternum that portrayed how Afek harvested the first ritual crystals from a great cavern and used them as the centerpiece of the great taro rituals that she instituted. In this final segment, he noted how these sacred crystals were used to replenish the extensive forests of the 'center place' and to ensure their continued fertility and how the sacrifice of honey to the animate, *finiik*-bearing crystals became the centerpiece of the rites of the regeneration of the forest.

In the course of this virtuoso narrative construction, Bosuurok had made use—at least in part—of almost all of the traditional models and canons for constructing a mythic framework for the interpretation of 'sacred meaning.' Indeed, his effort showed not only masterful "grammaticality" but also considerable ingenuity, enhancing his reputation as an outstanding ritual elder. There was only one challenge focused on the rationale for the pattern of selecting these particular vertebra segments in the order that he did, but he defended most of the selection and presentation on the grounds of the pattern that he had already established in his display and amended only one segment in response—illuminating the same focus but from a somewhat different vantage point in the Afek myth cycle. On the following day, however, when he turned to the construction of a myth-like narrative account of the coming of the European, the strategy of necessity changed dramatically. The constellation of Afek myth segments had been appropriately narrated in ritual language, although many of his appended elaborations were not. Indeed, he often elegantly juxtaposed both ritual and ordinary speech in order that the latter might elaborate the former since the former is characterized by rather restricted lexical and syntactic resources. In so doing, however, he made the structure of his construction exceptionally complex and dense. Nonetheless, this complexity and density, often created through sophisticated use of the rich figurative resources of the Bimin-Kuskusmin language, exposed numerous implications of underlying schemata concerning 'thinking/feeling' states and processes, the nature of *finiik* and social personhood, the character of initiation ritual, the assumptions of exchange, myriad classificatory schemes encompassing diverse flora and fauna, and so on.

In the historical narration, in contrast, the speech could not appropriately be cast in ritual language, nor were the various 'plant flesh,' 'animal flesh,' and 'bone' models applicable since they have reference *only* to 'sacred myths.' Bosuurok began by presenting a more or less chronological account of the sequence of events that had made the presence of the European known to the Bimin-Kuskusmin—an account that he knew in some detail, for he had lived through virtually all of the events and had been a central actor in all but the very first. He embellished this account by recalling his personal experiences of the mysterious steel axe from Feramin, the terror of the plane that roared out of the East, the shock of the shooting of the Oksapmin, the outrage at the denial of exchange, and the special sense of tragedy at the taking of the oil, for he had been the man who, fearing the threat of guns in the 'center place,' had finally shown the ever-persistent patrol the treasured oil seep. At each encounter, he paused to speculate on the moral constitution and 'thinking/feeling' processes of these strange beings who had come from beyond the farthest mountains of the known world. In this way, he sought to establish the significance of these interlinked events for the Bimin-Kuskusmin community and, thus, for the present interpretive effort.

When the prelude of this chronology had unfolded, Bosuurok turned attention once again to the display that he had created, and using the pattern of this display, somewhat replicated the 'bone' structure of his earlier mythic narration. In this instance, however, he adhered more to understandings about 'boundaries' and 'surfaces' in a sustained attempt to encase the narrative within the previous mythic framework through explicit comparison. Once again, nonetheless, he attended to linkages, but linkages cast more in terms of the mythic framework than in terms of the historical account. He noted that the European seemed not to have a ritual tradition of the splendor of that founded by Afek and Yomnok, commenting on the possible significance of rumors of missionary activity to the North. Yet, he also noted the hypothesis held by some that the European was Afek's lastborn child returned to the 'center place' with vast secrets from the ancestral underworld and voiced his skepticism about this view.

Once again, he repeated his perspective on the ritual impoverishment of the European. Then, the comparison—constructed almost entirely in reference to contrast—became more detailed with respect to the elements of his display. In contrast to taro, the pumpkin had neither ritual significance nor nutritive value. It occupied much garden space and offered little. It was associated with no known myths or rites of increase, and it was not *finiik*-bearing. It had no place in plant "genealogies." It exhibited a color that suggested polluting qualities. It was hollow and without solidity and was propagated by seeds. Indeed, it seemed a plant of the forest without qualities that might redeem it for garden planting. In contrast to the stone adze, the steel axe was splendid in its cutting strength, but it seemed to serve the European only for the cutting of trees. Although seemingly indestructible, it had no appreciable aesthetic value. It was hafted in a most inconvenient and uncomfortable way. One could not exchange true valuables for it.

Then, Bosuurok entered into the matter of the strange avoidance of exchange or any manner of reciprocity on the part of the European. Although a few items of European origin had long appeared in 'the center place' through distant trade, the transactions that produced them were unknown. What was known, however, was the European's early refusal to exchange and then the taking of the oil with threat and without reciprocity of any kind. Perhaps such men did not ordinarily live in communities, for mostly lone Europeans had been encountered. They had had no appreciation of the significance of the oil—no ritual understanding, no comprehension of the etiquette of exchange. The power of their weapons was extraordinary, but one had no sense of what modulated their violence. By plane and by foot, they invaded people's territory without request or truce or the sanctuary of kin.

The historical narrative was constructed briefly, contrastively, and largely negatively. Yet, each contrast was centered on particular elements not only in the display but also in the earlier mythic narration. Each element in the historical narrative was carefully described in several ways and, thus, bounded, for each element was seen to be overwhelmingly unique in most respects and not readily embedded in Bimin-Kuskusmin classificatory schemes. Bosuurok seemed unable, unwilling, or disinclined to probe beneath the 'surfaces' of the bounded European-centered events enough to enrich the semantic linkages *between* those 'surfaces' in any significant way except in terms of their fundamental implications for the moral personhood of Europeans. The events remained relatively discrete with respect not only to one another, but also to the Bimin-Kuskusmin mythic framework for interpretation. Indeed, there was no sustained attempt to embed these historical events in Bimin-Kuskusmin classificatory schemes beyond underlying issues of morality and personhood, which were held at some conceptual distance from the more immediate "fit" between narrative structures. Perhaps because the comparative effort in this instance was so emphatically contrastive in structure and negative in evaluative tone, the two narratives remained separated by a considerable gap, the framing boundaries held firm, and the mythic framework proved inadequate to encase the newly formed narrative in the often expected manner. Yet, the very separation that was maintained between the two narratives through contrastive linkage yielded a form of comparison and a somewhat fragile interpretation of 'sacred meaning.' The marked incongruity between the two narratives became a focus of concerted gathering of information and analytic attention, and much interesting comparative effort was invested in probing the nature of the gap; for a fundamental and disconcerting issue of the character and limits of personhood was seen to be at stake. Was the apparent moral gap between European and Bimin-Kuskusmin negotiable and, if so, on what grounds? If not, what would be the consequences? In time, two other and competing mythic frameworks for interpreting the 'sacred meaning' of the European presence emerged. One portrayed the distribution of morality vis-à-vis a traditional multi-ethnic landscape and sought to locate the European, by some analogy, on that map.[31] The other, and the one that Bosuurok had dismissed, continued to explore the entailments and consequences of viewing the European as Afek's lastborn child returning to the 'center place' with awesome ritual powers as manifested in matters of technology. To date, neither framework has clearly gained ascendancy, but both interpretive efforts—by virtue of the discursive, spatial, temporal, and other structures that encase them—are mnemonically retrievable in the collective memory of ritual elders who continue to resurrect them in impressive detail and to explore again their hidden significance in further 'work of sacred imagination' (*gaangan'nuuriin ogaak'khaa*).

This brief exploration of selected features of Bimin-Kuskusmin intellectual efforts to utilize mythic frameworks—to some extent locally recognized by ritual elders to be fabricated, to be of human design—as a way of confronting puzzles and dilemmas of the human condition has traversed a complex landscape of (1) concepts of person, *finiik*, 'thinking/feeling,' *aiyem;* (2) of metaphors of crystals, rainbows, shadows, and reflections; (3) of models of the structure of myth and the nature of *mythologique;* and (4) of ideas about the mythologically centered interpretation of historical events, without a familiar map. Yet, it is all too common in comparative history, mythology, philosophy, and religion to establish a framework of familiar—and often Western historical—categories to enhance comprehension by Western academic audiences and, thus, to lose sight of how non-Western peoples construct their own strategies and tactics for making sense of the world. In this chapter, I have moved in a somewhat different direction by attempting to provide a glimpse of Bimin-Kuskusmin views of epistemological, interpretive, and metaphysical issues in a manner that illuminates something of both the clarity and the ambiguity of their mode of intellectual and emotional struggle to comprehend a dramatically changing world and their place within it. By attending to their metaphors and the underlying cultural schemata that such metaphors identify and by recognizing that both the ambiguous and the coherent inhabit the realm of human reasoning, one encounters a set of issues about the local construction of understanding that comparative inquiry must develop ways of more sensitively encountering.

Despite the elaborations of this traditional design of mythic interpretation, however, one cannot ignore the ritual status, rhetorical skill, political prominence, and more implicit agenda of Bosuurok as narrator/interpreter. On the one hand, he draws on a sense of tradition in mythic interpretation with respect to which he has special powers, talents, and entitlements. In this regard, he lays claim to shaping 'historical events' as domesticated, managed, or controlled by a tradition that enfolds, transcends, and even colonizes them. They are made to appear neutralized or overpowered in mythically framed perceptions of new "forms of life" associated with Europeans. On the other hand, Bosuurok stands at the very center of key political interests reflected in the ideological implications of his 'sacred' interpretation. By disempowering the realm of the European, he has attempted to protect Bimin-Kuskusmin ritual paramountcy from the growing challenge of mission endeavors, to realign the configuration of ritual power in his cultural region, and to preserve the autonomy and superiority of a mythic tradition in the face of increasingly dramatic change. But this significant facet of mythic interpretation is noted in another essay.[32]

Notes

1.   The myths of Afek represent the centerpiece of the Bimin-Kuskusmin corpus of 'sacred myths' (*aiyem sang*) and of the final and most elaborate rite of the male initiation cycle and are associated with the primordial, androgynous, founding ancestor Afek, often represented as the cassowary, and "her" hermaphroditic consort Yomnok, typically portrayed as the echidna. A particular form of 'understanding' (*khaim'khraakkhaan*) is associated with the interpretation of these myths.

2.   The genre of 'images encased in words' (*kamiin feibaakiinan duu weeng*) or 'condensed, congealed speech' (*weeng waarak*) includes not only myths and some sixteen other types of tales, but also myriad proverbs, riddles, spells, chants, musical compositions, divinatory formulas, and other more or less structured, formulaic dicta and nonlanguage sound patterns, as well as representations of dreams, ritually induced "altered states of consciousness," and iconic ritual displays.

3.   See Poole, "The Voice of 'Thinking/Feeling,'" 1–30. The Bimin-Kuskusmin model of speech indicates that discourse inevitably is distortive of meaning in at least some senses and often hides as much as it reveals. Beyond the intentions and linguistic skills of the speaker, speech itself is said to be a 'crooked path' for the conveyance of meaning. The problem is most eloquently discussed in relation to verbal representations of dreams, ritually induced "altered states of consciousness," and iconic ritual displays, for which speech is deemed an impoverished representational resource.

4.   Field research among the Bimin-Kuskusmin (1971–73) was supported by the National Institutes of Health, the Cornell University/Ford Foundation Humanities and Social Sciences program, and the Center for South Pacific Studies of the University of California, Santa Cruz. The primary debt of gratitude, however, is owed to the Bimin-Kuskusmin people, and especially their ritual elders, for examplifying in word and deed the shapes, hues, and tones of 'wisdom' in unveiling the mysteries of myth.

5.   See D'Andrade, "The Cultural Part of Cognition," 179–95; and D'Andrade, "Cultural Meaning Systems," 88–119. Following D'Andrade, shared cultural schemata are fundamentally involved in perception, recognition, interpretation, problem-solving, and other modes of processing information that facilitate representation of, and enable or guide action in, those situations in which particular crystallizations of the schemata are instantiated. A schema usually consists of a small number of conceptual elements and their relations to one another as they are linked in semantic networks. The conceptual elements of a schema exhibit a typical range of values, can be variously interlinked within the schema or among other schemata, and can be variously bound to different aspects of the environ-

ment on different instantiations of the schema. The typical constraints on the concepts of the schema—that is, on their values and interrelationships—serve two critical functions: (a) they facilitate the use of the schema as a hypothesis about the identity or conceptual properties of an event or situation, and (b) they permit an interpretation to proceed beyond the information given in guiding inferences about unobserved, tacit, or ambiguous aspects of the situation or event. Yet, each conceptual element of a schema may itself be a complex schema, for schemata encompass subschemata in a hierarchical mode of organization that may be simultaneously activated *both* from the top down (that is, from whole to part) *and* from the bottom up (that is, from part to whole) as the construction of an instantiation and an interpretation proceeds. As D'Andrade implies, a distinctive attribute of most cultural schemata is that they are not precisely specified or explicit in all respects as they are represented in natural discourse. Indeed, certain aspects of such folk models remain tacit, ambiguous, or even opaque. Tacit dimensions presume other schemata that are implicated by, but are not explicitly embedded in or otherwise articulated with the focal folk model, and thus require implicit criteria of relevance and processes of inference to interconnect and to interpret these covert schemata. By virtue of some manner of intersubjective sharing of these cultural schemata in a community, certain aspects of folk models are often perceived as being obvious and "natural" facts of the world and need not be made explicit. These implicit aspects, however, are commonly the premises of the more explicit features of folk models. Ambiguous features of cultural schemata leave unresolved the problem of which of several potentially linked schemata, each with somewhat different implications for the hierarchical organization of *relevant* schemata, may be implied. Opaque features are lacunae in the structure of the folk model that are not readily articulated with other available cultural schemata and mark certain disjunctive aspects of the linkages among those concepts that are articulated by a schema. See also Langacker, *Foundations of Cognitive Grammar.* Langacker's notions of "base" and "profile" in his view of the cognitive foundations of grammar illuminate how various aspects of interlinked schemata or semantic networks may be foregrounded (specified) or backgrounded (left tacit) in the process of interpretation. These several characteristics of cultural schemata suggest that the interwoven networks of concepts that constitute a schema may variously exhibit strong and weak, complex and simple, dense and diffuse, and other variable qualities of connectivity or even gaps of articulation.

6. See Fortes, "On the Concept of the Person," 283–319. By personhood, following Fortes, I refer to those attributes, capacities, and signs that mark a moral career and its jural entitlements in a particular society. An interest in personhood invokes a concern with the cultural forms and social forces that together publicly render the individual present in a culturally constituted "human nature" that is socially encompassed and in some array of social positions that are the entitlements and the emblems of the achievement of particular kinds and degrees of personhood. Indeed, social personhood endows the culturally recognized indi-

vidual with those powers or capacities upon which human agency depends, enables and constrains his proper actions, casts him as possessed of judgment and thus responsibility, and calls him to account in a legal-moral-political-social order. Although the capacities of personhood may be anchored to the powers and limitations of the human body and thus seen as "natural" attributes, they are at once judgmental, social, and mystical capacities, and persons are essentially social beings who develop in different ways and to differing degrees over the course of the social life cycle. Thus, a person is fundamentally a social being with a certain moral status and is a legitimate bearer of rights and obligations. A person has a sense of self and of individuality, a notion of past and future; he can hold values, perceive goals, recognize resources, acknowledge contraints, make choices, and thus adopt plans that are attributable to him as a being with the conscious, reflective capacity to frame culturally appropriate representations of phenomena and to have purposes, desires, and aversions that require judgment. To be a person, or a moral agent, is to be sensitive to certain standards of the sociomoral order of the community and to suffer a sense of shame when their breach may be attributed to one's personal judgment and responsibility. Personhood, thus, is fundamentally a conceptual adjustment of a culturally constituted sense of "human nature" to a socially constituted jural-moral order.

7. See Poole, "Knowledge Rests in the Heart"; "The Ritual Forging of Identity," 99–154; "Cannibals, Tricksters, and Witches," 6–32; "Symbols of Substance," 191–216; "Erosion of a Sacred Landscape," 169–82; "Morality, Personhood, Tricksters, and Youths," 283–366; "Ritual Rank, the Self, and Ancestral Power," 149–96; "The Voice of 'Thinking/Feeling'"; "Cultural Schemata and Learning of the 'Sacred'"; and "Veils of Illusion, Kernels of Truth." It should be noted that Bimin-Kuskusmin view their myth-ritual complex as being the very core of their sense of an enduring, distinctive 'tradition' (*khaankharaak'khaan*). Indeed, it might be claimed that every community exhibits certain conceptual and institutional arrangements that are "their greatest elaborations and richest embellishments" (Tambiah, *Culture, Thought, and Social Action,* 13), and that an understanding of the significance of these sociocultural "centers"—and the metaphors and symbols in which they are cast—provides an important lens on a "form of life." For Bimin-Kuskusmin, that lens is very much embedded in the realm of myth and ritual.

8. Although this chapter is focally concerned with the logic and practice of mythic interpretations of historical phenomena as a genre of indigenous philosophy, some brief remarks on the general character of the "historical consciousness" of the Bimin-Kuskusmin vis-à-vis first contact are in order. The history noted here focuses on events surrounding the advent of the European into the mountain fastness of a remote Papua New Guinean people—on the encounter with an "Other" from a previously unimagined cultural world. This unsettling

encounter—with its aura of existential shock and epistemological uncertainty—led to the mobilization of cultural resources in the form of categories, values, and understandings to make a local sense of alien events and beings. The most privileged and authoritarian of these cultural resources have involved the elaborate schemas of mythic interpretations of historic events examined in this chapter. Indeed, Bimin-Kuskusmin ways of experiencing and understanding history and thus of constituting a sense of historicity are intimately bound up with constructions and representations of the past in mythic-ritual discourse.

The basic character of the events of first contact are well known to many older persons, for they occurred well within the lifetimes of most Bimin-Kuskusmin adults. Many reconstructions of these events have been drawn from conversations with men, and some women—although less entitled and more reticent to have a voice in such matters—have also presented their portraits of the coming of the first European. Reports of similar occurrences among the Telefolmin to the west have also been examined (D. Jorgensen, personal communication), and the accounts of the first patrol itself have been studied. There is considerable consistency among these accounts despite their inevitable variability in detail and emphasis. The constructions of these events as they are represented in the mythic interpretations of them explored here, however, are drawn primarily from the elaborated images of first contact presented by Bosuurok and Trumeng—the paramount male ritual elders of the ranking clans of the Bimin-Kuskusmin during fieldwork in 1971–1973. It is among such ritual elders that the detail of such historical events—invariably enfolded by the mythic interpretations placed upon them—is the richest, and they alone have the ritual authority to pronounce upon the significance of such events.

That the detail of this historical portrait should be so rich and vivid is intricately related not simply to its dramatic character but also to how it is encoded mnemonically. The mythic memory and narration of historical events is shaped by the interwoven "structures" of the mythic interpretation of such events. In turn, these "structures" are articulated with an image of a mythic "path" that traces a course up and down mountains from one named sacred site to the next from north to west to east across a ring of mountains. These sacred sites and the mountain path on which they are located are well known to all Bimin-Kuskusmin adult men who have walked the path many times in ritual and otherwise. Each successive site on the path may be associated with elements of the chronology of a narrative. This elaborate mnemonic, reminiscent of the kind of pattern described in F. A. Yates' (1966) *The Art of Memory* and known from other Oceanic societies, enables a great deal of detail, arranged chronologically with respect to a path, to be encoded and recalled with remarkable consistency in different accounts. Indeed, such remarkable recasting of the minutiae of first contact as represented in mythic interpretations was evident in the consistent retelling of the original mythic interpretations of first contact during brief visits to the field in

1981 and 1982 when new mythic interpretations of these events were being launched and explicitly compared with earlier ones.

9. See Beidelman, *Moral Imagination in Kaguru Modes of Thought.*

10. See Hallowell, *Culture and Experience.*

11. See Fernandez, *Persuasions and Performances.*

12. See Soskice, *Metaphor and Religious Language.* The significant role of metaphor in religious language represents a problem requiring both theoretical and empirical exploration.

13. See Lakoff, *Women, Fire, and Dangerous Things.* Despite the considerable promise of Lakoff's program, I strongly suspect that cultural schemata are not so much constituted by metaphor as indicated by metaphor and that the underlying structure of folk models, if not image-schematic (in Lakoff's term), is more likely some kind of story-like event-structure. One could argue that "event-ness" is as fundamental to human experience and existence as "embodiment." Cf. Potter, "Metaphor as Key to Understanding the Thought of Other Speech Communities," 19–35.

14. Poole, "Metaphors and Maps," 411–57.

15. See Pool, ibid.; Lakoff, op. cit.; Potter, op. cit.

16. Cf. Larson, "Introduction," 3–18; Rosemont, "Against Relativism," 36–70; Smart, *Concept and Empathy;* Smart, "The Analogy of Meaning and the Tasks of Comparative Philosophy," 174–83; Smith, *Map Is Not Territory;* and Smith, *Imagining Religion.*

17. See Scharfstein, "The Contextual Fallacy," 84–97. The "contextual fallacy"— that is, a misplaced sense of the irrevocable anchoring of meaning to situation under all circumstances—has often been too much of an unwarranted impediment to cross-cultural comparison. Furthermore, this sense of meaning-in-context has often denied the powers of abstraction to the peoples whom we study and has contributed to misguided assumptions underlying the notion of culture as a "seamless web," as a uniformly and tightly integrated pattern. See also Gellner, "Concepts and Society," 18–46; and Levine, *The Flight from Ambiguity.*

18. See Gyekye, *An Essay on African Philosophical Thought;* Horton, "African Traditional Thought and Western Science," 50–71, 155–87; see also Penner, "Rationality and Religion," 645–71. Cf. Larson, op. cit.; Smart, "The Analogy of Meaning," 174–83. Some of the key problems in Horton's program are interestingly dealt with in Penner's critical appraisal of his work.

19. See Rosemont, op. cit. Following Rosemont, I suggest that the enterprise of comparative philosophy must avoid defining its focus of comparison too narrowly and in terms of "concept clusters" that have had a varied existence in the

history of philosophy in the West. See also Larson, op. cit. From Radin's early attempt to locate philosophy in traditional societies to Gyekye's survey of the lineaments of Akan philosophy, there has been an unfortunate tendency to map indigenous concepts of various kinds onto what have been taken to be more or less stable and definitive Western philosophical categories with little recognition of the controversies pertaining to and the historical fluidities of the latter. See Radin, *Primitive Man as Philosopher,* and Gyekye, op. cit.

20.   For a fine discussion of these senses of praxis, see Lobkowicz, *Theory and Practice.*

21.   See Poole, "Cannibals, Tricksters, and Witches," 6–32; "Erosion of a Sacred Landscape," 169–82; and "Morality, Personhood, Tricksters, and Youths," 283–366. Bimin-Kuskusmin personhood is characterized by a distributive morality centered in the clearly bounded, ritually sanctified territory of the 'center place.' Indeed, the entire traditional territory of the Bimin-Kuskusmin is a ritually bounded space, despite the fact of land won by historical conquest and subsequently sanctified and enshrined in mythic maps of a contiguous whole. See also Smith, *Imagining Religion,* 53–65.

22.   Male substance refers primarily to plant or animal foods that are themselves *finiik*-bearing and appropriate for sacrifice, parts of the anatomy that are classified as 'male' and are enhanced by other male substances or mythic-ritual experiences, and certain hallucinogens that are used in particular rites by such ritual adepts.

23.   The knowledge that is bound up with male myth-ritual experience is held to be a distinctive corpus of knowledge, which associated with a complex, hierarchically organized sociology of knowledge that is elaborately marked by rules of entitlement and rules of taboo.

24.   Cf. Smith, *Man Is Not Territory.*

25.   Cf. Smith, ibid., 300.

26.   See Harris, *Casting Out Anger.* As Harris notes for the Taita, an important aspect of these rites is that they are at once inward-looking in reference to the bounded realm of ritual and outward-looking in reference to broader matters of sociocultural life.

27.   Cf. Firth, "The Plasticity of Myth," 181–88; Van Baaren, "The Flexibility of Myth," 199–206. More generally, Gellner, op. cit., and Levine, op. cit., have been at pains to observe that open-endedness, flexibility, inconsistency, incongruity, ambiguity, and the like are ordinary and essential characteristics of cultural systems, which all too often are portrayed as uniformly and tightly integrated, coherent *systems.* Both Gellner and Levine note that, both descriptively and theoretically, this aspect of sociocultural organization has gone largely unnoticed ethnographically and undeveloped theoretically.

28. See Poole, "Erosion of a Sacred Landscape," 169–82.

29. Although this divinatory aspect of mythically framed interpretation is significantly affected by political considerations, for successful interpretations are claims to ritual prestige and authority that diffuse into economic-political domains, I am not considering these political aspects of the process of achieving interpretive consensus here.

30. See Poole, "Erosion of a Sacred Landscape," 169–82; and "Cultural Schemata and Learning of the 'sacred.'"

31. See Poole, "Cannibals, Tricksters, and Witches," 6–32.

32. See Poole, "The Reason of Myth."

References

Beidelman, T. O.
　　1986 *Moral Imagination in Kaguru Modes of Thought*. Bloomington: Indiana University Press.

D'Andrade, R. G.
　　1981 "The Cultural Part of Cognition." *Cognitive Science* 5:179–95.

　　1984 "Cultural Meaning Systems." In *Culture theory*, edited by R. A. Shweder and R. A. LeVine, 88–119. Cambridge: Cambridge University Press.

Fernandez, J. W.
　　1986 *Persuasions and Performances*. Bloomington: Indiana University Press.

Firth, R.
　　1960 "The Plasticity of Myth: Cases from Tikopia." *Ethnologica* 2: 181–88.

Fortes, M.
　　1973 "On the Concept of the Person among the Tallensi." In *La Notion de personne en Afrique noire*, edited by G. Dieterlen, 283–319. Paris: Éditions du Centre National de la Recherche Scientifique.

Gellner, E.
　　1973 "Concepts and Society." In *Cause and Meaning in the Social Sciences*, edited by E. Gellner, 18–46. London: Routledge and Kegan Paul.

Gyekye, K.
1987 *An Essay on African Philosophical Thought.* Cambridge: Cambridge University Press.

Hallowell, A. I.
1955 *Culture and Experience.* Philadelphia: University of Pennsylvania Press.

Harris, G. G.
1978 *Casting Out Anger.* Cambridge: Cambridge University Press.

Horton, R.
1967 "African Traditional Thought and Western Science." *Africa* 37:50–71, 155–87.

Lakoff, G.
1987 *Women, Fire, and Dangerous Things.* Chicago: University of Chicago Press.

Langacker, R. W.
1987 *Foundations of Cognitive Grammar,* volume 1. Stanford, Calif.: Stanford University Press.

Larson, G. J.
1988 "Introduction: The "Age-Old" Distinction Between the Same and the Other." In *Interpreting Across Boundaries,* edited by G. J. Larson and E. Deutsch, 3–16. Princeton, Princeton University press.

Levine, D. N.
1985 *The Flight from Ambiguity.* Chicago: University of Chicago Press.

Lobkowicz, N.
1967 *Theory and Practice.* Notre Dame, Ind.: University of Notre Dame Press.

Penner, H. H.
1986 "Rationality and Religion: Problems in the Comparison of modes of Thought." *Journal of the American Academy of Religion* 54: 645–71.

Poole, F. J. P.
1976 "'Knowledge Rests in the Heart': Bimin-Kuskusmin Meta-Communications on Meaning, Tacit Knowledge, and Field Research." Paper presented at the 75th Annual Meeting of the American Anthropological Association, Washington, D.C.

———.
1982 "The Ritual Forging of Identity: Aspects of Person and Self in

Bimin-Kuskusmin Male Initiation. In *Rituals of Manhood,* edited by G. H. Herdt, 99–154. Berkeley: University of California Press.

――――.

1983 "Cannibals, Tricksters, and Witches: Anthropophagic Images among Bimin-Kuskusmin." In *The Ethnography of Cannibalism,* edited by P. Brown and D. Tuzin, 6–32. Washington, D.C.: Society for Psychological Anthropology.

――――.

1984 "Symbols of Substance: Bimin-Kuskusmin Models of Procreation, Death, and Personhood." *Mankind* 14:191–216.

――――.

1986a "Erosion of a Sacred Landscape: European Exploration and Cultural Ecology among the Bimin-Kuskusmin of Papua New Guines." In *Mountain People,* edited by M. Tobias, 169–82. Norman: University of Oklahoma Press.

――――.

1986b "Metaphors and Maps: Towards Comparison in the Anthropology of Religion." *Journal of the American Academy of Religion* 54:411–57.

――――.

1987a "Melanesian Religions: Mythic Themes." In *The Encyclopedia of Religion,* edited by M. Eliade et al., 9:359–65. New York: Macmillan.

――――.

1987b "Morality, Personhood, Tricksters, and Youths: Some Narrative Images of Ethics among Bimin-Kuskusmin." In *Anthropology in the High Valleys,* edited by L. L. Langness and T. E. Hays, 283–366. Novato, Calif.: Chandler and Sharp.

――――.

1987c "Ritual Rank, the Self, and Ancestral Power: Liturgy and Substance in a Papua New Guinea Society." In *Drugs in Western Pacific Societies,* edited by L. Lindstrom, 149–96. Lanham, Md.: University Press of America.

――――.

1987d "The Voice of 'Thinking/Feeling' and the Power of Speech: Ethno-Psychological Discourse among Bimin-Kuskusmin." Paper presented at the 86th Annual Meeting of the American Anthropological Association, Chicago.

――――.

1988 "Cultural Schemata and Learning of the 'sacred': Socialization,

Enculturation, and the Concept of *AIYEM* in the Bimin-Kuskusmin Culture of Children." Paper presented at the King's College Research Centre, Cambridge University, Cambridge.

———.

1992 "The Reason of Myth and the Rationality of History: The Logic of the Mythic in Bimin-Kuskusmin 'Modes of Thought.'" In *Religion and Practical Reason,* volume 2, edited by F. E. Reynolds and D. Tracy. Albany, N.Y.: State University of New York Press. June 1992.

———.

n.d. "Veils of Illusion, Kernels of Truth: Secrecy and Revelation in Bimin-Kuskusmin Ritual. Unpublished manuscript.

Potter, K. H.
1988 "Metaphor as Key to Understanding the Thought of Other Speech Communities." In *Interpreting Across Boundaries,* edited by G. J. Larson and E. Deutsch, 19–35. Princeton, N.J.: Princeton University Press.

Radin, P.
1957 *Primitive Man as Philosopher.* New York: Dover Publications.

Rosemont, H., Jr.
1988 "Against Relativism." In *Interpreting Across Boundaries,* edited by G. J. Larson and E. Deutsch, 36–70. Princeton, N.J.: Princeton University Press.

Scharfstein, B-A.
1988 "The Contextual Fallacy." In *Interpreting Across Boundaries,* edited by G. J. Larson and E. Deutsch, 84–97. Princeton, N.J.: Princeton University Press.

Smart, N.
1986 *Concept and Empathy.* New York: New York University Press.

———.

1988 "The Analogy of Meaning and the Tasks of Comparative Philosophy. In *Interpreting Across Boundaries,* edited by G. J. Larson and E. Deutsch, 174–83. Princeton, N.J.: Princeton University Press.

Smith, J. Z.
1978 *Map Is Not Territory.* Leiden: E. J. Brill.

———.

1982 *Imagining Religion.* Chicago: University of Chicago Press.

Soskice, J. M.
1985 *Metaphor and Religious Language*. Oxford: The Clarendon Press.

Tambiah, S. J.
1985 *Culture, Thought, and Social Action*. Cambridge: Harvard University Press.

van Baaren, Th. P.
1972 "The Flexibility of Myth. *Studies in the History of Religions* 22:199–206.

Yates, F. A.
1966 *The Art of Memory*. Chicago: The University of Chicago Press.

Chapter 2

Samantabhadra and Rudra: Innate Enlightenment and Radical Evil in Tibetan Rnying-ma-pa-Buddhism

Matthew Kapstein

Even a man who is fond of myths is in a way a philosopher, since a myth is made up of wonders.

—Aristotle, *Metaphysics, I.2.*

The Truth of Myth

Readers of *The Once and Future King* may recall Arthur's adventures among the ants, who know only two categories of thought: "done" and "undone." From the perspective of that formic adherence to the principle of bivalence, much of what follows will have to be allocated to the latter category. Reflections on folklore, philosophy, history, and religion all seem to have their proper roles in the diversion taking shape here, but I will not yet argue that I have figured out quite what these might be. One may also recall that the ants know but one song—a mind-numbingly repetitive tune whose sole lyric is "mammy." Raw/undone/*kaccha* though the present offering may be, I hope that at the very least it will provide something better in the way of melodic amusement.

To a large extent, the investigations presented in this volume and its predecessor turn on the relationship between philosophy and myth. The problem, posed in this manner, seems a disconcerting one, and one may feel that the question, "What is the nature of the relationship between philosophy and myth?" if not actually ill-formed, is somehow fishy. Consider, for example, Arthur Adkins's insistence that we study, in the context of classical Greek thought, not the relationship between mythos and *philosophia,* but rather the relationship between mythos and logos within *philosophia,*[1] and Philip Quinn, too, has suggested that we regard myth and philosophy not as contradictory categories, but instead see them both as belonging to a broader spectrum of discourse, of which each only covers a small part.[2]

Nonetheless, there does sometimes appear to be a peculiar relationship between myth and philosophical or scientific reason that is underscored when we turn to some now generally discredited theories of myth, for instance, Sir James Frazer's view that myth is "false science." Many, probably most, contemporary folklorists would insist that, regardless of the actual truth or falsehood of a myth, even assuming that to be capable of determination in any given case, the community in which a myth is transmitted traditionally regards it to be in some sense true. Given Frazer's assumptions, we can only conclude that myths are false explanations that are nonetheless taken to be true, for if they were *thought* to be false, they would no longer be myths. Indeed, this explains quite well a very common use of the term "myth" in contemporary English: "It's a myth that you can get AIDS from a handshake."[3]

While Frazer's view of myth as false explanation is no longer much adhered to by those who make it their business to specialize in the study of myth, there are nevertheless two points made in this connection that I think merit our continuing consideration: first, myth may often have some special relationship to reason, particularly to reasoned explanation, that neither legend nor folktale generally does, and second, we should attend carefully to the question of the truth-value of myths. A third point that I shall seek to emphasize in what follows relates to the common characterization of myths as narratives concerned with sacred history.

In its explanatory dimension myth engages reason by disclosing as intelligible what had otherwise seemed mysterious and by motivating appropriate human behavior in the light of what is thus explained, at least whenever the proper ordering of human agency is part of the mystery made intelligible, as it is in many important myths. For example, what we may term the "myth of our technological hubris" tells a certain community of believers among us that the mystery of much human misery may be understood with reference to humanity's over-reaching itself and sacrificing an essential, vitalizing harmony with nature in the course of a self-defeating and obsessive drive to attain control of nature. Apart from the truth or falsehood of any particular claims advanced in this connection, the believer may assert that, in the light of this myth, much of human misery is revealed to be an intelligible phenomenon, and so may be motivated to contribute to the alleviation of suffering by assisting in the effort to refrain from and limit our abuse of nature through technology. This, in turn, may or may not require that the believer master certain specific information about history or physical science.[4]

It is easy to see that the same points might just as well be made with reference to traditional myth narratives. Consider, for example, one of the myths that is told in connection with the cult of Bhāṭbhaṭinī, a deified minstrel couple widely worshipped by the Newars of the Kathmandu Valley in Nepal:

> Bhaṭinī, like Hāritī, had a taste for human flesh. But Viṣṇu, by means of Garuḍa, seized one of Bhaṭinī's own beloved brood, restoring it only on the ogress' promise to foreswear human flesh and to become instead a protector of children. It is apparently in this role that the blessing of Bhāṭbhaṭinī is invoked by parents of children thought to be bewitched or to be suffering from mental or physical disease.[5]

As long as there is a community affirming the authority of this myth, its members will continue to propitiate the minstrel couple to alleviate the illnesses of their children, and they will do so reasonably as long as the myth is not falsified for them in practice, as it might be if they were to conclude, for instance, that recovery of health was notably less likely for children of Bhāṭbhaṭinī worshippers than among the children of other Kathmandu Newars.[6]

These reflections, underscoring the relationship between mythic explanation and motivated action, lead us immediately to question the truth of myths. It may seem that in a certain sense they show truth to be virtually irrelevant here. The myths a given community considers authoritative, however, need not be thought to be true in the sense that they convey demonstrably true "factual" information: mythic matters seem to be more subtle than facts of the matter. The truth in myth may be thought to be expressed allegorically, metaphorically, or approximatively, or myth may be thought just to orient us toward truth so buried in mystery that no human discourse can disclose it directly. The truth in myth is thus conceived as veiled and obscure truth and this, of course, reinforces for some the conclusion that myths somehow stand outside of the domain of truth-value.

That conclusion, again, I believe to be wrong. For myth-truth, while not "factual" truth, is allied to pragmatic truth, in something approaching a Jamesian sense.[7] A myth is felt to be true whenever it functions in the discourse of a community to ground action that is itself felt to bring about the success of that community or of its individual members. It may thus be said to be true to the extent that it is felt by those who yield to its authority to promote *non-self-defeating ends*. Because it is probably impossible to remove the determination of human ends and their successful fulfillment from the domain of seeming, myth-truth cannot itself be more than a matter of seeming. But to say this is not to say that truth-value is irrelevant here, for the possibility of self-defeat entails that some myths may be *historically* revealed to be false to the very communities that, at an earlier time, had affirmed them.

Myth-truth, then, is essentially tied to a community's history, and myth makers may be said to know this. For even when, as is often the case, the time in which the events narrated in myth stand outside of historical time, it is nonetheless historical time—whether in terms of some of its particular features or the whole thereof—that is explained and interpreted through myth. Myth is in this respect metahistorical discourse. For this reason, myth may sometimes emerge as a powerful medium for philosophical and scientific thought: consider here the myths of the state of nature and the social contract in political philosophy since Hobbes, or that of the primal horde in the thought of Freud.[8]

Myths, in sum, engage our thinking in reason, truth, and history and so express and constitute the thinker's vision of these domains and of the manner in which they are related to one another. This being the case, we must avoid the error of associating mythical thinking preeminently with the "primitive" or the "archaic." Mythical discourse, as I understand it here, is part of the essential constitution of human discourse, though its precise role and value, and above all the specific manner of its articulation, may vary from one cultural-historical setting to the next.

The foregoing considerations permit us to clarify what we mean when we say, for instance, that "science is our myth."[9] This slogan is confusing because one may mean by it that *scientific discourse is mythical discourse*. But clearly we don't want to countenance the unbridled and arbitrary relativism that that would entail. What we should mean when we speak of science as our myth, if we wish to mean something sensible here, is that we have a (usually inexplicit) "story" we transmit in our culture concerning reason, truth, and history and authenticating the origins and underwriting the value and validity of science for us. It is precisely myth's role to do these things in a world of discourse, not science's. Notice, however, that "myth" as it is used in this instance no longer refers to a particular discourse genre but rather to any body of discourse that performs the tasks I have attributed here to myth as a particular genre of discourse. This is a derivative way of using the term "myth," and one that I shall employ from time to time, but it should not be conflated with the more primary signification of the term, which refers to a particular narrative category.

In Consideration of Context

Like some others who have contributed to these volumes,[10] I am concerned in this chapter with the study of a particular cultural sphere that is not our own, in this instance, the realm of Tibetan Buddhism. Investigations such as these tend to accentuate the apparent gulf separating descriptive and documentary scholarship from the domain of theory and interpretation, while at the same time repeatedly threatening to abolish the gulf altogether. It may appear that the matter gathered in historical and cross-cultural research is so much mythic grist for a meta-mythic mill. (If this is the case, our granaries are now stuffed to overflowing.) In construing our enterprise in this manner, we privilege ourselves and it: we think ourselves to be in a uniquely favorable position to understand what the myth makers say. We're so skillful, in fact, that we have come to conceal our presumption by focusing not on our supposed understanding, but on its uncertainty and its limits. No longer nouveaux riches, we have begun to be worried by the moral and material fragility of our wealth.

It seems desirable, in these circumstances, to give up altogether the attempt to resolve the problem of grist/mill dualism by tinkering with the construction of better meta-mythic mills: there is, I think, no all-embracing theoretical model that is going to permit us to make definitive sense of the relationships among myth, history, religion, and philosophy in our own cultural sphere or in any other. Against our implicit (and often explicit) retention of the familiar dichotomy between theory-philosophy, on the one hand, and that which theory-philosophy seeks to explain-interpret, on the other, we require a vision of human culture-forming discourse in which historical, philosophical, mythic, poetic, and other specific discourse genres may be seen to interact as possibly coequal conversation partners. In such culture-forming discourse conservation is indeed equivalent to creation, so that the conception is one of a dynamic system that is necessarily extended in time, subject to continuous change, generating itself anew in each cultural-historical instant.

Those engaged in cross-cultural and historical researches will at once recognize the problem of contextualization as one that calls to our attention the discomforting and irreducible necessity with which such multifaceted discourse domains—worlds of thought in which myth and science, history and metaphysics, and logic, poetry, and jokes come crashing together—impose themselves upon us. It seems unlikely that we should ever be able to provide a purely "methodological" account of contextualization that would also serve as an acceptable guide to practice.[11] We know that contextual background plays a crucial role in understanding, so we can't eliminate it. We can't seem to come up with a decisive formulation of what that role is to be, so we'd like to. We know that those who seem to do it best bring a wonderful array of skills to the task, which we seek to emulate: broad general learning, an eye for precise and relevant detail, incisive analytical abilities and far-reaching synthetic imagination, eloquence, the gifts of a story-teller. To put it plainly: the scholar as contextualizer is a myth maker. S/He must spin a tale of reason, truth and history, knowing which the actions/arts/sciences/myths of persons elsewhere and elsewhen become somehow more intelligible for us than they might have been otherwise. Because this is a form of myth making, we are always a bit suspicious of it—the eloquently told tale may always prove misleading: witness the varied constructions and deconstructions of the several Orientalisms.

The realm that I seek to explore in the reflections that follow, on two Tibetan myths, is here by no means conceived to be peculiarly "non-Western," much less "Buddhological" or "Tibetological," and in a more developed form the present exercise might well be explicitly comparative. Philosophical myth making belongs no less to the non-Eastern world than to any other. Though the material I consider below may strike some as exotic, my central concerns are, I believe, much in harmony with those of Martha Nussbaum, Charles Taylor, and other philosophers who have in recent years insisted upon the need for a fundamental reassessment of the relationship between philosophy and narrative, even in treating exclusively the Western tradition.[12]

Fragments from a Myth of Tibet

It will not be possible to examine the historical origins of the myths of Samantabhadra and Rudra in this chapter. Even limiting one's field solely to Buddhist materials, it would be essential to consider an extensive body of Indian literature, above all the many Buddhist tantras, even before seeking to elaborate peculiarly Tibetan developments. And in Tibet itself, we would have to investigate the manner in which the Indian versions of these myths were variously assimilated and transformed through the historical ramification of Tibetan Buddhism into a great number of distinct lineages and schools.[13]

My concern here, therefore, will be with the best known versions of these myths as transmitted in the Rnying-ma-pa tradition of Tibetan Buddhism, for which these myths have a special importance. I believe that some puzzling aspects of Rnying-ma-pa thought and practice become more readily understandable when we grasp something of the manner in which these myths are employed within that tradition.

The Rnying-ma-pa stand in a distinctive relationship to all other traditions of Tibetan religion. As its name, which literally means the "Ancients," suggests, the school maintains that it uniquely represents the ancient Buddhism of Tibet, introduced during the reigns of the great kings of Tibet's Imperial Age, i.e., seventh to ninth centuries C.E. In contradistinction to the organized Bon religion, it identifies itself as a purely Buddhist school, whereas, over and against the other Tibetan Buddhist schools and in harmony with the Bon, it insists upon the value of an autochthonous Tibetan religious tradition, expressed and exalted within a unique and continuing revelation of the Buddha's doctrine in Tibet. The following features of Rnying-ma-pa Buddhism are particularly noteworthy in connection with the present discussion.

The primordial Buddha Samantabhadra (Tibetan *Kun-tu bzang-po,* the "Omnibeneficent"), iconographically depicted as being of a celestial blue and naked, is regarded as the supreme embodiment of Buddhahood (shared with Bon). The highest expression of and vehicle for attaining that Buddha's enlightenment (which is equivalent to the enlightenment of all Buddhas) is the teaching of the "Great Perfection" (*rdzogs-chen,* shared with Bon). The paradigmatic exponent of this teaching, and indeed of all matters bearing on the spiritual and temporal well-being of the Tibetan people, is the immortal Guru Padmasambhava, the apotheosis of an Indian tantric master who played a leading role in Tibet's conversion to Buddhism during the eighth century, and who is always present to intercede on behalf of his devotees (distinctively Rnying-ma-pa, though the cult of Padmasambhava claims many adherents who are not otherwise Rnying-ma-pa). Finally, the teachings of the latter are continually renewed in forms suitable to the devotee's time, place, and circumstances, the agents for such renewal being "discoverers of spiritual treasure" (*gter-ston/-bton*), thought to be embodiments of, or regents acting on behalf of, Padmasambhava (in this form the tradition of "spiritual treasure," *gter-ma,* is distinctly Rnying-ma-pa, though non-Rnying-ma-pa *gter-ma* are known, particularly among the Bonpo).

While the Rnying-ma-pa adhere, as do other Tibetan Buddhists, to tantric forms of ritual and contemplative practice, their tantric canon is altogether distinctive, incorporating a great quantity of literature whose "authenticity" is challenged by many adherents of the other Tibetan Buddhist schools, as is the authenticity of their special teaching of the Great Perfection.[14] Hence, from relatively early times, their unique standpoint created for the Rnying-ma-pas a noteworthy justificatory problem, which has generated an elaborate apologetical literature, much of which is historical in character. Moreover, the peculiar Rnying-ma-pa emphasis on a way of practice that combines elaborate tantric ritualism, including a vast body of regulations and precepts, with the apparent antinomianism of the Great Perfection may appear to embody a remarkable contradiction. It is just this contradiction, in fact, that is both intensified and resolved by the conjunction of the myths considered here. The myths, therefore, may be regarded as part of the justificatory apparatus of the Rnying-ma-pa school.

In their thinking about the history of their own tradition, the Rnying-ma-pas have come to identify three phases in the lineage through which their special doctrines have been transmitted: the "lineage of the Conquerors' intention" (*rgyal-ba dgongs-brgyud*); the "symbolic lineage of the awareness-holders" (*rig-'dzin brda-brgyud*); and the "aural lineage of human individuals" (*gang-zag snyan-brgyud*).[15] The first of the "three lineages" is related to the primordial origination and disclosure in the domain of the Buddha's enlightenment of the doctrine in question, in this case, the Great Perfection teaching. The third concerns the successive transmission of that doctrine through a line of human individuals who are related each to the next as master to disciple and always thought to be placeable, datable persons, though the specifics may be much debated. The second lineage explains the beginnings of the transmission in the human world, the stages whereby a doctrine belonging to the timeless, inexpressible realm of awakening came to be expressed in time. While the conception of the three lineages in this way establishes a context in which some of what we would regard as purely mythic material is systematically distinguished from legend and history, the distinction is made here in terms of a specific narrative content, rather than in terms of narrative genre taken generally.

Of the myths to be considered here, that of Samantabhadra concerns only the "lineage of the Conquerors' intention," while the myth of Rudra sets the stage for the arising of the "symbolic lineage of awareness-holders." The latter may thus be placed, liminally, at the boundary of myth and legend, a characterization that seems in several respects to be appropriate. Some writers, for instance, do suggest that it is in principle possible to calculate the date of Rudra's subjugation,[16] but Samantabhadra is everywhere acknowledged to stand outside of ordinary temporal determinations.

Because it is possible to trace out a long incremental development of these myths, extending far back in Indian Buddhist literature—in the case of the myth of Rudra, the eighteenth-century Tibetan author Sle-lung Bzhad-pa'i rdo-rje has in fact assembled much of the required background[17]—there is no more reason to associate them particularly with the authors whose versions I consider here than there is to associate the Christian hell-purgatory-heaven cosmology particularly with Dante, or Satan's fall particularly with Milton. Nevertheless, there is also not much less reason to do so. If I risk overemphasizing here Klong-chen-pa's association with the myth of Samantabhadra or O-rgyan Gling-pa's with that of Rudra, it is nonetheless fair to say that these writers are particularly closely associated with the myths in question by Tibetans themselves.

Klong-chen Rab-'byams-pa (1308–63) and Yar-rje O-rgyan Gling-pa (b. 1323) belong to a critical period in Tibetan history, during which, in conjunction with the weakening and final collapse of Mongol power in China (1368), the Sa-skya-pa hegemony (1260–1358), which had successfully protected Tibet from outright Mongol invasion, grew feeble, with the result that Tibet was engulfed in a civil war from which the Phag-mo-gru-pa hierarchs eventually emerged victorious.[18] Loyalties shifted rapidly, and central Tibet found itself adrift in uncertainty. The formative tendencies of the Rnying-ma-pa school, already evident in the work of earlier writers,[19] now resurfaced as a powerful polemic, upholding the spiritual and temporal magnificence of Tibet's imperial past against the decadence and factiousness of contemporary hegemonic leadership. While both Klong-chen-pa and O-rgyan Gling-pa must be understood in this context, the historical setting in which they lived and worked, and despite their common sectarian affiliation, they appear as altogether distinctive personalities, expressing their common affirmation of the Rnying-ma-pa vision of the Buddhist enlightenment from fundamentally different perspectives.

Klong-chen-pa, to begin, had enjoyed a thorough Buddhist scholastic education; there are suggestions that during his youth he had something of the reputation of a brilliant dilettante.[20] Little of the large corpus of poetry and works on poetics attributed to him, and probably belonging to his earlier years, is now available, but the colophons of such poetical works as have come down to us make clear that he was exceedingly proud of his accomplishments in refined Tibetan composition modeled on Sanskrit *kāvya*.[21] Stylistic elegance would continue to characterize his writing, right down to his final testament. None of the philosophical writings (mostly commentaries) attributed to his early career appear to be currently available, though his command of the major traditions of Indian Buddhist philosophy known in Tibet is evident throughout his later expository writing on the Great Perfection.

When he was probably in his mid-twenties, Klong-chen-pa became disgusted with what he had come to regard as the pretensions of learning in the monastic colleges of central Tibet, and decided to seek his enlightenment among the itinerant yogins who dwelt in the isolated hermitages of the Tibetan wilderness. It was here that he came to encounter Kumārarāja (1266–1343), a renowned and saintly adept who specialized in the Rnying-ma-pa tradition of the Great Perfection. The inspiration derived from this teaching would motivate the entire course of Klong-chen-pa's later career, and the volume of his literary work devoted to it is enormous. Though he apparently sought to live as an exemplary yogin and teacher of the Great Perfection tradition, he was unable to avoid political entanglement completely and spent some years in exile in what is today Bhutan. However, his biography, by one of his disciples, provides little detail concerning the charges brought against him and the manner of their resolution, save to indicate that he had been falsely accused of being a partisan of a faction rivaling the Phag-mo-gru-pas.

The corpus of Klong-chen-pa's writings on the Great Perfection may be divided into two broad categories: (1) his contribution, as final redactor, to the eleven-volume collection of precepts, meditation texts, and ritual manuals known as the *Four-fold Innermost Spirituality (Snying-thig ya-bzhi),* this being a particular system (or rather a group of closely related systems) of Great Perfection practice; and (2) his numerous original treatises on the theory and practice of the Great Perfection.[22] The works making up the latter category reveal an extraordinarily rich blend of materials and genres—all branches of Indian and Tibetan Buddhist literature are drawn into his discussions, and he moves freely among allegory, rigorous philosophical argument, history, didactic poetry, and so on, as his discourses concerning the Great Perfection progress. So completely does the Rnying-ma-pa tradition regard him as epitomizing this teaching that Klong-chen-pa is called the "Second Samantabhadra"; hence, my belief that his formulation of the myth of Samantabhadra may be justly thought to be paradigmatic.

Of O-rgyan Gling-pa almost nothing reliable is known; the available hagiographies—which make him out to have been, like Klong-chen-pa, the object of some persecution at the hands of the Phag-mo-gru-pas—are all quite late.[23] However, the major works attributed to him are the products of an unusual *tour de force* and so do permit us to adduce a few generalities regarding their author.

All of O-rgyan Gling-pa's known writings belong to the class of texts known as *gter-ma,* "treasures," supposedly set down and then con-

cealed by Padmasambhava and his immediate disciples during the eighth
or ninth century. O-rgyan Gling-pa is presented as being merely their
rediscoverer. Though "treasures" of various kinds are attributed to him,
those for which he is best known are six "historical" works, relating the
legends of Padmasambhava and of Tibet under the reign of
Padmasambhava's royal patron, King Khri Srong-lde-btsan (who reigned
until 797). These six texts are always thought to form a pair: the *Testament of Padmasambhava (Padma bka'-thang)* and the *Fivefold Collection of Testaments (Bka'-thang sde-lnga)*. The first is a verse epic, in 108
cantos, telling of the coming of Padmasambhava and his conversion of
Tibet to Buddhism during Khri Srong-lde-btsan's reign.[24] The five texts
forming the second member of the pair develop aspects of the same
story from separate perspectives as documents concerning (1) the indigenous Tibetan gods and demons, (2) the Tibetan kings, (3) the queens,
(4) the ministers, and (5) the scholars.[25] Taken together, these works
elaborate a powerful vision of Tibet and its historically unique station in
the Buddhist universe. Their "prophetic" passages explicitly comment on
the political situation in mid-fourteenth-century Tibet, so that the
hagiographers' assertions that O-rgyan Gling-pa became the object of
political persecution seem not at all implausible.

The extraordinary body of tradition that finds its way into O-rgyan
Gling-pa's *Testaments* makes it clear that their author was greatly learned
in a certain sense but also that he was not the product of the same
refined scholastic upbringing that we know Klong-chen-pa enjoyed.
His writing is vigorous but coarse; stylistic fine points were of no interest to him, and this lends his work a peculiar raw power. If Klong-
chen-pa's harmonious marriage of poetic elegance and etherial spirituality suggests at times a Tibetan inspired by Dante's Beatrice, then O-rgyan
Gling-pa's pen would appear to have been blessed by Chaucer's Wife
of Bath.

What I wish to stress here, however, are some assumptions that
seem common to them both, that may be summarized briefly. Our world
is such that the full enlightenment of a Buddha is both a desirable and
realizable end for human beings; Tibet has historically become the guardian of the Buddha's doctrine, in which the means to realize that enlightenment are disclosed; and it is the ancient Rnying-ma-pa tradition alone
that possesses the quintessential revelation of that doctrine. The myths
under consideration here are both concerned, in particular, to underwrite
the first and last of these points.

Before closing this section it occurs to me that some may wish to
know something about the tradition of teaching I've been referring to as
the Great Perfection (*rdzogs-pa chen-po*). This is a very difficult question.[26] Suffice it to provide some remarks on this topic by Klong-chen

Rab-'byams-pa himself, though I recognize that, without further commentary, the terse discussion found here is bound to remain somewhat
obscure:

> The unsurpassed vehicle is the supremely esoteric Great Perfection
> that brings about real union with the spontaneously present expanse
> [of reality, *dharmadhātu*]. In the unchanging expanse of the ground,
> similar to space, the qualities of enlightenment are spontaneously
> present, like the sun, moon, planets and stars. Because they are
> spontaneously present from the very beginning, without having been
> sought out, the path is one of natural direct perception, without
> tiresome exertion. Its intention is equivalent to that of the Dharmākaya,
> self-abiding as the unconditioned maṇḍala of the expanse of inner
> radiance, and it is the supreme view of the abiding nature of reality
> that brings about [its] realization. Ephemeral obscurations are clouds
> in the expanse of purity: in the minds of beings bewildering appear-
> ances become manifest without veridical existence. . . . It is by
> knowing the nature of bewilderment as the appearance of what is
> not that one is freed. . . .
>
> Whatever consciousness arises is the self-liberated play of the
> body of reality, like water and waves, a single undulation in the
> body of reality. This is the intention of ultimate truth, the uppermost
> pinnacle among views; this is the Great Perfection.[27]

The Myth of Samantabhadra

Buddhist doctrine has generally affirmed the world to be entirely
law-like; there is a final and ultimate principle (or body of principles),
even though, at a certain point in the rarified atmosphere of Buddhist
discourse, this may become impossible to grasp in thought or in words.
The attempt to analyze the principles underlying apparent reality, and to
pursue the course of analysis until no further analysis is possible, has
given much of classical Buddhist thought a markedly "metaphysical" character, so that here, perhaps more than in many other instances where a
stream of thought not flowing from the Greek spring is termed "philosophical," we can retain this convention unapologetically.

A key problem for Buddhist philosophical thought, throughout its
long history, has been this: how can we resolve the triple tension arising
from the fundamental assumptions that (1) the world is law-like through
and through, (2) the world is such that there are ignorant beings who are
subject to a continual round of trouble due to their ignorance, and (3)
the world is such that these beings are possibly beings who overcome
their ignorance and the pain that it brings, thus attaining nirvāṇa. Tension
arises here because it may be thought that #1 determines #2 and so

precludes #3, that #1 determines #3 and so neutralizes #2, or that #2 and #3 jointly entail that #1 be weakened, i.e., the world is almost nomic but not quite. This is perhaps the Buddhist analogue to the West's headache concerning free will and determinism. The myth of Samantabhadra represents the formulation in Rnying-ma-pa Buddhism of a peculiar way of expressing the mystery of these three fundamental assumptions and their interrelationships.

Corresponding to the three assumptions, what I am terming the "myth of Samantabhadra" (the closest equivalent Rnying-ma-pa phrase is (b) just below), actually consists of three topics:[28] (a) how the ground became manifest in spontaneous presence (*lhun-grub gzhi-snang-gi shar-tshul*), (b) how Samantabhadra was liberated (*kun-tu bzang-po'i grol-tshul*), and (c) how ignorant sentient beings became bewildered (*ma-rig sems-can-gyi 'khrul-tshul*). In form, then, what we have here is a creation myth,[29] explaining certain broad features of our world, how it came into being as the peculiar sort of world that it is, and why things are such that it could be no other way. But it is a myth elaborated with a specific philosophical purpose, namely, through topics, (a), (b) and (c) to make three fundamental but not clearly compatible assumptions of Buddhist thought somehow cointelligible.

Klong-chen Rab-'byams-pa repeats the myth of Samantabhadra, with or without detailed exposition, at many points scattered throughout his writings. I shall discuss here only the versions found in his massive summation of the peculiar doctrines of the Great Perfection tradition, the *Jewel Treasury of the Supreme Vehicle (Theg-mchog rin-po-che'i mdzod)*. Here, the myth of Samantabhadra is summarized briefly at the very beginning of the text, to introduce the manner in which the Great Perfection teaching originated in the world. It is in this context that Rnying-ma-pas sometimes speak of the myth as representing the "lineage of the Conqueror's intention." Later in the same treatise, the myth is made the subject of a very detailed discussion, constituting the whole of the ninth chapter, upon which the discussion below will partially be based. The initial short version is as follows:

> Prior to everything, saṃsāra and nirvāṇa being not divided, nor dividing, nor to be divided, Samantabhadra, the teacher whose dominion is perfect, arose from the primordial ground—the expanse that is self-emergent pristine cognition, the nucleus of the Sugata—as the manifestation of the ground. In the instant that he emerged from the ground, because he recognized this to be self-manifest, then owing to the three self-emergent principles he seized his imperial realm in the spontaneously present precious enclosure, the great primordial purity that is the original site of exhaustion, the field of the vase-body of youth. The enlightened attributes of renunciation and real-

ization being perfected, he achieved buddhahood in the manner of
the dharmakāya, and abides thus inwardly clarified. . . . Subsequently,
from the expressive play that arises from the original ground as the
manifestation of the ground, mundane creatures appeared as if bewildered without cause for bewilderment, as in a dream. Seeing
them thus disturbed, his compassionate excellence was aroused.[30]

The original ground (*gdod-ma'i gzhi*) stands wholly removed from
the three temporal determinations of past, present, and future. For this
reason, it is sometimes spoken of in Rnying-ma-pa thought as being
"atemporal" (*dus-med*), or as being an "indeterminate time" (*ma-nges-
pa'i dus*), or a "fourth time" (*dus bzhi-pa*). The ground is pure potency,
possibly manifest as anything whatsoever (*chos ci-yang 'char-ba, ci-
yang snang-ba*). Its faculty for the actualization of its potencies is termed
"expressive power" (*rtsal*), and this is intrinsically noetic. The ground in
its indeterminacy is essentially empty (*ngo-bo stong*), in its unlimited
potency is characteristically open, or limpid (*rang-bzhin gsal*), and in its
expressive power is unimpeded spirituality (literally, "compassion," *thugs-
rje ma-'gags-pa*). In virtue of these three principles it is the ground of
primordial buddhahood, embodying the attributes of the three "bodies"
(*sku-gsum*) of reality (*chos-sku*), rapture (*longs-sku*), and emanation (*sprul-
sku*). The expressive power of the ground, being intrinsically noetic, is
possibly aware that it is itself the expressive power of the ground—it
may "recognize" itself (*rang-ngo-shes*). Because the self-recognition of a
timeless ground must belong to the ground in its timelessness, its self-
recognition is uniquely characterized as the attainment of buddhahood
by the primordial Buddha Samantabhadra. Whereas such self-recognition
is a *possibility* of the noetic aspect of expressive power, that power has
also primordially actualized non-self-recognizing cognition, which, alien-
ated from the ground from which it is no other by virtue of its non-self-
recognition, has become "bewildered" (*'khrul-pa*) and so has fallen into
multiplicity, projecting itself forward temporally. In this aspect, the expressive power of the ground is "limitless sentient beings." In the *Great
Auspicious and Beauteous Tantra (Bkra-shis mdzes-ldan chen-po'i
rgyud)*, cited by Klong-chen-pa, the primordial Buddha is made to speak
as follows:

Though I am free from bewilderment, bewilderment has emerged
from my expressive power. Though I do not come into being as
ground, my nature having arisen without impediment, unawareness
has spontaneously emerged from my spirituality that is without determination. Just as clouds do not intrinsically exist in the sky, but
emerge fortuitously, so there is no unawareness at all that belongs to
the ground.[31]

The passage from the indeterminacy and atemporality of the ground to the temporal projection of numberless sentient beings, without implying that the primordial Buddha must himself fall from his primordial enlightenment, is one that perhaps cannot be made without some element of apparent paradox. It is not, however, my concern to elaborate here a suitably purified Rnying-ma-pa cosmogony but rather to illustrate the manner in which the fundamental Rnying-ma-pa cosmogonic myth is itself constructed as an expression of Rnying-ma-pa speculative thought. What is crucial for the Rnying-ma-pa thinker is that this account establish an essential relationship between the primordial Buddha and sentient beings so that we can recover the ground of our being and thus participate in Samantabhadra's beginningless enlightenment.

The path of practice by means of which our recovery of Samantabhadra's enlightenment is to take place is, of course, the path of the Great Perfection, whose skillful means are intended precisely to introduce sentient beings directly to their affinity with Samantabhadra. When such introduction takes place, the goal of path may be realized almost immediately. As the Tibetan poet-saint Mi-la-ras-pa (1040–1123) was told by his Rnying-ma-pa teacher Rong-ston Lha-dga':

> This teaching of the Great Perfection leads one to triumph at the root, to triumph at the summit, and to triumph in the fruits of achievement. To meditate on it by day is to be Buddha in one day. To meditate on it by night is to be Buddha in one night.[32]

But what is one to do who is so bewildered by obscuration that she simply cannot perceive what the teaching of the Great Perfection is introducing her to? That was Mi-la-ras-pa's problem; perhaps it is also my problem, and it is possibly your problem too. The myth of Rudra offers the Rnying-ma-pa response to this dilemma.

The Matricide Rudra

In the Rudra episode of the *Testament of Padmasambhava*, the raw energy of O-rgyan Gling-pa's verse reaches one of its several pinnacles. The episode occurs early on and belongs to the section of the work treating the cosmological background for, and past lives preceding, the actual birth of Padmasambhava. In some its earlier forms, as in Indian Buddhist tantric literature, the myth concerns the defeat of Śiva by the Buddha and the manner in which their battle necessitated and prepared the ground for the appearance in the world of the tantras taught by the Buddha. Perhaps an antecedant can even be detected in the Buddha's confrontation with Māra. In one of the peculiarly Rnying-ma-pa tantras, the *Sūtra Gathering All Intentions (Mdo dgongs-pa 'dus-pa)*, the myth is enormously expanded, and becomes the organizing metaphor for the text as a whole.[33] It is this tradition that O-rgyan Gling-pa incorporates into his own work, where the fifth canto tells of Rudra's appearance in the world and the sixth of his final subjugation.[34] The translated text of the opening of the former, which relates Rudra's past life as the wayward monk Thar-pa Nag-po ("Black Liberation"), follows:

> After the teaching of Samantabhadra,
> In the land called 'Du-ljongs-mtshams,
> There was the householder Koukala,
> Who had a son named Kou kun-dkris
> And a servant, Pramadeva.
> The two were seen to be fit to be trained by the
>   two teachings.[35]
> To prevent the decline of the emanational body's teaching,
> [The master] took birth as the monk Thub-dka' gzhon-nu.
> To prevent the decline of the secret mantras, the teaching of
>   the body of rapture,
> He took birth as a great householder, a "family-maintainer."
> All men were exceptionally devoted to that monk,
> Known as one with one body but two names.
> Taking up the great path of five yogas[36] he practiced,
> And saw the skandhas' abode to be empty.
> At that time Kou kun-dkris grew faithful,
> And his doubts were resolved, whoever he asked:
> "What manner of teacher is Thub-dka' gzhon-nu?
> Does he teach the doctrine that without attaining
>   enlightenment,
> Without abandoning afflication, you may practice just as
>   you please?"
> "The monk teaches just that," they said.
> "To remove ignorance and realize nirvāṇa,
> Thub-dka' gzhon-nu is the best."
> Kou kun-dkris and Pramadeva
> Went to Thub-dka' gzhon-nu's abode.
> "May you, skillful in means, accept us
> To receive the mantras' intention, to behold the exalted truth
> In yoga by practicing as one pleases,
> Retaining doubts and the three afflictions."
> Praying thus, they bowed their heads to his feet.
> The teacher said, "So it is! Certainly! Fine!
> Men say that while the round of saṃsāra persists,
> The jewel of the saṃgha is best!"

Then both master and servant came forth as monks,
Ordained as Thar-pa nag-po and Dan-phag by name.
Dan-phag was elected to grasp the occasion for his liberation.
At that time the monk Thar-pa nag-po
Petitioned Thub-dka' gzhon-nu in these words:
"O mantra guardian, great holder of spells!
What is the path that causes release
From all extreme sufferings?"
The teacher, with radiant smile, responded:
"In what is as it is there's no contrivance.
Though you live practicing the four evil matters,[37]
They are just like clouds in the sky.
This is the path of genuine yoga.
If you don't realize this, throughout the three realms
No further stage among views will be found!"
So he well taught the investigation of mind.
Thar-pa and his servant rejoiced,
And worshiped him with offerings of devotion.
Singing his praises they went home.
Thar-pa practiced the doctrine literally;
Not realizing the definitive meaning, his afflictions were
    inflamed.
Engrossed in the four evil matters,
He maintained a religious deportment in body, while his mind
    became foul.
The servant Dan-phag realized the definitive meaning:
His intelligence grew while he practiced correctly.
Unengrossed, he knew to uphold just what the teacher had
    taught.
He maintained a deteriorating deportment in body,
While his mind, journeying on the certain path, deviated not
    in its view.
After some time had passed, master and servant,
Discordant in theory and practice, had occasion to quarrel.
The monk Thar-pa nag-po expressed his opinion:
"The two of us met with one single master.
How is it that we disagree on the meaning
And experiential cultivation of one phrase?"
Dan-phag gave Thar-pa nag-po this answer:
"I understand only confident meditation
Based on perfect equipoise."
Thar-pa nag-po responded:
"I have also practiced quite certainly,

So that my practice of secret mantras accords with the doc-
   trine."
And Thar-pa nag-po added in arrogance:
"Dan-phag, your theory and practice are wrong!
Affliction and pristine noesis have only a single basis.
By relative, tiresome virtues one achieves enlightenment not.
I am established in an absolute, effortless condition!"
To that Dan-phag made his reply:
"Consciousness purified of obsessive attachment is pristine
   noesis.
What is as it is, uncontrived, is the mantra-path.
Afflictions, like clouds, dissolve in the expanse.
One must strive, maintaining the three superior practices.[38]
This is teacher Thub-dka's intention."
When he said this, Thar-pa nag-po was enraged:
"Master Thub-dka' gzhon-nu, without contrivance,
Is no deceiver, but upright and honest!
Let's go—get up quickly!—to ask that great sage,
The world's doctrinal king, just what's what!"
Master and servant both went and asked.
The teacher, discerning the difference, said, "Dan-phag's right."
Thar-pa nag-po's mind flew into a rage of resentment:
"One master with two dissimilar viewpoints!
His entire teaching is perverse,
And always involves self-contradiction!"
With verbal abuse he fired his servant Dan-phag,
And, it being his way to wander down all evil paths,
Accusing him harshly, banished him to distant places.
"Like the disciple, the master's a common man.
Not just saying that we two were similar,
Teaching error, he really rebuked me.
That biased one, not allowed to live here,
Must be expelled. I'll seize the realm!" he thought.
He expelled him to the furthest frontier, abandoned him some
   place far away.

The apostate Thar-pa Nag-po now becomes increasingly vile—a
murderer, drunkard, and whoremonger. His path becomes a descending
spiral, traced through numberless lives, born in forms ever more despi-
cable, until he falls to the abysmal Vajra Hell. Aeons pass and he is
released only to be reborn among goblins and vermin for 20,000 more
lifetimes. And then:

After Buddha Dīpaṃkara's teaching,
Before Śākyamuni's teaching appeared,
Was an interval of many years without teaching.
In the demon-land called Laṅkākpurṇa,
There was a whore named "Wanders About."
In the evening she slept with a devil, at midnight with a king,
And at dawn with a god. In her womb he was conceived.
Because there were three fathers—god, devil and man—
After eight months a three-headed son was born.
He had six arms and four legs;
Spontaneously two wings burst from his body.
Each head had three eyes, nine in all.
His attributes were many and varied.
When he was born, evil omens appeared:
Ills of all kinds filled Laṅkā;
The whole mass of merit declined;
All auspicious portents fell away;
Famine, plague and the pox all spread;
As in nightmares, the host of ghosts gathered.
After his birth, in the ninth month, the childbirth
    illness returned,
And Wanders About herself passed away.
The locals said, "This evil bastard
Should be returned to his mother's womb!"
To the root of the charnel tree Fornication,
Where there sleeps Ignorance, the black charnel pig,
Where the poison snake Hatred coils the trunk,
Where the charnel bird Passion makes its topmost nest,
All dead demons were carried there.
Tigers and elephants made their abodes there,
And there all venomous snakes were entwined.
Ḍākinīs brought human corpses there.
At the root the demons build their charnel house.
The mother's corpse, with her son, was hauled out on a
    stretcher and left there.

The demon-child survives by devouring his deceased mother's body, eventually emerging from the charnel ground as a monster of extraordinary power. His conquests engulf the subterranean and terrestrial realms, until he seeks to bring even the domain of the gods under his sway, challenging all to do battle with him. The name by which he is feared is

"Matricide Rudra." The Buddhas and bodhisattvas of all times and places, responding to the terrified supplications of the gods, assemble to determine the means whereby this demonic force that threatens to engulf all saṃsāra might be at last defeated. Prominent among the Buddhas is Vajrasattva, the Adamantine Being, who, it so happens, is none other than Thub-dka' gzhon-nu, the banished master of Rudra's past life as the apostate Thar-pa Nag-po, while his former servant Dan-phag is now Vajrapāṇi, the Holder of the Adamantine Scepter. They are ordained by those assembled to assume the forms of Avalokiteśvara, the bodhisattva of compassion, and the savioress Tārā, who are then consecrated as the ferocious couple Hayagrīva, "Horse Neck," and Vajravārāhī, "Adamantine Sow," to do battle with Rudra. Hayagrīva, making himself minutely small, enters Rudra's "lower gate," the anus, and then explodes to tremendous proportion within his body. The demon, vanquished, vows to serve the Buddha's teaching as a powerful protector, and the elements of his broken body are transubstantiated to become the sacraments of tantric Buddhism. For this reason, Hayagrīva, as Avalokiteśvara's wrathful counterpart, is depicted as demonic in outer form, with a small horse's head emerging from the crown of the demon's skull; he is thus always garbed in the body of Rudra.

In O-rgyan Gling-pa's telling of it, the myth of Rudra is exceptionally complex, and the would-be interpreter of it must be wary of the seductions of possible reductionist readings. Robert Paul, the most perceptive interpreter of this myth to date, has focused primarily on the themes that can be clearly related to his overriding concern with exploring the structural problems posed by the continuity of generations in Sherpa and Tibetan society. Fraternal rivalry (i.e., the rivalry of codisciples), antagonism between father and son (master and disciple), matricide, and homosexual anal rape are among the key motifs in Paul's reading, which is markedly influenced by the psychoanalytic work of Géza Róheim.[39] It is not my concern to undertake to assess Paul's interpretations in general, and indeed, I think that Paul has suggested and begun to develop a powerful hermeneutic here. At the same time, however, he has necessarily bracketed those elements of the tale that have no apparent bearing on the proposed interpretation. What I should like to do, then, is to turn to some of the other aspects of O-rgyan Gling-pa's version of the myth, without attempting an overarching interpretation. In accord with the subject matter of the present investigations of philosophy and myth, let us concentrate on the apparently "philosophical" aspects of the first section of the Rudra tale translated above. Paul dismisses this entire passage in a single and, to my mind, misleading sentence:

Whereas Evil Pig [= *Dan-phag,* in my translation above; Paul is following Toussaint's problematic reading of the name as *Ngan-phag*]
understood and accepted the master's teaching, Universal Misery, or
Black Deliverance [= *Thar-pa Nag-po*], failed to see the value of a
doctrine which preaches the vanity of this world and nonattachment
to all things.[40]

Clearly O-rgyan Gling-pa's narration of the episode attaches more weight
than this to the "bad disciple's" failure of understanding: if Thar-pa Nag-
po's response to the teaching is to be summed up as a shrugged "I don't
get it," then it becomes very difficult to see how this long segment of the
story should be related to the brutal events that follow.

Let us return then to the beginning of the tale, to the assertion that
the events to be recounted take place *after* the teaching of Samantabhadra.
We have seen already how the Samantabhadra myth attempts to bridge
the gulf between time and eternity, between primordial enlightenment
and the bewilderment of sentient beings. The Rudra episode, by opening
with reference to this, begins by indexing itself to the temporal projection of mundane being that unfolds when the expressive power of the
ground has passed into bewilderment. *All* of the events that follow are
thus circumscribed by bewilderment.

As sentient beings, we have all already failed to see what Thub-
dka' gzhon-nu sought to reveal to his two disciples. Because we have all
thus failed in primordial time, it would be silly to regard that to be the
particular point O-rgyan Gling-pa is seeking to drive home here, for it
has already been driven home by placing the entire episode outside the
domain of Samantabhadra's teaching. What I think we should attend to,
rather, is the relationship delineated among simple failure to understand,
egocentric rebellion of the will, and radical evil. Saṃsāra is not merely
bewildering (after all, couldn't one be eternally subject to pleasant bewilderment?), but it is downright vicious, and to see why this is so we must
trace the temporal projection of saṃsāric being from the primordial origination of bewilderment to the point at which that bewilderment generates pride—it is not just error, but rather arrogant error, that condemns us
to the round of meaningless pain. The myth of Rudra is Buddhism's
closest approach to a myth of original sin.[41]

The myth of Rudra "explains" the origins of tantricism, in part because Rudrahood characterizes our nature as embodied persons, who
are constitutionally disposed to lust and self-protection, to arrogance and
rage. Tantricism, or something like it, is soteriologically necessitated by
the our being what we are, by our world's being as it is. So it is that the

Rnying-ma-pa practitioner, on days when penitential rites are required, recites a confessional litany entitled *Rudra's Lamentation*.[42]

Must the Message be Mythic?

If the "philosophical" readings of the myths of Samantabhadra and Rudra that I've begun to sketch out here (and admittedly, much remains to be filled in) reflect in part the manner in which these myths are understood within the Rnying-ma-pa tradition, then they will contribute to the formation of a contextualizing myth about Rnying-ma-pa Buddhism, in relation to which other features of Rnying-ma-pa practice and thought will be more intelligible to us than they might have been otherwise. I believe that this is in fact the case, that the peculiar Rnying-ma-pa synthesis of the Great Perfection teaching of the intrinsic enlightenment of all beings—a teaching which, like certain aspects of Ch'an, seems irreducibly subitist and antinomian—with the gradualist esotericism of the tantras, may be now seen as something more than jumbled eclecticism. For the combined argument of the two myths generates a view of the human condition according to which our inherent identity with the Omnibeneficent Buddha is concealed not only by the veil of unknowing but further by a profound and eminently evil act of rebellion—some may recognize here an intensified reformulation of the classical Buddhist doctrine of the "two obscurations."[43] It is thus only the violent inversion of the soul, catalyzed by the powerful means taught in the tantras, that can create within us the essential clearing in which the truth of the Great Perfection may be disclosed.

The myth of Samantabhadra as told by Klong-chen Rab-'byams-pa and that of Rudra as told by O-rgyan Gling-pa are thus seen to be constructed in order to convey, among other things, a number of "philosophical" messages concerning eternity and temporality, enlightenment and bewilderment, understanding and the rebellion of the will in ignorance. It is clear that both of these authors have deliberately incorporated these messages into their myth making; these are not cases in which apparent philosophical messages are "found" in "primitive" myths only thanks to the learned interpretations of modern (or postmodern) readers. It is equally clear that the messages in question can in some respects be separated from the myths in which they are found—not only our analysis but the commentarial tradition of Rnying-ma-pa Buddhism confirm that in practice.[44] Why then continue to tell the myths at all? Because they are more entertaining than cold, dry philosophy? Because they give the messages in question extra oomph? Or is there some essential element that is unavoidably left out, whenever the "philosophical" message is removed from the tale in which it is told?

Human thought, to repeat what an ancient and hallowed tradition tells us, is forever oscillating between two poles, and finding a lasting home for itself in neither: at one extreme it follows Plato into his heavens and takes up its dwelling among eternal and unchanging objects; at the other it steps into the stream with Heraclitus to be inundated by the surging flood of change. The abiding truths of the human condition, however, disclose themselves to us, if ever they do, precisely in the midst of the stream. For this reason we cannot desist from being tellers of tales: our fall and redemption are played out only in time. The philosopher who knows well to bathe in the Heraclitean stream, to warm his head beneath Plato's sun, will be content that both are present in the landscape of thought and recognize in narrative a path between them. Sometimes he will find philosophy walking along it, seeking out a fertile spot, trying to find the perfect balance of moisture and warmth.

So long as philosophy remains anchored in our common experience, it will have need of plentiful tales, and some of these tales will be myths. For these, indeed, are its anchor. Must the message be mythic? From the vantage point we've reached in our journey so far, it becomes difficult to see how it could be otherwise.[45]

Notes

1. Adkins (1990).

2. This suggestion was put forward in remarks to the fifth Conference on Religions in Culture and History, held at the Divinity School of the University of Chicago in October 1988.

3. Refer to Dundes (1984) for useful surveys of the leading attempts to define "myth," particularly in relation to the categories of "legend" and "folktale," and for general bibliographical background. For more recent work in this area, see especially Lincoln (1989), part 1.

4. In this context, readers may also wish to reflect on the so-called Gaia hypothesis of the British chemist James Lovelock, which regards our planet as forming a single organic system. In a popular review of recent scientific work on Gaia, *The Economist,* vol. 317, no. 7686/7687 (December 22, 1990), 107, commented that "[T]he strongest resistance to Gaia comes from those whose faith is grounded in another metaphor—'natural selection.' Nature is not a goddess who chooses, as Darwin knew full well. But the metaphor of choice was the best way to express his views. . . . Darwin's metaphor provided a great insight into the workings of the world. *If Gaia manages to do the same*—something which looks

unlikely at present, but not impossible—*then the objections to Dr Lovelock's metaphor will be forgotten, too*" [Emphasis added].

5.   Mary Shepard Slusser (1982), 1:364–65.

6.   There are, of course, many possible ways in which the adherents of a given body of myth might respond to changing technologies. In the present case, for instance, one might *both* continue traditional propitiation of the deity while seeking at the same time modern medical care. I believe that this observation, however, serves to reinforce my central point at this juncture, namely, that the possible falsification of a myth is not a matter of inadequation with respect to some reality to which the myth is supposed to correspond, but pertains rather to the historical experience of a community.

7.   See, in particular, "Pragmatism's Conception of Truth," and excerpts from "The Will to Believe," both in James (1948).

8.   See also Robin Lovin's contribution to this volume (Chapter 5). Besides these examples, consider Daniel (1990), where the topic investigated is the virtually ubiquitous presence of myth in early modern philosophy. Daniel's work, which I encountered only after writing this chapter, seems to develop a conception of myth essentially similar to that which I am exploring here. In his introduction (3), he writes, "What I mean by myth is a particular mode or group of functions, operative within discourse, that highlight how communication and even thought are themselves possible. Certain functions of discourse are mythic insofar as they reveal how discourse itself is possible."

9.   This phrase was heard frequently during the discussions that took place at the colloquium series from which the present volume is derived. It seemed to me that it was sometimes invoked as if it were a statement of a self-evident truth, without sufficiently questioning just what its exact meaning might be; hence, my interest in ferreting out the sense of it here.

10.   The contributions of Griffiths, Kasulis, Schrempp, Patton, Ziai and Clooney to Reynolds and Tracy (1990), and of Poole, Bantly, Kasulis, Campany, and Berling to this volume.

11.   Cf. Scharfstein (1988).

12.   Refer to Nussbaum (1986 and 1990) and Taylor (1989).

13.   For a general introduction to Indo-Tibetan Buddhist traditions, readers may consult Snellgrove (1987); for the distinctive elements of Tibetan religion, Tucci (1980); and for the Rnying-ma-pa school in particular, Dudjom Rinpoche (1991).

14.   Refer in particular to Kapstein (1989) and Karmay (1988). For an extended example of the traditional polemic concerning authenticity, see Dudjom Rinpoche (1991), vol. 1, book 2, part 7.

15.   Dudjom Rinpoche (1991), vol. 1, book 2, part 2.

16.   See, for instance, Karma Pakshi (1978), 1:402. Nonetheless, Karma Pakshi, like both Bsnubs-chen Sangs-rgyas-ye-shes (1987), whose work he is probably following, and Mkhan-po Nus-ldan-rdo-rje (1983), is primarily interested in the symbolic dimensions of the Rudra tale.

17.   Sle-lung (1979), 4–30. He is concerned here with the variant Buddhist tantric forms of the story of the defeat of Mahādeva (Śiva) by the Buddha or members of the Buddha's retinue, which is clearly the antecedent of the Rudra episode. For a very influential version of the story that is clearly related to that of Rudra, refer to Snellgrove (1987), 134–41.

18.   For the general background of Tibetan history during this period, refer to Shakabpa (1967), chapters 4 and 5.

19.   This is particularly evident in the writings of Nyang-ral Nyi-ma 'od-zer (1136–1204) and his associates, on which see especially Ruegg (1989), 74–92; Dudjom Rinpoche (1991), 755–59; and Kapstein (forthcoming).

20.   On the life and background of Klong-chen-pa, see Guenther (1975–6), 1:xiii–xxv; Thondup (1989), 145–88; and Dudjom Rinpoche (1991), 575–96. All of these accounts may be traced back to the biography authored by Klong-chen-pa's disciple Chos-grags bzang-po.

21.   This is very clear in the biographical accounts, such as those cited in the preceding note, and in his own poetical works: see, for instance, the colophons found in Klong-chen (1973), 1:95, 137, 149 and 2:622.

22.   Concerning the major writings, refer to Guenther (1975–76), 1:xvi–xx; and Thondup Rinpoche (1989), 149–58.

23.   For example, Dudjom Rinpoche (1991), 775–79. On O-rgyan Gling-pa's writings, see in particular Blondeau (1971 and 1980).

24.   Yar-rje O-rgyan Gling-pa (n.d.) and Toussaint (1933).

25.   Refer to Blondeau (1971).

26.   Dudjom Rinpoche (1991), 294–334, provides an extended doxographical account. For historical background, see Karmay (1988).

27.   Klong-chen (1973), 1:261. A complete translation of the text from which this passage is taken is given in Berzin et al. (1987).

28.   Klong-chen (n.d.), fols. 202b–221b.

29.   It is important to note, however, that the myth of Samantabhadra is not, and by Rnying-ma-pas is never taken to be, an actual creation myth: Samantabhadra is neither a creator god nor a demiurge; there is no divine volition posited,

through which the ground is thought to give rise to the primordial buddha and to sentient beings. Where, as in the quotation given below (p. 64), the ground is itself made to speak in the voice of the original buddha, there is no evidence to suggest that the tradition has ever regarded this to be other than a metaphorical representation. Nevertheless, some contemporary Western scholars have suggested there to be a quasi-theistic standpoint disclosed in certain aspects of Rnying-ma-pa discourse. See, for instance, Dargyay (1985). I am personally inclined to regard any attribution of literally intended theism to the Rnying-ma-pas as erroneous.

30.   Klong-chen (n.d.), fols. 3b–4a.

31.   Klong-chen (n.d.), fols. 206b–207a.

32.   Lobsang P. Lhalungpa, trans., *The Life of Milarepa* (New York: E. P. Dutton, 1977), p. 42.

33.   See Stein (1972). In the Sde-dge edition of the Tibetan Buddhist canon, the *Mdo dgongs-pa 'dus-pa* is given as text no. 829 (Tohoku Catalogue), where the Rudra myth is detailed in chapters 20 to 31. Commentary may be found in Bsnubs-chen (1987), chapters 20 to 31; Mkhan-po Nus-ldan-rdo-rje (1983), chapters 20 to 31; and Karma Pakshi (1978), pp. 401ff. Tibetan traditions concerning the controversial history of the transmission of the *Mdo dgongs-pa 'dus-pa* are detailed in Dudjom Rinpoche (1991), vol. 1, book 2, part 5.

34.   Yar-rje O-rgyan Gling-pa (n.d.), fols. 20a–38a. Toussaint (1933), 24–42. The translations given here are my own, with proper names transcribed as they are given in the Tibetan text. These names are themselves quite problematic: it is clear that O-rgyan Gling-pa is often engaging in wordplay in his composition of them, and Toussaint has attempted to reflect this in his French translation. Nevertheless, some of Toussaint's interpretations seem based on unusual readings that have little textual support (e.g., *Ngan-phag,* "Evil Pig," for the better attested *Dan-phag,* the precise signification of which is uncertain). Because these questions have little bearing on the present discussion, I have preferred not to consider them at length here.

35.   The exoteric teachings of the sūtras and the esoteric teachings of the Buddhist tantras.

36.   Various enumerations of five yogas are found in Rnying-ma-pa works. See, e.g., Dudjom Rinpoche (1991), 280–81, 369.

37.   Mkhan-po Nus-ldan-rdo-rje (1983), 630–35, gives two alternative enumerations of the "four matters": in their ordinary sense, they refer to the four prohibited actions of murder, theft, falsehood, and sexual misconduct; while, esoteri-

cally, they are the major categories of tantric vows that are abused when practiced literally and externally.

38. Morality, meditation, and insight.

39. Paul (1982), 53–58. The brief discussion of the myth found in Guenther (1984), 145–46, is surprisingly superficial.

40. Paul (1982), 153–54.

41. This is curiously suggested by a comment found in Bsnubs-chen (1987), 262–63, that "Rudra having been subject to a violation of voluntary obligation, sentient beings became subject to a natural violation." (*rudra ni bcas pa'i ltung bar gyur pas 'gro ba rang bzhin gyis ltung bar gyur to.*) Mkhan-po Nus-ldan-rdo-rje (1983), 660, however, emends this to read: "Rudra was subject to both natural violation and violation of voluntary obligation, and sentient beings became subject to natural violation." (*rudra ni rang bzhin dang bcas pa'i ltung ba gnyis kar gyur la, 'gro ba rnams ni rang bzhin gyi ltung bar gyur to.*) The notion of "natural violation" (Sanskrit, *prakṛtisāvadyam*) in normative Buddhist doctrine has nothing at all to do with Western Christian concepts of "original sin." Natural violations are those, like murder, that are regarded as being intrinsically wrong, quite apart from the specifications of any vows or religious commitments one has voluntarily assumed. It is the suggestion gound in Bsnubs-chen's wording, and avoided by Mkhan-po Nus-ldan-rdo-rje, that Rudra's violation is perhaps causally related to that of sentient beings which is remarkable here.

42. Khrag-'thung Las-kyi dpa'-bo (n.d.).

43. These are the obscuration with respect to knowledge (Sanskrit *jñeyāvaraṇa*) and the obscuration consisting of the psychological and emotional "afflictions" (Sanskrit *kleśāvaraṇa*).

44. Refer to the commentarial sources cited in note 33 above. Throughout his commentary on the *Mdo dgongs-pa 'dus-pa* Mkhan-po Nus-ldan-rdo-rje (1983) takes pains to specify which sections of the text he regards to be interpretable (*drang-don*) and which definitive (*nges-don*). His approach to the former is by no means allegorical in any straightforward fashion, for his interpretations of the texts allow for the contextual transformations of symbolic figures. As a brief example, consider his "demythologized" reading of the birth of Rudra: "Esoterically, [this means that] the Rudra of clinging-to-self has ripened. Losing sight of buddha-nature, the three poisons [aversion, desire, and stupidity] adhere to the poisonous tree of the self-aggregates. The child returned to its mother's corpse is the afflicted mind in its relation to the universal ground [i.e., the *ālayavijñāna*]. And this universal ground is now seized upon, as self" (Mkhan-po Nus-ldan-rdo-rje [1983], 642–43).

45. I wish to thank Professor Lee H. Yearley of the Department of Religion, Stanford University, for his comments on the original version of this essay, given at the Conference on Religions in Culture and History in April 1989. Lee's thoughtful and perceptive remarks did much to guide the task of revision. An abbreviated version was also presented at the national meeting of the American Academy of Religion in New Orleans, November 1990, where the remarks of Professor José Cabezòn, Iliff School of Theology, helpfully encouraged clarification of certain matters relating to Tibetan and Buddhist Studies. I am grateful, too, to Columbia University's Council on Research in the Humanities and Social Sciences for fellowship assistance contributing to the revision of this chapter for the present publication.

References

Tibetan Sources
Listed by author in Tibetan alphabetical order.

Karma Pakshi [1204–83]
1978 *Rgya mtsho mtha' yas kyi skor.* 2 vols. Gangtok: Gonpo Tseten. [This work was attributed by the publisher to Karma-pa III, Rangbyung-rdo-rje. Concerning the author's actual identity, refer to M. Kapstein, "Religious Syncretism in Thirteenth Century Tibet: The *Limitless Ocean Cycle*," in Aziz and Kapstein (1985), 358–71.]

Klong-chen Rab-'byams-pa Dri-med-'od-zer [1308–63]
n.d. *Theg pa'i mchog rin po che'i mdzod.* Gangtok: Dodrup Chen Rinpoche.

———.
1973. *Gsuñthor bu.* 2 vols. Delhi: Sanje Dorje.

Khrag-'thung Las-kyi dpa'-bo [Dates unknown].
n.d. *Ru tra'i smre sngags bshags pa.* A recent xylograph from Manali, Himachal Pradesh, in the author's collection.

Mkhan-po Nus-ldan-rdo-rje [*fl.* early twentieth century].
1983 *Dpal spyi mdo dgongs pa 'dus pa'i 'grel pa rnal 'byor nyi ma gsal bar byed pa'i legs bshad gzi ldan 'char kha'i 'od snang,* volume 1. Kalimpong, West Bengal: Dupjung Lama.

Bsnubs-chen Sangs-rgyas-ye-shes [ca. tenth century].

1987 *Sangs rgyas thams cad kyi dgongs pa "dus pa mdo'i dka' 'grel mun pa'i go cha lde mig gsal byed rnal 'byor nyi ma.* In *Rñiñ ma bka' ma rgyas pa*, volume 50, edited by H. H. Bdud-'joms Rinpo-che. Kalimpong, West Bengal: Dupjung Lama.

Yar-rje O-rgyan Gling-pa [b. 1323].

n.d. *O rgyan gu ru padma 'byung gnas kyi skyes rabs rnam par thar pa rgyas par bkod pa padma'i bka'i thang yig.* A recent xylographic print from Lhasa, Tibet, in the author's collection.

Sle-lung Rje-drung Bzhad-pa'i rdo-rje [b. 1697].

1979 *Bstan srung rgya mtsho'i rnam thar,* volume 1. Smanrtsis Shesrig Spendzod, volume 104. Leh, Ladakh: T. S. Tashigang.

Works in Western Languages
Adkins, A. W. H.

1990 "Myth, Philosophy, and Religion in Ancient Greece." In *Myth and Philosophy,* edited by F. E. Reynolds and D. Tracy. Albany, N.Y.: State University of New York Press.

Aris, Michael.

1989 *Hidden Treasures and Secret Lives.* London: Kegan Paul International.

Aziz, Barbara Nimri, and Matthew Kapstein, eds.

1985 *Soundings in Tibetan Civilization.* Delhi: Manohar.

Berzin, Alexander, Sherpa Tulku, and Matthew Kapstein, trans.

1987 *"The Four-Themed Precious Garland* of Longchen Rabjampa." In *The Jewel in the Lotus: A Guide to the Buddhist Traditions of Tibet,* 137– 69, edited by Stephen Batchelor. London: Wisdom.

Blondeau, Anne-Marie.

1971 "Le Lha-'dre bka'-thañ." *Études tibétaines dédiées à la mémoire de Marcelle Lalou,* 29–126. Paris: Maisonneuve.

———.

1980 "Analysis of the Biographies of Padmasambhave according to Tibetan Tradition: Classification of Sources." In *Tibetan Studies in Honour of Hugh Richardson,* 45–52. Edited by Aris and Aung. Warminster: Aris and Phillips.

Daniel, Stephen H.

1990 *Myth and Modern Philosophy.* Philadelphia: Temple University Press.

Dargyay, Eva K.
1985 "A Rñiṅ-ma Text: The *Kun byed rgyal po'i mdo*." In *Soundings in Tibetan Civilization*, 283–93, edited by B. N. Aziz and M. Kapstein. Delhi: Manohar.

Dudjom Rinpoche, Jikdrel Yeshe Dorje.
1991 *The Nyingma School of Tibetan Buddhism: Its Fundamentals and History*, translated by Gyurme Dorje and Matthew Kapstein. Boston: Wisdom Publications.

Dundes, Alan, ed.
1984 *Sacred Narrative: Readings in the Theory of Myth*. Berkeley: University of California Press.

Guenther, Herbert V.
1975–76 *Kindly Bent to Ease Us*, 3 vols. Emeryville, Calif.: Dharma Publications.

———.
1984 *Matrix of Mystery: Scientific and Humanistic Aspects of rDzogs-chen Thought*. Boston: Shambhala.

James, William.
1948 *Essays in Pragmatism*, edited by Alburey Castell. New York: Hafner Publishing Company.

Kapstein, Matthew.
1989 "The Purificatory Gem and Its Cleansing: A Late Tibetan Polemical Discussion of Apocryphal Texts." *History of Religions* 28(3):217–44.

———.
(In press). "Remarks on the Maṇi-bka'-'bum and the Cult of Avalokiteśvara in Tibet." In *Tibetan Buddhism: Reason and Revelation*, edited by R. Davidson and S. Goodman. Albany, N.Y.: State University of New York Press.

Karmay, Samten Gyaltsen.
1988 *The Great Perfection: A Philosophical and Meditative Teaching of Tibetan Buddhism*. Leiden: Brill.

Lincoln, Bruce.
1989 *Discourse and the Construction of Society*. New York: Oxford University Press.

Nussbaum, Martha.
1986 *The Fragility of Goodness: Luck and Ethics in Greek Tragedy and Philosophy*. Cambridge: Cambridge University Press.

———.

1990 *Love's Knowledge: Essays on Philosophy and Literature.* Oxford: Oxford University Press.

Paul, Robert A.

1982 *The Tibetan Symbolic World: Psycholanalytic Explorations.* Chicago: University of Chicago Press.

Reynolds, Frank E., and David Tracy, eds.

1990 *Myth and Philosophy.* Albany, N.Y.: State University of New York Press.

Ruegg, David Seyfort.

1989 *Buddha-Nature, Mind and the Problem of Gradualism in a Comparative Perspective.* London: School of Oriental and African Studies.

Scharfstein, Ben-Ami.

1988 "The Contextual Fallacy." In *Interpreting Across Boundaries: New Essays in Comparative Philosophy,* 84–97, G. J. Larson and E. Deutsch, eds. Princeton, N.J.: Princeton University Press.

Shakabpa, T. W. D.

1967 *Tibet: A Political History.* New Haven, Conn.: Yale University Press.

Slusser, Mary Shepard.

1982 *Nepal Mandala: A Cultural Study of the Kathmandu Valley.* Princeton, N.J.: Princeton University Press.

Snellgrove, David.

1987 *Indo-Tibetan Buddhism: Indian Buddhists and Their Tibetan Successors.* Boston: Shambhala.

Stein, Rolf A.

1972 "Étude du monde chinoise: Institutions et concepts." *L'Annuaire du Collège de France* 72:489–510.

Taylor, Charles.

1989 *Sources of the Self: The Making of the Modern Identity.* Cambridge: Harvard University Press.

Thondup Rinpoche, Tulku.

1989 *Buddha Mind.* Ithaca, N.Y.: Snow Lion.

Toussaint, Gustave-Charles.

1933 Trans. *Le Dict de Padma, Padma thang yig, Ms. de Lithang.* Bibliothèque de l'Institut de Hautes Études Chinoises, volume 3.

Paris: Librairie Ernest Leroux. [Translated from the French by Kenneth Douglas and Gwendolyn Bays as *The Life and Liberation of Padmasambhava,* 2 volumes. Emeryville, Calif.: Dharma Publications, 1978.]

Tucci, Giuseppe.
1980 *The Religions of Tibet.* Berkeley: University of California Press.

Chapter 3

Buddhist Philosophy in the Art of Fiction

Francisca Cho Bantly

It is a fact of academic inquiry that no category, concept, or construct has an indefinite shelf life. The most cherished assumptions and tools of our own inquiry eventually come under scrutiny as dictated by the prevailing winds of change. One major instance of this dynamic is the modern West's eroding faith in the power of Reason to illuminate truth or the thought habits of unfamiliar peoples. All too frequently, the ongoing debate on Reason is cast along disciplinary lines. The history of religions, for example, has challenged the supposed superiority of philosophical discourse by substituting mythical discourse in many cultural instances. A fundamental tenet operative here is that philosophy does not solely occupy the privileged position as a self-reflexive mode of discourse. Myth is just as capable of reasoned explanation as philosophy. Thus myth and philosophy merely constitute different discourse styles, both of which seek to persuade and explain.

There are some, of course, who still want to hold that the denaturalized discourse of philosophy imparts to it a greater persuasiveness that renders it more suitable for certain tasks. Paul Griffiths, for example, claims that denaturalized discourse "is aimed primarily at making available to its users what really exists"—that is, in making universal truth claims. Following this, he immediately adds that what "making available" means "can be unpacked in a variety of ways, depending largely upon the ontology with which a particular instance of such discourse is combined."[1] Griffiths allows for this variability, recognizing that a culture's conception of reality necessarily determines the form and manner of its realization. If ontology is so determinative of the way in which its highest truths are attained, then should it not also determine the type of discourse best suited to expound its claims? Thus it is surprising that an admission of the dependence of discourse style on the relevant ontology should accompany an assertion that those engaged in making ontological claims are best off using primarily one discourse above all others.

Within other discussions, however, myth has been overtly privileged over philosophy. Historians of religions and anthropologists have long privileged myth as the pristine vision articulated by the cultural seers at the beginning of human consciousness. In historical context, this stance represents a recoiling from philological reductions of myth, which see it as the elaborate explanations used to gloss over the misinterpretations of the language applied to natural phenomena—à la Max Müller. An alternative view seeks to deposit myth at the dawn of cultural sentience, as a configuration of the "radical metaphors" of existence. Ernst Cassirer describes these metaphors as the cognitive and emotive experiences which are simultaneously transfered and created by myth and language.[2] Philosophical, or "discursive," thinking develops later as a realization of the implicit potential in language to generate conceptual and generalized modes of thought. Although philosophy represents an advanced level of expression, it is still dependent on the prior work of myth and language in determining its categories of thought.

Before I attempt to add anything to this continuing conversation, there is one major aspect of Griffiths's statement which must be taken seriously. His point on the centrality of ontology in any discourse should be applied not only to the traditions that we study but to our own discourse as well. In other words, the ontological foundations of our own desires to rework the categories of myth and philosophy must be addressed. So far, current trends have displayed a willingness to throw both categories into the arena of "discourse" and "rhetoric," with the immediate effect of equalizing myth and philosophy as competing players in the field. Such a move, however, requires very little or no scrutiny of the ontology operative in our realm of academic practice. This particular ontology, as I hope to show, allows for the primacy of *both* philosophical and mythical discourses, each in its own turn. As such, the move to subsume myth and philosophy under the greater rubric of discourse requires very little ontological boat-rocking. Of course, one need not assume that a revolution is in order, but one can legitimately explore what might be gained by digging down to the foundations and envisioning new blueprints for reconstruction.

My contribution to this effort consists primarily of offering up an alternative ontology, specifically the ontological system of Buddhist-Taoist cultures, as a tradition far more flexible in its range of discursive representations. The comparative contrast this tradition offers us also confronts us with a question: how far are we willing to go in undermining some of our own ontological grounding for the sake of casting new molds for our understanding of cultural discourse? To push this point, it will be necessary to go outside the privileged realms of myth and philosophy and to uphold another category altogether. The particular mode I focus on here is that of fiction. The value of looking at fiction is significantly augmented by its marginal status as a narrative, especially where questions of truth values are involved. History purports to be an account of "true" events, and we have also come to generally affirm the "truth-value" of myth as a sacred narrative for its particular community. Fictive narrative presents a more complicated case because of our understanding of it as a deliberate artifice. Although it is hardly controversial to state that fiction may be edifying as well as entertaining, in what way can it be said to be persuasive or to illustrate reality?

The main body of this chapter attempts to answer this question with the thesis that in the Buddhist-Taoist ontology operative in East Asian cultures, fictional narrative not only provides a viable, but perhaps the most appropriate means of illustrating and substantiating its assertions of universal fact. The work in question here will be a Korean novel, *Kuunmong,* and my ultimate goal will be to demonstrate how discourse style and ontological content are mutually implicating practices.

Before moving on to this task, there is a need to characterize our own bases, the ones that have underscored the arguments of both the proponents of myth and the proponents of philosophy. I will begin with the argument for philosophy, since I have already alluded to it, and suggest that the insistence that universal truth claims about reality are best made through philosophy, or denaturalized discourse, itself makes tacit assumptions about that reality.

The dependence of modern Western epistemology on Christian dualist ontology must receive explicit consideration if we wish to uphold the category of discourse over philosophy. I do not claim here that all Christian cosmological speculations posit an explicit and radical disjunction between good and evil or the Creator and created, as in the philosophy of the Manicheans. The Neo-platonist strain in Christian thought by no means exhausts the religious tradition. It is warranted, however, to speak of a general cosmological map that recognizes two ontologically distinct spheres loosely labeled the sacred and the profane. The embeddedness of this distinction within Christianity is so pervasive as to need no constant articulation within the tradition itself. And yet the presence of this bifurcation asserts itself most loudly in the nondualist strains of thought—such as the assertion of the goodness of creation, or the simultaneous divinity and humanity of Christ—by provoking the paradox of one nature occupying two mutually exclusive ontological spaces.[3] The modern study of the history of religions in its early phases also betrays this cosmology in the manner that it organizes its research: it pivots on attempts to resolve the subjective experience of the transcendent with its objective manifestations in history.[4] Of central concern is the precise relationship between the transcendent and the nature of its historical existence—both as individual experience and as socially constituted phenomena. Given the discipline's allegiance to scientific investigation, it refrains from privileging the sacred over history. Yet the uneasiness of the relationship is apparent, with much of the tension stemming from the very threat of history to destroy the possibility of transcendence altogether.

In evading this threat, philosophy has claimed greater success. Of course, the modern Western philosophical tradition claims to have diverged from religion in fundamental ways. Its primary means of cognition is through the faculty of reason, which attempts to substantiate all propositions by applying them against criteria of validity. If the end result cannot guarantee certainty, at the very least it holds itself to rules of epistemological procedure that endow it with a rigor beyond the propositions based on pure belief, hope, or revelation. Modern philosophy, however, does not operate in a vacuum. Given its inception within an historical context—one that witnessed the collapse of absolute authority embodied in the Medieval Christian church—philosophy inherited a view of reality and a subsequent task disclosed by its reaction to historicism: that of absolute horror. The task of philosophy since the Reformation has been to overcome the limitations of historical existence in quest of the transcendent view, a task that connotes a "naive realism which regards the reality of objects as something directly and unequivocally given."[5]

It has been a recent academic fashion to challenge the claims of rationality, but too many attempts to discredit this pride of Reason have shied away from scrutinizing the foundations of this claim: the suspension of human beings between the Christian ontological realms of eternity and temporality. If humans are made in the image of God in that they are capable of reflecting upon, and therefore transcending, themselves, then the temptation to usurp the place of God is the ultimate sin carried through by the instrument of Reason. For all the apparent secularity of Reason, its profound participation in the Christian universe is maintained by upholding the latter's dualist cosmology. Truth is still transcendent and eternal by definition, and the limitation of humans is still identified with their temporal, historical nature. The Axial Age theory, which postulates the dawning of a distinct philosophical consciousness, goes far in revealing our own mythical self-image writ large on the level of history. The axial moment, in fact, attempts to resolve the dual ontological structure by having the eternal (as represented by self-reflexivity) descend onto historical space and time. Behind this drama, however, it is not too difficult to glimpse a cultural bias, itself rather temporal and limited in ultimate scope which responds in terror to the suspicion that our truth-concepts are only masks for our embedded interests.

I offer up this sketch of Western ontological dualism as an ideal, or pure type in the sociological tradition, rather than as a historical narrative. This kind of heuristic device proves useful in comparative enterprises of which this essay unequivocally is one. Lest history is lost sight of altogether, however, it is worth noting that the models that we use to represent the past to ourselves are in the final count hardly distinguishable from the "reality" they are supposed to point to. My position is in marked contrast to the tradition I am attempting to represent: that is, philosophy assumes the absolute referentiality of truth, as intimated by Cassirer's scoff at "naive realism." Ontological dualism, for our purposes, then, is best exemplified when pared down to the distinction between the "represented" and the "real." The implications of this symbol theory reach into the core of the theory of allegory, which is relevant in light of my ultimate concern with fictive narrative. In this instance, the philosophy of allegory concerns itself with "the relation between the literal text and its other meaning," or the "two-level correspondence between surface and depth."[6] This rendition of the process of reading a narrative text participates in a greater cosmology, which enjoins the reader to beware of confusing the symbol with its reference, and by implication, illusion with reality.

The pervasiveness of dualist ontology goes beyond the realm of epistemological concerns and penetrates, surprisingly enough, into our own discussions of myth. Our operative notion of myth seeks to elevate it through its significance as a body of literature. Although merely one of a vast corpus of narratives that cultures are apt to produce, the significance of myth—deriving directly from its close association with the dawn of cultural time—is that it is assumed to embody the archetypes of the collective cultural mind.

In this respect, the scholarly study of myth is also underscored by a dualist ontology in which the pristine vision—separated both in space and time—becomes the object of retrieval as well as nostalgia. This attitude is also linked to a reaction against historicism much along the lines of the backlash in philosophy. Mircea Eliade, the supreme representative of this school of mythology, contends that what he offers in his studies of mythically oriented societies is a philosophy of history.[7] What is most attractive to Eliade about "archaic ontology" is its rejection of all history that is not regulated by archetypes, which myths reveal. All events must repeat transhistorical models that "valorize" human existence, i.e., render it sacred. An attraction to this state of mind in and of itself does not imply that Eliade believes in the reality, or referentiality, of what he refers to as the "transcendent." He talks instead of two cultural models of history— the archaic and the modern—as part of a broader, personal articulation of the significance of history as he experienced it. As such, if I am to remain consistant with my prior remarks, it is a mistake to challenge Eliade's view of history. The mere articulation of his experience and the fact that it is representative of overriding sentiments of his epoch, is sufficient to render it "true."

It is instructive, however, to note that Eliade's historical schema displays its own repetition of some overriding Western archetypes, the most important of which is the rupture between the sacred and profane. Sacred history, as we have seen, is sacred because of its participation in cosmic models. Profane history, which is what modernity is condemned to, is either unwilling or unable to obtain the paradigms that offer trajectories into the transcendent because of the tyranny of historicism. The parallel between myth and philosophy at this level can again be stated in terms of symbol theory: the fear of history is founded upon a division between symbol (and myth, and rite) and its referent, which is ultimately the most significant object. Any act, including the ones within sacred history, is in and of itself meaningless; the significance lies in what it represents—the archetype, the transcendent, itself. No matter if the "reality" of this transcendence need not be taken for granted as in the case of philosophy. Cassirer, for example, is perfectly capable of privileging myth while simultaneously scoffing at the notion of referential, unmediated truth. If philosophy recoils from history because of the epistemological threat of ideology, then our valorization of myth reviles history because of the fear of our own triviality.

What I have attempted to demonstrate up to this point is that the disciplines of philosophy and myth, both being products of the Western experience, unsurprisingly reveal themselves to be ontological bedfellows. Because philosophy has come under suspicion of late, it follows that the foundations of the study of myth cannot be immune to these winds as well. Consequently, the latent tendency in the above discussion is to vitiate the privileged position of myth as a body of literature. This consequence, however, serves my own purposes of examining fictive narrative only too well. For if the superiority of philosophy to myth is to be challenged, it follows as a direct result that the gap between myth and fiction must be questioned as well. The underlying and unifying move in both these instances is the issue of how to resolve the question of the truth claims of all three modes of discourse—philosophy, myth, and fiction. In demonstrating that our current prejudices about the relative value of each discourse can only be understood at the level of our operative ontology, I merely set the stage to argue that the successful reconstruction of these categories is likewise dependent on a supportive ontology.

✎◑✌

The Korean novel known as *Kuunmong,* or *The Dream of the Nine Clouds,*[8] was written by Kim Man-jung, a scholar-official in the Yi Dynasty (1392–1910) court, at the end of the seventeenth century. Although the novel was originally written in Chinese, it was translated into Korean and circulated widely in the nineteenth century. This factor above all probably accounts for its survival to the present day. Believed by Korean scholars to be an example of vernacular literature, the work became the vehicle of enthusiastic, however misplaced, promotion of the excellence of native literature. As late as 1963, Cho Yun-je praises Kim Man-jung for raising the quality of the Korean novel and demonstrating the virtues of the mother tongue as an instrument of literary expression. The discovery of the oldest woodblock manuscripts (dated to 1803 and 1725), however, has evinced incontrovertible proof of its Chinese language origins.

Kuunmong is only one work in a vast corpus of Korean literature composed in literary Chinese. Often taking China as the physical setting of its stories, Korean-Chinese literature (Hanguo hanwen xiaoshuo) clearly models itself on Chinese literary standards, structures, and themes. Perceived as products of slavish imitation, which reflects premodern Korea's willing political and cultural subservience to the Middle Kingdom, this literary tradition has been generally ignored by Korean scholarship in its pursuit for the wellsprings of indigenous culture. The tradition, however, should prove worthy of the attention of scholars of comparative literature as well as promising to contribute new insights to the already thriving field of Chinese narrative studies.

Kuunmong already fulfills both of the above expectations by drawing attention to the prevalence of the dream theme in many fictive works. As Richard Rutt points out, "Chinese and Korean novels whose three-syllable names end with the character *meng* (Korean *mong*), meaning 'dream,' are legion."[9] The most prominent example from the Chinese side that comes to mind, of course, is the classic *Hongloumeng,* or *The Dream of the Red Chamber.* Already the object of much notable scholarship, most analyses of the *Hongloumeng* have confined the novel—for understandable reasons—to the context of Ming and Qing narratives. The unfortunate result, however, has been to obscure the novel's participation in an even broader literary tradition which Chong Kyu-bok terms the "fantasy structure," and which I render as the dream-fantasy (*menghuan*) genre.

Although this is not the appropriate place for a detailed analysis of the origins of this literary tradition, the main thesis adduced in order to argue for the actual existence of such a genre is worth noting. Chong claims (although he is not the first to do so) that the tradition began in India with the tale of Saranapiku contained in the Buddhist sutra known as *Zabaozangjing* (Korean *Chapbochangkyong*). The story created a tradition of dream tales in China and traveled through Korea to Japan, where the tradition became reconstituted through the branch of Noh drama known as *Mugen* (written with the same characters that depict the genre in question). Uniting this pan-Asian narrative tradition with its focus on the enlightening dream seems to be the common theme of "the nihility of life based on the Buddhist philosophy of emptiness."[10]

One frequent structural element of the dream tale is the frame-story pattern, in which the dream sequence (which comprises the central portion of the tale) is bracketed by a preface and epilogue. The *Hongloumeng,* for example, introduces the main protagonist, Baoyu, as a character in the mythical tale of the goddess Nu-gua, who repaired the dome of heaven. As the fretful stone that is rejected in this work of celestial construction, Baoyu is reincarnated into the young master of the Jia clan through the devices of the scabby old Buddhist monk and Taoist priest. At the end of the dream, Baoyu leaves the mortal realm of red dust with these same companions in what is understood to be a state of spiritual liberation.

The main character of the *Kuunmong,* Xingjen, also begins his tale in the immortal realm, this time the five sacred and mythical peaks of China. As the young Buddhist adept under the instruction of the Great Master Liuguan, Xingjen is his favorite disciple and destined successor, until one day he is banished into the mortal realm as punishment for his transgressions. His "transgressions," for as severe as the term sounds, consists more than anything else of a self-failing: the discovery by Xingjen that for all his years of religious training, he still has not achieved purity of mind. A flirtatious encounter with the eight fairy girls of the Taoist adept Lady Wei, who dwells on a neighboring peak, sends Xingjen into longing speculation about the pleasures, wealth, and fame enjoyed by a high-ranking Confucian bureaucrat.

Exiled into the mortal world of dust with the eight fairy girls, Xingjen and his compansions represent the "nine clouds" of the title. In the dream sequence, Xingjen, now reincarnated as the unusually gifted and handsome Shaoyou ("brief sojourner"), achieves all his previous dreams of wealth, honor, and fame. These attainments merely embellish his more central preoccupation with his two wives and six concubines, each of which is acquired in ecstatic erotic fulfillment. At the end of his success-ful career, however, Shaoyou ruminates on the emptiness of all his plea-sures and vows to seek the way that has no birth or death. At this moment, his old master reappears to awaken him from his dream, and Shaoyou discovers himself to be Xingjen once more, kneeling on his prayer mat in his austere cell.

To what extent do these cosmetic similarities in the way the two novels are structured point to meaningful links between them? Rutt points out that the frame-story pattern is a well-tried convention in many works of Chinese fiction and deemphasizes its thematic significance. In fact, of the two works in question, he says, "The Qing novel is of quite a differ-ent character from the Korean story, the religious element is much lower-keyed, and *Hongloumeng* was written seventy-five years later than *Kuunmong*."[11]

Rutt suggests a substantive criterion for determining whether or not the dream tale offers any significant and unified literary meaning—and that is the question of to what extent the dream device serves as a vehicle of religious import. In both *Kuunmong* and *Hongloumeng,* for example, the dream incarnation is set in the mortal realm. This equation of the ordinary world with a fleeting dream seems to reinforce the Bud-dhist message of the ephemeral, insubstantial nature of human life. But does this amount to an advocation of distinctly religious values?

Kuunmong is rather straightforward in its Buddhist identifications. Xingjen and his master are Buddhist adepts, and Buddhist ideals and lessons are plainly espoused. Most scholars of Kim Man-jung make much of the author's own biographical background in order to substantiate the Buddhist intentions of his novel. Although Kim was a successful scholar-official who achieved high rank, he often fell prey to the vicissitudes of political favor. At ease with the Confucian education and ethic befitting his station, Kim's literary works nevertheless express broader, perhaps even contrary, sensibilities.

Tradition has it that *Kuunmong* was written during one of his nu-merous political exiles, in an attempt to console his mother who was widowed in youth and now alone in her old age. The message of the novel would then seem to urge a detached perspective on her sufferings. This anecdote is unsubstantiated, however, and more responsible scholarship tends to focus on the literary qualities of the work itself. Although Buddhist practice was out of favor for much of the Yi reign and relegated to the remote mountaintops, imperial decrees could hardly succeed in banishing over a thousand years of Buddhist presence in Korea. Given the strictures of Kim's political position, which obliged him to an outward neo-Confucian appearance, it is not surprising that his metaphysical views should find outlet through his private pursuit of literary self-expression.

The question of which religious or philosophical tradition (if any) is most faithfully and explicitly represented in a given work is an issue continually at a low simmer on the back burner of Chinese literary studies. Perhaps one of the oddest and yet predictable result is that, given the high level of political and sectarian rhetoric which historically mark the interaction of Buddhism, Taoism, and Confucianism in East Asia, the interpreter who tries to focus on any one tradition is inadvertently drawn into the rhetorical war. Subsequently, the interpretor often reflects and perpetuates the sectarian stance of the tradition that he or she is interpreting.

One obvious arena in which this tendency is all too clear is scholarship that touches on any aspect of the conflict of Buddhist-Confucian ideals. As Anthony C. Yu points out, the momentousness of Baoyu's decision to become a Buddhist monk in *Hongloumeng* illustrates the historical antagonism between institutional Buddhist practice, which requires its novices to abandon household life altogether, and Confucian-based ethical ideals, which emphasize the individual's familial and social responsibilities.[12] The fact that the novelistic narrative faithfully mirrors this conflict of traditions, which has supplied grist for abundant polemics on both sides, should not entail joining the rhetorical fray in order to render a plausible interpretation of the novel. C. T. Hsia's analysis of *Hongloumeng,* for example, formulates an opposition between the Mencian-Confucian ideal, which posits compassion for one's fellow being as the most spontaneous and unalloyed aspect of human nature, and Buddhist metaphysics, which refuses to recognize the substantiality of egos and the existence of the individual.[13] This is a somewhat limited rendition of Buddhist ideals, which fails to recognize the intimate link that has long been maintained in Buddhist philosophy between such metaphysical wisdom and compassion for the suffering of others.[14]

My primary purpose is not to argue the finer points of Buddhist soteriological theory. The fact that the dream metaphor takes much of its language and symbology from Buddhist as well as Taoist sources hardly needs to be belabored.[15] But when it comes to assessing the precise function of the dream in fictive narrative, I believe an inquiry into the ontological dimensions that the dream metaphor both creates and operates in is more productive than an assessment of its religious doctrine. From this perspective, the dream becomes not so much prescriptive as illustrative of a vision of reality, which in the process of illustration, implicates its own medium of expression—that is, the fictive narrative itself. The final stroke of this process is delivered when fiction transcends its commonly understood function of merely expressing ideas and situations through its narrative medium to actually embodying the expressed truths in itself as a work of art.

To adequately explain how such a result might be obtained requires beginning again with the basics—that is, the operative ontology of the culture. Naturally enough, the relevant ontology here is in acute contrast to our own system, which positively maintains the separation of philosophical discourse and the illusion of art. The poles of eternity and temporality operative in Christian ontology dictates that art—although it may speak of the divine—must never be confused with it. Dante and Milton may have dealt boldly with the transcendent realm, but "we may point out that in both these cases what we see in Heaven is by no means the final vision, but rather its finite expression as filtered through the eyes of the poets and the veil of Scripture"[16] Philosophy's self-proclaimed access to the infinite view hardly challenges Christian cosmology but rather reinforces its own privileged status within the existing edifice. In fact, asserting the self-sufficiency of Reason requires a strict hierarchy of discourses, which relegates all other modes to the status of shadowy imitation.

The simple absence of the two-tiered cosmology in Buddhist-Taoist influenced cultures allows us to dispense with this hierarchy of discourses. Andrew Plaks's work on Chinese allegory has suggestively stated that:

> The distinction between the sublunar and the metaphysical, the finite and the infinite, which we have seen as the basis of most Western solutions to the problem of duality, is held by the Chinese thinkers to be just one more of the many complementary pairs included within a single, total frame of reference. The point is not that the Chinese thinkers are more naturally practical or this-worldly than their Western counterparts, but rather that they do not regard the distinction between the physical and the metaphysical aspects of existence as of absolute ontological significance. They are either both real or they are both illusory, but in any event they are commensurable.[17]

What Plaks manages to accomplish in a few short lines amounts to a double-whammy of ontological demolition. Not only are the physical and metaphysical planes sent into relative orbit in a common space, but the whole sphere is deposited in an indifferent ontological dimension that doesn't bother much about the distinction between illusion and reality. The extent to which the dream metaphor serves as a symbol of this unstructured attitude becomes clear in *Kuunmong* when Shaoyou awakens to his former identity as the Buddhist novice Xingjen. In realizing that his life as Shaoyou was a mere dream, Xingjen draws a rather simplistic moral from the tale, concluding that the dream was a device which offered a vicarious lesson on the illusoriness of worldly pursuits:

> He remembered: "I was reprimanded by my teacher and was sent to hell. Then I transmigrated and became a son of the Yang family. I came top in the national examination, and became Vice-chancellor of the Imperial Academy. I rose through various offices and finally retired. I married two princesses and was happy with them and six concubines, but it was all a dream. My teacher knew of my wrong thoughts, and made me dream this dream so that I should understand the emptiness of riches and honor and love between the sexes."[18]

When Xingjen encounters his master Liuguan, he thanks him profusely for having taught him through one dream what would normally have taken endless transmigrations to learn. Liuguan confounds Xingjen's understanding, however, by drawing on a famous Taoist anecdote to question Xingjen's impulse to privilege the dreamer over the dream:

> You went in search of pleasures, and came back having tasted them all. What part have I played in this? And you say that the dream and the world are two separate things, which proves that you have not yet woken from the dream. Chuang Chou dreamed he was a butterfly, and the butterfly dreamed it was Chuang, and which was real, Chuang or the butterfly, he could not tell. Now who is real, and who is a dream—Xingjen or Shaoyou?[19]

Before attending to Xingjen's own confusion, it is perhaps instructive for us to examine the above question as readers of the narrative to see what the art of fiction has to say about the nature of reality. As fictive creations, both Xingjen and Shaoyou are equally real (or unreal) as elements of the narrative. If anything, the character of Shaoyou takes on a more convincing presence, set as he is in the historical milieu of Tang China, and supported by a narrative that is accurate in its geographical and political representations. Of course, the dream sequence can hardly be held up as an example of literary realism, nor does it offer *Hongloumeng*'s wealth of historical detail on the management and occupations of polite society. As readers, however, there is no need for us to reject the dream sequence as any less a part of the narrative than the prologue and epilogue. Despite our understanding of the fact that Shaoyou is an illusion within the illusion of art, this does not diminish his importance in moving the fictive creation forward.

This observation on the construction of narrative reality can be imported wholesale to the metaphysical level with Liuguan's injunction to Xingjen: there is no reason to reject the dream for the reason that its nature is illusory. Inversely, Xingjen need not congratulate himself for having learned through a mere dream what might have taken many lifetimes of experience. As the novel suggests, dream and reincarnation are the same. In Buddhist doctrine, rebirth is fueled by one's failure to see through the illusoriness of the world (its dream-like quality), which in turn is engendered by excessive attachment to the world. If rejection of, or detachment from, the dream seems to make up for one's prior ignorance, the redemption is also illusory because this rejection itself is based on a persistant attachment to the supposed reality of the waking state. Ironically, the more enlightened posture would seem to entail, as an analogue to the rejection of "reality," the acceptance of illusion, both as dream and fiction. But perhaps the charge of casuistry is in order here. Can we not simply reduce the system to the maxim that all phenomena are illusory and therefore should be equally rejected?

Buddhist soteriology elicits the assumption that once life and all phenomena within it are pronounced to be illusory, the natural consequence must be to desire escape from this realm. Certainly within Christian cosmology, the ephemeral and temporal realm of creation lies in opposition to the eternal, spawning the desires of philosophers to transcend historicity for headier, immortal spheres. *Kuunmong,* however, provides a useful antidote to this schema by demonstrating that illusion need not be unpleasant. Unlike Baoyu, who rejects the world after a lifetime's worth of unfulfilled sentiments, Shaoyou's mortal journey meets with repeated realizations, especially in the realm of love.

Of course, it must be noted that in both narratives, the protagonist's circumstances and ultimate fate are mandated by prior karma. Furthermore, the narrative unfolding of both karmic destinies seems designed to teach a unifying lesson: that worldly success and failure both amount to a fleeting, momentary dream. For all his achievements, Shaoyou is tweaked at the end of his life by the feeling of the emptiness of it all. As Buddhist wisdom proclaims, even pleasure can become the occasion for suffering.[20] Even during the heights of the ectastic pleasures of lovemaking, the narrative cannot help sporting on the metaphysical ambiguity of Shaoyou's experience. When he beds the daughter of the Dragon King, the text announces, "they did not know whether it was a dream or reality, they had such joy together."[21] The tone of the narrative suggests a spoof, for at this moment in the story, Shaoyou—the dream incarnation—is himself dreaming of this encounter with the Dragon Princess. The joke is reversed, however, when the dream turns out to be "real," as indicated by the arrival of the Princess at the Imperial palace toward the end of the tale.

The novel frequently makes use of deception and transformation of identities in order to emphasize the existential fluidity of the nine main characters. Male becomes female and vice versa; human becomes fairy and ghost, and the dead come back to life; low-born are transformed into royalty, and beastly creatures are transformed into human beings. Often, these transformations are played as deliberate tricks by the nine "clouds" on each other. As the characters gaily set about deliberately off-balancing each other's sense of reality, however, the narrative simultaneously moves to a subtler tactic of questioning our own as well. When the concubine Chunyun tricks Shaoyou into believing that she is a fairy, their pleasure together is described thus: "It was like a dream, but it was not a dream. It seemed to be real, but it was not."[22] Shaoyou believes he is making love to an immortal, but we know better, or so we believe. Surely, since the woman is actually human, the pleasure between them is real and more substantial than erotic fantasy? Or perhaps the actuality of the pleasure is counterpoised by Shaoyou's own derailed sense of reality. The double-edged cut of the description of their gratification deliberately confounds our own understanding.

If we can only finally conclude that the pleasures of love are as evanescent as life itself, then the attainment of love—no matter how sweet and exalted the variety—does not necessarily lead to a greater satisfaction with the dream. On the other hand, the lack of attainment does not entail the rejection of the dream either. Both events are illusory, but their illusory nature does not render them unreal in some absolute metaphysical sense.[23] If the point of the dream is not merely to warn against the temporality of all phenomena in favor of some absolute, eternal solution, then what is the purpose of it? If Shaoyou's initial conclusions are wrongheaded, what reply does his master Liuguan have to his subsequent plea, "I am confused: I can't tell whether the dream was not true, or the truth was not a dream. Please teach me the truth, and make me understand"?[24]

What Xingjen demands is a clear distinction between the ontologically real and the ontologically false—a question any self-respecting metaphysician should be expected to address. The narrative ends rather abruptly at this point, however, and beyond offering a gatha from the *Diamond Sutra* through the mouth of Liuguan, the text is silent about the ultimate lesson that the young novice—and the reader—is expected to draw. This turn may provide a rather unsatisfying finale, but the artistic shortcoming cannot help but remind us of the Buddhist wisdom that any direct discourse on metaphysical nonduality is inherently self-defeating.

The most famous canonical observation of this point involves an even more pointed example of discourse through silence. The Bodhisattva Vimalakirti—another Buddhist adept noted for his active career in the mortal world—engages in a contest to see who can best discourse on the nature of nonduality. Only he understands the inherently discriminatory properties of language, and hence, its final uselessness in illustrating a contrary reality. Consequently, when the time for his lecture finally comes, he merely replies with wordlessness. Manjusri applauds him exclaiming, "Excellent! Excellent, noble sir! This is indeed the entrance into the nonduality of the bodhisattvas. Here there is no use for syllables, sounds, and ideas."[25]

Whether or not Kim Man-jung had this same ruse in mind when he closed his tale need not be ascertained in order to make the point. In any case, Chong's conclusion that the novel was written in order to convey the message that all "wealth, ranks, and fame on earth finally vanish like a spring dream"[26] is much too curt to do justice either to Buddhism or the agency of literature. If such understanding does not go far enough, then clearly the issue at hand is how one can discourse on ideas that defy discursive expression. Differently put, how can fictive narrative boldly go where procedural rationality is not allowed to tread?

If we choose to take Kim's own biography seriously as a factor in the composition of his art, then perhaps it is easy enough to identify the dream metaphor as a symbol of his own life, which he has awoken to. In that case, what Kim manages to bequeath to his readers by writing his narrative is aptly described by Yu's rendering of the parallel function of dream and fiction: they both teach by means of vicarious knowledge.[27] What the dream teaches Xingjen, the fiction is just as capable of teaching us. But if the lesson to be derived from both is that neither is real, then how are we to finally assess fiction as a mode of discourse?

The key to answering this question is to assert that, given the nondualist cosmology which *Kuunmong* operates in and affirms, the lessons of fiction go far beyond a purely vicarious mode. If life is illusion, in the way that we understand fiction to be, there is something poetic, almost economical, in using the illusion of art to talk about the illusion of life. For the subtle reader, this novel discourses on illusion not only by proclaiming that life is illusion but by existentially embodying the truth of illusion in itself as literary, fictive art. In this sense, fiction is an embodiment of "reality" as defined by the cosmology in force.

One must be careful here about the parameters of this current discourse on fictionality. Specifically, should a claim be made here that fictive/allegorical representation proffers special powers and qualities which draws attention to itself? To argue for such a position is best left to literary specialists. I, at any rate, do not wish to generalize my claims about fiction beyond the specific tradition that I have chosen to focus on. If I were to make such a move here, my act of comparing Western philosophy (and myth), with East Asian fiction would become rather peculiar. Why not compare Western and Eastern narrative traditions instead, rather than the present odd mix of discourses?

My motive for investigating philosophy, myth, and fiction is not to extract the essence of each discourse nor to show how they are all the same. The greater danger here, perhaps, is that of turning fictive representation into disembodied discourse, in the manner that the West has conceived of philosophy. My efforts are precisely to steer in the other direction by asserting that the effectiveness of any discourse is dependent on its context of praxis, rather than some inherent quality. Praxis, which stems from the communal and institutional settings in which discourses are maintained, both expresses and embodies the cosmological views of those societies. Subsequently, the relevant question becomes which form of discourse best conveys and embodies the praxis of each community. I have chosen philosophy, for example, as a primary representative of the West because both its foundations and methods replicate Western ontology. Thus we must understand philosophical discourse as tied to a praxis, which continues today mostly in the activities and concerns of the scholarly community.

Fiction, on the other hand, is an exemplary mode of discourse in late Imperial Korea and China, again, because it gives evidence of a particular form of praxis. This praxis both displays and embodies a cultural strategy that amounts to a historical and practical solution to the religious challenges of the time. In order to appreciate the situation, we must recognize that it is a standard wisdom (both our own and the native's) that Buddhism no longer existed as a viable tradition during the periods when *Kunnmong* and *Hongloumeng* were composed. A doubtful light is thereby cast on the authenticity of Buddhist sentiment in these texts, and they are in turn pointed to as evidence of the levels to which the tradition has fallen. Such opinion assumes particular views of "tradition" that identifies it with institutional settings and limited forms of explicit doctrinal articulation. This narrow definition of tradition problematizes the category of "folk," or "popular" culture, to which the East Asian novel can be positively traced. Here a difference in the depths of religious understanding on the part of various cultural groups supposedly exists. If one follows this view, the prevalence of religious concepts in *Kuunmong* does not display true piety but rather the vestiges of a once dominant point of view. This lingering presence may give evidence of the staying power of traditions, but it is a continuity composed primarily of empty symbols.

This view of cultural praxis is much too narrow and must be rejected here. The virtue of examining fiction as a form of praxis is that it breaks these very same restrictions by showing what can happen when more familiar avenues of cultural expression die out. Therefore, we must understand *Kuunmong* as an altered but authentic manner of religious expression engendered by and appropriate to its historical setting. The best way to begin is by going back to ontology, this time in order to refute the charges of religious meaninglessness in the novel.

If we go back to the use of symbols in Asian fiction, it becomes clear that the charge of "empty symbolism"—implying a lack of understanding of what the symbol points to—is rather peculiar. The art of Dante and Milton may be "to illumine the nature of unseen truth by analogical projection from a pattern of symbols presented on the level of visible images and events";[28] *Kuunmong,* however, lacks these referential and analogical qualities. If Western allegory is founded upon a hierarchy of discourses that differentiates between the symbol and its transcendent meaning, then *Kuunmong* represents the collapse of this hierarchy, in which the symbol becomes self-referential. William LaFleur's description of Buddhism and the literary arts is particularly relevant here: "Poetic depth involves more than the use of symbolism; it is not as much a move away from surfaces to seek inner essences and meanings as a move away from such inner 'meanings' to reaffirm the reality of the so-called surface."[29] When mere mortal words themselves embody sacred truths, the claims of philosophy and myth to provide privileged access to cosmic absolutes seem rather beside the point.

The Buddhist view of reality leaves little room for distinctions between processes of understanding traditionally utilized by us to hierarchicalize various levels of cultural practice. Fiction, both in its symbolic structure and in its link to popular culture, instantiates this reality. Although one can maintain distinctions between forms—fiction cannot be counted among the corpus of sacred scriptures, for example—one is obliged to include fiction as a central part of the cultural canon. One justification for this conclusion is that, as religious praxis, narrative creation can display an orthodox adherence to Buddhist views of reality. The better argument, however, goes beyond cosmological illustrations and inheres in the poetic manner in which fiction advances the central point of the cosmology: the imperative to seek enlightenment. This achievement comes about through the process of reading itself.

I have already made the case that fiction, in the present case, carries a religious meaning that goes beyond a vicarious illustration of metaphysical views. The multiple frames of illusion, of the dreams within the dream that the fiction creates, offers an aesthetically virtuous medium of expression which in the course of consumption becomes indistinguishable from the message itself.

There is a larger point to this. The Buddhist tradition has consistently upheld the decree that the goal of salvation supersedes questions of metaphysics. This position is in fact often taken up in rhetorical opposition to philosophical discourse.[30] Thus in judging the import of fiction as a religious practice, one must apply the internal criterion of the Buddhist tradition. That is, one must ask what is likely to be achieved toward transforming the practitioner—or, in this case, the reader.

The question becomes more pointed in light of the paradox Anthony Yu underscores about the process of reading. The extent to which the message that life is illusory becomes compelling depends on the virtuosity of the artistic creation—the better the illusion, the better it illustrates the truth of illusion. One must become engaged by illusion in order to learn the lessons which allow one to detach oneself from it.[31] As Yu queries, "If life is illusory like a dream or fiction, why is fiction about life such an engaging illusion?" The question leads to a critical distinction between Buddhist philosophy and the art of fiction:

> Whereas Buddhism draws from its "reading" the conclusion that detachment is the ultimate wisdom, the experience of reading fiction . . . is nothing if not the deepest engagement. In *Hongloumeng* therefore, the medium subverts the message, the discourse its language.[32]

The immediate challenge of this conclusion is posed to the integrity of theory and practice within the Buddhist tradition itself. Is it possible to demonstrate that the manner in which late Imperial Chinese-Korean novels function as "Buddhist texts" embodies a practice which remains consistant with its theory? I have thus far attempted to demonstrate their consistancy by showing their doctrinal fidelity to the Buddhist tradition, especially in the realm of ontology. But if it is accepted that salvation is the ultimate aim of religion, it is in this realm that one must demonstrate the virtuosity of fiction as a mode of praxis.

What *Kuunmong* and its discourse on illusion succeeds in achieving is obtained through its inverse quality, that is, its realism, in the sense of its trueness to life. In giving a synopsis of *Kuunmong* I have already suggested that in the narrative universe, illusion—exemplified by the figure of Shaoyou—is ontologically equal to the supposed reality of Xingjen. Both characters are equally necessary for the narrative reality. In reading the novel, however, Shaoyou takes on the more compelling literary presence; he is far more alive than the brief and sketchy figure of the

Buddhist monk. The fact that the illusion within the illusion should prove so compelling serves as a double-fisted example of the greater power of illusion, even in the more straightforward variety, such as fiction or life itself. Of course, the fact that life can be deceptively alluring is a truism upon which Buddhist efforts are built. Hence, there is an ontological identification of life with illusion, which is made not only to discourse on metaphysics but to cool the ardor of those taken in by the tantalizing illusion of life. The praxis of fiction demonstrates, however, the underside of this wisdom, which is a side that cuts with finer, more highly tempered observations: disengagement from suffering is also a process that entails the need for illusion. However much illusion and reality may be the same, the engaging nature of illusion is, without a doubt, soteriologically superior.

I began this chapter with a challenge to Griffiths's contention that philosophical discourse is the primary and most effective means of stating truth claims. Through the comparative example of fictive discourse in a Buddhist-Taoist society, I have sought to show that the means by which one can best express ontological truths depends significantly on the structure of that ontology itself. There is another level, however, on which Griffiths's claims must be taken very seriously, and that is the one concerning my own activity and purposes in making the arguments I have just made. By asking others to consider the fact that fictive discourse can illustrate an ontology, I am also supposing that this ontology should be taken seriously as well. The request is made not only in terms of personal assessment of this view of reality but also as a vehicle for grounding our academic enterprise of redefining the nature of discourse. My own metapractice as a member of the academic community, then, includes pushing some truth claims of my own. And as Griffiths suggests,

> if it is to be explicated, made attractive, and defended to those outside the intentional community that engages in it, this can only be done by laying bare the ontology that underlies and informs its axiology and its metapractice: and this will, because it must, involve a descent into the very denaturalized discourse that the classificatory and descriptive-analytical metapractice seeks to treat solely as an object.[33]

Here, the importance of denaturalized discourse exists not so much as the object of our study (as in attempting to define philosophy over and against myth) but rather as "a vehicle for the expression and justification of our metapractice."[34] Indeed, although I have attempted to represent

Buddhist-Taoist ontology as faithfully as the powers of my own understanding allow, the manner and vehicle of presentation has been determined by the existing standards of academic discourse. The irony of this
process is that my own purpose in utilizing this discourse is to put forward an ontology which challenges the one that spawned it. If denaturalized discourse—now defined explicitly as the practices and intentions of
the academy—can survive the subversion of its own origins, then perhaps we have cultivated a procedural principle, however institutionally
and historically determined, worth refining. The ultimate emphasis, however, must remain on the importance of praxis in the determination of
proper discourse. For if I reflect on my own praxis in the course of this
chapter, I am forced to concede that it is determined by the demands of
my community, which is the academic one. Therefore, my discourse
here on fiction is appropriately in the mode of philosophy.

Notes

1. See Griffiths's essay "Denaturalizing Discourse: Abhidmarikas,
Propositionalists, and the Comparative Philosophy of Religion" in *Myth and Philosophy,* 65, edited by Frank Reynolds and David Tracy (1990).

2. Cassirer, *Language and Myth,* 88.

3. Saint Augustine refers to just such a paradox in his *Confessions,* 192, which
is concerned with the relationship between God the creator and his act of creation: "For did any new motion arise in God, and a new will to make a creature,
which He had never before made, how then would that be a true eternity, where
there ariseth a will, which was not? For the will of God is not a creature, but
before the creature; seeing nothing could be created, unless the will of the
Creator had preceded. The will of God then belongeth to His very Substance.
And if aught have arisen in God's Substance which before was not, that Substance cannot be truly called eternal. But if the will of God has been from eternity
that the creature should be, why was not the creature also from eternity?"

Such speculation clearly illustrates the ontological distinctiveness of the sacred
and profane, to the point that the Eternal's association with the created becomes
very problematic indeed. The magnitude of the paradox would almost seem to
dictate that all must be either eternal or created; the mutual exclusiveness of the
two spheres makes it difficult to find a cosmological town big enough for the
both of them.

4. Some examples of this approach include Rudolph Otto's notion of the rational and nonrational in religion, G. Van der Leeuw's essence and manifestations,

Joachim Wach's experience of Ultimate Reality and its social organization, and Mircea Eliade's notion of hierophany.

5. Cassirer, *Language and Myth*, 6.

6. Plaks, *Archetype and Allegory*, 89.

7. See his forward in *Cosmos and History*.

8. The title of this novel has been variously rendered. James S. Gale's 1922 translation gives it as *A Cloud Dream of the Nine*, whereas Richard Rutt's more recent 1974 version styles it *A Nine Cloud Dream*. I offer up the title of *The Dream of the Nine Clouds* because the suggestive ambiguity of this rendering allows both senses of the previous translations to be preserved. The tale either offers a dream of nine clouds or the tale is itself dreamed by them. The net effect is to suggest that both the dreamers and their dreams are as wispy as clouds.

9. *Three Virtuous Women*, 12.

10. *Kuunmong Yongu*, 340.

11. *Three Virtuous Women*, 12.

12. See his essay, "The Quest of Brother Amor," 60–63.

13. See Hsia's chapter on *The Dream of the Red Chamber* in his *The Classic Chinese Novel* (New York: Columbia University Press, 1968), 245–99.

14. The figure of the Bodhisattva personifies the merger of wisdom and compassion in Mahayana Buddhism. The implicit paradox, of course, is that the Bodhisattva maintains his compassion for other beings even while recognizing the ultimate nonexistence of those very beings. If the contradiction is recognized, textual sources seldom address it directly; the prevalent tendency is to simply link the two qualities of wisdom and compassion together, as if they were two sides of the same metaphysical coin:

> When the Yogin courses in wisdom, the best of perfections,
> He engenders the great compassion, but no notion of a being.
> Then the wise becomes worthy of the offerings of the whole world,
> He never fruitlessly consumes the alms of the realm.
> The Bodhisattva who wishes to set free the gods and men,
> Bound for so long, and the beings in the three places of woe,
> And to manifest to the world of beings the broad path to the
>   other shore,
> Should be devoted to the perfection of wisdom by day and
>   by night.
> —*Perfection of Wisdom in Eight Thousand Lines*, p. 52

15. Roberto Ong notes, "it can readily be seen that there is some affinity be-

tween the Buddhist and Taoist views of the dream. Small wonder that, in the Chinese popular mind, the cliché 'Life is but a dream' is indifferently attributed to Buddhist or Taoist origins" *The Interpretation of Dreams in Ancient China*, 102.

16. Plaks, *Archetype and Allegory*, 106.

17. Ibid., 109.

18. Rutt, *Virtuous Women*, 175.

19. Ibid. The story of Chuang Chou and the butterfly appears at the end of chapter two of the *Chuang Tzu*.

20. This is preached as part of the First Noble Truth expounded in the first sermon of the Buddha—the *Dhammacakkappavattanasutta*. Given the impermanence of all conditioned states, including that of pleasure, suffering is created by the inevitable disassociation from the pleasant, which leads to craving and desire.

21. Rutt, *Virtuous Women*, 103.

22. Ibid., 61.

23. As Indologists are apt to inform us, the notion of illusion, or *maya*, which prevails in Buddhism is inherited from prior Hindu definitions of the term as the power of the gods to create. This creative power hardly constitutes metaphysical nihilism; instead, it is likened to artistic creation, with its derivative notions of magic, illusion, and deceit. See O'Flaherty, *Dreams, Illusion and Other Realities*, 118.

24. Ibid., 176.

25. *The Holy Teaching of Vimalakirti*, 77.

26. *Kuunmong Yongu*, 329.

27. "The Quest of Brother Amor," 82.

28. Plaks, *Archetype and Allegory*, 106.

29. *Karma of Words*, 96.

30. In the *Majjhima-Nikaya* of the Pali Canon, the Buddha compares philosophers to a man who has been wounded with a poisonous arrow, but who refuses medical treatment until he has learned the name, background, and physical characteristics of his assailant as well as the make of the arrow that has entered him. In drawing this famous analogy, the Buddha points out that such questions "tend not to edification." Likewise, "Whether the dogma obtain . . . that the world is eternal, or that the world is not eternal, there still remain birth, old age, death,

sorrow, lamentation, misery, grief, and despair, for the extinction of which in the present life I am prescribing" Warren, *Buddhism in Translation,* 121.

31. The power of illusion for the purposes of illumination is not lost even on those who operate within Western ontology. Philip L. Quinn, who addresses the methods of ethical theory, notes that life itself "is a process with a narrative structure." He continues, "The extent to which an ethical theory made in the image of the theories of science can generate a blueprint or model of a life is problematic. . . . Fortunately there are other resources at our disposal. Among them are the lives narrated in history and literature. As models or analogies, they can contribute to our understanding of what it would be like to lead lives of various sorts and thereby help to guide us in constructing our own lives. Reflection on literature and history can in this way serve the ends of ethical thought" ("Tragic Dilemmas," 83).

32. Yu, "Quest of Brother Amor," 90.

33. "Denaturalizing Discourse," 81.

34. Ibid.

References

Cassirer, Ernst.
   1946 *Language and Myth.* New York: Harper and Brothers.

Cho, Yun-je.
   1963 *Hanguk Munhaksa.* Seoul: Dongguk Munsa.

Chong, Kyu-bok.
   1973 *Kuunmong Yongu.* Seoul: Koryo Daehakkyo.

Conze, Edward, trans.
   1973 *The Perfection of Wisdom in Eight Thousand Lines and its Verse Summary.* San Francisco: Four Seasons Foundation.

Eliade, Mircea.
   1959 *Cosmos and History.* New York: Harper and Row.

Griffiths, Paul.
   1990 "Denaturalizing Discourse." *Myth and Philosophy.* Albany, N.Y.: State University of New York Press.

Hsia, C. T.
1968 *The Classic Chinese Novel*. New York: Columbia University Press.

LaFleur, William.
1983 *The Karma of Words*. Berkeley: University of California Press.

O'Flaherty, Wendy Doniger.
1984 *Dreams, Illusion and Other Realities*. Chicago: University of Chicago Press.

Ong, Roberto.
1985 *The Interpretation of Dreams in Ancient China*. Bochum: Studienverlag Brockmeyer.

Otto, Rudolf.
1958 *The Idea of the Holy*. London: Oxford University Press.

Plaks, Andrew.
1976 *Archetype and Allegory in the Dream of the Red Chamber*. Princeton, N.J.: Princeton University Press.

Pusey, Edward B., trans.
1961 *The Confessions of Saint Augustine*. New York: MacMillan.

Quinn, Philip.
1989 "Tragic Dilemmas, Suffering Love, and Christian Life." *Journal of Religious Ethics* 17/1:151–183.

Reynolds, Frank, and David Tracy, eds.
1990 *Towards of Comparative Philosophy of Religion: Myth and Philosophy*. Albany, N.Y.: State University of New York.

Rutt, Richard, trans.
1974 "A Nine Cloud Dream." In *Virtuous Women: Three Classic Korean Novels*. Seoul: Kwang Myong Printing Co.

Thurman, Robert.
1983 *The Holy Teaching of Vimalakirti*. University Park, Pa.: Pennsylvania State University Press, 1976.

Van der Leeuw, Gerardus.
1938 *Religion in Essence and Manifestation*. London: Allen & Unwin.

Wach, Joachim.
1958 *Sociology of Religion*. Chicago: University of Chicago Press.

Warren, Henry Clarke, trans.
1979 *Buddhism in Translations* New York: Atheneum.

Yu, Anthony C.
1989 "The Quest of Brother Amor: Buddhist Intimations in The Story of the Stone." *Harvard Journal of Asiatic Studies* 49(1):55–92.

Section II

Myth and Practice
in Philosophy

Chapter 4

On Demythologizing Evil

Philip L. Quinn

The relation of morality to religion has been one of the perennial topics of philosophical discussion. Plato's Socrates famously asks: "Is what is holy holy because the gods approve it, or do they approve it because it is holy?"[1] Tracing a pedigree for their concerns back to the *Euthyphro,* contemporary philosophers generalize the question as follows: Is *x* good because God wills it or does God will *x* because it is good? In his contribution to the series of New Studies in the Philosophy of Religion, W. W. Bartley III has provided a critical survey of views of the relations of morality and religion.[2] He argues against the reduction of morality to religion advocated by theological voluntarism, according to which morality depends wholly upon the will of God, and he also argues against the reduction of religion to morality espoused by R. B. Braithewaite, who was notorious for holding that one could be a Christian merely by adopting an agapeistic behavior policy and entertaining without believing Christian stories. In the concluding chapter of this book, Bartley tries to render plausible his own view that morality and religion are inseparable.

The debate among philosophers about the problematic relations of morality and religion is of more than merely theoretical interest. In modern pluralistic societies there is competition among spheres of culture for moral authority; traditional religions vie with secular political ideologies such as Marxism. If morality is grounded in religion, then religious institutions have a legitimate claim to a decisive role in shaping moral practice. For example, religious experts will be in a privileged position to solve moral problems if the religious myths and narratives they interpret are genuine moral paradigms. But if morality is independent of religion, then religious institutions have no such legitimate claim. For instance, secular moral theorists will have the expertise to solve moral problems if moral authority rests with some theoretical position such as utilitarianism capable of being justified entirely in terms of nonreligious reasons. Also at stake in this debate is the fate of competing claims to control institutions of moral pedagogy. In the United States, where a constitutional wall of separation between Church and State has been erected, this renders politically sensitive the issue of whether secular public schools should be in the business of inculcating moral values in their students, since there are conflicts between the values it would be legally permissible to teach in the schools and those taught by some religious communities. So Bartley's view that morality and religion are inseparable is fraught with consequences for the claim that religion can and should settle questions of moral theory, pedagogy, and practice in our own society.

It is also a view with a long and rich history in Western thought. Understanding something about that history can help us to explain why many today in our culture continue to find it compelling. Such historical self-understanding will in turn stand us in good stead in the larger comparative enterprise of trying to grasp with precision what separates us from Eastern traditions in which different historical contingencies have forged rather different links between morality and religion. Thus the historical study undertaken in this chapter can be seen as a contribution to the project of writing comparative history of philosophical ideas about the relations of morality and religion. It can also be seen as a case study that reveals the complexity of the interactions among myth, philosophy, and practice within a single religious tradition.

It is of some interest to see how Bartley conceives of morality and religion in making the claim for their inseparability. Referring to some remarks by J. M. Keynes, Bartley takes Keynes to be drawing a distinction "between one's religion—which is said to concern one's own inner states and one's attitude towards the ultimate—and one's morals—which are said to be directed towards the outside world and what Keynes calls the 'intermediate,' which, amongst other things, are those things which are less than ultimate."[3] Bartley is of the opinion that this distinction will not bear much examination. More important, "it hinders understanding of the development of either personal or social morality, understanding of the soul's conquest of evil."[4] But in order to conquer evil one must first become aware of the evil of which one is oneself capable, and so the quest will be largely inner and self-directed. Bartley proposes to call it religious for just this reason. In order to convey a sense of the inner evil he has in mind, he resorts to retelling some stories from psychology casebooks. One of them involves Christopher, whom Bartley characterizes as "a shockingly clever wicked little good boy."[5] It takes place when Christopher was eight years old and begins early in the morning of the first day after the end of Christmas vacation.

> We find him lying slumbering in bed, sleeping late, as he had done on many of the mornings during the holiday. Suddenly he is abruptly and painfully awakened: his mother seizes his hair, yanks him out of bed, and spanks him. She had been calling him repeatedly to rise, to wash and dress, and prepare for school. But he had not heard; he had slept on; he was still on holiday. But not for long. Less than an hour later, on the way to school, trudging through the snow with his little sister, Mary, five years old, whom Christopher had to guide to and from school each day, he begins to cross-examine her about their mother. 'What do you feel about Mommy?' Christopher asks repeatedly. 'Don't you really hate her?' Sister protests her love of her mother; but Christopher is stubborn and persuasive—and he promises not to tell. Eventually, as they near school, Mary submits, and agrees that she really does hate their mother. That evening, after returning home from school, Christopher takes aside his mother to tell her: 'Mommy, Mary told me today that she hates you.' And then mother spanks Mary.[6]

To live without self-deception or self-delusion involves becoming aware of a capacity within oneself for the same sort of evil one recognizes in the Christopher of the story. Such self-awareness is, Bartley thinks, required if one is to have a proper sympathy for others, to avoid projections in evaluating social situations, and to escape feelings of moral revulsion where such feelings are inappropriate. So partial success at least in the religious quest to overcome inner evil is a prerequisite of a morally sensitive response to the social environment. Such a deep appreciation of the evil of which one is capable might be expressed, Bartley says, "as one's 'sinfulness,' as it might be within the Christian tradition, or as a recognition of one's knavery, to speak in terms that could be given an entirely pagan interpretation."[7]

I find something quite puzzling in the way in which Bartley takes inner evil against which one must struggle to show the inseparability of morality and religion. To be sure, many religions contain both a diagnosis of inner evil and prescriptions for therapy. But these things do not appear to be essentially religious. As Bartley himself notes, they can be given a pagan interpretation. I would add that they also permit wholly naturalistic interpretations. There are, for example, familiar explanations that depth psychology proposes for behavior such as that recounted in the story about Christopher; indeed, it may well be that this is why that story is to be found in a psychology casebook. More generally, there would seem to be no logical or empirical barrier to an entirely secular morality both recognizing the phenomenon of the capacity for inner evil and recommending techniques for taming it.

Yet Bartley is not the only philosopher to discern a special connection between religion and the inner capacity for moral evil. Over a hundred years earlier Jakob Friedrich Fries had expressed similar ideas in the work whose English translation bears the title *Dialogues on Morality and Religion*. In the eleventh dialogue, called "Man's Sense of Guilt," Philanthes, who acts as a mentor to German youth, enumerates what he takes to be the three fundamental ideas of faith. We believe, he says: firstly, "in the truthfulness of our reason and in the personal dignity of our eternal and free spirit." Secondly, "in God, the holy creator of all things, and in the universal dominion of his Eternal Love." Thirdly, we have "the feeling of the moral inadequacy of each person, but, at the same time and on account of Eternal Love, we also have the assurance of the eternal purification and purgation of the will."[8] The conversation between Philanthes and his pupil Otto then continues as follows:

PHILANTHES: Now, attend for a moment to the following question. What is the supreme principle of this view of the world held by faith?

OTTO: The holiness of God and belief in the universal dominion of Eternal Love.

PHILANTHES: With respect to the universe, this is quite certainly the supreme and dominant idea which is the foundation of everything. But what about its status subjectively for us, for man's view of the world?

OTTO: Here I see two, so to speak, conflicting ideas. On the one hand, I see the ideas of the self-confidence and independence of the spirit, and of the freedom of the will. On the other hand, I see consciousness of our moral inadequacy, the consciousness of guilt within our own heart, or however we are to express the matter.

PHILANTHES: What I would say to you is this: subjectively, for man, *consciousness of moral inadequacy is indeed to be designated the fundamental idea, without which we could not introduce any agreement into our convictions* [my emphasis].[9]

Philanthes goes on to claim that "consciousness bestows upon each person the feeling of moral inadequacy."[10] The religious significance of the moral consciousness of guilt resides in the humility it evokes, for "this humility is the deepest fundamental consciousness of the religious view of our life."[11] Jakob Friedrich Fries was an avowed follower and elaborator of Kant's philosophy.[12] And so it might be said of him that he replaced the Kantian trinity of practical postulates of God, freedom, and immortality with a new trinity of God, freedom, and guilt as fundamental ideas of faith. From the human point of view, consciousness of guilt is the most fundamental of this trio, for the humility associated with it is the deepest consciousness involved in the religious view of life.

But this too is puzzling. No doubt there is a kind of religious sensibility at whose roots lies a consciousness of guilt or moral inadequacy. Fries, however, has Philanthes make a much bolder claim than the evidence would seem to warrant. It seems plain that there are varieties of religious sensibility not rooted in guilt. Hence, it is close to obvious that it cannot be subjectively fundamental to religion from the human perspective generally if this is meant as a descriptive claim about the full range of cases that would be conceded to be instances of authentic religiousness. Indeed, the claim does not even hold if its scope is restricted to the Judeo-Christian tradition within which Fries himself is situated. Since Fries is otherwise a perceptive and careful thinker, charity demands that we not attribute to him silly mistakes if this can be avoided, and so I think we must take his claim about the depth of guilt in the religious view of life as at least partly normative. It is religion rightly understood for which guilt is subjectively fundamental, where rightness of understanding imports normative considerations. But this can only intensify the puzzlement. Why should one think that religion rightly understood must be seen as rooted in a consciousness of moral inadequacy?

Both Bartley and Fries then see a tight linkage between religion, on the one hand, and an acknowledgment of interior evil or a sense of moral inadequacy, on the other. It is as though religion as such is being taken for a response to moral guilt. Looked at in the abstract, this is a perplexing picture. After all, there appear to be other sources of religion than moral unworthiness, and there surely are wholly nonreligious ways of dealing with inner evil. But I am of the opinion that Bartley and Fries are moved by a deep and influential current in our culture, and so I think that there is a story to be told that will account for their common perception of the inseparability of religion and moral evil. In this chapter I shall sketch salient features of that story. A part of what makes the story interesting is that it exhibits some of the complexity of historical interactions among myth, interpretation, theological and philosophical theory, and demythologization. So it can be hoped that the story will suggest lessons about the uses and limits of those categories. And, of course, since the story is partly about moral matters, it will also have practical implications that I shall pause to emphasize from time to time in the course of the narrative.

Myth and Its Interpretations

Our narrative begins in myth. It is the story of the fall of humankind recounted in Genesis 3. The serpent tempts the woman, Eve, to eat the forbidden fruit, and she, finding the fruit desirable for gaining wisdom, chooses to eat of it. She gives some to her husband Adam, and he too eats it. As a result, they become aware of their nakedness and so make for themselves loincloths of fig leaves. They hide themselves from God when he moves about in the garden. God asks Adam who had told him he was naked and accuses him of having eaten from the forbidden tree. Adam replies that he ate the fruit because Eve gave it to him. God then asks Eve why she did such a thing, and her answer is that the serpent tricked her into it. The punishment God metes out to the serpent includes crawling on its belly and eating dirt. To the woman he says:

> I will intensify the pangs of your childbearing; in pain shall
> you bring forth children.
> Yet your urge shall be for your husband, and he shall be your
> master.[13]

To the man God says:

> Because you listened to your wife and ate from the tree of
> which I had forbidden you to eat,
> Cursed be the ground because of you!
> In toil shall you eat its yield all the days of your life.
> Thorns and thistles shall it bring forth to you, as you eat of the
> plants of the field.
> By the sweat of your face shall you get bread to eat,
> Until you return to the ground from which you were taken;
> For you are dirt, and to dirt you shall return.[14]

God clothes Adam and Eve in leather garments. He says: "See! The man has become like one of us, knowing what is good and what is bad. Therefore, he must not be allowed to put out his hand to take fruit from the tree of life also, and thus eat of it and live forever."[15] So God banishes him from the garden and sets the cherubim with the fiery sword to guard the way to the tree of life.

This charming story wears some of the marks of myth on its face. It is a narrative of origins set in primordial time.[16] It offers an account of sorts of deeply disturbing aspects of the human condition such as suffering, toil, death, and perhaps, by implication, of the alleged sexual dependency of womankind. Biblical literalists and inerrantists of various stripes to the contrary notwithstanding, it is not now plausibly construed as historically accurate in all its details. Though it is pregnant with religious significance, its import is indeterminate enough to permit subsequent interpreters to project their quarrels backward into their readings of it. But, for all of that, we should not at the outset side with those gnostics who treat the story, reductionistically, merely as spiritual allegory, "not so much *history with a moral* as *myth with meaning*."[17] For one thing, that would be to get ahead of ourselves in our own narrative, since some of our characters do take the story to be history with a moral. More important, it would beg the question against those among us who profess to find a kernel of historical truth buried in the story under layers of fantasy; it would, after all, be a bit rash to suppose it is absolutely certain that the inclination of the human will toward moral evil is not the result of some debilitating catastrophe in the distant past. So when we subsume the story of the fall under the category of myth with meaning, we would do well not to make the gnostic assumption that this precludes its also being, at least in part, history with a moral.

The myth of the fall contains, I have said, a kind of explanation of such features of the human condition as suffering, toil and death. Those things were visited upon Adam and Eve by God in consequence of their disobedience of a divine command, and so we are invited to construe them in the first instance as punishments deserved in virtue of guilt. Though we have inherited them from our first parents, the story does not, on the face of it, force us to conclude that they are also to be thought of as punishments in our case. Nor does the story clearly suggest that we have also inherited from our first parents a burden of guilt. It is going to take some pretty fancy hermeneutical footwork to read the story of the fall as conveying such ideas. The next two episodes in our historical narrative represent stages in the process by which this was accomplished, with momentous consequences for the history of Western Christianity.

The protagonist of the first episode is Paul. Since his concern is to appropriate Jewish history for Christianity, he reads it as history with a moral. The basic interpretive strategy for driving the moral home involves seeing that history as rife with foreshadowings of things that only come to fruition in the life and death of Christ. The underlying polemical purpose is to reinforce in readers the conviction of the spiritual merits of Christianity. In a passage of great rhetorical power, Paul contrasts Adam and Christ in order to press the point:

> Therefore, just as through one man sin entered the world and with sin death, death thus coming to all men inasmuch as all sinned— before the law there was sin in the world, even though sin is not imputed when there is no law—I say, from Adam to Moses death reigned, even over those who had not sinned by breaking a precept as did Adam, that type of the man to come.

> But the gift is not like the offense. For if by the offense of the one man all died, much more did the grace of God and the gracious gift of the one man, Jesus Christ, abound for all. The gift is entirely different from the sin committed by the one man. In the first case, the sentence followed upon one offense and brought condemnation, but in the second, the gift came after many offenses and brought acquittal. If death began its reign through one man because of his offense, much more shall those who receive the overflowing grace and gift of justice live and reign through the one man, Jesus Christ.
>
> To sum up, then: just as a single offense brought condemnation to all men, a single righteous act brought all men acquittal and life. Just as through one man's disobedience all became sinners, so through one man's obedience all shall become just.[18]

It seems plain that this passage adds to the myth of the fall in the course of interpreting it. To refer only to the topic that is the concern of our narrative, verse 19 seems to say with tolerable explicitness that all bear a burden of guilt as a result of Adam's disobedience and thereby to make a commitment that goes beyond anything in the original story. At least, unless this is so, what appears to be a carefully constructed and detailed contrast is actually a clumsy failure. For the obedience (positive moral status) of one man (Christ) is said to be that through which all shall become (future) just (positive moral status), and so, in order for the set of contrasts to be complete, the disobedience (negative moral status) of another man (Adam) must be that through which all became (past) sinners (negative moral status). And this implies both that all became sinners through Adam's disobedience and that being a sinner is a negative moral status, which would be easily explained on the assumption that negative moral status is somehow transferred from Adam to his progeny in a way that parallels the transfer of positive moral status from Christ to those who benefit from his atonement. Moreover, although this involves a controversy about which more will be said later, it is both natural and traditional to read verse 12 in a way that suggests the same ideas. Thus, for example, the explanatory gloss on that verse in the translation I have been quoting reads as follows: "Sin, i.e., man's guilt before God which merited the punishment of death and loss of grace, began with Adam and *infected* the entire human race (v. 12)" [my emphasis].[19] The notion of infection evokes an epidemiological picture according to which sin is transmitted like a disease from Adam to his progeny.

How shall we categorize the kind of interpretive activity embodied in this Pauline text and others of its kind? It seems to me seriously misleading to describe it as mythopoeic. It is too self-consciously interpretive and argumentative for such a description to be entirely apt; it occupies a reflective standpoint that, so to speak, looks at myth from a metalevel. But I think it would be equally misleading to describe it as philosophical. For one thing, it lacks the distance from and critical attitude toward myth already to be found in Plato's work. More important in terms of our narrative line, it also lacks the preoccupation with theory characteristic of philosophy and systematic theology. Paul does not even appear to be concerned with what will come to be central explanatory questions such as specifying a mechanism by which Adam's disobedience might influence his progeny in such a way as to be instrumental in making them sinners. This merely reinforces the by now familiar thought that mythos and logos are not exhaustive categories and reemphasizes the need for one or more analytical categories in which to comprehend interpretive activity that, as it were, falls in the continuum between them, sharing features with the ideal types at both ends of the spectrum. But though Pauline commentary on the myth of the fall is not yet fully philosophical, it represents a step in that direction.

Another step occurs in our next episode whose protagonist is Augustine. He undertakes to perform the philosophical task of proposing a mechanism whereby sin is propagated from Adam to his progeny. In a famous passage, Augustine claims that

> When the first couple were punished by the judgment of God, the whole human race, which was to become Adam's posterity through the first woman, was present in the first man. And what was born was not human nature as it was originally created but as it became after the first parents' sin and punishment—as far, at least as concerns the origin of sin and death.[20]

We are born sinful and guilty because we are born with human nature in its postlapsarian state, that is, human nature as it became after the fall. And the explanation for this is that the whole human race was, in a way yet to be specified, present in Adam. But how are we to understand this claim? Should we, for example, invoke a Platonic model of preexistence and imagine that we were in Adam in the sense of being, unbeknownst to ourselves, present at the fall and willing participants in the sin of our first parents? Not according to Augustine. He offers a sketch of a physical understanding of our presence in Adam.

> Although the specific form by which each of us was to live was not yet created and assigned, our nature was already present in the seed from which we were to spring. *And because this nature has been soiled by sin and doomed to death and justly condemned, no man was to be born of man in any other condition* [my emphasis].[21]

What only seemed explicit in Romans 5:19 has become unmistakably clear in *City of God* 13, 14. We are born in the condition of being soiled by sin, doomed to death and justly condemned, and this is to be explained in terms of physical causation. Because this condition propagates from Adam to his posterity by means of the semen itself, it is part of what we would today refer to as our genetic endowment.

It has been claimed that Augustine derived this astonishing theory from a misinterpretation of Romans 5:12.[22] It is alleged that, because he read the verse in Latin and so ignored or was unaware of the connotations of the Greek original, he took it to say that through one man sin entered the world and with sin death, death thus coming to all men, *in whom* all sinned, and mistakenly supposed that the final clause referred to Adam. And this error is supposed to be the basis for his conclusion that Adam's sin brought upon all men not only universal death but also universal sin. But even if we concede that Augustine made the alleged mistake in reading that is being attributed to him, as I am prepared to do, we are not driven to the conclusion that his view that Adam's sin brought sin upon all men rests entirely on that error. As should be obvious in light of the previous discussion, the claim that Adam's sin brought sin upon all men is supported also by the statement in Romans 5:19 that through one man's disobedience all became sinners. What seems to rest entirely on the mistake in interpretation is not the doctrine of universal inherited sin but rather the doctrine that the whole human race was present in Adam, which is what is involved in claiming that he is the man *in whom* all sin. But the latter doctrine is a bit of an embarrassment to the Augustinian position in any case, since Augustine himself admits that it was not the specific form which individuates me but only the generic nature which I share with other humans that was seminally present in Adam.

In other words, Augustine does not share the view of preformationists in embryology, who held that in Adam's semen there were homunculi who would be his children, and in their semen smaller homunculi who would be his grandchildren, and so on *ad infinitum* or, at least, *ad indefinitum*. So a consistent Augustinian could easily accept correction with respect to the interpretation of Romans 5:12 and abandon the doctrine of universal presence in Adam, since it is no part of the Augustinian picture to claim literal truth for that doctrine, while continuing to hold that the doctrine of universal inborn sin derives its scriptural warrant from texts other than Romans 5:12. But this exegetical controversy should serve to remind us that Augustine's philosophical theorizing does not deal directly with the myth of the fall. It comes to Augustine filtered through Paul, and so his activity involves second-order interpretation. And, of course, there is no denying the enormous influence of Augustine's misreading of Romans 5:12. One has only to recall what the *New England Primer* teaches: in Adam's fall, we sinned all. Popular piety, however, is not the subject of our narrative.

There are implications of Augustine's theory that are part of our tale. Elaine Pagels suggests a connection between the success of the theory and its political utility. It is this:

> By insisting that humanity, ravaged by sin, now lies helplessly in need of outside intervention, Augustine's theory could not only validate secular power but justify as well the imposition of church authority—by force, if necessary—as essential for human salvation.[23]

Though she emphasizes she is not claiming that Augustine or the bulk of his followers held the theory on account of its potential benefits to secular or ecclesiastical authorities, she does commit herself to the view that the primary reason for the great influence of Augustine's teaching on this subject throughout Western Christendom for a millenium and a half is this: "It is Augustine's theology of the fall that made the uneasy alliance between the Catholic churches and imperial power palatable—not only justifiable but necessary—for the majority of Catholic Christians."[24] Unfortunately, no evidence is offered in support of this sweeping causal claim about what made the alliance of spiritual and temporal powers acceptable to most Catholics. Since I am skeptical of single-cause explanations of complex social phenomena spread out over centuries, I doubt that any one thing made that uneasy alliance palatable. But there is some plausibility in the suggestion that Augustine's theology played a more modest causal role in this process.

Of course, the enormous influence on Western culture of the fundamental features of Augustine's understanding of the fall cannot be gainsaid. Perhaps the most striking part of the Augustinian legacy is its doctrine of innate and inherited moral evil. I consider it reasonable to suppose that we hear echoes of this doctrine in Bartley's thought that the conquest of inner evil is a religious project and in Fries's notion that consciousness of moral inadequacy is the subjective foundation of faith. And the genetic mechanism Augustine proposed for the transmission of hereditary moral evil was also endorsed and elaborated by some of his theological and philosophical successors.

But it is easy to see that this doctrine, for all its distinguished ancestry, is deeply problematic from a philosophical point of view. If we allow ourselves the latitude normally granted to authors of science fiction, it is not hard to imagine that mortality is a consequence for humanity of some evil action in the distant past. For we may imagine that a long time ago the genetic constitution of humans was such that they were then naturally immortal but that they brought catastrophe upon themselves by tampering with their own genetic material and so irreversibly altering it in such a way that humans thereafter would be mortal by genetic inheritance. Though I suppose this scenario lacks empirical plausibility, there seems to be nothing logically impossible in it. So one could hold that death is a hereditary consequence of some primordial moral evil. But if one thought about death in this way, one would be committed to viewing mortality as a natural fact about those subject to it, a misfortune but not itself morally evil. After all, we are not properly praised or blamed for our biological inheritance; a person's genetic endowment is, as John Rawls aptly puts it, the result of a natural lottery and so does not ground desert of either reward or punishment. But moral evil does deserve condemnation or punishment. Since those guilty of it must be accountable for it, it cannot be inherited. And it would seem that all sin is moral evil, for sinners are said by Augustine and others to be justly condemned by God. It seems therefore that there can be no such thing as inherited sin or guilt.

There is, then, a tension, if not an outright conceptual absurdity, at the heart of the Augustinian understanding of the moral of the myth of the fall. The remaining episodes in our narrative exhibit attempts to deploy philosophical resources for the purpose of reducing this tension.

Medieval Theological Elaboration

Anselm of Canterbury continues the Augustinian project of specifying a causal mechanism to explain the heritability of sin. Anselm's work progresses beyond Augustine's in terms of such desiderata of theories as clarity, rigor, systematic unity, and articulation of detail. But they are both in search of an explanatory logos, and in this sense both are engaged in the enterprise of philosophical theory construction.

Some would dissent from this way of putting things and classify Augustine and Anselm as theologians rather than philosophers. As they see it, philosophy and systematic theology are distinct theoretical activities. Both search for explanatory logoi, and they share such values as clarity, rigor, systematicity, and articulation. Nonetheless, there is an important methodological distinction between them. The starting points of philosophy must be exclusively things known from sources other than revelation; theology may include the data of revelation among its starting points. On this view, Augustine and Anselm are theologians rather than philosophers because they assume the historical truth of the story of the fall on the authority of scripture and without independent empirical confirmation. Though it is slightly anachronistic to look at Augustine and Anselm in these terms, there is a conceptual point worth making here. Let us take philosophy in the narrow sense to be philosophy in the sense in which it contrasts with systematic theology, and let us take philosophy in the broad sense to be that genus of theoretical activity, focused on the search for explanation, under which both philosophy in the narrow sense and systematic theology fall as species.

Using this distinction, we can say, for example, that Thomas Aquinas is a philosopher in the broad sense and both a systematic theologian and a philosopher in the narrow sense. His *Summa Contra Gentiles* is meant to be a work of philosophy in the narrow sense and not of systematic theology, but his *Summa Theologiae* is a work of systematic theology and not of philosophy in the narrow sense. When philosophy is contrasted with myth and other things such as exegesis, it seems that what is ordinarily meant is philosophy in the broad sense. So I think it would not be misleading to say that the theories about the inheritance of sin proposed by both Augustine and Anselm play a role in our narrative that is philosophical, although those theories are theological rather than philosophical in the narrow sense.

Theory construction is, of course, not the only task of theology. Theologians also have direct practical concerns with liturgy and religious education. But faith does seek understanding. If what a community of believers wants to understand is something as perplexing as the Augustinian doctrine of innate and inherited moral evil, its theologians have some explaining to do. Systematic theology attempts to meet such demands for explanation and quickly turns theoretical.

Anselm's theory is set forth in his *De Conceptu Virginali et Peccato Originali,* which begins with a sharp and irreducible contrast between original sin and personal sin. A metaphysical presupposition of this contrast is the distinction between nature and person. Each human being is metaphysically composite and includes both a nature, which makes him or her human like others, and a principle of individuation, which makes him or her a particular person distinct from all others. Original sin is sin that one contracts with human nature at the very origin of one's existence as a person; personal sin is sin one commits at some time after one has begun to exist as a person.[25] Being contracted with one's human nature, original sin is inherited; it is innate and unavoidable. Being committed after one has begun to be an individual person, personal sin is evildoing; it is not innate and is avoidable. The two seem as different as chalk and cheese. What could they have in common in virtue of which both are kinds of sin?

Anselm's answer is that both are injustice. He defines justice as uprightness of the will preserved for its own sake.[26] In a rational creature, the upright orientation of the will consists in the will being subject to the will of God. Since injustice is no positive thing but a mere absence, it is to be defined negatively as the absence of due justice. In other words, injustice is the lack of justice where justice ought to be, namely, in the will. So both justice and injustice reside in the will and, strictly speaking, there alone.[27] Because all sin is injustice, it too resides only in the will. A sinful will is one in which there ought to be but is not an upright orientation preserved for its own sake, and it is also one that should be but is not subject to the will of God. So sin consists in the will being disordered both with respect to its own proper orientation and in relation to God's will.

It is easy enough to see how to apply these considerations to the elucidation of personal sin. To commit a personal sin is to disobey God in deed. The sinner's will, which should have remained subject to God's by obeying his commands, refuses to be subject to God's will when it disobeys his commands. On that account, it lacks upright orientation and so is characterized by an absence of due uprightness preserved for its own sake. Because such an absence is injustice, personal sin is injustice. It is more difficult to make sense of the notion that original sin too is injustice. One who suffers from original sin must begin to exist as a person already lacking an upright orientation of the will; when such a person contracts human nature, along with it must come a will already not subject to God's will. By itself this may not be so very difficult to understand. Perhaps there is no logical problem in grasping what it would be like to come to be a person with a will already so damaged and disordered that it lacks upright orientation and is not subject to the will of God, and maybe this misfortune could be conceived of as a consequence of a catastrophe in the distant historical past. So the absence of justice in the will when one begins to be a person need not, on its own, be a source of fatal perplexity. But injustice is not merely the absence of justice; it is rather the absence of justice where justice ought to be. Thus we must further suppose that one who suffers from original sin begins to exist as a person with a will that ought to possess justice, despite the fact that it is innately lacking in justice. To make this supposition, however, is to endorse the claim that the lack of uprightness from the very beginning of personal existence in the will of one who suffers from original sin is, despite being unavoidable for the sinner, a moral evil for which the sinner deserves condemnation by a morally perfect judge. This is a disturbing thought.

Faced with this apparently unpalatable consequence of Anselm's views, one might well pause to wonder whether he really means it. Could it be that he only means to claim that we begin to exist as persons with wills from which uprightness and so justice are absent? Must we read him as asserting also that this absence is unjust and so sinful? I think we must. Anselm explicitly considers the objection that original sin is no more real sin than a painted man is a real man. In response, he notes that, if this were so, infants who die unbaptized, having no sin but original sin, either would not be condemned or would be condemned without sin. But, says Anselm blandly, "we do not accept any of these consequences."[28] He holds that infants who die without baptism, having committed no personal sins, are condemned. Since they are condemned by God, who is a morally perfect judge, they are not condemned without sin. Hence, original sin is real sin. It is a moral evil for which unbaptized infants deserve condemnation by a morally perfect judge, even though it is innate in and so unavoidable for unbaptized infants. Moreover, Anselm explicitly denies that an unbaptized infant's inability to possess justice excuses its lack of justice. He claims that the absence of uprightness of the will preserved for its own sake is unjust and so sinful in unbaptized infants because justice is required of infants before Baptism and there is no excuse for its absence in them.[29]

Whence comes this terrible fault? Anselm agrees with Augustine in proposing a causal mechanism by way of response to this question but differs with Augustine about the nature of that mechanism. According to Anselm, the causal pathway by which sin is propagated from Adam and Eve to their descendents passes through human nature. Anselm initially puts this point in terms of what we might think of as a two-way transmission principle. He says: "as what is personal passes over to the nature, so what is natural passes over to the person."[30] Thus, by the first half of this principle, the sin of Adam and Eve passes over to human nature, and by its second half, the sin of human nature passes over to their descendents. By a two-step process, then, sin is handed on from Adam and Eve to their progeny. Of course, this formulation of the principle is a bit crude. It is apt to mislead us into thinking of sin as a sort of stuff that could literally be transmitted from one person to another via some intermediary like the viral particles that cause a communicable disease. And if we operated under the influence of this picture, we might well be tempted to think that the sin which is in infants from the very moment they begin to exist as persons is the same as, or at least a part of, the sin of Adam and Eve. But, if that were so, infants who die unbaptized and so are condemned would be condemned for the sin of others. This Anselm will not allow, presumably because a morally perfect judge would not condemn one person for the sin of another.

Anselm is at pains to insist that the sin of Adam and Eve is discernible from the sin of the infant. Adam and Eve were unjust, not because someone else abandoned required justice, but because they themselves did; newly born infants are unjust, not because they abandoned required justice, but because someone else did.[31] Hence, by the principle of the indiscernibility of identicals, the sin of Adam and Eve is diverse from the sin of the infant. When an infant is condemned for original sin, Anselm insists, the infant is not condemned for the sin of Adam and Eve; the infant is condemned for a sin of its own, for it would not be condemned unless it had a sin of its own. So what we should say, strictly speaking, is that the sin of Adam and Eve causes the sin of the infant. Accordingly, a more precise version of Anselm's two-way transmission principle is this: what is personal causes what is natural, and what is natural causes what is personal. Thus the persons Adam and Eve make human nature sinful by the first half of this principle; they do this by personally deviating from the uprightness of will with which they were created and which their creator empowered them to preserve. And sinful human nature in turn makes the descendants of Adam and Eve sinful in their own right, from the very first moment they possess it, by the second half of this principle; it does this by a natural necessity with which the nature's destitution of required justice causes those in whom the nature propagates also to be destitute of required justice and so unjust.[32]

This attempt to specify more precisely a causal mechanism for the transmission of inherited sin and guilt obviously does nothing to resolve the philosophical tensions implicit in the Augustinian tradition.[33] Many of Anselm's successors played other variations on Augustinian themes; they include Aquinas, Luther, and Calvin. Though some of these variations are interesting in their own right, considering them would make a long story even longer, and so our narrative must leave them to one side in order to hasten to its climax in the modern era. Its concluding episodes have a deflationary air about them, for they involve relieving the Augustinian tension by rejecting some of the assumptions that generated it.

Modern Philosophical Revisions

John Locke rejected the doctrine of inherited sin and guilt. But there is no reason to doubt his sincerity when he calls himself a Christian; during the late autumn of 1704, Lady Damaris Masham read Scripture by his bedside as life slowly deserted him.[34] He was not prepared to deny all historical truth to the story of the fall recounted in Genesis 3 and to treat that story as a mere fable. However, as we have seen, it takes two steps to get from the unadorned story of Genesis 3 to its Augustinian interpretation; a Pauline layer of interpretation lies between the unadorned story and its fateful Augustinian reading. Locke's thoroughly modern strategy is to drive a wedge between the Pauline and Augustinian strata of interpretation; his aim is to undercut Augustine by reinterpreting Paul.

We can see this deconstructive strategy at work in Locke's paraphrase and notes on Romans. His procedure is to quote a verse, then to offer his own paraphrase of it, and finally to argue in support of the paraphrase in an appended note. Here, for example, is the application of that procedure to Romans 5:12. First Locke quotes his text:

> Wherefore, as by one man sin entered into the world, and death by sin: and so death passed upon all men, for that all have sinned.

Next he paraphrases it:

> Wherefore, to give you a state of the whole matter, from the beginning you must know, that, as by the act of one man, Adam, the father of us all, sin entered into the world and death, which was the punishment annexed to the offence of eating the forbidden fruit, entered by that sin, for that all Adam's posterity thereby became mortal.

Having, in effect, substituted "became mortal" for "have sinned" at the end of the verse, Locke has neatly blocked both the inference that sin is inherited as well as death and the inference that death is a punishment for sin in Adam's posterity; we are to understand the text as saying no more than that death was the punishment for Adam's sin and is inherited by his posterity. And Locke tries to justify this substitution in a note that begins as follows:

> "Having sinned," I have rendered became mortal, following the rule I think very necessary for the understanding St. Paul's epistles, viz. the making him, as much as is possible, his own interpreter. I Cor. xv. 22, cannot be denied to be parallel to this place. This and the following verses here being, as one may say, a comment on that verse in the Corinthians, St. Paul treating here of the same matter, but more at large. There he says, "as in Adam all die," which words cannot be taken literally, but thus, that in Adam all became mortal. The same he says here, but in other words, putting, by a no very unusual metonymy, the cause for the effect, viz. the sin of eating the forbidden fruit, for the effect of it on Adam, viz. mortality, and, in him, on all his posterity: a mortal father, infected now with death, being able to produce no better than a mortal race. Why St. Paul differs in his phrase, here, from that which we find he used to the Corinthians, and prefers here, that which is harder and more figurative, may perhaps be easily accounted for, if we consider his style and usual way of writing, wherein is shown a great liking of the beauty and force of antithesis, as serving much to illustration and impression. In the xvth chapter of I Cor. he is speaking of life restored by Jesus Christ, and, to illustrate and fix that in their minds, the death of

mankind best served: here, to the Romans, he is discoursing of righ-
teousness restored to men by Christ, and therefore, here, the term
sin is the most natural and properest to set that off. But that neither
actual or imputed sin is meant here, or ver. 19, where the same way
of expression is used, he, that has need of it, may see proved in Dr.
Whitby upon the place.[35]

Having laid out his argument at length in this note, Locke can be brief in
his treatment of Romans 5:19. First he quotes the text:

For, as by one man's disobedience, many were made sinners: so, by
the obedience of one, shall many be made righteous.

The paraphrase is just what one would expect:

For as, by one man's disobedience, many were brought into a state
of mortality, which is the state of sinners; so, by the obedience of
one, shall many be made righteous, i.e. be restored to life again, as if
they were not sinners.

And the justificatory note is quite terse:

"Sinners." Here St. Paul uses the same metonymy as above, ver. 12,
putting sinners for mortal, whereby the antithesis to righteous is the
more lively.[36]

Thus is Paul reinterpreted in the interest of cutting the ground out from
under the Augustinian doctrine of innate and inherited sin. Even if one is
not wholly persuaded, as I am not, by Locke's reading of Romans 5:19, it
does at least serve to illustrate an interesting possibility for philosophy. If
the Lockean strategy were successful, there would be no need for philosophy to provide an explanatory account of hereditary sin, for the
Augustinian doctrine of inherited moral evil would have been shown to
rest on a mistake. But, like the other humanistic disciplines, philosophy
is interpretive. So it need not conceive of itself as restricted to constructing theories to explain hard data that cannot be challenged. Often the
alleged data are, as in the present case, products of a long and complicated history of interpretation and are not so hard after all. In some such
cases, it will be appropriate for philosophy in the broad sense defined
above to engage in the project of reinterpretation and to argue that the
putative explanatory problem does not really exist since the alleged data
that had been thought to pose it are themselves products of misinterpretation. Of course, not all arguments of this kind will succeed. But the
Lockean episode in our narrative nicely illustrates the fact that this option
is available to philosophy when it confronts myth buried beneath layers
of interpretation. In short, philosophy can be archeological, clearing away
accumulated layers of interpretive rubbish, as well as architectural, erect-
ing vast theoretical superstructures.

Could it turn out that, once the process of stripping off interpretive layers begins, what philosophy discovers is rubbish all the way down? I suppose so. It seems that many people would have our narrative conclude with this discovery; since the Enlightenment we have known, it might be said, that the story of Genesis 3 expresses nothing but pernicious falsehood and produces only pathological feelings of guilt if taken seriously. It is therefore fitting to make Kant the protagonist of the final episode in our narrative. For he more than anyone else epitomizes the Enlightenment's rationalism in philosophy, and yet there is a sense in which his view of human nature is as harsh as that of his Lutheran and Augustinian forebears.

As the very title of his major work on religion indicates, Kant was self-consciously a philosopher in the narrow sense defined above.[37] His topic is religion within the limits of reason as those limits are defined in the context of his larger philosophical system. This work got him into trouble with the state censors, who read it as controverting the teachings of the Bible, and brought down upon him the wrath of the king, who wrote him a threatening letter.[38] Kant rejects the Augustinian doctrine of inherited sin and guilt. He says explicitly that "however the origin of moral evil in man is constituted, surely of all the explanations of the spread and propagation of this evil through all members and generations of our race, the most inept is that which describes it as descending to us as an *inheritance* from our first parents."[39] But Kant also holds that humans are, in a sense, by nature morally evil because there is in them a morally evil propensity to evil. It is this propensity that stands in for original sin in Kant's philosophy of religion; he even calls it *peccatum originarium.*[40]

A propensity is one among several ways in which the faculty of desire can be related to its objects. It is, Kant tells us, a predisposition to crave a delight which, when once experienced, arouses in the subject an inclination to it.[41] For example, some people have a propensity to eat chocolate. Before tasting it they have no desire for it, but once they have sampled it they immediately develop a craving for it. The propensity to eat chocolate is innate in those who possess it; presumably its presence in them can be explained in terms of inheritance. Kant describes propensities of this sort as physical because they pertain to their possessors considered as natural beings determined by causal laws.[42] If all propensities were physical, then even if there were a propensity to evil in humans, it would not itself be morally evil and so would not make the humans who possessed it morally evil by nature. For Kant, whatever results entirely from natural laws is morally indifferent, and so physical propensities are morally indifferent.[43] Hence, there must be at least one nonphysical propensity if a propensity to evil is to make the humans who possess it morally evil. Kant characterizes the postulated nonphysical propensity as moral because it pertains to its possessors considered as moral beings, who freely determine themselves to action. And since nothing is morally evil but free action and what derives from it, a propensity to evil that is itself morally evil has to be a product of the exercise of freedom. Though the propensity to evil can be represented as innate, Kant tells us it should not be represented merely as innate; it should also be represented as brought by humans upon themselves.[44] Indeed, it must be so represented if it is to be thought of as a moral propensity that makes its possessors morally evil.

But how can a single thing be coherently represented both as innate in its possessors and as brought by them upon themselves? Kant's response to this question appeals to his account of free human actions. If an action is to be free, there must be something at its roots that is completely subject to the spontaneity of the agent.[45] Kant takes this to be the maxim of the action. A maxim for an action provides a characterization of the action that incorporates both a description of what is to be done and a description of the incentives for doing it. The agent is free with respect to adopting maxims for actions, but once a maxim is adopted, the incentives incorporated into it determine the agent's will to action. So, although the will of the agent is determined to action by incentives, the agent is, in effect, free to choose among incentives in virtue of being free with respect to the choice among maxims incorporating different incentives or patterns of incentives. Kant's bold reductive stroke consists of extending this idea to the analysis of the propensity to evil. The agent's freedom extends beyond choice of conduct to choice of character. The propensity to evil is the underlying common ground in the agent, itself a maxim and so freely adopted, of all particular morally evil maxims of individual actions.[46] This supreme maxim, Kant tells us, is "a rule made by the will for the use of its freedom."[47] We may think of it as a general policy, freely adopted by one who has it, for adopting maxims of individual actions. It is, as it were, a metamaxim that applies to the whole use of the agent's freedom.

According to Kant, the morally evil propensity to moral evil so conceived is susceptible to a double representation. It can be represented as innate in its possessors because, as the underlying ground of all morally evil actions, it is to be thought of as present in its possessors antecedent to all such actions and so represented temporally as present from birth in them. But it can also be represented as brought by its possessors upon themselves because it is a maxim whose adoption is an free act on their part and so is something for which they are accountable. Humans are, therefore, by nature morally evil only in the sense that the morally evil propensity to evil is, as far as we can tell on the basis of the empirical evidence available to us, universal among humankind. As Kant puts it, given what we know of humans through experience, we may presuppose moral evil to be subjectively necessary to every human, even to the best of them.[48] But they are not causally determined to moral evil by events in the remote past.[49]

Kant's account of the morally evil propensity to evil cuts both causal and evidential ties to the story of the fall recounted in Genesis 3. Since each human who possesses it brings the propensity to evil upon himself or herself, it is no part of anyone's genetic endowment. Hence, there is no need to postulate a causal mechanism to explain its transmission from Adam and Eve to their progeny. And our evidence for belief in such an evil propensity is not for Kant the authority of scriptural stories but an induction from our experience of human affairs. As he sees it, the existence of such a propensity "need not be formally proved in view of the multitude of crying examples which experience *of the actions* of men puts before our eyes."[50] To be sure, Kant does say that his account agrees well with the manner in which the origin of evil in the human race is presented in Scripture.[51] However, upon examination it becomes clear that this agreement consists in nothing more than the fact that what is primary in the Kantian account, namely, humans bringing upon themselves a morally evil propensity to evil, is represented in the scriptural myth as having occurred first in time. Agreement to this extent plainly does not commit the Kantian account to the truth of any historical claims about the scriptural story of the fall of Adam and Eve. When Kant endorses the formula "in Adam all have sinned," he means only to be saying that the story of the sin of Adam and Eve provides a kind of symbolic representation of something that actually occurs, as far as we can tell, in each human life.[52] And, as if to bring us full circle, there occurs at this point in the Berlin edition of Kant's *Religion Within the Limits of Reason Alone* a footnote referring to Romans 5:12, alluding to the problematic relation of its Greek text to the Latin translation and suggesting the influence of that translation on Augustine.[53]

There are practical implications of Kant's willingness to accommodate an innate and morally evil propensity to evil within the limits of reason. The most important of them arises from the picture the postulate of the morally evil propensity to evil gives us of the starting point of our moral lives: we begin from evil. According to Kant, the consequence for moral discipline is that "we cannot start from an innocence natural to us but must begin with the assumption of a wickedness of the will in adopting its maxims" and "since this propensity [to evil] is inextirpable, we must begin with the incessant counteraction against it."[54] It is this rather deflationary estimate of human character that most strikingly sets Kant apart from the currents of facile optimism found elsewhere in Enlightenment thought. It is preserved in the work of his disciple Fries. Speaking of our fundamental moral inadequacy, his character Philanthes says: "But, of necessity, we pronounce this moral condemnation of each person, even the best."[55] And its emphasis on the need for incessant counteraction against the will's interior wickedness is even reflected in Bartley's notion of the moral project as the soul's struggle to conquer inner evil.

So our narrative does trace historical associations of religion and morality in Western Christian culture. But the moral this history teaches is not, as Bartley supposes, that religion and morality are inseparable. Contingent historical circumstances account for the fact that a doctrine of innate evil became part of the dominant interpretation of the biblical myth of the fall in Western Christianity. By rendering that doctrine evidentially independent of religious myth, Kant contributed, perhaps without meaning to do so, to the separation of morality from religion by demythologizing moral evil. Fries follows his master in taking the demythologizing turn. In the course of instructing his pupils about the universal moral inadequacy of humanity, Philanthes remarks:

> As you know, these ideas have been expressed by means of the images of man's fall away from God, and in the doctrines of eternal reward and punishment. It was natural that these latter ideas should have been borrowed from civil life where we work for reward, and then transferred metaphorically to religious ideas. But it is manifest that they have no meaning here.[56]

Metaphor without meaning is all that remains of Augustine's savage claim that we are all born soiled by sin, doomed to death, and justly condemned. And, of course, Bartley too is aware that the conquest of evil is a project that can sensibly be undertaken in a wholly secularized setting without appeal to religious myth or theological theory. Picking up on his previous reference to Keynes, he concludes his book with a tribute to denizens of Cambridge or Bloomsbury, such as Russell, Moore, Keynes, Leonard and Virginia Woolf, and Morgan Forster. He says of them:

> Although these individuals were, then, engaged in a conquest of evil, although they even were, one might say, searching for salvation, it is well to remember that they were hardly Christians: they often referred to themselves as pagans.[57]

No doubt these people deserve admiration; they were cultivated, creative and, for the most part, morally earnest. But it will not do to think of them as searching for salvation if the notion of salvation is reserved for "those visions that see a type of transmoral destiny for humankind."[58] Nor, I suggest, can we conceive of their struggles with evil as religious without emptying the notion of religion of all mythological and theological content. So I take the upshot of both Bartley's own example and our narrative to be that morality and religion are separable in both theory and practice.

Conclusions

Our narrative is, of course, history at least in outline, and I hope to derive some methodological morals from it. To be sure, induction from a single case study is mainly of heuristic value, and so the lessons I claim this narrative teaches will need to be tested for generality against other cases. But I am of the opinion that they have an air of commonsense plausibility that makes it worthwhile to spell them out.

The first lesson is the importance of history for understanding the complex interactions of myth, philosophy, and practice. What the historical perspective reveals in our case study is a picture that suggests geological analogies. Myth is transformed by an interpretive process like sedimentation in which successive layers of interpretation pile up on the mythic substrate, and the explanatory theories of philosophy and theology are superstructures erected upon the higher interpretive layers. There also occurs a process like erosion in which older interpretive layers are stripped away as a result of critical reinterpretation, and this process can undermine the foundations of philosophical or theological superstructures by dissolving the explanatory problems they were constructed to solve. And at every stage of these processes intellectual activity is both under pressure from existing practice and helps to shape subsequent practice.

The remaining lessons are about the categories of myth, interpretation, philosophy, theology, and practice employed by students of religion. Consider first myth. There is a way of thinking about things according to which, even if myth is taken seriously, *myth with meaning* and *history with a moral* are treated as exclusive categories. I tend to think that this way of mapping the terrain has serious disadvantages. For one thing, it is often partisan. As our narrative shows, the historicity of the biblical story of the fall is contested within the traditions of Western Christianity. In the Middle Ages, that story was taken for sober historical truth; more recently, it has become an object of skeptical suspense of judgment or open disbelief. To classify it as myth in the exclusive sense would be to depart from descriptive neutrality and to take sides in this quarrel. In addition, such a procedure can be patronizing and insulting to the natives being studied, a group which, in the case under discussion, includes the fundamentalist Christians among us. They are apt to see such a move as a rather crude power play by secular humanists, a way of rejecting the legitimacy of their beliefs by terminological fiat. If classification were a subject for negotiation with the natives, the story of the fall would not be classified as myth in the exclusive sense. Because I am convinced that these considerations are generalizable, I favor a concept of myth that leaves the question of historical truth open. By way of methodological advice, I suggest that students of religion owe both their audiences and the natives candor about whether their talk of religious mythology carries with it this exclusive implication.

As I read it, the genealogy of the doctrine of original sin demonstrates the utility of deploying a category of nonphilosophical interpretation of myth. Paul is the key figure in this connection. Romans 5:12–19, for instance, clearly involves interpretation of the story of the fall, but it does not much resemble the paradigm cases of philosophical theorizing about that story. Its technique of elaborate parallel contrasts is rooted in rhetoric rather than logic, and its main aim is persuasion rather than theoretical explanation. It posits no explanatory structures or mechanisms to match Plato's Forms, Aristotle's four causes, Augustine's seminal causation, Anselm's two-way transmission principle, or Kant's free choices of character. Hence, I consider it illuminating to think of Paul as representing a prephilosophical interpretive moment interpolated between the mythopoeic moment of Genesis 3 and later philosophical moments that derive from Augustine. On this view, mythos and logos are not exhaustive categories; exegesis may fall between myth and philosophy.

Locke raises an interesting question for this way of looking at things. His paraphrases and notes on the Pauline Epistles are exegesis done by a philosopher. But are they philosophy? There seem to me to be arguments on both sides of this question. On the one hand, it might be claimed that they are philosophy because they are part of a larger argument aimed at undermining theories of the inheritance of sin in the Augustinian tradition by dissolving the explanatory problem those theories were constructed to solve. On the other hand, it might be claimed that they are not philosophy just because they advance no new explanatory theories. I suspect that this is an issue that calls for stipulation rather than for further argument and that it does not make much difference how we settle the matter. If we say that the Lockean paraphrases and notes are philosophy, then the categories of philosophy and interpretation will overlap partially. Some interpretations will be philosophical and some will not; presumably contextual factors will help to determine which are which. If we say that the Lockean paraphrases and notes are not philosophy, then we can regard philosophy and interpretation as exclusive categories and think of Locke as a polymath who sometimes practiced philosophy but occasionally dabbled in exegesis. My own preference for the former picture rests on the belief that interpreting the texts that are the past of philosophy is itself a philosophical activity, but I would not strenuously object if someone were to classify that activity as the history of ideas. So the only methodological lesson I wish to extract from the case of Locke is that it is important for students of religion to be clear about how they conceive of the relation between interpretation and philosophy.

A similar point about the relation between philosophy and theology is worth emphasizing. If we think philosophy must operate within the limits of reason alone, philosophy in this narrow sense and systematic theology will be mutually exclusive. On this proposal for cutting up the pie, Kant's *Religion* will turn out to be a work of philosophy but Anselm's *De Conceptu Virginali* will not. But for some purposes it may well be more illuminating to stress the resemblances between Anselm and Kant. Both are in search of the kind of logos to be secured by constructing explanatory theories, and both are driven to postulate explanatory causal structures, transmission of sin via human nature in Anselm's case and free choice of character in Kant's. So there is something to be said for including both Kant's *Religion* and Anselm's *De Conceptu Virginali* within the class of works that are philosophical in a broader sense. On this taxonomic proposal, both philosophy in the narrow sense and systematic theology will be subclasses of philosophy in the broad sense. But since texts do not fall neatly into natural kinds, taxonomy in the humanities is bound to be more arbitrary than taxonomy in chemistry or biology. Clarity about one's classificatory apparatus is, of course, a methodological virtue. However, apart from their consequences for academic turf wars, I can see nothing substantive that hangs on such terminological decisions.

The allusion to turf wars brings up questions of practice and power. The moral I wish to draw from the history of the doctrine of original sin is that myth, interpretation, and philosophical theory in various combinations can be used to rationalize or justify practices at three, if not more, distinct levels. The first is the level of individual morality. Thus, as Kant notes, the postulate of innate evil forces us to picture the moral life as an incessant struggle against that evil and, at best, a difficult climb from bad to better. This picture places such virtues as self-discipline, restraint, and conscientious attention to duty in an attractive light, and it at least suggests suspicion of such character traits as spontaneity and sincerity. The second is the level of internal ecclesiastical politics. Pagels claims that Augustine's theory of innate sin could be used to justify the imposition by force of church authority. Augustine himself clearly used that theory and the interpretation of Paul on which it rested as weapons in the ideological struggle against Pelagius for the heart and mind of Christendom, and Locke's reinterpretation of Paul was an ideological weapon in a campaign against the Augustinian legacy in the Church of England. And, finally, there is the level of external ecclesiastical politics. Pagels speculates that Augustine's theology of the fall rationalized the uneasy alliance between temporal and spiritual powers for most Catholic Christians. Kant's rationalistic deviations from Augustinian orthodoxy plainly provoked the wrath of the allied powers of the Lutheran Church and Prussian State at least in part because they represented the practice of exercising academic freedom from control by church or state.

Since the Enlightenment, criticism of the authoritarianism of religious practices and institutional structures from the point of view of a morality centered on individual autonomy has become increasingly common in our culture. The result is a characteristically modern relation of antagonism between morality and religion, which adds a new dimension to the perennial philosophical discussion of their relations.[59]

Notes

1. *Euthyphro* 10a. I quote the translation by L. Cooper in *Collected Dialogues.*

2. Bartley, *Morality.*

3. Ibid., 53.

4. Ibid., 55.

5. Ibid., 57.

6. Ibid., 56–57.

7. Ibid., 64.

8. Fries, *Dialogues,* 200. This volume consists of selections from the second edition of the German *Julius und Evagoras,* which was published in 1822.

9. Ibid.

10. Ibid., 203.

11. Ibid.

12. Mourelatos, "Fries."

13. Gn. 3:16. I quote from The New American Bible.

14. Gn. 3:17–19.

15. Gn. 3:22.

16. Eliade, *Sacred,* chapter 2.

17. Pagels, *Adam,* 64.

18. Rom. 5:12–19.

19. New American Bible, New Testament, 225.

20. Augustine, *De Civitate Dei,* 13, 3. I quote the translation by Walsh, Zema, Monahan, and Honan.

21. Ibid., 13, 14.

22. For discussion and additional references, see Pagels, *Adam,* 109 and 143.

23. Ibid., 125.

24. Ibid., 125–126.

25. Anselm, *De Conceptu Virginali et Peccato Originali,* 1. I make use of the translation by Colleran.

26. Ibid., 3. This definition originates in Anselm's *Dialogus de Veritate.*

27. Ibid.

28. Ibid.

29. Ibid., 29.

30. Ibid., 23.

31. Ibid., 26.

32. Ibid., 23.

33. For a more detailed exposition and criticism of Anselm's theory, see Quinn, "Adam's fall."

34. Spellman, *Locke,* 152.

35. Locke, "Paraphrase," 323. Dr. Whitby is Daniel Whitby of Salisbury, whose own study of Scripture, *A Paraphrase and Commentary upon All the Epistles,* was published in 1700.

36. Ibid., 328.

37. Kant, *Religion Within the Limits of Reason Alone.*

38. Greene, "Historical context," xxxii–xxxvii.

39. Kant, *Religion,* 35.

40. Ibid., 26.

41. Ibid., 24.

42. Ibid., 26.

43. Ibid., 18.

44. Ibid., 24.

45. Ibid., 19.

46. Ibid., 16.

47. Ibid., 17.

48. Ibid., 27.

49. For a fuller exposition of Kant's theory and a defense of it against some objections, see Quinn, "Adam's fall."

50. Kant, *Religion,* 28.

51. Ibid., 36–37.

52. Ibid., 37.

53.   Ibid., 37–38.

54. Ibid., 46.

55. Fries, *Dialogues,* 202.

56. Ibid., 204.

57. Bartley, *Morality,* 66.

58. Reeder, *Source,* 100–101.

59. An earlier version of this chapter was discussed by the Notre Dame Discussion Group in Philosophy of Religion and at the University of Chicago Divinity School Colloquium on Religions in Culture and History. I am grateful to the participants in those discussions and especially to Frank Clooney, who was my commentator at the Chicago Colloquium, for stimulating criticism. Because the

paper had to be severely cut in revising it for publication, I was not, to my regret, able to incorporate everything I learned from my critics into the final version.

References

Anselm of Canterbury.
1969 *Why God Became Man* and *The Virgin Conception and Original Sin*. Translated by J. M. Colleran. Albany, N.Y.: Magi Books.

Augustine of Hippo.
1958 *The City of God*. Translated by G. G. Walsh, D. B. Zema, G. Monahan, and D. J. Honan. Garden City, N.J.: Doubleday.

Bartley, W. W.
1971 *Morality and Religion*. London: Macmillan.

Catholic Biblical Association of America.
1970 *The New American Bible*. Translated by members of the Catholic Biblical Association of America. New York: P. J. Kenedy.

Eliade, M.
1959 *The Sacred and the Profane: The Nature of Religion*. Translated by W. R. Trask. New York: Harcourt, Brace and World.

Fries, J. F.
1982 *Dialogues on Morality and Religion*. Translated by D. Walford. Totowa, N.J.: Barnes and Noble.

Greene, T. M.
1960 "The Historical Context and Religious Significance of Kant's Religion." In *Religion Within the Limits of Reason Alone*, by I. Kant, ix–lxxviii. New York: Harper Torchbooks.

Kant, I.
1960 *Religion Within the Limits of Reason Alone*. Translated by T. M. Greene and H. H. Hudson. New York: Harper Torchbooks.

Locke, J.
1824 "A Paraphrase and Notes on St. Paul's Epistle to the Romans." In *The Works of John Locke*, volume 7, 271–427. London: C. and J. Rivington et al.

Mourelatos, A. P. D.
1967 "Jakob Friedrich Fries." In *The Encyclopedia of Philosophy*. Edited by P. Edwards, volume 3, 253–55. New York: Macmillan and Free Press.

Pagels, E.
1988 *Adam, Eve, and the Serpent*. New York: Random House.

Plato.
1961 *The Collected Dialogues of Plato*. Edited by E. Hamilton and H. Cairns. New York: Pantheon Books.

Quinn, P. L.
1988 "In Adam's Fall, We Sinned All." *Philosophical Topics* 16(2):89–118.

Reeder, J. P.
1988 *Source, Sanction, and Salvation: Religion and Morality in Judaic and Christian Traditions*. Englewood Cliffs, N.J.: Prentice-Hall.

Spellman, W. M.
1988 *John Locke and the Problem of Depravity*. Oxford: Clarendon Press.

Chapter **5**

The Myth of
Original Equality

Robin W. Lovin

Isaiah Berlin once noted that modern thought is characterized by a presumption in favor of equality. A policy that overtly aims at greater equality has from the outset at least one reason in favor of its adoption, while policies which would increase inequality must present a very strong case to overcome the presumption against them. There may be difficulties of implementation or other overriding moral reasons that lead us to choose against the egalitarian policy, but the burden of proof lies with those who would widen the differences of wealth, status, and power, while those who would narrow them get the benefit of the doubt.[1]

Berlin called attention to a political assumption that is at once so pervasive as to go unnoticed and so profound as to require explanation. The drive for political and social equality in modern Western institutions, and indeed, in modernizing societies throughout the world, appears initially as just the "natural" direction of social development, but it contrasts sharply with the hierarchies of the premodern West and many other traditional societies.

Any discussion of equality that keeps an eye on comparative questions must therefore begin with an examination of this presumption. Important debates about the differences between substantive equality and equality of opportunity or about the relationships between the various forms of political, social, and economic equality will be suspended in this chapter so that we may direct our attention to the idea of human equality itself. How does the idea of human equality enter into modern Western thought? What kinds of evidence are used to support the claim that human beings are equal? How do the different evidences and claims subtly alter the conception of equality itself?

Seventeenth- and eighteenth-century authors in the liberal tradition attempted to answer that question by returning to origins. They argued a case for freedom and political equality that gained strength from the suggestion that the original condition of human life was one of equality. Speculation about human origins was thus intended to shape modern political practice, and the facts that entered into those speculations were reshaped into something quite like a myth of origins, an account of how all things began that sets the terms for present practices. Mandeville, Swift, and Shaftesbury all used myth or fable in explicit responses to the basic political questions of their day.[2]

Hobbes and Locke, the major theorists of liberalism, introduced into this discourse a split between the rational and the imaginative elements of these political myths that was already noted by their contemporaries.[3] They were interested in facts about human nature and history, and the role of moral speculation had to be strictly limited. To set the parameters of equality within societies organized by modern, liberal principles, Hobbes, Locke, and later Rousseau each began with a discussion of people living in a "state of nature." This idea referred to the condition of persons who have no common ruler over them and thus have no recognized authority to whom a dispute between them might be referred. This condition apart from the restraints of human law provided a useful contrast by which to point up the essential features of government and the commitments of the citizen or subject. Given the diversity of political systems found among the European states, or reported by travelers to other parts of the globe or learned from records of previous cities, states, and empires, a general concept of government could not be established by observation. The world had grown too large for Aristotle's catalogue of constitutions! A more direct method involved reflecting on persons with no government of any kind, in contrast to which situation the essential features of every kind of government should become apparent.[4]

The mythic elements in the formulation of the state of nature are apparent to a twentieth-century observer.[5] For the early liberal authors, however, it was an important part of this myth that it was *not* a myth. The attenuation of narrative and imaginative elements in the theoretical accounts of the state of nature was deliberate. As Stephen Daniel puts it, imagination and imagery have a place in Locke's idea of political education "only insofar as the reader of fables needs entertainment in the process of acquiring good sense or needs devices to aid memorization."[6]

This methodological constraint had substantive, as well as literary, consequences. As a result of the effort to reduce or eliminate imaginative or mythic elements in the account of origins, equality in a "state of nature" carried into the theories and practices of liberal democracy only part of a broader idea of equality found in earlier Western traditions. The social thought of Western Christianity, especially the theological movements of the Protestant Reformation, included an aspiration for human equality based on divine command and human love, rather than on humanity's original condition. The characteristic features of *equality as condition* that mark the state of nature coexist in some tension with this *equality as aspiration.*[7] Political liberalism resolves these tensions by eliminating the elements of aspiration producing an account that apparently rests only on those evidences of equality that are demonstrable facts. When these facts are traced through their operation in a primordial state of nature, they provide a justification for the equality that is crucial to the liberal idea of government and society. That equality, however, falls short in important ways of the aspiration to equality that was also an important part of the social, religious, and political movements that gave rise to liberalism. A full understanding of equality as a normative idea in modern society will require a recovery of equality as aspiration alongside equality as condition.

The State of Nature

Ungoverned persons were not readily available for observation, the state of nature being populated perhaps only by the natives of the newly discovered Americas, but it was easy enough to suppose that there must have been a time before governments were first formed, when everyone was in the state of nature. Assuming a certain uniformity and continuity in human characteristics, we could say something about what persons in that state were likely to do and what idea of government was likely, initially, to come into their heads. The political ideas of early liberalism thus rested on a speculative reconstruction of how human needs and desires would play themselves out in a setting unconstrained by government.[8]

Given this uniformity of method, different authors gave remarkably different accounts of just what this state of nature would have been like. For Hobbes, it was a war of all against all, in which life was, to quote his memorable phrase, "solitary, poore, nasty, brutish, and short."[9] John Locke imagined a more congenial setting of industrious cultivators and primitive economic cooperation, not unlike the bucolic *polis* in Book II of the *Republic*, though Locke's primitives give more attention to commerce and less to dinner than do those described by Socrates.[10] In Rousseau's state of nature the development of reason, trade, and property fall somewhat below the levels imagined by Locke, or even by Hobbes, but the possibilities for human freedom and cooperation actually exceed those ordinarily achieved in civil society.[11]

Different as they otherwise may be, all authors agree that in the state of nature people are equal. For Locke, this is almost a theological truth. For people who had not themselves set up a sovereign, the only conceivable source of inequality would be the "evident and clear appointment" of a natural ruler by God, and it was evident to Locke that no such appointment had been made.[12] For Hobbes and Rousseau the ground of equality is stated more straightforwardly as the equality of natural human powers. We shall see that despite his more theological formulation, Locke's account of original equality comes down to the same thing.

This speculation about equality in the state of nature did not lead to the immediate practical conclusion that persons living in civil societies should be equal in the same way that their predecessors in the state of nature were equal.[13] Rather, original equality sets the conditions for subsequent developments. Between the equal persons in the state of nature, the only form of government that could come into being would be one that all of them could accept as an extension of their own aims. The authors we have mentioned offered various accounts of just what this government would be like, but they would have agreed that where the rules of law cannot be explained as developments from this point of original equality, some form of tyranny or oppression has intruded on the arrangements legitimated by the consent of the governed.

Myths of Inequality

From a broader historical and comparative perspective, this theoretical formulation of the equality of persons in a state of nature was a startling innovation. The conclusion of the liberal authority is clearly a minority report in the wider Western tradition.

The philosophers' state of nature recalled the Biblical myth of Eden, or at least the accounts of the early stages of human history in which people lived without rulers (Genesis 4:17–5:32). Genesis says little about equality or inequality in this state, but many had interpreted its descriptions of early Hebrew patriarchy as the warrant for a society in which all legitimate power descends from father to son. Locke and other writers in the seventeenth century were obliged to take that argument very seriously, and it has not entirely lost its power even today.[14]

More definitive statements about equality and inequality could be found among the Greeks. Plato's world was a world of original *inequality*. According to his myth in the *Republic* (414d–417b), persons are born with differing temperaments and skills, and these gifts can be ranked in a hierarchy that corresponds to the order of powers that distinguish human life from other beings. In some persons, the distinctively human powers of reason predominate, while in others, the animal spirits that make for martial valor hold sway. Others are characterized by the simpler vegetative powers by which all life sustains itself. Lest there be any doubt about how these powers are ranked, Plato distinguishes the three classes as gold, silver, and bronze, respectively. In a well-ordered society, Plato suggests, the golden people who have the greatest powers of reason will rule, even as reason dominates the other powers in a well-ordered human life.

This Platonic ordering of human value was but one segment of a larger hierarchy of being that later became the principal doctrine of Neoplatonists and so entered into a fateful combination with Christian interpretations of the Hebrew creation myth to produce a worldview in which all things proceed from and return to God. The *exitus et reditus* theme, while it accords to all things a common origin and destiny, nonetheless assures that in the time and space of God's creation, the creatures differ radically in power and in value. Human inequality is an obvious correlate of these ontological inequalities.[15] In the dominant forms of medieval theology, the assumption of original inequality was as obvious and unchallenged as the assumption of equality is in liberalism today.[16] To rank persons in a hierarchy of birth, privilege, and power was the "natural" way to regard human differences in the premodern West, as it has been in most societies until very recent times.[17]

Equality in Love

Alongside this ontological inequality, however, the scriptures of Christianity and Judaism also suggest an aspiration for equality based on love for one's neighbors and obedience to God. The Holiness Code of Leviticus forbids acts of violence and deceit against one's neighbors, but it also enjoins treating them with the same love held for oneself. "You shall not take vengeance or bear any grudge against the sons of your own people, but you shall love your neighbor as yourself. I am the LORD" (Leviticus 19:18 RSV). The Gospels of Matthew and Luke explicitly link this requirement of neighbor love with the "great and First" commandment to love God with all one's powers, and in the Lukan narrative, Jesus follows this pronouncement with a parable that suggests that the "neighbor" here must include everyone in need (Matthew 22:34–40; Luke 10:25–37).[18]

This clear insistence that the neighbor is an object of love equal to oneself, coupled with the dramatic story of the "Good Samaritan" to reinforce its universalistic implications, occupied an important place in Christian moral teaching. While this teaching does not directly contradict the idea of ontological differences between persons, it prescribes an attitude toward them that is quite different from the classical maxim that justice is "to render to each what is due to each." The biblical norm completely bypasses the scrutiny and assessment of individual merits that Aristotle assumed was an essential first step to knowing how properly to treat someone.[19] As the social differentiations that marked premodern European society began to lose their apparently "natural" quality, this suggestion that they might for moral purposes be ignored altogether gained in importance.

Equality in Covenant

One way to diminish the claims of ontological inequality was to repudiate God's role in the creation of hierarchy and to stress instead God's eschatological leveling of human distinctions. The common destiny of persons is no longer viewed as the fulfillment of their hierarchically ordered roles in God's creation, but as their liberation from the burdens imposed by the powers of this world into the freedom and unity of the children of God. This eschatological equality antedates the Protestant Reformation in heretical groups that formed a marginal but not insignificant part of the Christian population of Europe in the Middle Ages. It was lived out in a variety of pacifist and militant forms in the Radical Reformation and survives into the present in groups that insist on their vocation to live out the life of the redeemed community in the midst of the present world which is passing away.[20]

The groups that formed the mainstream of the Protestant Reformation and exercised the greatest influence on the development of modern European politics rejected the formulations of the radical egalitarians and reformers and mistrusted the subversion of social order that their apocalypticism implied. Nevertheless, their own more moderate political programs included an account of human equality that undermined the old relationship between creation and social hierarchy. Even Martin Luther, much maligned for his defense of the established order against the peasants in 1524, saw the community of Christians as a community of equals united in love, rather than ruled by law.[21] Where Luther differed from the radicals was in his insistence that in practice it is impossible to live out the equality of Christians in a political world in which most people remain unchristian.

> Therefore it is out of the question that there should be a common Christian government over the whole world, nay even over one land or company of people, since the wicked always outnumber the good. Hence a man who would venture to govern an entire country or the world with the Gospel would be like a shepherd who should place in one fold wolves, lions, eagles, and sheep together and let them freely mingle with one another and say, Help yourselves, and be good and peaceful among yourselves. . . . The sheep, forsooth, would keep the peace and would allow themselves to be fed and governed in peace, but they would not live long; nor would any beast keep from molesting another.[22]

Despite the pessimistic realism of this assessment, there is no doubt that for Luther, the connection between divine creation and social hierarchy is decisively broken. The princes who wield the power of civil government are no more than glorified hangmen. Their offices have only a functional significance, and their honors are owed to God, rather than to the men who hold the offices. "Our God is a great Lord, and therefore must have such noble, honorable and rich hangmen and beadles, and desires that they shall have riches, honor and fear, in full and plenty, from every one."[23]

Calvin placed a higher value on politics, stressing that the civil authorities are ordained of God not only to restrain evil but also to improve human life and declaring that those who undermine law and government not only threaten the people's peace but deprive them of their humanity.[24] The egalitarian implications of Christian community received even more explicit recognition in Calvinist circles than among the Lutherans. Christianity not only constitutes a fellowship of love in which earthly differences lose their significance within the community; the relationship within the community overcomes in important ways the distinctions of degree that mark relationships in the wider society.

In Calvinism, these secular relationships do not disappear, but they are transformed by the *covenants* that reconstitute human relationships on the basis of choice and consent, and include God as one of the participants in the relationship. Persons continue in their roles as husbands and wives, owners or laborers, magistrates or citizens, but these natural roles are transformed, so that the differences between persons are never absolute, and even the relationships of authority and submission become matters of mutual acceptance, in which whatever authority is allowed is exercised under the scrutiny of the divine covenant partner.[25] Puritan preachers did not hesitate to elaborate the egalitarian implications of this convenantal relationship:

> If we consider it, it is an exceeding great mercy, when we think with ourselves, he is in heaven, and we are on earth; he the glorious God, we dust and ashes . . . and yet he is willing to enter into covenant, which implies a kind of equality between us. As when *Jonathan* and *David* made a covenant, though there was a difference (the one was a king's son) yet notwithstanding, when the covenant of friendship was made, there did rise a kind of equality between them. So it is between the Lord and us, when he is once willing to enter into covenant with us.[26]

Covenantal equality tended to increase political accountability, not only before God but to the human covenant partners as well. Calvin's suggestion that the lower magistrates, like the ephors of ancient Sparta, have a positive duty to rein in the excesses of a tyrannical ruler was incorporated into a more general idea of political community based on covenant. The ruler clearly stands within the constraints of the covenant and not outside of it. The ruler holds power from God only in partnership with the people.[27] Hence, the exemplary leader in covenantal politics not only permits but must indeed invite criticism from all ranks. Hierarchy is not eliminated, but the rigid requirements of social order now accommodate a freedom to call the ruler to account if the terms of stewardship are violated. "Wherein, if we fail at any time, we hope we shall be willing (by God's assistance) to hearken to good advice from any of you, or in any other way of God; so shall your liberties be preserved, in upholding the honor and power of authority among you."[28]

The Covenant and the State of Nature

The importance of these covenantal themes for the development of American democratic politics has long been recognized, and there can be little doubt that the religious idea of covenant community exercised important moral and rhetorical influences on the formation of American constitutionalism. Conceptually, however, there are sharp differences between the political equality of a Lockean democracy and the equality shared by members of a covenantal community. These differences require further comment and exploration.

Perry Miller, Harry Stout, Robert Bellah, and others have traced the persistence of covenantal theology in the praxis of the post-Revolutionary era of constitution building. It is no doubt true, as Harry Stout has shown, that Puritan ideas of call and covenant continued to influence the ideas and public commitments of Americans long after Locke and Hobbes, Francis Hutcheson, and Jean-Jacques Burlamaqui had become the chief suppliers of political vocabulary to their intellectual leaders.[29] Americans arrived at liberal democracy not by abandoning their Calvinist heritage but by developing it and indeed, by taming some of its more radical egalitarian implications.

It is also important, however, to attend to the practical differences between covenantal and liberal versions of human equality. Most obvious among these is that covenant equality extends to a more restricted group of persons. Even allowing for property qualifications for voting, the general exclusion of women from the franchise, and the nervousness about "mob rule" that afflicted many American leaders at the end of the eighteenth century, their liberal political community treated as equals a more diverse group of persons than the covenantal communities of Puritan New England had included as full partners in civil and ecclesiastical affairs. Liberal equality begins with original equality, the Jeffersonian presumption that "all men are created equal." In the covenant, equality begins with an experience of spiritual regeneration that may not be widely distributed and may take effect rather late in life.[30]

Nor are those who are already members of the covenant community obliged to acknowledge this gift simply because someone claims to have it. In a community where "all men are created equal," it is difficult in principle to deny human rights to anyone who is evidently human. In a community where equality rests on a common spiritual experience, we might expect that those who are assured that they have had the experience will exercise a rigorous scrutiny of those who claim it. That, of course, was how matters were conducted in the early years of the colony in Massachusetts Bay. Far from being created in a state of equality, persons who share in the equality of the covenant must meet high standards to be treated as equals. Also, as Luther warned, it may be dangerous to extend equality to those who do not meet the standards.

This does not imply that covenantal communities were rigid or exclusivistic in the way that most Americans collectively remember their Puritan ancestors. Puritan pastors were often skillful counselors, shepherding those in their charge to a self-awareness that could prepare the way for the experience of regeneration.[31] In the nineteenth century, as the predestinarian theology gave way to views that allowed more role for human cooperation in divine salvation, the emphasis on scrutiny

shifted to a concern for nurture that sought to prepare persons for covenantal participation and recognized the potential for transformation,
even in those lives that seemed to give the least evidence of the grace
required for that participation.

It is this nineteenth-century humanitarianism, rather than the liberal
doctrine of political equality, that has the best claim to be regarded as the
secular reformulation of the covenantal community. Evident in movements as diverse as abolitionism, temperance crusades, and efforts to
reform the treatment of prisoners and the mentally ill, this humanitarianism has a sense of social responsibility for the welfare of all individuals
that is missing from the laissez-faire liberalism that accords to each individual, created equal, an equal opportunity for success or ruin. If it is
more hesitant to treat everyone as an equal from the beginning, it is
more concerned to arrive at a point where everyone will be equal in
some important dimension of life.

Equality in covenant, then, is a version of equality as aspiration. It
is limited in scope but is steadily realized in the interactions among those
who share in it, and attentiveness to the movements of spiritual regeneration in oneself and one's neighbors marks an aspiration to share this
equality as widely as the mercies of God will allow.[32]

God and Humanity in the State of Nature

The aspiration for equality in covenant follows, in large part, from
the mutual, personal relationships that persons have with each other and
with God. In the liberal theories, by contrast, relationships between persons and God and between persons themselves receive less attention.
The relationship between persons and their property is key, and where
the relationship to God is considered, it is reinterpreted in light of this
possessive relationship.[33]

Locke's account of equality in the state of nature incorporates a
well-developed theological argument. Persons in the state of nature are
equal because they are artifacts of God's work. They are thus God's
property, and just as no one is to disturb the property of another person,
so no one should presume to employ God's property for personal use.

> For Men being all the Workmanship of one Omnipotent, and infi-
> nitely wise Maker, all the servants of one Sovereign Master, sent into
> the World by his order and about his business, they are his Property,
> whose Workmanship they are, made to last during his, not one
> anothers Pleasure. And being furnished with like Faculties, sharing
> all in one Community of Nature, there cannot be supposed any such
> *Subordination* among us, that may Authorize us to destroy one an-

other, as if we were made for one anothers uses, as the inferior ranks of Creatures are for ours.[34]

The original equality seems to include a divine intention, mediated to us as a dictate of natural reason, that we should treat one another as equals. Locke, however, does not develop this into a reasoned assessment of what we want or expect from other persons. Indeed, in his account of men as the creation—and hence, the property—of God, what Locke largely eliminates is their relationship to one another. If we ask about the practical implications of our original equality, Locke's answer is given largely in terms of our relationships to things.[35] We have a right to those things on which we have expended our creative energies, the things with which we have "mixed our labor."[36] We have a right, too, to defend our property against those who would assert their own claims over it, just as we claim our own freedom against anyone who would assert a human dominion over that bit of God's property which we are.

Hobbes and Rousseau make even less use of the traditional mythic elements in their accounts of human origins, and consequently cannot begin with natural rights as a moral status resulting from a person's relationship to God. There is no property, human or divine, in the state of nature described by Hobbes and Rousseau.

Hence, for Hobbes, the rights available to us in the state of nature do not offer us a protected moral status, but only permission to act:

> The Right of Nature, which Writers commonly call *Jus Naturale,* is the Liberty each man hath, to use his own power, as he will himselfe, for the preservation of his own Nature; that is to say, of his own Life, and consequently, of doing any thing, which in his own Judgement, and Reason, hee shall conceive to be the aptest means thereunto.[37]

In the absence of any restrictions imposed by law, persons in the state of nature are free to make their own assessments of their need and to procure the objects they conclude they require—if they can. That is just what makes people in the state of nature so fearsome to one another.

Rousseau thought Hobbes had the correct understanding of natural right but that he had got the facts about human wants and desires wrong. A man in the state of nature has a "right he justly claims to all he needs," but it is precisely in this state that "the care for our own preservation is the least prejudicial to that of others." It is only when we confuse the modest wants of natural humanity with the "gratification of a multitude of passions that are the work of society" that we arrive at the notion of a war of all against all that characterizes the state of nature for Hobbes.[38]

Hobbes and Rousseau, then, differ in their account of the attitudes and dispositions that persons in a state of nature would have, but they

both offer a thoroughly naturalized account of the rights that they have
to act on these characteristic features of their humanity.[39] In both cases,
the equality of persons in a state of nature stems from the rough parity of
their natural powers. Hobbes does not overlook the differences in strength,
skill, and cunning that obviously distinguish one person from another,
but he asserts that these differences effectively cancel each other out, so
that no one emerges as able to dominate others, or effectively to prevent
others from pursuing their natural right to self-preservation.

> Nature hath made men so equall, in the faculties of body, and mind;
> as that though there bee found one man sometimes manifestly stron-
> ger in body, or of quick mind then another; yet when all is reckoned
> together, the difference between man, and man, is not so consider-
> able, as that one man can thereupon claim to himselfe any benefit,
> to which another may not pretend, as well as he. For as to the
> strength of body, the weakest has strength enough to kill the stron-
> gest, either by secret machination, or by confederacy with others,
> that are in the same danger with himselfe.[40]

For Rousseau, the same observation about this rough parity of natural
powers holds. The *natural* differences between persons are far smaller
than the differences that emerge as a result of difference in education
and conditions of life in civil society. More important, perhaps, the relationships between persons in a state of nature are so attenuated that
many of the strengths and skills that convey advantages in modern society are virtually useless against others in the state of nature. Whatever
advantages we might seize from another by brute strength, we could
hardly, in a state of nature, subject the other to a domination that would
alter the fundamental condition of equality between us.

> One man, it is true, might seize the fruits which another had gath-
> ered, the game he had killed, or the cave he had chosen for shelter;
> but how would he ever be able to exact obedience, and what ties of
> dependence could there be among men without possessions? If, for
> instance, I am driven from one tree, I can go to the next; if I am
> disturbed in one place, what hinders me from going to another?
> Again, should I happen to meet with a man so much stronger than
> myself, and at the same time so depraved, so indolent, and so barba-
> rous, as to compel me to provide for his sustenance while he himself
> remains idle; he must take care not to have his eyes off me for a
> single moment; he must bind me fast before he goes to sleep, or I
> shall certainly either knock him on the head or make my escape.
> That is to say, he must in such a case voluntarily expose himself to
> much greater trouble than he seeks to avoid, or can give me.[41]

There are important conceptual differences between Locke's right
of nature, which protects persons from encroachment by others, and the

same right understood by Hobbes and Rousseau as a permission to act for one's own preservation. Locke's right seems to guarantee a form of property in the state of nature, while Hobbes and Rousseau can at best identify particular things as the objects of human interests and labors. Locke's natural men expand their lives by acquiring dominion over things in nature under the shelter of a divinely granted inviolability, while those in the state of nature envisioned by Hobbes and Rousseau swing from tree to tree, clutching what they can carry with them.

No doubt there is an element in Locke's thought which resists the reductionism that treats the state of nature as a set of bare facts from which morality must be reconstructed by a race of prudent egoists. Locke does not *want* a state of nature like the one depicted by Hobbes, but the way he develops his argument undercuts his case against it. For when we ask how the rights we have in a state of nature come into practical effect, the answer is that we must put them into effect for ourselves.

> And that all Men may be restrained from invading others Rights, and from doing hurt to one another, and the Law of Nature be observed, which willeth the Peace and *Preservation of all Mankind*, the Execu- *tion* of the Law of Nature is in that State, put into every Mans hands, whereby every one has a right to punish the transgressors of that Law to such a Degree, as may hinder its Violation. For the *Law of Nature* would, as all other Laws that concern Men in this World, be in vain, if there were no body that in the State of Nature, had a *Power to Execute* that Law, and thereby preserve the innocent and restrain offenders, and if any one in the State of Nature may punish another, for any evil he has done, every one may do so. For in that *State of perfect Equality*, where naturally there is no superiority or jurisdiction of one, over another, what any may do in Prosecution of that Law, every one must needs have a Right to do.[42]

The rights and property we enjoy in Locke's state of nature practi- cally depend on the exercise of those same natural powers that Hobbes and Rousseau identify. In a Lockean state of nature, one's claims to property and even to life itself are only as good as strength, cunning, and confederacy can make them. That, indeed, is one of the principal "incon- veniences" of the state of nature that leads people to form governments as an alternative. Moreover, Locke must believe, as Rousseau and Hobbes do, that these powers are more or less evenly distributed. Otherwise, the persons of greater powers could successfully defend their rights against others, while the others would have no recourse against them. Locke explicitly states that no one would enter a contract of government if it made him worse off than he was in the state of nature, "[f]or no rational Creature can be supposed to change his condition with an intention to be worse."[43] Since a naturally superior person would be worse off by giving up natural rights, Locke's move from the state of nature to civil government, which requires that *everyone* surrender the power to execute judgments that he has in the state of nature, would never get off the ground. Only if the equality between persons created equal by God comes down to the natural equality of powers observed by Hobbes and Rousseau can Locke explain why everyone would choose to leave the state of nature.

The State of Nature as Myth and Antimyth

Despite the important differences between Hobbes, Locke, and Rousseau, in the end they present a unified understanding of the state of nature. It is a state in which the characteristic features of humanity, unrefined by the arts of government or society, come into view in an especially clear way. These human characteristics are dictated largely by the requirements of individual physical survival, and relationships between persons are mediated chiefly through relationships to the material goods that survival requires. What we can predict about how human actions will develop and what the likely results will be depends on the observation that the unimproved human capacities relevant to physical survival are roughly equal between persons.

To the critical eye of a twentieth-century historian of religion, the idea of the state of nature has several important features that allow one to construe it as a myth.[44] The concept concerns the origins of the world of nature and society as we know it. It gives order to the contrary evidence about human nature that emerges in experience. It identifies a political community and explains how one becomes a part of it. And although it is presented as a sort of narrative, its details cannot have any relationship to historical truth as that is understood today, or for that matter, to historical truth as understood in the time that the concept was developed.[45] Rather, what we have is a narrative that reconstructs the past. The relationship of this reconstruction to actual history is ambiguous, for events in the state of nature take place at no particular time but are relevant to all times. Because the first formation of governments and societies is beyond the reach of history in the ordinary sense, the only things we can know about it are the things that must have been the case if we are to account for the facts of our own time—not just the specific details of this present time and place but all times and places where people now live together in civil society. The formation of the original contract takes place in this peculiar mythic time, before or outside of ordinary history. What happens in the state of nature happened *in illo tempore*.[46]

The mythic reconstruction draws on observations that can be made of humans in their present state. They do share a broad range of physical powers that make them all competitive in the unregulated combat that characterizes the state of nature. Their intellects are at least so far equal that, as Descartes had observed, no one readily acknowledges inferiority to another in mental powers.[47] But the reconstruction is also a persuasive reconstrual. It highlights the appearances of parity and directs attention away from the differences that are also observable. Most important, it ties its observations to a framework of meaning, so that the facts and the meanings are mutually reinforcing.

This also suggests, however, that a different set of facts might plunge us into quite different politics. Despite the reassurances of Hobbes and Rousseau, it is not difficult to imagine someone whose strength and cunning so far exceed those of others as to overawe and master them. The natural ruler is not inherently less plausible than the natural liberty of Rousseau's savage. Nor is it implausible that, were we to pay more attention to human relationships and less to material needs, we would postulate a natural patriarchy, arising from the strength of the father and the inherent weakness and dependence of the human infant. A closer attention to the requirements of species survival might lead us to emphasize differentiated capacities to breed, bear, and raise offspring rather than the roughly equal capacities for individual survival. Indeed, each of those alternative readings of the facts of human similarity and difference generated its own myth in the century or so after Rousseau. Nietzsche's superman, Freud's primal horde, and Darwin's account of the origin of species each turned observations of present facts into a quite different assessment of the origins of equality and inequality. These alternative accounts aroused controversies of their own, precisely because they are not simply speculations about a distant and irretrievable past but a threat to whole systems of meaning in the present. Without the conviction that the facts indicate a rough parity of natural powers, the mythic reinforcement of the liberal system of individual rights and government accountable to the people collapses.

Both the state of nature depicted by the liberal theorists and the nineteenth-century accounts of human and social origins that supplanted it have elements that suggest that they are best understood as myth, rather than history, science, or psychology.[48] Those mythic aspects of the idea of the "state of nature," however, largely escaped those who first developed the idea. They present it, not as a competitor to the Christian scriptural account of origins but as a rational replacement for it. Hobbes drew sharp distinctions between reason, revelation, and prophecy and announces retrospectively at the beginning of chapter 32 of *Leviathan*

that the foregoing discourse has concerned a commonwealth understood by natural reason alone.[49] Rousseau, probably to avoid an argument with the censors, designates the stories of Adam and Moses as "the
facts," only to lay them aside in favor of "conditional and hypothetical
reasonings."[50] Locke devotes virtually the whole of his first treatise on
civil government to a refutation of the idea that the proper patriarchal
form of human government is laid down already in the text of Genesis.
In Locke's Christian context, that exegesis, if true, would render the
second treatise's speculative account of human beings created free and
equal quite irrelevant.[51]

The most obvious consequence of this extreme naturalization of
the story of origins is that the myth of the state of nature can contain no
account of God's action. For Hobbes and Rousseau, this is dictated by
the rigorous distinction between natural and supernatural knowledge.
For Locke, although God's creative action frames the conditions of the
state of nature, only human agents, with their limited and equal natural
powers, act in that state.

An equally important practical consequence, however, is that even
the human actors in the state of nature lose their exemplary, paradigmatic roles and become merely agents of their own purposes. In contrast
to myths that summon people to emulate the virtues of the beings present
at the beginning and to repeat their creative and ordering actions in the
present, the myth of the state of nature does not urge us to imitate what
has been done *in illo tempore*. The attitudes and dispositions ascribed to
people in the state of nature are not virtues for us to copy. The relationships they had to one another are not to be recreated among ourselves.
Indeed, those relationships have been definitively abolished by the steps
they took to remove themselves from the state of nature, with its dangers
and inconveniences. What they have passed on to us is not their freedom
and equality, but the limitations on freedom and equality to which they
once consented and the consequences of the sovereignties they first
established.

The point of the concept of the state of nature is not that we should
emulate our unknown ancestors, but precisely that we may *not* undo the
bonds of the contract they have made. Only an unspeakable catastrophe
could plunge us into a state in which the civil society we live in would be
dissolved and the motives and actions of persons in a state of nature
could once again become relevant to us. The imperative is rather to
consent to what they have given us and get on with business within the
framework of relationships that their contract has created.

Persons in the state of nature are merely persons, not exemplars.
They represent only themselves. Thus the equality that holds between

them loses the aspiration for equality in relationship that characterized the earlier covenantal understanding of equality. Persons in the state of nature are not regarded as fallen, or as selfish in inordinate ways. Indeed, Rousseau supposes that they are generally morally better than their counterparts in the civil society he knows. But the naturalized account of the state of nature means that the equality of persons in that state is equality as condition. It can only constrain relationships in civil society. It cannot prescribe them.

The equality of persons in the state of nature is not a model for their relationships in contemporary life. What we know about those relationships from the beginning has nothing to do with human aspirations or with the virtues of our ancestors. We only know that, given the rough parity of natural powers between persons in a state of nature, rational self-interested persons would not have consented to arrangements that left them worse off than they could expect to be in a state of nature. Permanent, disabling inequalities of status are thereby ruled out, and that is no small point for contemporary politics. But substantial inequalities based on achievement are still possible, and nostalgia for the primitive equality that set the stage for these differences of wealth and power is irrelevant. Original equality constrains the arrangements that govern society today. The aspiration for equality in the present, however, acquires no normative force from an understanding of the state of nature. In eliminating the characteristic features of myth from their accounts of the state of nature, the early liberal theorists thus sharply reduced the scope of its practical implications. They may also, as we shall now see, have undercut their own interest in equality.

The State of Nature and the Aspiration for Equality

The idea of the state of nature served important purposes in the development of liberal political thought. Because it appeared to rely only on an assessment of human powers that could be confirmed by observation, eliminating appeals to revelation and to moral sentiments or intuitions, it satisfied a quest for certainty in politics at a time when cultural consensus and religious sanctions for political arrangements were breaking down. The safest generalizations seemed to be those based on empirical observation, and the most reliable predictions of human behavior seemed to be based on individual self-respect. The liberal theory of government did not range very far from those dependable sources of knowledge.

To achieve this degree of certainty, however, liberalism had to abandon a large part of the Western tradition of thinking about politics and human relationships. Equality as aspiration gave way to a more reliable emphasis on the desire for safety and security. Complex situations of benevolence, gratitude, and loyalty between persons gave way to the more straightforward relationships between persons and their property. Accounts of how people should relate to each other could be reconstructed from that starting point. The vagaries of love, or as the eighteenth century would put it, sympathy, could be replaced by the more predictable motives of self-interest.

As long as the liberal theory of society and politics was accompanied, as it was through most of the eighteenth century, by an affirmation of moral sentiments that give us an immediate interest in the welfare of others,[52] liberalism was an effective vehicle for the reforming work of equality as aspiration. Only when those subjective, relational elements of ethics were lost to a reductive naturalism that found no normative power in them did equality as condition become the only basis for claims to equality in politics and society. At that point, liberalism could legitimate the differences in power and privilege that had grown up on the basis of consent to the original contract as easily as it could provide an ideology of equality.[53]

The increasing distance, in theory and in practical politics, between liberalism and aspirations to equality, has led to a reaction in favor of equality and against the liberal politics that once was the bearer of that ideal. Radical political thinkers insist that it is only by abandoning liberalism, with its individualistic, property-centered assumptions, that we can hope to achieve equality. Radical theologians insist that it is only by abandoning all claims to equality based on the facts of the case and substituting a theonomous demand to treat persons as equal, in spite of the facts of inequality, that we can begin to achieve the equality to which we aspire.

Those reactions may underestimate liberalism's potential for further social transformations. Nevertheless, it seems clear that the naturalized account of political equality, with its sharp differentiation between myth and philosophy, is not adequate to the aspiration for equality which gave it birth and which continues to move persons to action in modernized and modernizing societies today. If we are to preserve the achievements of liberalism, we will have to find a way to affirm the normative role of those aspirations, to acknowledge the facts of human sentiment that cannot be naturalized into facts about the world. That will require a different sort of myth from the state of nature, a myth in which the relations between persons, rather than their relations to their property, give definition to their common life.

Notes

1. Isaiah Berlin, "Equality as an Ideal," in Frederick A. Olafson, ed., *Justice and Social Policy* (Englewood Cliffs, N.J.: Prentice-Hall, 1961), 128–50.

2. See Stephen Daniel, *Myth and Modern Philosophy* (Philadelphia: Temple University Press, 1990), 86–110.

3. Daniel, *Myth and Modern Philosophy*, 104.

4. Cf. G. D. H. Cole, in his introduction to Jean-Jacques Rousseau, *The Social Contract and Discourses* (New York: E. P. Dutton, 1973), xxii–xxiii.

5. See pp. 238–40 below.

6. Daniel, *Myth and Modern Philosophy*, 105.

7. To avoid terminological confusions, it is perhaps important to note that what I call "equality *as* condition" refers to the claim that certain forms of equality between persons can simply be demonstrated as a matter of fact. Literature on equality frequently refers to "equality *of* condition," meaning a condition of actual equality between persons, as distinct from "equality of opportunity," the equal chance persons have to compete for rewards that may be quite unequal. In the terms of this essay, a commitment to "equality *of* condition" would be an expression of equality as aspiration.

8. The device was very widely used, not only for political speculation, but to develop arguments about the "natural," as opposed to artificial, socially developed characteristics of human beings. Neither Kant nor Hume, for example, gives much credit to the political idea of an original contract, but both employ speculation on an original human condition as a way to present, logically and persuasively, their ideas about human nature. See Hume, "Of the Original Contract," 474. See also Kant, "Mutmaßlicher Anfang der Menschengeschichte," 108–24.

9. Thomas Hobbes, *Leviathan*, edited by C. B. Macpherson (Harmondsworth, England: Penguin Books, 1968), 186.

10. John Locke, *Two Treatises of Government*, edited by Peter Laslett (New York: New American Library, 1963), 328–44.

11. Rousseau, *Discourses*, 72–73. Interestingly enough, this benign view of the propertyless state of nature was largely endorsed by Adam Smith when he first presented Rousseau's work to English readers in the *Edinburgh Review*. See Smith, *Essays on Philosophical Subjects* (Indianapolis: Liberty Classics, 1982), 250–54.

12.   Locke, *Two Treatises,* 308. See also page 231 below.

13.   Andrzej Rapaczynski, *Nature and Politics: Liberalism in the Philosophies of Hobbes, Locke, and Rousseau* (Ithaca, N.Y.: Cornell University Press, 1987), 226.

14.   See, especially, Robert Filmer, *Patriarcha,* edited by Peter Laslett (Oxford: Oxford University Press, 1949). Filmer's work, little read today, is known chiefly because it goaded Locke to write the first of his *Two Treatises of Government* in refutation of it.

15.   See I. S. Robinson, "Church and Papacy," in S. H. Burns, ed., *Cambridge History of Medieval Political Thought* (Cambridge: Cambridge University Press, 1988), 261–63; J. R. Pole, *The Pursuit of Equality in American History* (Berkeley: University of California Press, 1978), 3–7.

16.   We must note in passing the Stoic ideas of human equality which were an inheritance from the classical age and provided a kind of "minority report" to accompany the dominant medieval emphasis on ontological inequality. The Stoic texts themselves were, of course, largely unknown or ignored until the revival of classical learning in the Renaissance. See Quentin Skinner, *The Foundations of Modern Political Thought* (Cambridge: Cambridge University Press, 1978), I:84–88.

17.   On this point, see, most generally, Louis Dumont, *Homo Hierarchicus: The Caste System and Its Implications* (Chicago: University of Chicago Press, 1980).

18.   By putting the formulation that links love of God and love of neighbor in the mouth of a "lawyer" (*nomikos*), Luke suggests that this conjunction was already a commonplace of Jewish moral teaching. Jesus' contribution was to extend its application beyond "the sons of your own people."

19.   Aristotle, *Nicomachean Ethics,* 1130b–1134a.

20.   See, generally, Ernst Troeltsch's treatment of the eschatological element in Christian social thought in his *Social Teaching of the Christian Churches* (Chicago: University of Chicago Press, 1976), I:326–43.

21.   Martin Luther, "Secular Authority: To What Extent It Should Be Obeyed," in John Dillenberger, ed., *Martin Luther: Selections from His Writings* (Garden City, N.Y.: Doubleday, 1961), 368–69.

22.   Luther, "Secular Authority," 371.

23.   Ibid., 389.

24.   John Calvin, *Institutes of the Christian Religion* (Philadelphia: Westminster Press, 1960), II:1487.

25.   See Robin W. Lovin, "Covenantal Relationships and Political Legitimacy," *Journal of Religion* 60(1980):1–16; James T. Johnson, *A Society Ordained by God* (Nashville: Abingdon Press, 1970).

26.   John Preston, *The New Covenant or the Saint's Portion* (London: Nicolas Bourne, 1624), 331. Spelling and punctuation have been modernized.

27.   Calvin, *Institutes*, II:1519. Anonymous, "Vindiciae contra tyrannos," in Julian H. Franklin, ed., *Constitutionalism and Resistance in the Sixteenth Century* (Indianapolis: Bobbs-Merrill, 1969), 146.

28.   John Winthrop, *The History of New England from 1630–1649*, edited by J. Savage (Boston: Little, Brown and Company, 1853), 282.

29.   See especially Perry Miller, *Errand into the Wilderness* (Cambridge,: Harvard University Press, 1956); Robert N. Bellah, *The Broken Covenant* (New York: Seabury, 1975); and Harry Stout, *The New England Soul* (New York: Oxford University Press, 1986), 314–16. See also Robin W. Lovin, "Equality and Covenant Theology," *Journal of Law and Religion* 2 (1984):241–62.

30.   Even in predestinarian theologies, which hold that the persons who will receive this gift are determined by God from the beginning so that the equal partners in the covenant are in some sense created equal, recognition of the gift is expected to be a matter of considerable soul-searching.

31.   David D. Hall, *The Faithful Shepherd: A History of the New England Ministry in the Seventeenth Century* (New York: W. W. Norton, 1972).

32.   There is also in the Western Christian tradition a version of equality as condition: The equality in sin which afflicts all who share in Adam's fall. Equality in sin, in contrast to the covenantal equality among the elect, extends to everyone, but it limits by its very nature the extent to which this original equality can be preserved in society. The unrestrained greed and lack of common purpose that mark the condition of equality can only be controlled by elevating some persons to the role of powerful authorities, and perhaps, in the more sophisticated, Calvinist versions of the idea, promoting some others to a special status in which they may watch the watchers. Sanford Lakoff developed the political implications of this "equal depravity" some years ago. Lakoff's interpretation perhaps ties the idea too closely to Calvin, but his book is an important corrective to studies of the religious origins of modern politics that concentrate too narrowly on Puritan covenantal themes. See Sanford A. Lakoff, *Equality in Political Philosophy* (Boston: Beacon Press, 1968), 38–48.

33.   On the importance of property relationships in this period generally, see C. B. Macpherson, *The Political Theory of Possessive Individualism: Hobbes to Locke* (London: Oxford University Press, 1962).

34. Locke, *Two Treatises,* 311.

35. Ibid., 328–29.

36. Ibid., 338–40.

37. Hobbes, *Leviathan,* 189.

38. Rousseau, *Discourses,* 65.

39. Rapaczynski, *Nature and Politics,* 224.

40. Hobbes, *Leviathan,* 183.

41. Rousseau, *Discourses,* 74–75.

42. Locke, *Two Treatises,* 312.

43. Ibid., 398.

44. Cf. the account of myths in eighteenth-century political discourse in Daniel, *Myth and Modern Philosophy,* 5–10, 111–12.

45. Hume's criticism of the idea of an original contract shows us that. "In vain are we asked in what records this charter of our liberties is registered. It was not written on parchment, nor yet on leaves or barks of trees. It preceded the use of writing, and all the other civilized arts of life. But we trace it plainly in the nature of man, and in the equality, or something approaching equality, which we find in all the individuals of the species." Hume, "Of the Original Contract," 474. Though Hume mocks the idea of an original contract as history, he clearly shares the main beliefs of Hobbes, Locke, and Rousseau regarding natural human equality.

46. Cf. Mircea Eliade, *The Sacred and the Profane* (New York: Harper and Row, 1961).

47. Wolfgang von Leyden, *Hobbes and Locke: The Politics of Freedom and Obligation* (New York: St. Martin's Press, 1982), 203, n.2. Hobbes appears to allude to this remark of Descartes, and Locke and Rousseau would both have known it.

48. On the nineteenth-century myths, see especially the study of Freud by Lee Yearley and of Marx by Douglas Sturm in Robin W. Lovin and Frank E. Reynolds, eds., *Cosmogony and Ethical Order* (Chicago: University of Chicago Press, 1985).

49. Hobbes, *Leviathan,* 409.

50. Rousseau, *Discourses,* 45. See also G. D. H. Cole's interpretation of this dismissal of the "facts," on 313n.

51. Cf. Locke, *Two Treatises,* 257–303. Because Locke regularly declines to undertake rational reconstructions in moral matters when definitive teachings are

available in scripture, it is important to him to establish that the scriptures do not settle the questions about the origins and authority of government with which he deals in his second treatise.

52. For a good recent account of moral sense and moral sentiment in the eighteenth century, see V. M. Hope, *Virtue By Consensus* (Oxford: Oxford University Press, 1989). The classic study remains D. D. Raphael, *The Moral Sense* (Oxford: Oxford University Press, 1947).

53. Charles S. Maier, *Recasting Bourgeois Europe* (Princeton, N.J.: Princeton University Press, 1988), 23.

References

Anonymous.
  1969 "Vindiciae contra tyrannos." In *Constitutionalism and Resistance in the Sixteenth Century*. Edited by Julian H. Franklin. Indianapolis: Bobbs-Merrill.

Bellah, Robert N.
  1975 *The Broken Covenant*. New York: Seabury Press.

Berlin, Isaiah.
  1961 "Equality as an Ideal." In *Justice and Social Policy*. Edited by Frederick A. Olafson. Englewood Cliffs, N.J.: Prentice-Hall.

Calvin, John.
  1960 *The Institutes of the Christian Religion*. Edited by John T. McNeill. Translated by Ford Lewis Battles. The Library of Christian Classics. Philadelphia: Westminster Press.

Daniel, Stephen.
  1990 *Myth and Modern Philosophy*. Philadelphia: Temple University Press.

Dumont, Louis.
  1980 *Homo Hierarchicus: The Caste System and Its Implications*. Translated by Mark Sainsbury, Louis Dumont, and Baisa Gulati. Chicago: University of Chicago Press.

Eliade, Mircea.
  1961 *The Sacred and the Profane: The Nature of Religion*. Translated by Willard R. Trask. New York: Harper and Row.

Filmer, Robert.
1949 *Patriarcha*. Edited by Peter Laslett. Oxford: Oxford University Press. [First published 1680.]

Hall, David D.
1972 *The Faithful Shepherd: A History of the New England Ministry in the Seventeenth Century*. New York: W. W. Norton.

Hobbes, Thomas.
1968 *Leviathan*. Edited with introduction by C. B. Macpherson. Harmondsworth, England: Penguin. [First published 1651.]

Hope, Vincent M.
1989 *Virtue by Consensus*. Oxford: Oxford University Press.

Hume, David.
1985 "Of the Original Contract." In *Essays Moral, Political and Literary*. Edited by Eugene F. Miller. Indianapolis: Liberty Classics. [First published 1748.]

Johnson, James T.
1970 *A Society Ordained by God*. Nashville: Abingdon Press.

Kant, Immanuel.
n.d. "Mutmaßlicher Anfang der Menschengeschichte." In *Immanuel Kants Populäre Schriften*. Berlin: Deutsche Bibliothek. [First published 1785.]

Lakoff, Sanford A.
1968 *Equality in Political Philosophy*. Boston: Beacon Press.

Locke, John.
1963 *Two Treatises of Government*, revised edition. Edited by Peter Laslett. New York: New American Library.

Lovin, Robin W.
1980 "Covenantal Relationships and Political Legitimacy." *Journal of Religion* 60:1–16.

———.
1984 "Equality and Covenant Theology." *Journal of Law and Religion* 2:241–62.

Lovin, Robin W., and Frank E. Reynolds, eds.
1985 *Cosmogony and Ethical Order: New Studies in Comparative Ethics*. Chicago: University of Chicago Press.

Luther, Martin.
1961 "Secular Authority: To What Extent It Should be Obeyed." In *Martin Luther: Selections from His Writings.* Edited by John Dillenberger. Garden City, N.Y.: Doubleday.

Macpherson, C. B.
1962 *The Political Theory of Possessive Individualism: Hobbes to Locke.* London: Oxford University Press.

Maier, Charles S.
1988 *Recasting Bourgeois Europe.* Princeton, N.J.: Princeton University Press.

Miller, Perry.
1956 *Errand into the Wilderness.* Cambridge: Harvard University Press.

Pole, J. R.
1978 *The Pursuit of Equality in American History.* Berkeley: University of California Press.

Preston, John.
1624 *The New Covenant: Or the Saint's Portion.* London: Nicolas Bourne.

Rapaczynski, Andrzej.
1987 *Nature and Politics: Liberalism in the Philosophies of Hobbes, Locke, and Rousseau.* Ithaca, N.Y.: Cornell University Press.

Raphael, David Diaches.
1947 *The Moral Sense.* Oxford: Oxford University Press.

Robinson, I. S.
1988 "Church and Papacy." In *Cambridge History of Medieval Political Thought.* Edited by S. H. Burns. Cambridge: Cambridge University Press.

Rousseau, Jean-Jacques.
1973 *The Social Contract and Discourses,* revised edition. Translated with introduction by G. D. H. Cole. Revised by J. H. Brumfitt and John C. Hall. New York: E. P. Dutton. [First published 1755.]

Skinner, Quentin.
1978 *The Foundations of Modern Political Thought,* 2 volumes. Cambridge: Cambridge University Press.

Smith, Adam.
1982 *Essays on Philosophical Subjects*. Indianapolis: Liberty Classics. [First published 1756.]

Stout, Harry.
1986 *The New England Soul*. New York: Oxford University Press.

Troeltsch, Ernst.
1976 *The Social Teaching of the Christian Churches*, 2 volumes. Translated by Olive Wyon. Introduction by Richard Niebuhr. Chicago: University of Chicago Press.

Von Leyden, Wolfgang.
1982 *Hobbes and Locke: The Politics of Freedom and Obligation*. New York: St. Martin's Press.

Winthrop, John.
1853 *The History of New England from 1630–1649*. Edited by J. Savage. Boston: Little, Brown and Company.

Section III

Metapractical Discourse: Comparative Studies

Chapter 6

Philosophy as Metapraxis

Thomas P. Kasulis

This chapter explores some general issues about the role of philosophy in religion. As a way of introducing the *problematik,* let us begin with some observations about a specific case. In the twentieth chapter of the Gospel of John, the risen Jesus appears to his disciples and says, "Peace be with you. As the Father has sent me, even so I send you." The account in verse 22 then describes the action in this way: "And when he had said this, he breathed on them, and said to them, 'Receive the Holy Spirit.'" At least that is what the Revised Standard Version says he said. In the *Anchor Bible,* Raymond E. Brown is a bit more cautious.[1] He translates the risen Jesus' words as "Receive a holy Spirit," removing the definite article from the English since it is not there in the Greek and relegating "holy" of "holy Spirit" to the lowercase.

As we know from the Johannine account, Thomas was not there during that appearance of the risen Jesus. Neither were we. Like him, we may have our doubts when we have only other people's accounts. We may have even greater doubts when we have only translations of others' accounts, especially by translators who also were not present. We may wonder specifically how the Greek word *pneuma* should be translated here. It does, after all, mean "breath" and "wind" as well as "spirit." How do we know that we should not translate the sentence as: "And when he had said this, he breathed on them, and said to them, 'Receive a holy breath?'" The Gospel of John apparently uses the word in different senses: In the third chapter, for example, even the RSV translates *pneuma* in verse six as "spirit" (contrasted with "flesh"), but in verse 8 as "wind."[2] So how do we know in a given instance, one as contextually ambiguous as John 20:22, which translation is best? On prima facie evidence alone it is more sensible to associate Jesus' exhalation with breath than with the entrance of another divine person. Or, at least, when does the polysemous word *pneuma* deserve some hedging in the translation so its physical meanings can complement its metaphysical senses in the minds of the English readers?

Clinton Morrison's *Analytical Concordance* informs us that *pneuma* occurs in the New Testament 378 times and the RSV translated it as "breath" three times, as "mind" twice, as "wind" twice, and as "spirit" a whopping 371 times.[3] Apparently, the RSV translators (and the King James translators before them) found the context of almost all occurrences of the Greek term unequivocal. They used "spirit" as the norm to translate *pneuma*, a norm with only seven exceptions out of 378 instances. They literally took the breath out of the text.

As scholars of ancient religious texts, we should want our reading to reflect as much as possible the conceptual frameworks of the time. Most biblical scholars interpret the Greek word *pneuma* in light of the Hebrew Bible's use of the term *ruaḥ*, for example. After all, Jesus was a Jew, not a Greek-speaking Gentile. This connection with the Hebrew tradition does not solve our problem, however. Robert Koch explains:

> The primary meaning of *ruaḥ* may be taken to be *wind*, the mysterious and irresistible power of which Yahweh avails himself in the execution of his designs in salvation and creation. On the human plane it designates the *breath* with all its concomitant manifestations which permeates the lives of men (and beasts) from the first moment of their existence to the last. This breath of air and of life comes from on high, from God, and it permeates, brings to life and maintains all the inhabitants of the world together (see Wis 1:7; Acts 17:28). In this sense it is omnipresent (Ps 139:7).[4]

So, the issue remains: How do we know when we should translate *pneuma* as "breath" or "wind" and when as "spirit?" To associate *pneuma* with *ruaḥ* seems to make the problem only all the more pressing.

Perhaps our hermeneutic queasiness derives from an overindulgence in philology, and we could more readily resolve the difficulties by a more theological exegesis. By examining those 378 occurrences of the word *pneuma* in the New Testament as a whole, we might be able to uncover in the texts themselves a theory of *pneuma* and especially *pneuma hagion*, the "Holy Spirit." It is perfectly possible that the writers of the New Testament were trying to stretch the semantic range of the Greek word and the Hebraic metaphysics of *ruaḥ*. Yet, in attempting this more constructive theological reading, let us not leave behind Thomas and his hermeneutic of suspicion. If we want to reconstruct what the writers of the New Testament really meant, let us take care not to read into their words the ideas of a later Christian agenda.

In his article on "Spirit" for the *Encyclopedia of Theology*, Lourencino B. Puntel takes our discussion in an interesting direction.

> The philosophical concept of spirit was first worked out in Greek thought, though there is no one Greek word which has all the connotations of our "spirit." The word *pneuma* "wind, breath" came to be used for the "breath of life" but except in religious and poetical use never quite lost its etymological meaning. It was the word *nous* which underwent the changes of meaning in which the specifically Greek understanding of spirit was arrived at, which was to have such influence on Western thought.[5]

In his historical sketch of the theological notion of "spirit," Puntel goes on to discuss such ideas as *nous* in Anaxagoras, Parmenides, Plato, and Aristotle. For the medieval period he discusses *mens* and *animus* in Augustine and *mens* and *spiritus* in Thomas.[6] His discussion continues into a survey of the modern era. The noteworthy point for us is the following. In discussing the theology of "spirit," in trying to examine the historically central ideas having "all the connotations of our 'spirit,'" Puntel virtually ignores the word *pneuma*. And *pneuma* is a term that, he himself noted, "never quite lost its etymological meaning of 'wind' or 'breath.'"

What is missing in Puntel's discussion is more striking when we go on to the very next entry in the *Encyclopedia of Theology*, Josef Sudbrack's article on "Spirituality." His first section, "'Spirit' in Scripture," begins with a discussion of the now familiar themes of *ruah, pneuma*, life-force, and so forth. So, it seems when we want to consider "spirituality," we should think of the biblical term *pneuma* and its associations with breath and wind as well as spirit. Yet, when we want to capture the philosophical or theological idea of "spirit," we should apparently look to other terms, terms without those associations. On the surface at least, this seems odd: We were wise to bring our doubting Thomas with us.

The distinction between a theological account of spirit and one of spirituality suggests a distinction between a discussing a theory and discussing a praxis. A theory of spirit raises ontological and metaphysical questions whereas a theory of spirituality raises issues more existential and practical. In so cavalierly translating *pneuma* as "spirit," are we either consciously or inadvertently concealing the practical and the existential in favor of the theoretical and metaphysical? Is our translation, and ultimately our reading, of *pneuma* colored by Neoplatonic assumptions about mind and spirit? Is our facile move from the Greek word *pneuma* to the English rendering "the spirit," and by extension, "the Holy Spirit" a residue of Trinitarian and Christological debates in, say, the fourth century? Are we failing in the attempt to capture the life of the text as it breathed in the early second century? To think of *pneuma* whenever possible as "the Spirit" serves Trinitarianism much better than would thinking of it as the divine "breath." As the Hebrew tradition suggests, "breath" seems a characteristic of God, not a separate person or agent.

We may be missing what other scholars find obvious. Then again, we may be questioning what others only think obvious. As scholars of religion, we should be concerned how religious thought relates to praxis. We may wonder whether one could, or should, understand the passage from John in relation to religious behavior as well as to religious metaphysics.

The hermeneutic connecting *pneuma* with spirit rather than with breath supports theological arguments about the ontology and nature of the Holy Spirit. For example, that ontological orientation reads the passage as proof that the breath of life as the Holy Spirit came into the disciples through Jesus. Western Christendom has used that interpretation to support its case for the *filioque* clause in its debate with the Eastern Church: The passage gives textual evidence that the Holy Spirit proceeded from the Son as well as from the Father. Of course, we would disallow that evidence if it turned out that the risen Jesus only exhaled a holy breath, and not the Holy Spirit. So, we may wonder, could someone just as easily understand the passage in relation to religious praxis, instead of the theoretical relation between Jesus and the Holy Spirit? Certainly they could and indeed they have.

In his detailed note on the biblical passage in question,[7] Brown explains that some commentators have wondered whether the Johannine account reflects an early Christian ordination rite in which the spirit is breathed into the recipient of the sacrament. This seems possible. Information from the history of religions adds strength to this thesis since, as Brown notes, we know the practice of insufflation has been a part of the ordination rites in some later forms of Christian practice.

> The most famous example of this was the custom of filling a skin bag with the holy breath of the Coptic Patriarch of Alexandria, tying it up, and transporting it up river to Ethiopia where it was let loose on the one designated to be the Abuna or head of the Ethiopian church.

Brown's reference to "a holy breath" could presumably be translated as *pneuma hagion*. Why, then, did Brown not say they put "a holy spirit" in the skin bag? How does he know the context is different from what he translated in John 20:22?

The Coptic case shows that the passage has had implications for religious practice. Its interpretation has not been limited to theological debates on the nature of the Trinity and the *filioque* clause. Brown's discussion continues with the following observation.

> Lootfy Levonian, *The Expositor,* 8th Series, 22 (1921), 149–54, discussing such beliefs and practices in relation to John xx 22, says (with confidence!) of the latter custom: "No one can doubt apostolic succession when it comes in this form."

To Brown's apparent consternation, Levonian understood the Johannine passage not only as leading to a particular religious practice, or as describing a practice that may have been part of the early Church, but also as *justifying* it. Does Brown's parenthetical exclamation reflect the Western Church's insistence that the passage is about orthodoxy, but not orthopraxis?

The Coptic ritual reminds us of the importance of breathing in prayer for other traditions of Eastern Christianity, especially the contemplative tradition of hesychasm and the praxis of the Jesus prayer or the prayer of the heart. The association of breath control with the Jesus prayer has been explicitly part of the tradition since the thirteenth century and has roots in hesychasm going back at least to the fifth century.[8] Historians of religion have documented well the connection between religious praxis and breath control or breath awareness in a variety of traditions across cultural and historical boundaries.[9] From the historian's study of comparative praxiology, Western Christianity's relative lack of breathing-related rituals might be more an anomaly than the norm. It is an especially striking anomaly since *ruah* and *pneuma* are such important metaphysical concepts in its tradition. In asking why this apparent anomaly might have developed, we confront this paper's central concern.

As noted at the outset, we want to focus on the role of philosophical thinking within religious traditions. The complexity of how to interpret and translate a single verse from the Gospel of John has furnished a background against which we can depict some relevant issues. In particular we are underscoring the difference between reading the passage in question as a statement about ontology and reading it as a statement about praxis. This occasions our making a few distinctions and stipulative definitions.

First, we are not simply posing a distinction between theory and praxis. There would be a fundamental error in saying that the "spirit" oriented interpreters wanted to develop a theological theory whereas the "breath" oriented interpreters wanted to develop a religious praxis. Levonian's claim about apostolic succession was just as theoretical as any discussion about the relationship between Christ and the Holy Spirit. The difference lies in what the theories are about and what they are trying to do. The former is a theory about the nature of divine reality; the latter is a theory about the activity of the believers and the function of their praxes as a basis of community. This difference is crucial but commonly overlooked in both philosophical accounts of religion and descriptive accounts about the role of philosophy within religion. Philosophy within a religious tradition can as readily reflect on the nature of the religion's praxis as on its understanding of reality.

This leads to a distinction between the metaphysical and what we will call the "metapractical" role of religious philosophizing. By "metaphysics," we will mean simply the development of a philosophical theory about the nature of reality. Basing our sense of the term on its philological components instead of historical etymology, we can say metaphysics theorizes about what lies "behind" or "beyond" (*meta*) "natural things and powers" (*physis*). By analogy, "metapraxis" is the development of a philosophical theory about the nature of a particular praxis, in this case, religious praxis. It theorizes about what lies behind or beyond the practices of a religious tradition. Several points about these two enterprises require further discussion.

First, we are considering them as philosophical activities. By that we mean that they present and defend a position about what is the case with some appeal to rational justification. A simple description is neither metaphysical nor metapractical. A metaphysics or a metapraxis must include an attempt to show why it is better than competing views of reality or of religious praxis. The latter point is what distinguishes metapraxis from praxiology, for example. Praxiology, an activity often pursued by historians of religion, is the descriptive study of the behavior or practices in a religious tradition. Metapraxis, on the other hand, advocates a religious praxis over other alternatives, actual or possible. In so advocating that position, a metapraxis must give reasons for the integrity or superiority of the praxes it defends. Religious metaphysics grounds orthodoxy whereas religious metapraxis grounds orthopraxis.

Second, the prefix "meta-" also bears for us the meaning of "after." A religious metaphysics arises as the reflection on our religious involvement in the natural world. A religious metapraxis is the reflection on our activities within a religious community or tradition. In the sense we will be using the terms, both metaphysical and metapractical thinking are responses to the human situation. When we go beyond asking what things are to asking why they are that way, or whence they came, and whither they go, we discover metaphysical issues. When we encounter, or devise on our own, competing answers to those questions and try to decide rationally which of those answers is better, we are doing metaphysics.

Analogously, we find ourselves in socially and culturally defined communities with activities that we label "religious." When we go beyond asking what we do as members of that community and start asking why we do it, we undertake metapractical considerations. When we encounter, or devise on our own, competing answers to those questions and try to decide on rational grounds which answer or which praxis is the better one, we start doing metapraxis. So, in our use of the terms, metaphysics and metapraxis are not detached, abstract fields of inquiry or branches of philosophy. Rather, they refer to the reflective moment in our religious understanding of the world and of our religious activities in it.[10]

Third, a metapraxis may relate to, but is not the same as, a "theory of praxis."[11] A theory of praxis tries to interpret the nature of praxis in general instead of within a particular religious tradition. Although such a theory may advocate its interpretation of praxis, it does not advocate one praxis over another (except insofar as any theory is, in one sense, the expression of an academic praxis). This difference does not imply, however, that metapraxis is always independent of a theory of praxis. A metapractical theory may involve in its articulation a general theory about praxis, its nature, and proper function, and then particularize that general theory into the specifics of interest to the tradition. For example, a religious metapraxis may sometimes assume a particular philosophical anthropology in justifying its tradition's religious praxis. That anthropology may itself include an understanding of the role of praxis for human life in general.

In this context we can now specify how the case of interpreting the passage from the Gospel of John relates to the main theme of this paper. Our brief discussion of traditional interpretations of John 20:22 gives us a specific instance of what is at stake in the distinction between metaphysics and metapraxis. As we have seen, some commentators and translators have taken an approach emphasizing the ontological character of the Holy Spirit. Others have taken an approach emphasizing the ritualization of the transmission of the spirit from one person to another. In effect, these interpretations differ in whether they focus on how the passage illuminates metaphysical or metapractical concerns. Since the dominant interpretation has obviously become the metaphysical rather than metapractical, we might speculate on how this emphasis developed in the history of Christian thought.

Certainly, the Hellenistic emphasis on metaphysics and ontology alongside its psychological and epistemological concerns about "mind" (*nous*) might have influenced the early Christian tradition to establish its own metaphysical orthodoxy. In the move from Jerusalem to Athens, Christianity confronted a different, highly sophisticated, philosophical worldview. It was perhaps natural that it would respond by trying to formulate its metaphysics in conceptual schemes that would clarify similarities and differences between the Christian and Hellenistic philosophies. This would account for the phenomenon we have discussed already in terms of Puntel's comments on the theology of "spirit": Terms like *nous* in Greek and *mens* and *animus* in Latin displaced some original physical and practical nuances of *pneuma* as "breath" or "wind."[12]

An aspect of Christian philosophy's Hellenization was the specifically Neoplatonic devaluation of the body. This devaluation followed Plato's tirade against the body in such dialogues as the *Phaedo:*

> We [philosophers] are in fact convinced that if we are ever to have
> pure knowledge of anything, we must get rid of the body (*sōma*)
> and contemplate things by themselves with the soul (*psyche*) by
> itself.[13]

It is not surprising that the Pauline dichotomy of spirit (*pneuma*) and flesh (*sarx*) would be read in this light, completely overlooking the positive senses of "body" (*sōma*) often found in Paul. For Paul, of course, the struggle between spirit and flesh was primarily a struggle within the spiritual dimension. It was not simply a conflict between some immaterial spirit and material body. Paul even had his own tirade against the Greeks who sought wisdom (*sophia*) in the philosophical sense Plato advocated:

> For Jews demand signs and Greeks seek wisdom, but we preach
> Christ crucified, a stumbling block to Jews and Greeks, Christ the
> power of God and the wisdom of God. (I Cor 1:22–24)

In short, to fit the model of Hellenistic philosophizing, the Christian tradition changed its vocabulary for discussing the metaphysical implications of its scriptures. In so doing, it marginalized the somatic aspects of *pneuma*. To develop a metaphysical account more palatable to the Gentile philosophers, it tended to forsake *pneuma*'s relation to the breath and to a tangible presence like the Hebrew *ruaḥ*. With the diminished emphasis on the somatic qualities of the *pneuma,* the theme of praxis receded into the background of the Christian pneumatology.

Not all Greek traditions demeaned the somatic as much as Plato and the Neoplatonists. We might wonder, for example, whether the Aristotelianism of the late medieval Scholastics allowed a more positive evaluation for the body's role in religious life. In some ways it did. Thomas, for example, wrote the following against the Platonists:

> Others said that the entire nature of man is seated in the soul, so that
> the soul makes use of the body as an instrument, or as a sailor uses
> his ship. . . . But the Philosopher [Aristotle] sufficiently destroys this
> foundation (*De Anima, ii.*2), where he shows that the soul is united
> to the body as form to matter. . . .
>
> Other things being equal, the state of the soul in the body is
> more perfect than outside the body, because it is a part of the whole
> composite. (*Summa Theologica, Supplement, Q75*)[14]

As much as this approach returns us to the importance of the body, it still
follows an Aristotelian rather than Hebraic analysis. That is, Thomas sees
the body as in-formed matter, whereas the *ruaḥ* tradition sees it as inspired matter.

Of course, the somatic and practical aspects of spirit are never
completely lost in the Christian tradition. The Christian concept of spirit
is not simply metaphysical but also experiential. The Holy Spirit may be
an ontological personal entity, but its function is also to fill the individual
Christian with its "gifts." This raises the issue of how the metaphysics, the
praxis, and the metapraxis of a religious tradition may be interrelated.

As historians and social scientists like to remind philosophers, religion is a social and personal activity, not simply a set of intellectual
beliefs. Rarely in human history do we encounter the birth of a totally
new religion. Most often, people find themselves born into an already
existing tradition. They assimilate the communal religious praxes alongside the other cultural forms of language, gesture, etiquette, social structure, and so forth. As with the other inherited cultural forms, the religious
praxes are not initially reflected upon. When they are, the philosophical
moment enters religious experience and that reflective activity can go in
two directions, the metaphysical or the metapractical.

The metaphysical reflection arises out of questions about what the
praxis means or to what it refers. Religious praxis has, to use a phenomenological term, a "thetic" component, that is, it implicitly or explicitly
posits something as real. To pray to someone or something, for example,
is to assume that someone or something is real. But in what sense of real?
How is the reality of this entity related to the reality of other experienced
entities (for example, the disease or drought that precipitated the prayer
in the first place)? What are the relations among the various entities?
Once raised, these questions do not readily go away without some focused reflection and analysis.

If there are already highly developed theories of reality outside the
religious tradition, the situation becomes more complex: there may be
alternative accounts of what things are real and how they are real. To
return to our opening example, when entering the Gentile world, the
early Christians needed to respond to the entrenched Hellenistic philo-

sophical world view with its concepts of *nous* and *sōma*. Competing accounts of reality have to be either reconciled or one preferred to the other in some respect or in some specified circumstances.

Again, there is a tendency to conceive of this metaphysical speculation as an abstruse, systematic, comprehensive form of intellectual activity limited to the elite. Yet, metaphysical reflection can operate on the most ordinary levels of thought as well. This point struck home years ago when I was reading my four-year-old son a children's version of the creation story from the beginning of *Genesis*. To check his comprehension I asked him to repeat the main details of the story. When he got to the sixth day of creation, he explained that God then created the first human being. He paused for a moment and then said, "That must have been when God was a monkey. And then, on the seventh day—" "Wait. What do you mean God was a monkey?" "Well, before we were people, we were monkeys. And God made Adam to be like God. So, God must have been a monkey then." Obviously, the four-year-old had heard two accounts of the same event. Instead of seeing them as conflicting or alternative stories, he had decided to reconcile them. He was doing metaphysics and, in effect, had produced a primitive process or evolutionary theology. His was not a full-bodied, theological metaphysics of the classical sort. Yet, his activity differed not so much in kind as in complexity and the number of factors integrated.

Let us turn now to metapraxis. It arises out of questions about the purpose and efficacy of the religious praxes. Religious praxis generally has either a participatory or transformative function. It participates in, to use Rudolf Otto's term, the "numinous." It is transformative in its improving the person or community in some spiritual way (purifying, healing, reconciling, protecting, informing, and so on). Metapractical reflection inquires into the purpose and efficacy of the practice in terms of these participatory and transformative functions. Something happens, or at least is supposed to happen, in and through religious praxis. Metapraxis analyzes and evalutes that happening. What does the praxis change? Is something remembered? Reenacted? Empowered? If so, exactly how does the praxis work? And why should we prefer our traditional praxis as more effective than another?

Because metapraxis is a less familiar term than metaphysics, it will require a more detailed analysis. Before exploring those theoretical heights, let us remind ourselves that, like metaphysics, metapraxis need not be an abstruse, complex, systematic activity reserved for the elite. As with metaphysical reflection, children may engage in it. Whenever a child asks the reason for a particular praxis, the discussion may venture into metapractical discussion and speculation. Often the precipitating cause of the discussion is an encounter with another tradition and, therefore, an alternative set of praxes. I recall a discussion between a Jewish father and his seven-year-old daughter at a picnic. The father tried to answer the girl's questions about why Gentiles can put cheese on their kosher beef hamburgers, but they could not. The discussion involved issues dealing with tradition, ethnicity, and the meaning of dietary restrictions. Finally, the girl said, "You mean if I weren't Jewish, it would be all right for me to eat a cheeseburger? Gee, sometimes it's hard to be Jewish instead of being like other people."

The little girl's comment points to two primary reasons for the appearance of metapractical reflection. First, a religious praxis always involves effort, and the effort must be justifiable. Second, where there is an awareness of other traditions with different praxes, one's own praxes necessarily undergo scrutiny. Religious praxis takes effort, time, and often financial or physical sacrifice. It is natural, then, that the question of "Is it worth it?" will periodically arise. The praxis must be justified in some sense, especially if the religious community is aware that other groups do not perform that same praxis.

It is crucial again to keep clear the difference between a metapractical theory and a general theory of praxis. As we noted already, a metapraxis arises out of the reflection on one's own praxis as a way of understanding and justifying that particular praxis. A theory of praxis, on the other hand, is a reflection on the purpose and significance of praxis in general. For example, an anthropologist, philosopher, psychologist, or historian of religion might develop a theory of why so many traditions have rituals to mark the arrival of puberty or adulthood. If the theory is adequate, it explains the presence of the observable phenomena. Yet, it does not describe or explain the particular praxis as a lived experience. To explain the behavior, a theory of praxis necessarily stands outside it for the purpose of generalization.

A metapractical theory, on the other hand, arises from within the praxis itself for the sake of the people involved in that praxis. It justifies their activity at least to themselves and possibly to some outsiders. It explains not a general theory of dietary restrictions as a religious phenomenon, but why that little girl might decide to maintain those restrictions throughout her entire life. It explains to her what she as an individual can derive from that particular praxis. It appeals to her as a member one community rather than another. It explains her particular Jewishness, not just her universal humanness.

How do traditions justify their praxes? We might go about answering this question empirically. We could collect information about as wide a variety of religious phenomena as possible and see what different traditions count as good reasons for undertaking a religious praxis. For example, continuity of tradition sometimes counts as a necessary condition for justification. That sense of tradition might be defined in a variety of ways. It may be what our canon prescribes, what the elders say we have always done, what we agreed to do at some council in the past, and so forth. In other cases, empirically verifiable efficacy might be a criterion. Did the praxis do what it was supposed to do in curing the illness, ending the drought, winning the battle, or whatever?

As a philosopher of religion, I do not intend in this paper to explore extensive information about a variety of religions. Instead, let us analyze how a rational justification of praxis might proceed. This analysis will show that a particular condition is necessary for a fully adequate justification: In a given tradition, its metaphysics and its metapraxis must be compatible with each other. Ideally, they should not only be compatible but fully integrated.

We would not want our discussion of the relationship between metaphysical and metapractical theories to become too abstract. So, let us begin by briefly discussing an instance of the type of integration at issue. We will consider the structure of the religious system of Kūkai (774–835 C.E.), the founder of Japanese Shingon Buddhism. In fact, I first developed the idea of metapraxis in my efforts to understand and then explain Kūkai's philosophy of "esotericism" (*mikkyō*). For our purposes, we need not examine the historical background of that tradition. Nor must we sift through which ideas were Kūkai's and which he drew out of the thirteen centuries of Buddhist philosophy preceding him. We will also try to avoid the technical vocabulary of Shingon Buddhism as much as possible, since it can easily overwhelm the nonspecialist. Our interest is simply to see how Kūkai integrated Shingon praxis, metaphysics, and metapraxis.

Let us begin with Shingon praxis, since it is the experience out of which its metaphysics and metapraxis are philosophical reflections. As an esoteric tradition, Shingon emphasizes complex rituals that masters teach and interpret directly to their disciples. Although the actual rituals are intricate and of a seemingly infinite variety, there are three basic elements of performance involved: meditating on mandalas (schematic maps of the Shingon worldview presented in a geometric and highly symbolic form), chanting mantras (sacred words or phrases), and performing mudras (sacred postures or gestures). To enact these rituals diligently under the proper guidance is to merge with the powers of the universe and to achieve insight into the basic nature of all things. Shingon Buddhists believe various thaumaturgic powers generally accompany this level of accomplishment.

Let us turn now to Kūkai's metaphysics or theory of reality. What is the praxis's meaning? What reality does it assume? According to Kukai, the cosmos as a whole is the Buddha called Dainichi. As a person,

Dainichi is a process defined by the three forms of enactment: thought, word, and deed. As an enlightened person, Dainichi's thoughts, words, and deeds are also enlightened. The Buddha's words are, therefore, "truth-words" (*shingon*) or mantras. Dainichi's continuous chanting of these truth-words emits the resonances constituting the building blocks of the universe. For example, the basic elements of the universe are the macrophysical manifestation of these microcosmic resonant energy states. They in turn form the compounds making up the world of everyday life. In a parallel fashion, Dainichi's enlightened mental activity gestalts the world into the form it has, patterns that can be depicted from different perspectives as the various mandalas. Lastly, the Buddha's enlightened deeds are the gestures (mudras) that give a fixed style of movement to all things. In this way, Kukai's system gives a comprehensive theory of what is, what appears, and how things relate in different dimensions of reality.

The key phrase encapsulating this metaphysics is *hosshin seppo,* "the dharma-body (the Buddha as cosmos) expounds the dharmas (true doctrines) as the dharmas (all phenomena)." It is depicted especially well in one of the two major traditional mandalas, the Womb Mandala. Dainichi is portrayed there as the nucleus out of which all other buddhas and ultimately all other phenomena emanate as his "symbolic expression" (*monji*).

Let us now consider Kūkai's metapraxis. How does Shingon praxis work? Whence derives its power to transform? How is it able to partici-pate in the sacred? According to Shingon, since the cosmos is itself an enlightened being, we are already part of that enlightenment. Yet, we are unaware of this because we act in disharmony with the natural patterns around us. The purpose of Shingon practice is to effect a harmonization with the natural patterns so that we can feel Dainichi's power within us. Shingon praxis is effective because it forces us into the patterns of enact-ment descriptive of enlightenment. By chanting the seed mantras, for example, we attune ourselves to the seed mantras that Dainichi is chant-ing. We harmonize ourselves, as it were, into the song that is already being sung. As singers feel empowered when they join in the harmony of a chorus, we are empowered by Dainichi's chanting. In a parallel way, we merge with Dainichi's meditation through the mandalas and with Dainichi's style through the mudras. In adding our voice, images, and style to the chorus, we increase the power of the cosmic harmony and overpower disharmonious elements (disease, drought, human ignorance). This empowerment (*kaji*) is the Buddha's energy at work, but to outsid-ers it seems the Shingon Buddhist practitioner has gained thaumaturgic capabilities.

The encapsulating phrase for Kūkai's metapraxis is *sokushin jōbutsu,* "achieving the buddha in, through, and by means of this very body." We can relate the metapraxis to the other major mandala of the Shingon tradition, the Diamond Mandala. The Diamond Mandala depicts the deepening praxis and more profound levels of wisdom spiraling inward in nine stages until one reaches the center, the image of Dainichi.

Kūkai's brilliance as a philosopher is in his working through the system's details. Our concern, however, is simply to see how the structure of Shingon praxis, metaphysics, and metapraxis dovetail into each other. A gesture, image, or mantra from a ritual leads naturally into a philosophical reflection on both the nature of reality and the nature of Shingon praxis. In fact, the units of meaning (mantra, mandala, and mudra) are the same for the discussion of praxis, metaphysics, and metapraxis. The polysemous character of the system allows an aspect of praxis, a characterization of ultimate reality, and a reflection on one's own spiritual development as a person to be expressed in the same words. In this way, the praxis, metapraxis, and metaphysics establish the foundation for each other. Each pair serves to justify the third.

The polysemous character of Kūkai's system is not simply fortuitous. It derives from a rational commitment to coherence and completeness. By coherence, we mean a logical accord among the three religious dimensions of praxis, metaphysics, and metapraxis. Let us consider a hypothetical case. Imagine a religious tradition that maintains a metaphysical monism, rejecting the world of diversity and change. Advaita Vedānta might be an example. The praxis of such a tradition could not be based simply in empirical verification. Sense experience yields diversity, not singularity. It is not surprising, therefore, that the praxis of an Advaita Vedāntin is not the same as the praxis of a research scientist or a logical positivist. There must be a praxis (contemplation or meditation, for example) supporting the metaphysics of monism and participating in its sacred reality.

Yet, as explained so far, there is still something missing in our hypothetical example of a religious system. It lacks completeness. Suppose someone asks why the results of the particular yogic meditation should be trusted more than the results of empirical observation. The praxis of empirical observation supports a pluralistic metaphysics and vice versa. The yogic meditation supports a monistic metaphysics and vice versa. How can we decide between the two systems?

As Kant argued through his discussion of the antinomies, we cannot settle a metaphysical disagreement on the grounds of pure reason alone. In the case of empiricism, its implicit metaphysical assumption is the validity of the principle of verification. Yet, that principle itself cannot be proven by verification. Conversely, the monist's mistrust of sense experience cannot be proven through pure reason alone either. Hence, Kant maintained that metaphysical principles can only be justified as regulative for praxis, thus leading to his analysis of "practical reason." In this sense, Kant resorted to a type of metapraxis to justify his metaphysical claims about freedom and God.

This Kantian generalization has implications for our theory of metapraxis. There is no logical algorithm for deciding between two internally consistent but mutually exclusive metaphysical systems. In the end, once we have determined the two to be equally valid logically, we decide between competing metaphysics in terms of their likelihood. Which better fits our experience of the world as we think about it and act in it? The way we act in the world is our praxis. If we are members of a religious tradition or community, our praxis includes religious activity. As we reflect on the nature and meaning of these praxes from which we derive spiritual identity, that is, as we develop our religious metapraxis, we become more acutely aware of the premises according to which we act out our spiritual lives. A Kantian may see these as the "regulative principles of practical reason."

Traditional Kantianism errs mainly in seeing these principles as universal, as independent of the praxes of a particular cultural and religious system. Kant understood his principles as the (transcendentally) necessary presuppositions for any human action. I contend they were the necessary presuppositions for a particular Judeo-Christian, Western Enlightenment form of praxis. If Kant had been a Theravāda Buddhist instead, for example, his regulative principles might have included conditionedness instead of freedom and insubstantiality instead of God.

In effect, Kant had mistaken a metapraxis for a theory of praxis. He confused the regulative principles for a particular praxis with the regulative principles for praxis itself. Later philosophers rejected Kant's contextless praxis for such rich notions of meaning, enactment, reflection, and praxis as Husserl's *lebenswelt* and Wittgenstein's *lebensform*. The development of the sociology of knowledge, the Marxist interpretation of praxis and ideology, and Foucault's concern for knowledge and power are also modes of interpretation that soften the sharp distinction between the practical and reflective. All these post-Kantian developments have affirmed, in one way or another, the interdependence of praxis, metapraxis, and metaphysics. Although much of this chapter has striven to distinguish the three dimensions, our analysis has suggested that the rational search for coherence and completeness requires an interdependence among the three. Through the use of polysemous terms, in fact, the very boundaries separating the three may become permeable. To this extent, this chapter does not radically depart from the concerns of other twentieth-century Western philosophical views.

For the study of religion, however, our distinctions have more far-reaching implications. In particular, the study of religion has frequently been too facile in its division between theory and praxis. The theory, typically limited to metaphysical theory, has become the domain of theologians and philosophers of religion. The study of praxis has been left to historians of religion and anthropologists. The distinction between "high" and "low" religion has only contributed more to the confusion. It separates out those traditions or aspects of tradition with a highly developed metaphysics and a weak sense of praxis from those with a strong sense of praxis and little metaphysical development. As long as we do not bring metapraxis more into the foreground of our analyses, we cannot fully bridge that separation between theory and praxis.

A greater sensitivity to the nature and role of metapraxis might enhance our studies of religion in a variety of ways. In the last section of this paper, let us consider some of the effects such a heightened sensitivity might have on the history of religions and the philosophy of religion conceived in their broadest terms. Using our previous analysis of John 20:22, we can also relate our considerations to the study of Christianity as a specific case.

History of Religions

The history of religions is a field with multiple subdisciplines. For our purposes, let us consider three projects that the historians of religion often undertake: the study of a tradition's historical development, the study of sacred texts, and the anthropological observation of religious behavior.

The Study of a Tradition's Historical Development

From our discussion of John 20:22, it would seem that in any study of a particular religious tradition, we would do well to keep metapractical and practical issues in mind along with the metaphysical. Even further, if our general point about the interpenetration of the three dimensions has merit, we should be sensitive to how the three support each other. For example, in discussing the Christian case, the early debates about Trinitarianism and Christology seem to be metaphysical disagreements. Was there a relation to praxis and metapraxis? We do know, for example, that the eleventh-century schism between the Eastern and Western Church was as much about metapractical issues dealing with the sacramental use of leavened and unleavened bread (*enzyma* and *azyma*) as about the metaphysical implications of the *filioque* clause.[15] If the leavening was associated with the Holy Spirit, as seems to be the case, did the liturgical use of bread have implications for the metaphysical relationship between the Holy Spirit and Christ?

On the other hand, the Reformation seems to have been mainly about metapractical issues (justification by faith versus justification by works, iconoclasm, the status of the sacraments, the translation of the Bible into the vernacular, and so on), but were there also implications for praxis and metaphysics? In fact, what exactly does praxis mean in the various strands of Protestantism? Is there an implicit metapraxis to the congregation's singing of hymns or of the Word as presented in the voiced homily from the pulpit? If so, could that metapraxis be related to a metaphysical pneumatology, thereby recapturing the practical sense of *pneuma* as breath since the Spirit moves the breath in both singing and in preaching? What were the metapractical justifications for the Protestant departure from the Catholic praxis of formulaic prayers? Did the Catholic tradition develop or revert back to a previous metapraxis in order to justify the continuation of that praxis? What were the practical and metaphysical implications?

These types of questions can be fruitfully asked of the historical account of any religious tradition. Whenever we find a historical issue that seems to be only about praxis or only about metaphysics or only about metapraxis, we might do well to look more carefully at the materials to see if there are interrelated phenomena in the other two dimensions. Liturgical disagreements may teach us about differences in the philosophies of reality and of praxis. Metaphysical disagreements may grow out of differences in praxis and theories about those praxes.

The Study of Sacred Texts

In reading the sacred texts of any tradition, we should be vigilant in identifying polysemous terms or phrases that might refer to praxis or metapraxis as well as to metaphysical realities. Texts generally arise out of existing religious communities. They typically do not create traditions but reflect them. Religious texts are themselves already a reflection on the religious experience as lived in a communal context. If this is correct, then we must be aware of the metapractical implications in any religious text we are interpreting or translating. It is too facile to look at a text and classify it as either narrative (including myth) or metaphysics. Many passages may be about praxis or metapraxis. Polysemous terms or even images may be clues to how the three dimensions of praxis, metaphysics, and metapraxis relate in a specific tradition. In the examples discussed in this paper, we have seen how difficult it can be to separate the metaphysical, practical, and metapractical denotations of a term like *pneuma* in Christianity or *mantra* in Shingon Buddhism. Textual scholars should be alert to the function of such polysemous terms in the works they study.

The Anthropological Observation of Religious Behavior

The anthropological approach to the study of religion sometimes disdains the philosophical dimension of religious life. The claim is that philosophy in religion is limited to the speculations of a small cadre of elitist intellectuals. This interpretation may result from identifying philosophy in religion with the construction of disembodied, abstract metaphysical systems. Such an identification leads to the odd romantic assumption that "real" religious life is unreflective, that it is all praxis without any philosophizing. Without giving attention to the reflective dimension of religious life, our analysis of a Native American rain dance would resemble an analysis we might give of the honey bee's dance. Such a simplistic approach overlooks the fact that under the right conditions a cheeseburger or a monkey can be the catalyst for a metapractical or metaphysical reflection.

Furthermore, without the cognizance of religious agents as reflective beings, the so-called phenomenological study of religion can easily degenerate into becoming naively empirical rather than truly phenomenological. In defining phenomenology as the return "to things" (*zu den Sachen*), Husserl explicitly meant things as intended within human consciousness. Husserl's project was not to classify phenomena in a taxonomic way but rather to reveal the functions by which experience is constituted and the manner in which meaning is formed. If we are to understand what a *bar mitzvah* means to a Jew or a Confirmation ritual to a Christian, we must go beyond the taxonomy that labels them simply as rites of passage into puberty. We should investigate how the event gives specific meaning to the Jew or to the Christian involved. By looking at the way the specific tradition permeates the meaning-bestowing context of the lived experience, we discover more than what the event means for a universal characterization of religion. We also discover what that event means for the very people enacting that ritual. In other words we will have not merely a universal theory of practice, but a tradition-dependent metapraxis as well.

By being phenomenological in the true Husserlian sense, we engage the polysemous character of terms and symbols. This opens us to the multidimensional world of religious meaning where praxis, metaphysics, and metapraxis all meet. In such a project, we may discover that the philosophizing within a tradition may be as much an internal reflection on praxis, relating it to an associated worldview, as the construction of the metaphysical world view itself. Religious reflection in any tradition may analyze what we mean by what we believe. It is just as likely, however, to analyze what we mean by what we do. A truly phenomenological study of religion would consider both possibilities.

The more the philosophers of religion and theologians turn their attention to metapractical matters, the more useful corroboration can occur between those disciplines and the social sciences. This brings us to our comments on the philosophical approaches to the study of religion.

Philosophy of Religion

The philosophical study of religion is also diverse and has various subdisciplines. For our purposes, let us consider two: the study of philosophical doctrine in a particular religion and the study of the nature of religion itself. For convenience, let us call the former "doctrinal study" and the latter "the comparative philosophy of religion."

Doctrinal Study

In theistic religions we generally use the term "theology" to indicate the study of religious doctrine from within the tradition itself. If the line of argument in this paper is generally correct, we would do well to look at religious doctrine as a complex phenomenon bridging praxis and theory in various ways. In particular, religious doctrine is often consciously or unconsciously seeking a coherence and completeness as a system of praxis, metaphysics, and metapraxis.

Our discussion of the pneumatology of John 20:22 raises the question of whether a particular theology or system of doctrine may overemphasize the metaphysical to the detriment of the metapractical. In another paper[16] I have compared Karl Rahner's and Kūkai's views of spirituality, especially the criteria used in evaluating the spirituality of traditions outside their own. In the process I submitted Kūkai to Rahner's criteria for qualifying as an "anonymous Christian." Kūkai qualified. I then submitted Rahner to Kūkai's system for ranking religious philosophies, his scheme of the "ten mind-sets." Rahner qualified easily for at least level nine, the highest level of exoteric teaching. Qualification on level ten, the esoteric level, requires certain metapractical as well as metaphysical commitments. In the end I concluded Rahner probably was an "anonymous Shingon Buddhist," mainly because of the way he worked out his "theology of the symbol" in terms of the sacraments.

The comparison between Rahner and Kūkai underscores a point central to our concerns in this paper. Rahner's criteria for anonymous Christianity include three major points to which one must agree if one is to qualify as an anonymous Christian. We can elliptically cite them as follows:[17]

1. By looking within ourselves, we discover that every concrete thing reveals itself to be limitless in its being.

2. Being and knowing are essentially one and the same act.

3. This being and knowing are "incarnated" in the person's daily activity. By knowing one's own incarnate functions, one comes to know the perfect Incarnation of the sacred (as Christ, if one is explicitly a Christian).

The first two criteria are essentially metaphysical, whereas the third is the basis for a metapractical theory. When we compare this with Kūkai's discussion, we find a difference in emphasis, however. Rahner's third criterion for anonymous Christianity states, in effect, that praxis is necessary. For Kūkai, on the other hand, the highest level of the ten mind-sets requires a much more detailed metapractical vision, one that explicitly includes, for example, coherence with the metaphysical assumptions. In short, Kūkai's theory is more demanding in setting criteria for a specific way of relating one's incarnate activities to the larger metaphysical scheme. Rahner does, as already mentioned, undertake broader metapractical discussions when he analyzes specific rituals and practices. Furthermore, he does establish coherence between his metaphysical and metapractical theories. (Note the polysemous character of the term "incarnate" in the third criterion, for example.) The difference, however, is that what qualifies Kūkai as an anonymous Christian is not exactly what would qualify Rahner as anonymous Shingon Buddhist. The latter requires a more explicit metapraxis, including its relation to metaphysics and praxis.

I suspect most Christian theologians today would fit the Rahnerian pattern. Indeed, as a Roman Catholic theologican, Rahner is perhaps more sensitive to liturgical aspects than most systematic theologians. The question is whether Kūkai's requirements about the explicit interrelationship between metapractical and metaphysical considerations make his religious system not merely different, but philosophically superior, to a system without that requirement. If the general argument of this chapter is correct, the answer would seem to be yes. The coherence of a tradition's metaphysics and metapraxis is a demand of rationality, not merely an optional aesthetic principle. Religious knowledge must be knowable through the religious praxes in a manner consistent with the character of that reality. The theory of what is known must be in accord with the theory of how it is known. Kūkai's system formally recognizes that basic principle.

Theologies of the body, especially if they are grounded in a comprehensive theological anthropology, might be a way of bringing praxis and thereby metapraxis, back into the domain of theological thinking.[18] Work in this direction has begun, much of it within a feminist context. Of course, a comprehensive system would have to raise issues beyond gender to that of a more general religious anthropology. As Rahner often argued, the incarnate character of Jesus Christ can be understood only as we understand our own incarnate natures—presumably not just as women or men, but also generally as human beings.

The Comparative Philosophy of Religion

Through most of the modern period and especially in the past half century, philosophers have tended to analyze religion primarily as a system of belief instead of as a system of praxis. Especially in the Anglo-American tradition, much attention has been the analysis of whether religious beliefs can be justified. This approach may lead to the wrong assumption that the only philosophical dimension of religion is metaphysics, losing sight of the fact that religious beliefs can be a philosophical reflection on praxis as well. By disconnecting religious metaphysics from religious praxis and metapraxis, we run the danger of devising a disembodied model of religious personhood. As we noted already, this view is at odds with a major thrust of the rest of philosophy in our century emphasizing the embeddedness of philosophizing within a *lebenswelt* or a *lebensform,* or a theory-praxis matrix, or a community of discourse, and so on.

A philosophy of religion can also generate confusion when the only form of knowledge it recognizes is epistemic. The tradition of phronesis or even of Kant's practical reason would seem to provide more useful paradigms but may have been sometimes ignored on naively positivistic grounds. Furthermore, an overly positivistic analysis of language handicaps our capacity to deal with polysemous terminology. As Western philosophers turn increasingly to the analysis of tropes and figures of speech, we may become more skilled in evaluating the functions of religious language.

For these reasons, we philosophers may want to rethink our discipline's approach to religion. We can begin to deal more directly with the concrete phenomena of religious life itself and less with the rarefied metaphysics contemplated by a disembodied, Neoplatonic *nous.* As this chapter has itself exemplified, the philosophical treatment of religious systems outside the Western tradition (in our case, the study of Shingon Buddhism) can give us a new perspective on issues within our own religious heritage. In this regard, philosophers of religion would profit from more direct dialogue with historians of religion and less with those theologians who wish to rehash the traditional problems from the Judeo-Christian tradition (proofs for the existence of God, the problem of theodicy, the tension between divine omniscience and human free will, and so forth). Such comparative and cross-disciplinary interaction would enhance our philosophical understanding of religious praxis and of the two reflective responses to it—metaphysics and metapraxis.

Notes

1. Raymond E. Brown (ed.). *The Anchor Bible: The Gospel According to John.* (New York: Doubleday, 1984), 1018.

2. The Vulgate, however, even denies the sense of "wind" in this sentence, translating *pneuma* as *spiritus,* "spirit" or "breath," rather than as *ventus,* "wind."

3. Clinton Morrison. *An Analytical Concordance to the Revised Standard Version of the New Testament.* (Philadelphia: Westminster Press, 1979), 736.

4. In the article on spirit in Johannes B. Bauer (ed.). *Encyclopedia of Biblical Theology.* (New York: Crossroad Publishing Company, 1981), 872–73.

5. Karl Rahner (ed.). *Encyclopedia of Theology: The Concise Sacrementum Mundi.* (New York: Seabury Press, 1975), 1619.

6. Puntel does not mention this point, but it should be noted that although the Latin word *spiritus* can mean "breath" as well as "spirit," Thomas Aquinas generally wants to distinguish the two senses. For example, he writes in the *Summa Theologica* (Part I, Question 41, Article 4, Reply to Objection 4)

> The other passages quoted [in the objections] do not refer to the Holy Spirit, but to the created spirit (*spiritus creatus*), sometimes called wind (*ventus*), sometimes air (*aer*), sometimes the human breath (*flatus hominis*), and also sometimes soul (*animus*) or any other invisible substance (*substantia invisibilis*).

It is clear from this passage that Thomas recognizes the polysemic character of the word *spiritus,* but he is primarily interested only in its sense of "spirit" in relation to the "Holy Spirit."

7. The Anchor Bible, op. cit., 1023.

8. On the hesychastic tradition of the Jesus prayer and the prayer of the heart, see George A. Maloney's *Prayer of the Heart* (Notre Dame, Ind.: Ave Maria Press,

1981) and Jean Gouillard's *Petite Philocalie de la Prière du coeur* (Paris: Documents Spirituels, vol. 5, 1953). For a brief selection of traditional writings on these prayers in the orthodox tradition, see also Chariton of Valamo's *The Art of Prayer: An Orthodox Anthology,* trans. E. Kadloubovbsky and E. M. Palmer (Boston: Faber and Faber, 1966), 75–123. Those selections are, in turn, mainly derived from the Russian orthodox anthology, *The Philokalia.* The first three of the projected five volumes have been translated into English: St. Nikodimos of the Holy Mountain and St. Makarios of Corinth (compilers). *The Philokalia: The Complete Text,* trans. G. E. H. Palmer, Philip Sherrard, and Kallistos Ware (Boston: Faber and Faber, 1979—)

9.   For a brief discussion of the role of breathing in religious ritual from the standpoint of the history of religions, see the article on "Breath and Breathing" by Ellison Banks Findly in Mircea Eliade (ed.), *The Encyclopedia of Religion* (New York: Macmillan, 1987), 2:302–8. After tracing the philosophical views of breath in various traditions, he examines the religious praxes in Hindu yoga, Buddhist meditation, Taoist yoga, Islamic prayer, and Christian prayer (where he discusses the hesychastic tradition).

10.   The theologian Dietmar Mieth has used the term "meta-practice" in a related way. Mieth sees praxis itself as being an inherently reflective act. In his article "What is Experience?," [*Concilium* 14 (1978)], he argues:

> it is through practice that the insight gained [in a "formative experience"] acquires a dimension of distance from the action and the effect produced by it. This dimension cannot exist without practice, because it is determined by the nature of cross-reference, while at the same time exceeding what can be achieved by practice. This dimension, without which practice is reduced to mere pragmatism, we call 'meta-practice.' (page 49)

Although Mieth's use of the term "meta-practice" is consonant with my metapraxis, my term has a more specialized meaning in denoting reflection about, as well as his sense of reflection arising out of, religious praxis.

11.   In the preface to his book, *Praxis and Action: Contemporary Philosophies of Human Activity* (Philadelphia: University of Pennsylvania Press, 1971), Richard J. Bernstein gives a pithy and insightful discussion of the term "praxis" and why he wishes to distinguish it from the ordinary senses of "action" (and, I would add, "practice"). On page xi, he points out that Marx was the first of the left Hegelians "to develop a thorough, systematic and comprehensive *theory of praxis,"* an evaluation with which I agree. Marx's theory of praxis, as described by Bernstein and others, is one of paradigms I have in mind in distinguishing a theory of praxis from a metapraxis. More recent theories of praxis would include, for

example, the interpretation developed in Pierre Bourdieu's *Outline of a Theory of Practice* (New York: Cambridge University Press, 1977).

12.   For a related example of translation as transformation, see William C. Placher's discussion of the difference between the Greek senses of *hypostasis* and the Latin senses of *persona* as one basis for the disagreements about Trinitarian issues between the Eastern and Western churches: *A History of Christian Theology* (Louisville, Ky.: Westminster Press, 1983), 79ff.

13.   Other typical quotations from this section of the *Phaedo* assure us that Plato is unequivocal on this point.

> When the soul tries to investigate anything with the help of the body, it is obviously led astray. (65B)

> Then here too—in despising the body and avoiding it, and endeavoring to become independent—the philosopher's soul is ahead of all the rest. (65C–D)

The translations are by Edith Hamilton and Huntington Cairns in *The Collected Works of Plato* (New York: Pantheon, 1963), 47–48.

14.   Translation from Aquinas's *Summa Theologica* by Fathers of the English Dominican Province (New York: Benzinger Brothers, 1948), 3:2875–76.

15.   On the leavening controversy, see, for example, Harry J. Magoulias's *Byzantine Christianity* (Detroit: Wayne State University Press, 1982), 112–16; and John Meyendorff's *The Orthodox Church* (New York: Pantheon, 1962), 54–57.

16.   "Kōbō Daishi and Karl Rahner: The Ground of Spirituality" in Goenki kinen shuppan hensan iinkai (eds.), *Kobo Daishi to gendai* (Tokyo: Chikuma shobo, 1984). ("Kōbō Daishi" is the posthumous honorific title conferred on Kūkai by imperial edict.)

17.   These are condensed from the criteria presented in the essay "Anonymous Christians" found in Karl Rahner's *Theological Investigations,* trans. Karl-H. and Boniface Kruger (New York: Crossroad Publishing Company, 1982), 390–98; see especially pp. 391–95.

18.   For a provocative philosophy of the body posed within the context of Eastern spirituality, see YUASA Yasuo's *The Body: Toward an Eastern Mind-body Theory,* ed. T. P. Kasulis, trans. NAGATOMO Shigenori and T. P. Kasulis (Albany, N.Y.: State University of New York Press, 1987).

References

Bernstein, Richard J.
1971 *Praxis and Action: Contemporary Philosophies of Human Activity*. Philadelphia: University of Pennsylvania Press.

Bourdieu, Pierre.
1977 *Outline of a Theory of Practice*. New York: Cambridge University Press.

Brown, Raymond E.
1984 *The Anchor Bible. The Gospel According to John (xiii-xxi)*. New York: Doubleday.

Chariton of Valamas.
1966 *The Art of Prayer: An Orthodox Anthology*. Translated by E. Kadloubovbsky and E. M. Palmer. Boston: Faber and Faber.

Findly, Ellison Banks.
1987 "Breath and Breathing. In *Encyclopedia of Religion,* volume 2, 302–8. Edited by Mircea Eliade. New York: Macmillan.

Gouillard, Jean.
1953 *Petite Philocalie de la Prière du coeur*. In *Documents Spirituels,* Volume 5. Paris.

Kasulis, Thomas P.
1984. "Kōbō Daishi and Karl Rahner: The Ground of Spirituality." In *Kōbō daishi to gendai* [Kōbō Daishi today], 57–74. Edited by *Goenki kinen shuppan hensan iinkai*. Tokyo: Chikuma shobō.

———.
1990 "Kūkai (774–835): Philosophizing in the Archaic." In *Myth and Philosophy,* 131–50. Edited by Frank Reynolds and David Tracy. Albany, N.Y.: State University of New York Press.

Koch, Robert.
1981 "Spirit." In *Encyclopedia of Biblical Theology,* 872–73. Edited by Johannes B. Bauer. New York: Crossroad Publishing Company.

Kūkai.
1983–85 *Kōbō Daishi Kūkai Zenshū* [Complete works of Kōbō Daishi Kūkai], 8 volumes. Tokyo: Chikuma shobō.

Magoulias, Henry J.
1982 *Byzantine Christianity*. Detroit: Wayne State University Press.

Maloney, George A.
1981 *Prayer of the Heart*. Notre Dame, Ind.: Ave Maria Press.

Meyendorff, John.
1962 *The Orthodox Church*. New York: Pantheon Books.

Mieth, Dietmar.
1978 "What is Experience?" In *Concilium* 14.

Morrison, Clinton.
1979 *An Analytical Concordance to the Revised Standard Version of the New Testament*. Philadelphia: Westminster Press.

St. Nikodimos of the Holy Mountain and St. Markarios of Corinth
1979 *The Philokalia: The Complete Text*. Translated and edited by G. E. H. Palmer, Philip Sherrard, and Kallistos Ware. Boston: Faber and Faber.

Otto, Rudolf.
1950, second edition. *Idea of the Holy*. Oxford: Oxford University Press.

Placher, William C.
1983 *A History of Christian Theology*. Louisville, Ky.: Westminster Press.

Plato.
1963 *The Collected Works of Plato*. Edited and translated by Edith Hamilton and Huntington Cairns. New York: Pantheon Books.

Puntel, Lourencina B.
1975 "Spirit" In *Encyclopedia of Theology: The Concise Sacramentum Mundi, 1619–23*. Edited by Karl Rahner. New York: Seabury Press.

Rahner, Karl.
1982 "Anonymous Christians." In *Theological Investigations,* 6:390–98. Translated by Karl-H. and Boniface Kruger. New York: Crossroad Publishing Company.

Sudbrack, Josef.
1975 "Spirituality." In *Encyclopedia of Theology: The Concise Sacramentum Mundi*, 1623–29. Edited by Karl Rahner. New York: Seabury Press.

Thomas Aquinas.
   1948 *Summa Theologica*. Translated by Fathers of the English Dominican Province. New York: Benzinger Brothers.
Yuasa Yasuo.
   1987 *The Body: Toward an Eastern Mind-body Theory*. Edited by
   T. P. Kasulis. Translated by Nagatomo Shigenori and T. P. Kasulis.
   Albany, N.Y.: State University of New York Press.

Chapter 7

Xunzi and Durkheim as Theorists of Ritual Practice

Robert F. Campany

Introduction

It is no longer possible for Western academicians to presume that the other communities we study lack analogues to ourselves or to our ways of studying them. Until quite recently, our discourse on other cultures and religions was premised—almost totally unconsciously—on at least one fundamental difference between "us" and "them": we had the theory, while what they could provide amounted only to "raw" data; we theorized about their practices; we philosophized, they acted. A growing and increasingly sophisticated body of work has begun to deconstruct this notion as well as to imagine what our study of religions will look like in its absence. We are beginning both to recognize something analogous to our theories and philosophical discourses among the others we theorize about and to view our own theoretical and philosophical discourses as modes of cultural practice that might repay comparative study.

    This chapter is intended as a small contribution toward that effort. I want to consider *theory about ritual practice,* or what might be called the philosophy of ritual, as itself a form of cultural practice; for this is an area in which the difference between "us" and "them" has been particularly clearly linked to the difference between "thought" and "practice."[1] To study ritual theory as a mode of practice is to "look [in some detail] at what we [and others] *do* when we theorize" about ritual. It is to become aware of the range of purposes served by ritual theory.[2] And, for the historian of religions, whose practice is always inherently comparative, it is to become aware of ritual theory as the locus of a *human* problem—not simply a modern Western problem—by searching for analogous practices across cultural, religious, and spatiotemporal boundaries.

The theorist of ritual to whom I will devote most of my attention here is the Chinese author Xun Kuang or Xunzi ("Master Xun"), whose name adorns the collectively authored text produced by a school of Ruist (or "Confucian") thinkers in the state of Qi sometime during the third century B.C.E.[3] Near the end, I will briefly sketch a few analogies with the work of Emile Durkheim (1858–1917), who, more than two millennia later and a world away, helped to lay the foundations for much of the subsequent comparative study of religions, and whose work continues to be an important part of its canon. In Xunzi and Durkheim we have two thinkers widely disparate in time, space, and culture who demarcated a certain realm of human practice as particularly important and problematic, who thought it possible and indeed necessary to "theorize" about that realm of practice, and who, as we will see, in some respects theorized about it in similar ways and for similar purposes. The point of this chapter is, first, to highlight certain features of Xunzi's ritual theory by comparison with a theory most readers of this volume are probably more familiar with; second, to reinforce by means of the comparison the claim that Xunzi's theory of ritual is sophisticated and deserves to be taken as seriously as that of a figure such as Durkheim; and finally, perhaps to cast a ray of new light upon aspects of Durkheim's ritual theory that appear particularly salient when compared with Xunzi's theory.[4]

The questions that have shaped my reading of each of these figures are three: (1) What does each conceive a "theory" of ritual to be, and why does each think it necessary to construct a theory of ritual? (2) What specific shape does the theory take? In other words, what strategies does each writer use to describe, interpret, and explain ritual practice? (3) In the service of what larger social, moral, and religious aims does each construct a theory of ritual?

My answers to these questions have helped me to wrestle with a larger problem that arises from the linked dichotomies of us/them (or outsider/insider) and theory/practice. The problem is this: if we assume, as I think we must, that all practitioners of rituals have some self-understanding of why they do what they do and could offer some coherent account of what their practice "is" or "accomplishes" or "means," then how does a "theorist" of ritual differ from a "practitioner" of ritual—or is there a difference?[5] To put it another way: if we reject the notion, crudely put, that we as academic outsiders have a monopoly on thought about action, a monopoly we exercise as we think about others' action (where the "other" is virtually *defined* as one who acts, in contrast to the academic self, one who thinks), and if we replace it with the twin notions that all thought is already a species of action and that all actors already exercise thought about their action (or are "metapractitioners"), are there not still different—*practically* different—modes of thinking about action that might roughly be distinguished as "theoretical" versus "practical"? If so, what precisely is the difference?

Let us begin with Xunzi.

Xunzi's Ritual "Theory": What and Why?

In what sense does Xunzi offer a "theory" of ritual? Why does he consider it necessary to theorize about ritual at all?

I begin by noting some simple facts. From the total spectrum of human action, Xunzi isolates a particular sphere with its own distinctive form and coherence. In assigning that sphere a name—*li,* a term translatable both as a specific body of rites ("the" rites) familiar to Xunzi and his audience and as something like "ritual" in the generic sense—he already marks it off as somehow distinct from other sorts of activity. And in writing a treatise about it—*Li lun,* "A Discourse on Rites"—he already suggests that the rites are a sphere of activity that have become peculiarly problematic or opaque, requiring an effort of interpretation or explanation. These facts already point toward what constructing a "discourse" (*lun*) on ritual might have meant for Xunzi.

Consider further the following. Knowing that Xunzi belonged to the Ruist school, and that he looked upon the skillful performance of rites as an extremely valuable activity, we can assume that he, like most of his social class and orientation, participated in the rites he describes. Nevertheless, in writing a treatise on the rites—a treatise that, as we will see, goes far beyond merely describing performance, and that is in no sense a ritual manual or set of instructions for performance—Xunzi adopted a stance toward rites quite different from that of a participant in them. In fact, in doing so he engaged in a discourse that presumed a kind of cognitive distance from its object. By writing about ritual in the ways he did, he removed himself from the framework of ritual and placed its moments and gestures within an extra-ritual framework of his own devising. This remains true no matter how closely he thought his account of the rites matched their "real" meaning and purpose, and it remains true even if he valued ritual performance itself over mere writing (and reading) about ritual as a vehicle of culture. The point is that, in considering it possible and necessary to give a written account of ritual, he had already distanced himself from the arena of ritual no matter how sympathetic he was to its distinctive merits. He had become a spectator, which is exactly what a "theorist" is, etymologically speaking.[6]

Xunzi is no more explicit than some modern Western writers on what exactly he sees himself doing in his account of ritual, or why he is doing it. The best way to guess at his self-perception is to examine what he in fact does in his treatise, a task to which I will turn shortly. But embedded in his language we find a few subtle hints of Xunzi's stance toward his object and his task. At one point, writing of the need for personal examples when learning, he remarks that "rites and music provide models (*fa*) but no explanations (*shuo*)"; the implication seems to be that these performative genres—to each of which Xunzi devotes a chapter—are not immediately intelligible to the novice and require oral or written interpretation. We might speculate that Xunzi conceives of the *books* he goes on to cite as conversely providing "explanations" without "models," and thus find here a prototheory of the relation between written and performative genres; but Xunzi himself does not say this.[7] At another point he speaks in the first person of "being present as an observer at the community libation ceremony" and drawing conclusions from that experience about the way a true king should govern through ritual.[8]

In setting out to "explain" (*shuo*) or "discuss" (*lun*) ritual, as I said above, Xunzi suggests that the rites were the locus of a particular problem, that in his time they *needed* explanation or discussion, for as Charles Taylor has observed, "People reach for theories in order to make sense of a . . . universe which is full of conflict and rival interpretations, and which moreover everyone agrees is partly opaque."[9] Taylor's phrases aptly characterize the state of the "universe" of ritual in third century B.C.E. China. Consider for a moment the options on the table at that time.

Roughly three centuries before, Confucius had initiated a revolutionary understanding of the ancient rites of the Zhou dynasty as a medium for the cultivation of one's inner dispositions and for the perfect expression of one's humanity. He had declared that "one who knows the 'explanation' (*shuo*) of the [royal] sacrifice to the highest ancestor" would be able to govern the world "as easily as if holding it in his palm";[10] and he had set the "explanation" of rites on a new footing by removing it from a "theological" ground, on which an account would be given of how the rites effected proper relations with ancestral spirits and with heaven and earth, to what I would call a "performative" ground: "Sacrifice to the spirits *as if* the spirits were present."[11] On this new demythologized ground, this ground of "as if" or "necessary fiction,"[12] "explanations" of rites now took the form of elucidations of the ways in which their performance expressed emotions or embodied moral principles.

Mencius had taken the new Ruist understanding of the rites one step further in this "performative" direction by grounding *li* as a disposition in the very nature of the self. For him, *li* was a realm of action generated by one of the four "germs" or "sources" (*duan*) of morality innate in human nature. Ritual—or more accurately, the attitudes of respect and modesty that find expression in ritual—well up spontaneously from the self unless obstructed.[13] Xunzi attacked this view—explicitly naming its proponent—in his famous chapter, "Human Nature is Evil," in part because it undercut what he saw as the compelling need for rites as the basis of human cultivation and social order.[14] One of Xunzi's opponents on the battlefield of rites, then, was the Ruist wing that portrayed rites as a natural, effortless flowing out from the self of certain of its innate dispositions.

Other schools had produced different sorts of challenges. Mozi and his followers decried many rites—especially the Ruist mourning ceremonies—as wasteful consumption of precious material resources; on the other hand, they advocated the old "theological" understanding of the rites, seeing them as expressions of gratitude and efforts to please the spirits, although belief in spirits was in turn advocated on purely pragmatic grounds.[15] The Taoists agreed with the position adopted by Xunzi (against Mencius) that the rites are a human artifice, the result of deliberate activity (*wei*), but they differed from him in seeing such artifice as an undesirable activity, a falsification of and disastrous departure from primordial simplicity and nondifferentiation.[16] The Legalists, who played the variant traditionalisms of the Confucians and the Mohists off against one another to good effect, proposed to replace the rites with a "behaviorist" system of rewards and punishments.[17] Finally, a crucial adversary for our purposes was a view that has been called "divinistic" or "shamanic naturalism";[18] it sought to explain the efficacy of rites by reference to either spiritual or cosmic "responses," not by reference to the human sphere. This view to some extent approximated that of the "commoners" on why rituals were performed and were efficacious. Its exponents rivaled the Ruists for imperial recognition and patronage.[19]

These competing understandings of the nature and significance of ritual are the background against which Xunzi's view of the need for and nature of a "theory" of ritual must be understood. From the above it can clearly be seen that in discussing ritual Xunzi is taking up a topic that has become a well-worn problem and a battleground on which various philosophical and religious issues were contested. To theorize about rites was therefore necessarily to take up this "transmit" of problems and to adopt a stand on some of the issues that had become attached to the interpretation of rites. We are not dealing with disinterested speculation about rites for its own sake; we are dealing with a world in which the understanding of rites has become a vehicle for debate among competing visions of how to organize a society and live one's life. It follows that the particular shape of Xunzi's theory of ritual must be understood, in part at least, as a response to the challenges posed by these other schools of interpretation. When set in its social context and viewed as a mode of practice, Xunzi's ritual theorizing, not surprisingly, comes to be seen as a vehicle of ideological contestation and moral-religious reform.

But we risk misunderstanding Xunzi if we forget that it is about *ritual* (among other things), after all, that he writes. His analysis of ritual performance cannot therefore be reduced to a mere pretext for ideological debate. The reason why the rites had become such fertile ground for disagreement, I suspect, is that their origin and purpose had to some extent been forgotten. They constituted so many "survivals" of an archaic, feudal world long since past. New life forms demanded reevaluation of an area of life now cut free from its old social and ideological moorings: should the rites be preserved, and if so, how could they now be understood?[20] Rites perhaps continued to provide pattern and order to the lives of at least some among the literate segments of Chinese society (although there is evidence that even here they were being departed from), but their rationale had become obscure. Since they could no longer be adequately understood from within the framework of the rites themselves, external (even if ritually derived) principles of explanation had to be brought to bear—a process initiated by Confucius and now to be continued (though in a new way) by Xunzi. The rites' opacity had made a *theory* about them both necessary and possible, and constructing a "theory" about them meant giving an account of them from some point of view other than themselves, a stance already adumbrated in the very act of *writing a treatise*. Ritual theory in China, in this sense, was born at the moment when the rites became a cognitive and religious *problem*— when they were something that demanded explanation instead of being the basis upon which other realms of activity were explained.

What shape, then, did Xunzi's theory of ritual take?

Xunzi's Strategies for the Description, Interpretation, and Explanation of Ritual

My goal here is not to summarize Xunzi's discourse on ritual but rather to characterize certain strategies used by Xunzi in his account, making explicit what are usually implicit moves made by him. For convenience I divide these strategies into descriptive, interpretive, and explanatory types, although I am aware that these categories often overlap, that (for instance) there is no "pure" description.

Description as Analysis

How does Xunzi describe ritual performance? He does so in a way that already presumes a spectator's distance in at least two senses: he never gives the sort of instructions that would be necessary to perform the ritual or participate in it, and with rare exceptions, he does not give a flowing narrative of the events of ritual performance from beginning to end, choosing instead to *analyze* the ritual process into discrete parts.

In his descriptive analysis of ritual, Xunzi uses an array of what we might call "registers"—schematic devices in terms of which he breaks ritual performance down into parts and against which he plots those parts. He "describes" ritual, in other words, by providing a succession of lists of those of its aspects that fit under certain rubrics. His analysis is fairly clearly meant to give a rationale for particular aspects of the rites.

One of Xunzi's analytical registers for the organization of information about ritual performance is the set of human sensory faculties and body parts. Asserting that rites belong to that area of human activity concerned with "nourishing" or "bringing to maturity" (*yang*), he divides certain ritual acts and implements into categories according to the aspects of the body through which they nourish human nature. Thus, sacrificial foods nourish through the mouth; the odors of plants used during rites, through the nose; ornamentation of ritual objects, through the eye; musical instruments, through the ear; the spatial setting of ritual, through the body (13.1a–b; W89). At another point, he divides bodily modes for the expression of joy and sorrow: one's facial countenance and voice, what one eats and wears, where one dwells, are each described as markers of auspicious and inauspicious occasions (13.13a–14a; W102).

Time is another of Xunzi's analytic registers—or rather times, for Xunzi speaks of several kinds of duration. One kind is calendrical: he gives rationales for the number of days required for each of the stages of funeral ritual (13.11a; W99) as well as for the various lengths of mourning observed for those with whom one is related in different ways (13.18b–20b; W106–9).

Elsewhere, Xunzi seems more clearly to be dividing ritual duration into discrete segments and implying that each segment has (what we would call) a distinct "meaning." At one point, he tries to link different ritual acts according to the processual phase to which they belong: for instance, filling a goblet with water (an unfermented drink), laying out uncooked fish on the altar, and presenting unflavored soup, are all linked together as moments when raw food is offered;[21] other phases are those in which food or drink are not (or are only partially) consumed by the impersonator of the dead, those in which a particular ritual phase is about to begin, and those in which rough or unfinished materials are used or music is performed in a deliberately imperfect way (13.5a–6b; W93–94). Elsewhere he charts the phasal structure of "all [the] rites" (*fan li*) as beginning in "simplicity" or a state of unadornment (*zho*, early glossed as *tuo*), coming to fulfillment in "form" or "pattern" (*wen*), and ending in "joy" or "pleasure" (*le*) (13.6b; W94). He also writes of how, "in all funerary rites" (*sangli zhi fan*), successive changes in the state of the dead are embodied in ritual display (*bian er shi*): the corpse is moved ever farther away from the living (*dong er yuan*) until a phase of rest or equilibrium is obtained (*jiu er ping*) (13.12a; W99). In all of these passages Xunzi is charting the structure of ritual process: the discrete phases of one rite are classified with similar phases in other rites, a move that presumably aided understanding (although it is not clear just how), and individual ritual phases are linked with corresponding emotions or successive states of being.

Occasionally, Xunzi seems to want to correlate one analytical register with another, as if searching for ritual "principles." For example, he links the register of raw/cooked with that of temporal frequency: the greater the extent to which a food is cooked, the more frequently it is offered (13.4b–5a; W92–93). Elsewhere he links the nonconsumption of offerings by the impersonator of the dead (eating/not eating) with the completion phase of rites (incomplete/complete): when the impersonator no longer eats or drinks, invariably the rite is concluded (13.5b; W93).[22] These sorts of strategies lead us beyond Xunzi's descriptive analysis of ritual to his *interpretation* of it.

Interpretation: Decoding Ritual as Mimesis and as Expression

Symbolic Indirection

Xunzi is acutely mindful of what we might call "symbolic indirection" in ritual performance. In other words, he is concerned to show that certain ritual gestures and objects do not always "mean" what they seem to mean, that they are sometimes used in a nonapparent way to refer to something less than obvious. Ritual for Xunzi is a realm of "imitation" or "symbolization" (*xiang*). Further, while he thinks (as we will see below) that ritual performance has real, practical effects on human nature and social life, he wants to mark it off as a realm of practice distinct from other, "ordinary" forms of life by virtue, in part, of its "symbolic" or "indirect" nature.[23] His views on these topics can be seen most clearly in his analysis of funerary rites.

Xunzi gives the following principle for funerary and mourning rites: "One performs rites for the dead as though they were living, roughly imitating [or symbolically enacting, *xiang*] what one would do if they were alive while yet sending them to their final death."[24] Everything turns, then, on the tension between the ways in which one treats the living and the reality of the death of the person for whom the rites are performed. For Xunzi, funerary and mourning rites play across the contradiction and the gap between life and death: at times they seem to deny the contradiction and span the gap, while at other times they bespeak the contradiction and reveal the gap.

After this introductory passage he proceeds to analyze the symbolism of specific gestures and objects in the four basic ritual phases: preparation for burial, burial, mourning, and sacrificial offerings. Particularly in the case of the rites of preparation and burial, Xunzi's discourse takes the form of comparing the services rendered to the dead with those one would render to the living. This comparison allows him to isolate what we would call the "symbolic" quality of the ritual gestures. In preparing the corpse for burial, for instance, one washes, combs, and feeds it, here "imitating" (*xiang*) what one would for the living despite one's knowledge that the person in this case is dead. On the other hand, one seals off its orifices, thus "opposing" (*fan*) what one would do for a living person. In dressing the corpse and providing it with supplies, finally, one performs acts whose subtle ambiguity bodies forth the tension between our *connection with* and *separation from* the dead. One arranges the hair but adds no pin, provides jars but puts nothing in them, presents musical instruments but does not tune them, buries a carriage but takes the horses back home. Aspects of the burial—the "forms" (*mao*) of various constructed objects—likewise "imitate" or "symbolize" aspects of the world of the living from which the dead person is now separate: the form of the grave mound imitates (or symbolizes) that of a house, coffins imitate carriages, coffin covers imitate wall hangings in a room, and the wood lining of the grave pit imitates the railing and roof of a house (14b–18a; W103–5).[25]

Throughout this treatment, the key term is *xiang*, which I have translated as "imitate" or "symbolize." It is used repeatedly as (what we would term) a "verb" to specify how objects or gestures in the sphere of death ritual refer to, are modeled on, resemble, or reenact the forms appropriate to life. Xunzi's use of this word recalls the *Yi jing (Book of Changes)* account of how the ancient sages "were able to survey all phenomena under heaven and, considering their forms and appearances, 'symbolized' (*xiang*) things and their proper attributes. These were called 'symbols' (*xiang*)."[26] These mimetic signs reproduce in writing—a medium subject to human manipulation—the structure of nature and can thus be made to disclose the hidden patterns of cosmic change. Xunzi implies something similar of death ritual: that its elements, like graphic signs, imitate life forms while operating in a realm once removed from life, a realm of action and speech which is in fact (in this case) directed toward the opposite of life.[27] Ritual forms presume and play across a gap between ordinary life and the arena of ritual performance; they also, like the written signs of the *Yi jing*, allow a manipulation of ordinary life—or at least a real effect on it—by virtue of the mimetic correspondence between ritual gestures and life forms.

Conversely, it is this correspondence which allows Xunzi to "interpret" ritual, where "interpretation" entails linking ritual events with the external "meanings" to which they refer. This can be seen most clearly in a rare passage which seems to show Xunzi envisioning a "pure performance" that does not refer to anything outside itself and that is thus, strictly speaking, uninterpretable.

> How can one know the meaning (*yi*) of the dance? I say: the eyes cannot see it, the ears cannot hear it; and yet, when all the posturings and movements, all the steps and changes of pace are ordered and none are lacking in proper restraint, when all the power of muscle and bone are brought into play, when all is matched exactly to the rhythm of the drums and bells and there is not the slightest awkwardness or discord—*there*, in all these manifold actions of lively intensity, is the "meaning" of the dance![28]

We have here the exception that proves the rule: an area of ritual practice whose "meaning" Xunzi is unable or unwilling to locate anywhere but within itself. The dance *is* its "meaning," that is, it is intrinsically meaningful; there exists no *other* register onto which one could map its gestures or in terms of which one could decode its symbols.[29] This passage is striking in its contrast to the many others in which Xunzi engages in "interpretation" and finds rites to have extrinsic meaning and function.

Expression

Xunzi also speaks of ritual as "expressing" through action states and dispositions internal to the self, although no single term in the text carries precisely the same range of connotations as our word "to express." One of the closest analogues is *jin*, "to exhaust," as in the phrase (said of the ways people should deal with their emotions through ritual) *lei zhi jin zhi* (13.14a), translated by Watson as "to express [them] completely and properly" (W102) and by Dubs as "made to fit the situation, completely expressed."[30] Other analogues include *fa*, "to issue from," "to burst out," and *xing*, "to be embodied," both of which appear in the following rationale for ritual music and dance: "Since people cannot help feeling joy, their joy must issue forth (*fa*) in the sound of the voice and be embodied (*xing*) in movement."[31]

Xunzi's notion of how ritual "expresses" inner states and dispositions is best seen in the dialectic he sets up between "emotion" or "sentiment" (*qing*) and "[ritual] form" (*wen*), each of which is ideally balanced against the other in ritual.[32] "When rites are performed at their best, emotion and form are both fully realized; next best is when emotion and form prevail by turns; last is when everything is based on emotion alone" (13.7a; W94). Elsewhere he imagines ritual "forms" to have been established as channels or outlets for human emotions that would otherwise lack proper media for expression (13.18a, W105; 13.21a, W109; 13,21b–22a, W110). In the lyrical conclusion to his chapter on rites, he even speaks of ritual as the literal *embodiment* of what would otherwise have no shape or image: "One serves the dead as though they were living, one serves the departed as though they were still present, thus giving body to that which has no shape or image. In this way are constituted the forms [of ritual]."[33]

But Xunzi's language of "embodiment" does not privilege inner emotions as the ultimate and unreachable source of ritual form. On the contrary, emotions—along with other aspects of human nature (*xing*)—are themselves subject to formation by ritual practice at the same time that they find expression in that practice. The rites constitute "models" or "molds" (*fa*) for a human nature that is pictured as naturally depraved but eminently malleable toward good.[34]

In Xunzi's chapter on "Self-Cultivation" we are told that "one who is without models (*wu fa*) is lost and without a guide"; that "ritual is the means whereby one can rectify oneself" (*zheng shen*), that "if you do unerringly as ritual prescribes, this means that your emotions have found rest in ritual (*qing an li*)"; and finally, that ritual (*li*) is itself the "model" (*fa*) one should adopt: "to reject ritual is to be without a model. . . . 'Learning' (*xue*) means learning to regard ritual as your model" (W30; 1.22a–b). So while, on one hand, ritual is pictured as channeling the expression of inner emotions into appropriate outward forms, on the other hand, it is also pictured as shaping emotions, informing by deliberate activity (*wei*) what is formless and entropic in human nature (*xing*).[35] In fact, Xunzi views human nature itself as split between innate dispositions (*xing*), on the one hand, and, on the other, dispositions instilled by conscious activity (*wei*) and directed by a mind capable either of direct-

ing desire or detaching itself from desire and becoming a "spectator."
That is, the bipartite structure of the human self mirrors the bipartite
distinction between inner, innate dispositions and the outer, learned "models" which are comprised in ritual. The structure of action is introjected
into the self.[36]

We have now left Xunzi's methods of *interpreting* ritual, however,
and have begun to approach his view of its *functions,* by means of
which he seeks to *explain* its origin, its rationale, and its peculiar power.

Explanation: The Origins and Functions of Ritual

Origins

The strategy of searching for the *origins* of something as a way of
explaining its existence and meaning is a familiar one. Xunzi's "Discourse on Ritual" opens with an account of the origins of ritual, an
imaginative reconstruction of the conditions under which ritual first arose,
not unlike the "state of nature" imagined by modern Western thinkers to
explain the social contract.

> From whence did ritual arise? I reply: People are born with desires
> (*yu*). If they are unable to get what they desire, then they cannot
> help seeking it (*qiu*) all the more. If their seeking is not regulated
> and set within prescribed boundaries (*fen jie*), they will unavoidably
> contend with each other. Contending, they will grow disorderly;
> disorderly, they will wear themselves out. The ancient kings hated
> such disorder, so they established ritual principles (*li yi*) in order to
> contain (*fen*) it by training people's desires and providing that which
> they sought. By these means they ensured that desire did not ex-
> haust the goods desired and that goods did not fall short of what
> was desired. By thus holding these two [goods and desires] in bal-
> ance, each was allowed to flourish. This is how ritual arose (13.1a;
> cf. W89).

What is significant about this account is that, while it locates the origins
of ritual in the distant past with the "ancient kings"—who were the subject of a fair amount of mythologizing on the part of other writers before
and after Xunzi—it *explains* ritual's *rationale* by seeking to lay out general principles of human nature and behavior. It grounds ritual's origin,
and hence its authority, not so much in the greatness and wisdom of its
ancient inventors as in its efficacy for overcoming a fundamental obstacle
to human flourishing anywhere and any time.[37] Ritual is that area of life
that allows the expression of emotion (*qing*) and the fulfillment of human nature (*xing*) while at the same time enabling human community to
exist by mitigating the innate, disorderly tendencies of human nature.

Here, too, ritual involves a kind of indirection, only this time "functional" rather than "symbolic"; by obeying the dictates of ritual, which constrain one to act in a way one might not act by nature, one would appear to forfeit the objects of one's desires, because unlike ordinary life ritual is not about the direct pursuit of desires. But in fact it is only through the indirection of ritual that one's desires can be satisfied; if one attempts to satisfy them directly, one will fail (see 13.2b–3a; W90–91).

Xunzi gives another sort of explanation of the origins of ritual when he speaks of its "bases" (*ben*). At one point he says that "ritual has three bases: heaven and earth (*tiandi*), one's ancestors (*xianzu*), and one's lords and masters (*junshi*)" (13.3a–b; W91). This tripartite division sums up the categories of beings for whom one made offerings or performed rites in Xunzi's day. Xunzi seems to suggest that ritual performance is grounded in human relations with these types of beings; those relations are the context in which ritual becomes a meaningful activity.

In accounting for ritual's origins and rationale, then, Xunzi offers a view of what ritual *does:* in other words, he speaks of its functions.

Functions

Xunzi characterizes the functions of ritual with a rich array of metaphorical images. He first gives a "cosmic" characterization in which all natural processes, from the movements of heavenly bodies to the activities of human beings, are said to achieve their proper order through rites: "it is through ritual that the sun and moon shine, the four seasons proceed in order, the stars and constellations march, the rivers flow," and so on.[38] He next gives a "cultural" or "social" characterization in which it is through rites that human communal life reaches perfect form and apparent opposites (high and low, root and branch, beginning and end) are unified. Then comes a series of "directional" metaphors: ritual provides human life with requisite standards of measurement and degrees. To ignore these is to be "without direction" (*wufang*), while to abide by them is to "possess direction" or to be "oriented" (*youfang*); the sage is one who "possesses direction." Finally Xunzi describes the functions of ritual by resort to "habitative" metaphors: the rites are "the constant habitat and dwelling of the gentleman" because they allow a balance between "form and principle" (*wenli*), on the one hand, and "emotion and [practical] use" (*qingyong*) on the other. They constitute, in other words, the *world* of the gentleman, the environment in which he is comfortable, performs at his best, and achieves the full stature of humanity (13.8a–b; W94–96).[39]

These images do not exhaust Xunzi's views on the functions of ritual, however. We have already seen how, from the point of view of the individual participant, ritual functions as a vehicle not only for the expression but also for the transformation of emotions (which Xunzi conceives of as dispositions).[40] Concerning funeral rites, for instance, Xunzi says that they serve to channel disgust and loathing of the corpse—emotions that are natural but inappropriate—into a performance characterized by reverence (*jing*), which is what differentiates our approach to death from that of beasts (13.12a; W100).

Furthermore, from the point of view of the human community, ritual functions to reinforce social hierarchy and maintain social order. In the first place, the rites themselves encode distinctions (*bie* or *bian*) between hierarchical levels. For instance, the suburban sacrifice to heaven may be performed by the emporor (Son of Heaven) alone; altars of the soil (*she*) may not be established by anyone lower than a feudal lord (*zhuhou*). In this way "the rites distinguish [and make clear that] the exalted ritually serve the exalted and the humble serve the humble, that great corresponds to great and small to small" (13.4a; W91). Elsewhere we read that the three-year mourning period serves "to distinguish the ritual duties owed to near versus distant kin, to the eminent versus the humble" (13.18a; W105). The rites, then, are a domain given over to the marking of distinctions—not only, as we have seen, distinctions between different states and phases of the process of life (life/death, auspicious/inauspicious, joy/sorrow), but also distinctions between different social roles and hierarchical levels (ruler/noble/commoner, close/distant kin).

For Xunzi, ritual functions to preserve hierarchical social *distinctions* at the same time that it creates and maintains social *harmony*. A society must have status divisions in order to be unified and harmonious. The way in which Xunzi thinks ritual accomplishes this emerges quite clearly in his detailed analysis of the community libation ceremony (*xiang*).[41] As he moves through a rather lengthy narrative account of the gestures comprised in this ritual, he occasionally pauses to observe how they embody a particular principle of social distinction. For example:

> The host goes in person to fetch the guest of honor and his attendants, while the other guests [by contrast] come of their own accord. . . . This makes clear the principle of distinction between eminent and humble (14.5a; W118).

In his analysis of the *xiang* ceremony, then, Xunzi seeks to show how it functions to display the principles on which the community is built as well as to constitute the community as a cohesive group.[42]

Having discussed the ways in which Xunzi describes, interprets, and explains the origins and functions of ritual, we are now in a position to step back from these particular strategies and reflect on the larger aims of his theoretical project.

The Aims of Xunzi's Ritual Theory

As stated earlier, Xunzi's theory of ritual is not just a theory of ritual. To construct a theory of ritual in his day was to engage in a religious and ideological debate with others who had constructed other theories; it was to advance certain moral and religious aims. What Xunzi's own aims were can best be seen by considering the theories to which he fashioned an alternative, and how he responds to those theories in his text. Having briefly characterized above several of the competing academic theories of ritual current in his time, I will focus now on one particular competing view of ritual that apparently held sway among most of the common people as well as among a group of elite academicians who (to some extent at least) represented them.

I begin with the following passage, which comes near the end of Xunzi's "Discourse on Ritual."

> Only a sage can fully understand ritual. The sage has a clear under-standing of it, the gentleman finds comfort in practicing it, the offi-cial takes it as something to be preserved, and the common people accept it as custom. To the gentleman it is the way of being human (*ren dao*); to the common people it is a matter of serving spirits (*gui shi*) (13.21b; W110).

This utterance is double-edged. On the one hand, it introduces a hierar-chy of different ways of understanding and embracing the nature and significance of ritual performance. To one who understands its true na-ture it is seen for what it really is, "the way of being human." This is the view of ritual that Xunzi has been developing and would like his readers to accept. To see ritual as "the way of being human" is to see it as a symbolically and functionally "indirect" activity that is not, contrary to appearances, directed at the gods and ancestral spirits (save insofar as these are themselves symbolic entities) but at the human community and the human self. By contrast, to those who do not understand its true nature—the "hundred surnames," who are also lower on the status scale, whose entire social role is quite different—it is "a matter of serving spir-its." This is one of the understandings of ritual Xunzi has been arguing against and to which he offers his own view as an alternative.[43]

Yet, on the other hand, each of these ways of participating in ritual—from understanding it to merely accepting it as custom, from seeing it as "the way of being human" to taking it as "a matter of serving spirits"—has a niche in what is an inclusive hierarchy of levels of participation. Ritual is a domain in which all participate (though in different ways corresponding to different social levels); it is a body of *practice* that members of all social levels share. It is only in their respective *under-standings* of those practices that they differ. That difference is a crucial one for Xunzi, but at the same time, he seems to admit that his theory is not for everyone, that there will always be some who view ritual in ways he takes to be not so much false as limited, partial, or less than ultimate.

We have seen how Xunzi constructs a theory of ritual—involving a particular way of describing it, an account of its symbolism, and an explanation of it based on its origins and functions—in order to open up a ground from which ritual could be viewed as a "way of being human." In this respect his theory is aimed at countering the naive view of ritual as a matter of serving the gods and spirits. In a similar vein, he argues elsewhere that prayers for rain are best viewed in the way the gentleman views them, as "ritual forms" (*wen*), and not as the common people view them, as "[concerned with] spirits" (*shen*) (11.18b; W85); that visions of ghosts are due to overexcitement and not to real spectral appearances (W135), and so on.[44] Put simply, he is attempting to shift the meaning of ritual from the divine to the human sphere.

The difficulty facing him in this task is that, if taken "literally" or "at face value," rites seem to be about nothing if not the service of gods and spirits. Victims are immolated; food is laid on altars; divine beings are invited to eat; ancestral spirits are impersonated by a ritual performer who eats, drinks, and converses with the living participants; grave goods are buried with corpses for their use in the other world; ancestors' names are inscribed on tablets. Then there is the fact, to which Xunzi himself attests, that most ordinary people in his day—most ritual participants— view the rites as a way of serving spirits. If the rites do not really serve spiritual beings, then whom or what *do* they serve? If these various gestures do not accomplish what they seem to, then what *do* they accomplish? And why, if the rites cannot be taken "literally," do they take the "divinistic" forms that they do, and why do so many participants view them literally?

We have already seen Xunzi's answers to the first two of these questions: ritual serves to train human desires, to express human emotions, to give structure and coherence to human society, to provide a total cultural habitat in which virtue and wisdom can flourish. But I do not think he provides answers to the last two questions. Xunzi does not tell us, that is, why rites that really serve humanity appear to serve spirits, nor does he explain why so many have misunderstood their real nature and function. He creates a notion of what I have called the "indirection" of ritual gestures and functions as a way of interpreting and explaining these, but he fails to explain why the indirection was necessary in the first place.

Now the most important difference between what we might call the "popular" or "received" account of ritual's nature and function, on the one hand, and Xunzi's account, on the other, is this: Xunzi's account seeks to shift the discourse on ritual from the ritual sphere to another sphere. Bypassing the apparent or surface-level referents of ritual acts, he seeks to put ritual on a different footing. Another way of saying this is that he gives an account of ritual from a point of view outside ritual.

In this respect, his discourse on ritual resembles that offered by other contemporary schools—Taoist, Mohist, Legalist, Mencian, Logicist, and others. Members of each of these other schools shared with Xunzi the quest to place ritual on some nonritual footing, to understand it not by reference to the world defined by its own internal logic but by reference to some other ground of knowledge or value they took as more fundamental. They differed over the ground on which ritual was to be set: was it to be natural processes, social utility, rewards and punishments, a self innately disposed toward good, linguistic analysis, or as Xunzi thought, a self innately disposed toward selfish action but capable through training of other-regarding action? For Xunzi, none of the other schools offered a satisfactory account of what ritual was, how it worked, what it accomplished, and most importantly, *why it was worth preserving.*[45]

Xunzi's key purpose in theorizing about ritual is to retrieve and preserve ritual as the center of human life, the locus of value and beauty. None of the other schools provided sufficient justification for the continued performance and preservation of ritual. The received or popular view of ritual, on the other hand, no longer sufficed to justify its practice, for it was being undermined by the various school theories each of which took ritual as secondary and other areas of life (or aspects of the self) as fundamental. Ritual had become opaque, the locus of a problem; it could no longer be defended from within, or justified internally in terms, as it were, of ritual itself. Paradoxically, then, in order to place ritual on a more secure footing, Xunzi had to resort to explaining it in nonritual terms; by adopting a stance outside of ritual he sought to justify ritual. He therefore adamantly maintains the *real function and effect* of ritual performance, but at the same time, he maintains that ritual performs functions and generates effects *indirectly,* not in the way that would be apparent from a point of view located inside the world of ritual. Ritual's demonstrated indirection saves it from agnostic or sceptical attack.

We are now in a position to return to one of the big questions mentioned at the outset as having generated this paper: given the breakdown of the old dichotomy between thought and action, is there any remaining way in which a theorist of ritual practice differs—in terms of practice—from a ritual participant? There is. Everyone involved in ritual performance, at least in principle (if often not in practice), has an account to offer of why they do what they do, what it means, what their practice essentially is; so far, the practitioner and the theorist are indistinguishable. The real difference is not one between those who think and those who act. Nor is it one between a discrete group of participants and a discrete group of observers: Xunzi himself is probably an example of a person who was a "participant" and a "theorist" by turns. The essential difference is one between two *points of view* or roles, even if these are occupied at different moments by the same person. It is a difference between two ways of thinking about ritual practice (not one between thought and nonthought).

Quite simply, *theoretical* thinking about ritual practice is thinking from the point of view of a spectator, and this entails giving an account of ritual from a point of view outside ritual, using a language and a framework of understanding that are not derived from the ritual world but in terms of which that world is nevertheless described. "Theories" of ritual may take many forms, but they will all shift the discourse on ritual to some nonritual ground. Nontheoretical statements about ritual—statements made from within the realm of ritual—will take ritual itself as their point of departure; they will often use ritual itself as the reference point for explaining or describing other areas of life. For the theorist, ritual can no longer be the place from which to start, for *it* has become *the problem;* recourse must be had to some more secure foundation.

If ritual theory is an account of ritual from some point of view outside ritual, it is never a point of view outside *practice.* Theorizing about ritual is no less a mode of practice for being "theoretical": it is a project that takes on a particular shape, adopts a certain set of strategies, and perhaps most importantly, is undertaken for definite reasons. These reasons usually have to do with changing the way people live their lives—often even changing the way they participate in ritual. Ritual theory, in other words, often seeks to alter ritual practice as a social reality. This was certainly true of Xunzi and his contemporaries: those for whom they wrote about ritual were themselves participants in ritual. Paradoxically, Xunzi's aim in gaining an extra-ritual perspective on ritual was to enable his readers to perform and appreciate ritual in a new and better way.

Durkheim as Ritual Theorist: A Brief Analogical Exercise

If ritual is a ubiquitous human activity, ritual theory in the sense I have specified is hardly less so: wherever ritual has become a cognitive, moral, or religious problem, ritual theory will not have been far behind. We need more studies of premodern and non-Western ritual theory, and we need to know more about how modern Western theorists compare with their counterparts in other cultures and eras.[46] The following brief remarks are offered in that spirit, as a rough sketch for future work; space does not permit anything approaching a thorough comparison of Durkheim and Xunzi here.

In Durkheim we have a twentieth-century European who not only theorizes about ritual but does so in ways often strikingly analogous to those of Xunzi. In what follows I will highlight what are to me some of the most illuminating similarities and differences.

Like Xunzi, first of all, Durkheim views ritual gestures as subject to "symbolic indirection." Rites, like other religious practices and ideas, act as "symbolic expression[s]" or "allegories" or in the role of "mythological intermediary" for "forces" that are really moral, that is, social. They therefore need to be decoded; Durkheim seeks, as he says at one point, to "disengage [moral forces] from their symbols [and] present them in their rational nakedness."[47] Ritual objects and gestures are symbols of society created by society, which, however, has long forgotten that those symbols are its own.

> Between society as it is objectively and the sacred things which express it symbolically, the distance is considerable. It has been necessary that the impressions really felt by men, which served as the original matter of this construction, should be interpreted, elaborated and transformed until they became unrecognizable.[48]

We have seen that Xunzi, who came to something like the same conclusion, never explained why the "real" meaning and function of ritual gestures should be concealed by symbolic indirection. Durkheim has an explanation, arrived at with the aid of Kant and Hegel: humanity must undergo self-alienation in order to arrive at self-knowledge; to know the self is perforce to come to terms with an "other." "Since collective sentiments can become conscious of themselves only by fixing themselves upon external objects, they have not been able to take form without adopting some of their characteristics from other things" (EF 466). This fixation of sentiments upon external objects takes place during periods of "collective effervescence," in which

> vital energies are over-excited. . . . A man does not recognize himself; he feels himself transformed and consequently he transforms the environment which surrounds him. In order to account for the very particular impressions which he receives, he attributes to the things with which he is in most direct contact properties which they have not, exceptional powers and virtues which the objects of everyday experience do not possess (EF 469).

It is society that creates the objects and categories of knowledge, that indeed creates the individual person as an entity. But here a particularly thorny problem confronts Durkheim, a problem from which Xunzi was relatively free: the dichotomy, inherited from his ancestors who discoursed on ritual, between thought and action, or belief and rite. Early on in this great decoding enterprise, he had maintained that "it is possible to define the rite only after we have defined the belief" (*EF* 51). But by the end, because of his stress on the collective as prior to the individual, he is forced to grant primacy to action—particularly ritual action—over belief or thought.[49] Rites, then, are metapractices that rejuvenate communal solidarity by recalling the primal acts and representations generated during "collective effervescence."[50] Again, although initially he says otherwise, rites for Durkheim do not simply reflect or "express" beliefs or sentiments: "The cult is not simply a system of signs by which the faith is outwardly translated; it is a collection of the means by which this is created and recreated periodically" (*EF* 464). One thinks of Xunzi's insistence that rites do not simply express inner dispositions but actively shape those dispositions.[51]

Durkheim, like Xunzi, seeks to "demythologize" ritual: by means of the notion of "symbol" and the dynamic of indirection, he criticizes the "theological" understanding of rites held by most of those who participate in them and substitutes another set of objects and forces to which ritual acts refer. And, as in Xunzi's case, those objects and forces are human, communal, and moral. It is society itself to which rites symbolically refer; it is the power of the collective upon which ritual power is based. Once again, as with Xunzi, Durkheim is concerned above all to maintain that the referents of ritual are *real* and that rites exert *real effects*. In decoding rites of sacrifice, for instance, Durkheim seeks to show that they are in fact an exchange between society and the individual, not between a god and an individual. Moreover, they effect "internal and moral regeneration": by the act of offering, persons periodically renew within themselves their social aspects, or their attachment to the collective (their "social sentiments"), which are otherwise in danger of decay (EF 384–90).

This leads us to another analogy: just as for Xunzi, for Durkheim the self is split into two parts, the religious symbols for which are body and soul: the one is "individual," is "rooted in our organisms," and tends toward selfishness, while the other is not merely "social" in disposition but is an aspect of the self that is *created and implanted* by society.[52] The condition in which the self's individual aspect dominates and runs rampant, tearing the self loose from its social and moral moorings, is anomie, which often results in suicide.[53]

The key motivation for theorizing about ritual, then, for Durkheim as for Xunzi, is *education*. People must be taught the true and "rational" essence underlying the superficially absurd and outmoded forms of ritual and belief. Ritual must be set on a new foundation, that of human society and self cultivation; the alienation that characterizes unreformed religion must be abolished. Durkheim is more sensitive than Xunzi, however, to a problem inherent in this procedure: once society and its attendant moral code are stripped of the authority formerly lent them by religious symbols, and reduced to their "rational nakedness," whence comes their authority? It is an acute problem for Durkheim, who speaks of his desire to retain morality's old "sacred" character, to enable the schoolmaster to keep his sense of mission, so that he can feel himself to be "speaking in the name of a superior reality" as in the old days (*Moral Education*, 10). The only solution he arrived at was the modern Western social theorist's old standby: the voluntary association as the new locus of social solidarity—for children, the school; for working adults, the occupational group, a form of association well suited to the modern division of labor.[54]

There are many other, perhaps less significant analogies between these two fertile thinkers: each holds out the possibility of what Durkheim calls "pure practice without theory" and what Xunzi sees exemplified in the dance, a realm of "pure" or "raw" practice that refers only to itself and cannot be decoded as ritual can;[55] each sees social solidarity as dependent on clear social divisions which are often embodied in ritual action; each stressed the different levels at which ritual may be understood, and each sought to raise the level of his audience's understanding to the point at which ritual's mask could be raised and ritual seen for what it "really is." Each, that is, engaged in ritual *theory* in the sense developed here: each described, interpreted, and explained ritual practice in nonritual terms, but for the eminently practical purpose of preserving its real and salutary social, moral, and psychological effects.

There are, however, at least two massive disanalogies. The first is that, unlike Xunzi, Durkheim felt it possible and helpful to reflect on the problem of ritual through the indirect vehicle of analyzing *other people's* rites—rites in which he never personally participated or even directly observed. His ritual theory gets refracted through what we noted at the outset to be a characteristically Western mode of encounter with "primitive" others. The second disanalogy is closely related: Xunzi wrote for a community of readers largely (if ideally) defined by its shared participation in a body of rites, whereas Durkheim wrote precisely because such a body of rites was lacking in his time and place. Too briefly put, Xunzi the premodern dealt with ritual in search of adequate theory, while Durkheim the modern dealt with theory in search of adequate ritual.

Each of these disanalogies carries implications that cannot be explored here, perhaps the most salient is the extent to which a fully nuanced comparison of theorists (at which this essay only gestures) must take careful account of the total cultural and religious contexts in which their theories take on meaning as creative responses.

Conclusion

I would like to return to the point from which I departed: the question of the extent to which "we" (by which I mean late-twentieth-century Western-trained students of comparative culture and religion) are analogous to those we study, or the extent to which our "theories" are analogous to theirs. The notion that ours is to think, while theirs is to do, is happily departed from our midst. There is no more raw action or sheer actor. "They" turn out to be just like "us." But are they really? A book such as James A. Boon's *Other Tribes, Other Scribes* points up the problem sharply: when it is found that both the anthropological and the (say) Balinese communities are "dialectical" and "reflexive" and that both use signs in the Saussurian sense of engaging in an inherently contrastive enterprise, are we not still "dialectical" and "reflexive" and "Saussurian" in a way that they are not when we write a book about them—especially a book that compares ourselves to them—and gather around a table (in Chicago, say) to talk it all over? In the very stance of "studying" others are we not already placing ourselves on a level of practice definitionally distinct from theirs? In writing a chapter, as I have here done, consisting of a theory of theories of ritual (which are already themselves "metapractices" and not merely "raw practice"), have I not thereby mock-triumphantly asserted my—and our—distance and difference from the makers of those theories, thus starting the problem all over again?

Notes

1. On the pervasiveness of the distinction between thought and action in modern Western ritual theory (the very label for which already betrays the divide), including its relationship with the ways we differentiate ourselves from those we study, see Bell, "Discourse and Dichotomies." I have also learned much from Sullivan, *Icanchu's Drum*, chapter 1. I am grateful to Professors Frank Reynolds and David Tracy and Dean Franklin Gamwell for allowing me to serve as assistant to the Religions in Culture and History project while a graduate

student at the University of Chicago. I would also like to thank the members of the sixth colloquium of the project, held in April 1989, for their thoughtful responses to an earlier draft of this chapter, and in particular Dean Judith Berling, who gave a careful critique. My only regret is that space did not permit a more thorough incorporation of some of their suggestions in the revision.

2. I here follow Charles Taylor's mandate (see *Philosophy and the Human Sciences*, 116) to study social theory as a mode of practice. See also Bellah, "The Ethical Aims of Social Inquiry."

3. I am skirting here numerous problems of authorship and attribution that are more properly the work of the specialist. In what follows, I will often refer to the person named Xunzi as though I took him to be the sole author of the text called *Xunzi*, but this is of course a matter of convenience. As an excellent synopsis of the evidence concerning the author, the text, and the Ruist school to which both belonged, I have relied on the important work of my colleague Robert Eno, *The Confucian Creation of Heaven*, especially chapter 6, which he kindly loaned me in its manuscript form. Other discussions of Xunzi in his historical and social context include Dubs, *Hsüntze, the Moulder of Ancient Confucianism*, and Fehl, *Rites and Propriety in Literature and Life*.

4. I realize that in many contexts it might be important to distinguish between a "theory" and a "philosophy" *of* something, including ritual, but for the purposes of this paper I make no such distinction. I henceforth use the term "theory" when characterizing the discourses on ritual produced by Xunzi and by Durkheim, and what I mean by that term will become clear shortly.

5. This is, of course, not to deny what anyone knows who has questioned informants concerning their ritual practices: that not every individual is able (or willing) to articulate such a self-understanding when called upon to do so; as Taylor puts it, "the understanding is [often] implicit in our ability to apply the appropriate descriptions to particular situations and actions" (*Philosophical Papers*, 2:93).

6. Such was, apparently, the earliest English sense of the word: deriving from the Latin and Greek root *theoria*, the English *theorie* meant "a looking at, a viewing"; it also designated what offered to the viewer a particularly noteworthy "sight" or "spectacle" (this from *theoros*, a spectator). (I have consulted the *Oxford English Dictionary*, s.v. "theory." A 1605 sermon by Bishop Andrewes is cited to illustrate the sense of theory as a "spectacle": "Saint Luke . . . calleth the Passion *theorian* a Theory or Sight. . . . Of our Blessed Saviour's whole life or death, there is no part but is a Theorie of it selfe, well worthie our looking on.") In classical Greece, the same word in a more specialized sense also denoted a solemn legation of festal envoys sent by a state to observe religious rites in a

220 ROBERT F. CAMPANY

neighboring state—a body of men who were apparently *sent to watch*. On this see Burkert, *Greek Religion*, 283. Compare Bourdieu, *Outline of a Theory of Practice*, 1, who, however, wants to return to the notion that there can be a "pure practice without theory."

7. For the context of this passage see Watson, *Hsün Tzu*, 20; I have consulted the annotated Chinese edition of Wang Xianqian, ed., *Xunzi jijie (Xunzi with Collected Commentaries)*, 1.9b (26). When citing Watson's translation I will henceforth abbreviate, for example, as W20. When citing the Chinese edition I will give the *juan* (chapter) number, followed by a period and the page number ("a" and "b" indicating recto and verso respectively). All translations from the Chinese are my own unless explicitly attributed to Watson, but in all cases I give the location in Watson if one exists (his is only a partial translation). I have also occasionally consulted the older translation by Dubs, *The Works of Hsuntze*.

8. See 14.5a (539): *wu guan yu xiang er zhi wangdao zhi yi yi ye;* cf. W118.

9. Taylor, *Philosophical Papers*, 2:106. Cf. 2:93: "We could say that social theory arises when we try to formulate explicitly what we are doing, describe the activity which is central to a practice, and articulate the norms which are essential to it."

10. I refer to *Analects* 3.11; cf. the translation in Lau, *Analects*, 69.

11. *Analects* 3.12: *ji shen ru shen zai;* cf. the translation in Lau, *Confucius: The Analects*, 69. Compare the things of which "the Master would not speak" mentioned in 9.1 and 7.21; most of them involve "spiritual" and "divine" matters.

12. I borrow this phrase from Yearley, "Hsün Tzu: Ritualization as Humanization," from which I have learned a great deal. I would like to thank Professor Yearley for kindly lending me his paper. I would also here like to thank Sally Gressums for lending me her unpublished paper (for which a title was lacking in my copy) on Xunzi, from which I also learned much.

13. See especially *Mencius* 2.A.6.

14. See W158ff. On Xunzi's response to Mencius, particularly as regards his alternative view of the mind and of human nature, see especially Yearley, "Hsün Tzu on the Mind," 465–68, and Lau, "Theories of Human Nature."

15. I do not pretend to have done justice to the fascinating subtleties of the Mohist position on rites and the spirits in such a short synopsis. For more thorough treatments, see Fehl, *Rites and Propriety*, 90–92; Schwartz, *The World of Thought*, 138–45 and 151–56; Mote, *Intellectual Foundations*, 87–89; and Graham, *Later Mohist Logic*, 270–72. Particularly relevant passages in the *Mozi* include sections 25, 31, and 32; see Watson, trans., *Mo Tzu*, 65ff. and 94ff.

16.   See Schwartz, *The World of Thought*, 309–11. On certain of Xunzi's views on the mind and heaven as responses to Taoist "naturalism," see Yearley, "Hsün Tzu on the Mind," and Eno, chapter 6.

17.   See Watson, trans., *Han Fei Tzu,* 118ff., and Schwartz, *The World of Thought,* chapter 8.

18.   Eno, 142ff., gives an excellent discussion of this tendency of thought and how it differed from Xunzi's views on many points.

19.   This is probably the view that later informs the specialists known as *fangshi,* on which see Ngo, *Divination,* and DeWoskin, *Doctors, Diviners, and Magicians.*

20.   On the turbulent social changes that were culminating in Xunzi's day, see especially Hsu, *Ancient China in Transition.*

21.   Watson's interpretation, though based on the Chinese commentarial tradition, that Xunzi thinks all of these acts "indicate respect for the basic materials of the meal" (W93), seems to me inadequate. All I am really sure of is that these gestures, in contrast to others used in the rites Xunzi describes, all involve *raw* foods; Xunzi's view of the significance of this fact remains unclear, though it is of course tempting to read him here as a proto–Lévi-Strauss.

22.   "Completion" of ritual is a plausible but uncertain interpretation of what Xunzi is getting at in this passage.

23.   I think Xunzi would agree, therefore, with the thesis advanced particularly clearly by Beattie, "On Understanding Ritual." I think he would disagree with the view advanced by Staal (in "The Meaninglessness of Ritual") concerning participants in ritual, that "there are no symbolic meanings going through their minds when they are engaged in performing ritual" (3), although he would agree with Staal and many other modern Western theorists that ritual is a "useless" activity in the sense that it is noninstrumental (or at least not *directly* instrumental) action (see 11–12). In any case, Xunzi clearly wants to affirm what Staal denies, that "ritual . . . consists in symbolic activities which refer to something else" (ibid.), and deny what Staal affirms, that "ritual . . . is meaningless, without function, aim or goal, or also that it constitutes its own aim or goal" (9). Indeed, Staal himself contradicts this, for he names a function performed by ritual, viz., the creation of a realm of perfect, risk-free activity, which has "a pleasant, soothing effect" (10). All of this is curious, since Staal cites Xunzi's opening passage on rites as a corroboration of his argument (14–15).

24.   13.14b: *sangli zhe yi shengzhe shi sizhe ye da xiang qi sheng yi song qi si ye;* cf. W103.

25. The term *mao,* which I have here rendered as "forms," connotes more specifically the *outward form taken by something that originates within,* and it usually refers to facial "expression." One of its classical lexical definitions is "whatever appears on the outside of something," the proof text being, significantly, another early text on ritual, the *Li ji* (*Ru xing* chapter): *Lijie zhe ren zhi mao ye,* "The rites and customs are the outward forms of benevolence [or humaneness—*ren*]" (cited in *Ci hai,* s.v. *mao*).

26. *Yi jing, Xi ci* section 1, 8.1; cf. the translations given in Wilhelm and Baynes, trans., *The I Ching or Book of Changes,* 304, and Legge, trans., *I Ching,* 360.

27. In his chapter on music—which immediately follows the chapter on rites in the received text of today—Xunzi also uses *xiang,* along with the semantically similar term *si,* when discussing the "symbolism" of musical instruments used in rites, what each "represents" and "resembles"; see W117–18, 14.4aff. For similar Ruist discourse on the symbolism of instruments, see Legge, trans., *The Li Ki,* chapter entitled *Li qi* (Ritual Implements), especially 1:398ff.

28. 14.4b–5a; cf. W118.

29. In other words, this is the one passage I have found in which Xunzi seems to be adopting something like Staal's position that ritual is, strictly speaking, "meaningless." Compare this statement by Staal: "To performing ritualists, rituals are to a large extent like dance, of which Isadora Duncan said: 'If I could tell you what it meant there would be no point in dancing it'" ("The Meaninglessness of Ritual," 4).

30. See *The Works of Hsüntze,* 234.

31. 14.1a; cf. W112 and Dubs, *The Works of Hsüntze,* 247.

32. Peter Boodberg has argued, in fact, that the very term *li,* translated here as "rites" or "ritual," has the root etymological meaning of "form." See Boodberg, "The Semasiology of Some Primary Confucian Concepts," 34–35.

33. 13.22b: *shi si ru shi sheng shi wang ru shi cun zhuang yu wu xingying ran er cheng wen;* cf. W111.

34. I am here reminded of Geertz's well known observation that religion provides models *of* as well as *for* human life. See Geertz, *The Interpretation of Cultures,* 93–94.

35. Compare the passage in the "Discourse on Rites" 13.14a–b, translated at W102–3, which speaks of rites as "trimming or stretching, broadening or narrowing"—in short, forming and adjusting—the primal emotions of joy and sorrow, as a mode of "conscious activity" (*wei*) that works upon the "raw material" (*caipu*) of human nature and its attendant spontaneous emotions.

36. The clearest treatment of this topic may be found in Yearley, "Hsün Tzu on the Mind," passim.

37. On the "universal" as distinct from merely "conventional" aspects of Xunzi's thought, see Yearley, "Hsün Tzu on the Mind," 476–79.

38. Yearley ("Hsün Tzu: Ritualization as Humanization," section 7) notes that this characterization of ritual is out of tune with most of his other statements in that it shifts discourse on ritual from the human to the natural sphere; he accounts for Xunzi's "cosmic" language, in a way reminiscent of Fingarette, by referring to "an experience many of us can have when humane order and power are at their most effective." But I think the passage is better seen as a cooptation of Taoist-style "naturalism": on the one hand, ritual belongs to the realm of *wei* or conscious activity and not that of *xing* or innate nature, but on the other hand, to the extent that ritual is patterned on the structure of, and can have real effects on, the course of nature itself, it takes on a "natural" dimension (no longer a mere human artifice) which lends it greater power in the eyes of Taoist opponents. I think Xunzi, in other words, is here trying to have his cake and eat it too, in direct response to the Taoist challenge—much as Eno convincingly shows Xunzi's theory of heaven to have been a response to Taoist naturalism. For examples of other, roughly contemporary "naturalistic" or "cosmic" characterizations of ritual emanating from the Ruist school, see Legge, trans., *The Li Ki*, 1:386–87 and 391.

39. I have omitted mention of a section of this passage (W94–95) in which Xunzi seems to be saying that one cannot measure ritual in certain other terms; I will consider it below, note 45.

40. On this see esp. Yearley, "Hsün Tzu on the Mind," 466.

41. On this ceremony see further Legge, trans., *The Li Ki*, 1:435–45; I have consulted the Chinese edition of Wang Meng'ou, 2:797–806.

42. Xunzi often speaks as if it is the particular function of music and dance to create social harmony, whereas ritual serves principally to reinforce social distinction. See, e.g., 14.3b; W117: "Music embodies an unchanging harmony, while rites represent unalterable reason. Music unites that which is the same; rites distinguish that which is different."

43. Note that the Taoist "naturalist" view—that people in their activities (though not in ritual activities as the Ruists understood these) should conform with natural patterns external to them and from which they have "fallen"—is structurally similar in locating the source of value outside the human realm. It comes under Xunzi's attack for just this reason, as in this passage: "Zhuangzi was obsessed by thoughts of heaven [that is, nature] and did not understand the importance of humanity. . . . He who thinks only of heaven will take the Way to be wholly a

matter of harmonizing with natural forces" (W125–26). This passage comes in the context of a litany of the mistakes made by various academic schools, and in each case, their characteristic mistake could be applied to the realm of ritual, though space does not permit me to do so here.

44. On this line of argument in Xunzi, see esp. Machle, "Hsün Tzu as a Religious Philosopher," and Yearley, "Hsün Tzu: Ritualization as Humanization," who invokes the categories of "false consciousness" and "masochistic religion" to characterize Xunzi's objections to what I above called "divinistic naturalism" or a "theological" understanding of ritual practice and belief.

45. This explains the important passage, alluded to above, on 13.7b/W94–95, which seems to say that the "principles" (*li*) of ritual are incapable of being fathomed in terms of certain other standards. The first of these other standards is clearly that of the Logicians; the academic identity of the other two is unclear to me. But the essential point is that this passage does *not* say that ritual cannot be understood from any external point of view; it *does* say that ritual cannot be understood from three particular sorts of viewpoint, none of which, of course, Xunzi espouses.

46. A perusal of a recent work such as Grimes, *Research in Ritual Studies,* for instance, turns up nothing of this sort.

47. The quoted phrases are from Durkheim, *Moral Education,* 10–11.

48. Durkheim, *Elementary Forms,* 426. Hereafter abbreviated as *EF.*

49. "Society cannot make its influence felt unless it is in action, and it is not in action unless the individuals who compose it are assembled together and act in common. It is by common action that it takes consciousness of itself and realizes its position. . . . The collective ideas and sentiments are even possible only owing to these exterior movements which symbolize them" (*EF* 465–66).

50. On this point, see especially O'Keefe, *Stolen Lightning,* 189.

51. A key difference, however, is that Durkheim always speaks of this "shaping" in both *moral* and *cognitive* terms. In Durkheim and Mauss, *Primitive Classification,* for instance, social practice is pictured as the source of epistemological categories. Xunzi focuses much less on cognition and the source of epistemic categories, and more on the formation of dispositions to act appropriately.

52. The key locus for this idea is Durkheim's essay "The Dualism of Human Nature and Its Social Conditions," in Bellah, ed., *Emile Durkheim on Morality and Society,* 149–66. See also *EF* 298 and Bell, "Discourse and Dichotomies," 101.

53. I have relied especially on Giddens, *Capitalism and Modern Social Theory,* chapter 6.

54. See especially *Moral Education,* part 2, hints of which had already been given in Durkheim, *The Division of Labor.*

55. See especially Durkheim, *Education and Sociology,* 101.

Glossary of Chinese Characters

ben 本

bian er shi 變 而 飾

bian 辡

bie 別

caipu 材 朴

dong er yuan 動 而 遠

duan 立耑

fa (issue forth) 發

fa (model) 法

fan li 凡 禮

fangshi 方 士

fen 分

fen jie 分 界

gui shi 鬼 事

jin 盡

jing 敬

jiu er ping 久 而 平

junshi 君 師

le 樂

li 禮

lijie zhe ren zhi mao ye 禮 節 者 仁 之 貌 也

Li lun 禮 論

li yi 禮義

mao 貌

qing 情

qingyong 情用

qiu 求

ren 仁

rendao 人道

sangli zhe yi shengzhe shi 喪禮者從生者飾死者也
sizhe ye da xiang qi sheng yi song qi si ye 大象其生以送其死也

sangli zhi fan 喪禮之凡

she 社

shi si ru shi sheng shi wang ru shi cun zhuang yu wu xing
ying ran er cheng wen 事死如事生事亡如事存狀乎無形影然而成文

shuo 說

si 似

tiandi 天地

Wang Xianqian 王先謙

wei 偽

wen 文

wenli 文理

wufang 無方

wu guan yu xiang er zhi wangdao zhi yi yi ye
吾觀於鄉而知王道之易易也

xianzu 先祖

xiang (community libation ceremony) 饗 (sometimes 鄉)

xiang (symbol) 象 (sometimes 像)

xing (embodiment) 形

xing (nature) 性

xue 學

Xunzi 荀子

Xunzi jijie 荀子集解

yang 養

yi 意

Yi jing 易經

youfang 有方

yu 欲

zho 梲/ ./ tuo 脫

zhuhou 諸侯

References

Beattie, J. H. M.
1970 "On Understanding Ritual." In *Rationality,* 240–68. Edited by Bryan R. Wilson. Oxford: Basil Blackwell.

Bell, Catherine.
1987 "Discourse and Dichotomies: The Structure of Ritual Theory." *Religion* 17:95–118.

Bellah, Robert N.
1973 *Emile Durkheim on Morality and Society.* Chicago: University of Chicago Press.

———.
1983 "The Ethical Aims of Social Inquiry." In *Social Science as Moral Inquiry,* 360–86. Edited by Norma Haan. New York: Columbia University Press.

Boodberg, Peter.
1979 "The Semasiology of Some Primary Confucian Concepts." *Philosophy East and West* 2 (1953):317–32; reprinted in Alvin P. Cohen (ed.): *Selected Works of Peter A. Boodberg.* Berkeley: University of California Press.

Boon, James A.
1982 *Other Tribes, Other Scribes: Symbolic Anthropology in the Comparative Study of Cultures, Histories, Religions, and Texts.* Cambridge: Cambridge University Press.

Bourdieu, Pierre.
1977 *Outline of a Theory of Practice.* Translated by Richard Nice. Cambridge: Cambridge University Press.

Burkert, Walter.
1985 *Greek Religion.* Translated by John Raffan. Cambridge: Harvard University Press.

DeWoskin, Kenneth J.
1983 *Doctors, Diviners, and Magicians of Ancient China: Biographies of "Fang-shih."* New York: Columbia University Press.

Dubs, Homer H.
1927 *Hsüntze, the Moulder of Ancient Confucianism.* London: Arthur Probsthain.

Dubs, Homer H., trans.
1928 *The Works of Hsuntze.* London: Arthur Probsthain.

Durkheim, Émile.
1933 *The Division of Labor in Society.* Translated George Simpson. New York: Macmillan.

———.
1956 *Education and Sociology.* Translated by Sherwood D. Fox. Glencoe, Ill.: Free Press.

———.
1961 *Moral Education.* Translated by E. K. Wilson and Herman Schnurer. New York: Free Press.

———.
1965 *The Elementary Forms of the Religious Life.* Translated by Joseph Ward Swain. New York: Macmillan, 1915; reprinted in Free Press Paperback Edition.

Durkheim, Émile, and Marcel Mauss.
1963 *Primitive Classification.* Translated by Rodney Needham. Chicago: University of Chicago Press.

Eno, Robert.
1990 *The Confucian Creation of Heaven: Philosophy and the De-*

fense of Ritual Mastery. Albany, N.Y.: State University of New York Press.

Fehl, Noah Edward.
1971 *Rites and Propriety in Literature and Life: A Perspective for a Cultural History of Ancient China*. Hong Kong: The Chinese University of Hong Kong Press.

Geertz, Clifford.
1973 *The Interpretation of Cultures*. New York: Basic Books.

Giddens, Anthony.
1971 *Capitalism and Modern Social Theory: An Analysis of the Writings of Marx, Durkheim and Max Weber*. Cambridge: Cambridge University Press.

Graham, A. C.
1978 *Later Mohist Logic, Ethics and Science*. Hong Kong: The Chinese University of Hong Kong Press.

Grimes, Ronald L.
1985 *Research in Ritual Studies: A Programmatic Essay and Bibliography*. Metuchen, N.J.: The American Theological Library Association.

Hsu Cho-yun.
1965 *Ancient China in Transition: An Analysis of Social Mobility, 722–222 B.C.* Stanford, Calif.: Stanford University Press.

Lau, D. C.
1953 "Theories of Human Nature in Mencius and Shyuntzyy." *Bulletin of the School of Oriental and African Studies* 15:541–56.

Lau, C. C., trans.
1979 *Confucius: The Analects*. Harmondsworth, England: Penguin.

Legge, James, trans.
1926 *The Sacred Books of China: The Texts of Confucianism*, Parts 3 and 4: *The Li Ki*, 2 volumes, 2nd ed. Sacred Books of the East volumes 527–28. Oxford: Oxford University Press.

———.
1973 *I Ching: Book of Changes*. New York: Causeway Books.

Machle, Edward.
1976 "Hsün Tzu as a Religious Philosopher." *Philosophy East and West* 26:443–61.

Mote, Frederick.
1971 *Intellectual Foundations of China.* New York: Knopf.

Ngo Van Xuyet.
1976 *Divination, magie et politique dans la Chine ancienne.* Paris: Presses Universitaires de France.

O'Keefe, Daniel Lawrence.
1982 *Stolen Lightning: The Social Theory of Magic.* New York: Vintage Books.

Schwartz, Benjamin I.
1985 *The World of Thought in Ancient China.* Cambridge: Harvard University Press.

Staal, Frits.
1975 "The Meaninglessness of Ritual." *Numen* 26:2–22.

Sullivan, Lawrence E.
1988 *Icanchu's Drum: An Orientation to Meaning in South American Religions.* New York: Macmillan.

Taylor, Charles.
1985 *Philosophical Papers,* volume 2: *Philosophy and the Human Sciences.* Cambridge: Cambridge University Press.

Wang Meng'ou, ed.
1980 *Li ji jinzhu jinyi,* 2 volumes. Taipei: Taiwan Commercial Press.

Wang Xianqian, ed.
1959 *Xunzi jijie (Xunzi with Collected Commentaries).* Taipei: Yiwen Yinshu guan.

Watson, Burton, trans.
1963 *Hsün Tzu: Basic Writings.* New York: Columbia University Press.

———.
1963 *Mo Tzu: Basic Writings.* New York: Columbia University Press.

———.
1964 *Han Fei Tzu: Basic Writings.* New York: Columbia University Press.

Wilhelm, Richard, and Cary F. Baynes, trans.
1977 *The I Ching or Book of Changes,* 3rd ed. Princeton, N.J.: Princeton University Press.

Yearley, Lee H.
1980 "Hsün Tzu on the Mind: His Attempted Synthesis of Confucianism and Taoism." *Journal of Asian Studies* 29:465–80.

———.
n.d. "Hsün Tzu: Ritualization as Humanization." Unpublished paper to appear in Wei-ming Tu, ed., *Confucian Spirituality,* volume 11 of *World Spirituality: An Encyclopedic History of the Religious Quest.* New York: Crossroads.

Chapter 8

Embodying Philosophy: Some Preliminary Reflections from a Chinese Perspective

Judith Berling

Mythos, Logos, Praxis

Mythos and logos (or myth and philosophy) present competing or alternative accounts of reality. After all, both offer an account or depiction of the world in the medium of words. It is often possible to identify the philosophical dimensions or implications of a myth, or the mythic assumptions or motifs underlying a philosophical stance, but the two are far from reconcilable. They serve different cultural purposes, invoke different sorts of authority, legitimate different styles of leadership, and present themselves in different literary forms. Praxis, however, is another matter. Not being fundamentally verbal, it need not structurally compete with mythos or logos, but is seen as having a relationship to both.

Praxis, like mythos and logos, is a complex and multivalent term used differently in different contexts. Praxis is often contrasted with theory, or more precisely, *theoria;* as contrasted with theory, *praxis* often suggests the application or living out of theories or principles as for instance, the difference between a system of ethical thought and the living out of a set of ethical principles. In Marxist terms, praxis refers to the productive behaviors (means of economic production, and so on) that produce social structures; theory emerges from praxis and social relationships. In religious communities praxis often refers to the rituals, religious disciplines, or formal obligations of the community to shape their actions according to communal standards. Some contemporary thinkers maintain that every community of interpretation has its practices: that philosophizing itself is a practice that needs to be analyzed as such. In this chapter all of these layers of praxis will be invoked, with some attempt to show how they inform each other.

Most scholars have viewed the relationship between mythos and praxis as close and mutually supporting. Durkheim and those who follow him argue that myths provide a narrative justification and foundation for the relationships and institutions, i.e., the practices which comprise the social order. Mircea Eliade posited that myths provide the account of the sacred beginnings, and rituals (praxis) reenact them. In Eliade's account of the views of *homo religiosus,* rituals and religious practice derive from and reenact myth; hence, practice is derivative and myth is foundational. However, the myth is believed to reflect the actions of the gods, or of the founders in the sacred time; in that sense, action is primary and myth is derivative. At a fundamental level, the two arise together and reinforce each other; they are not really separable.[1]

Views of the relationship of logos (philosophy, reason, or knowledge) and praxis (action) have been complex and varied. It is beyond the scope of this chapter and the expertise of this author to review the history of philosophical positions on this matter. Until relatively recently, however, the dominant stream of Western philosophical writing has assumed that logos, or theoretical speculation, transcends and should shape practice. This dominant notion emerged in part from a "myth" about the origins of a distinctively new mode of thought among the Greeks during the so-called Axial Age, which has become a cultural myth defining "philosophy." According to the myth of the emergence of Greek philosophy, it was at this point in history that logos emerged from mythos, creating a tradition: universalizing reason guided by the spiritual faculties of the human mind and transcending the particularities of self (body) and community; true philosophy seeking abstract and disembodied universals which could clarify understanding and guide ethical behavior; universal reason as the hope of human civilization.[2] This account may be called a myth for two reasons: (1) it simplifies and reconstructs reality to make a particular point which defines a community or tradition (Western philosophy), and (2) it has been a powerful story that functioned to define and justify certain cultural divisions without submitting them to the scrutiny of rational argument.

Although many "modern" philosophers were by no means Platonists, the myth of the triumph of philosophy over mythology has profoundly influenced Western understandings of what counts as philosophy. It was this view of philosophy as argumentative, abstract, disembodied, and aspiring to universals that has reinforced a common bias in Western philosophical writings to see abstract reason as higher than and thus a guiding force for appropriate behavior, or praxis. In this view, for instance, religious practices follow from beliefs; hence, in confronting any religious community one asks first about beliefs as the key to all other aspects of the community. In this view also ethical behavior is rule-governed, or at least governed by general principles; behaviors follow logically from the general principles.

Although the primacy of reason and theory over practice has long dominated Western culture, a number of scholars are trying to offer a different picture (or myth, or theory) about how reason and practice actually function and interact in human society. Some of the impetus for this has emerged from the social sciences, which have a commitment to describe adequately the ways in which human society actually operates. That is to say, the social sciences are focused centrally on human behavior, practices, and institutions.

One is Pierre Bourdieu, who in his *Outline of a Theory of Practice* sought as an ethnologist to challenge the notion of rule-governed behavior to get at the logic of practice itself; he sought to articulate the practical coherence of symbolic systems. He writes,

> Symbolic systems owe their *practical coherence,* that is, their regularities, and also their irregularities and even incoherences (both equally *necessary* because inscribed in the logic of their genesis and functioning) to the fact that they are the product of practices which cannot perform their practical functions except insofar as they bring into play, in their practical state, principles which are not only coherent—i.e. capable of engendering intrinsically coherent practices compatible with objective conditions—but also practical, in the sense of convenient, i.e. immediately mastered and manageable because obeying a "poor" and economical logic.
>
> One thus has to acknowledge that practice has a logic which is not that of logic, if one is to avoid asking of it more logic than it can give, thereby condemning oneself either to writing incoherences out of it or to thrust upon it a forced coherence.3

For Bourdieu, the logic of practice is not the logic of a consistent set of rules but the principles implicit in a practicable, functioning, and manageable set of behaviors. These practices, if they accomplish their goals with an economy of effort and are easily learned, have a logic of their own.

In Bourdieu's view, practices demonstrate their logical coherence when they flow from the habitus (i.e., the concrete experiential realities of a society). In that case, they support those means of production, those social interactions, and those institutional practices through which the society accomplishes its goals. In his view, both mythos and logos are generated to justify and reinforce the set of coherent practices. While his view owes a great deal to Marxist forms of analysis, Bourdieu's agenda moves in a distinctive direction, seeking to address directly the analytical problem of identifying the coherence in patterns of behavior.

Bourdieu's approach turns the common Western philosophical bias on its head. He sees persons in society manipulating the "rules" in order to accomplish the goals of their distinctive social positions; in other words, their practical ends drive the use they make of the mythos and logos of society. He gives little or no role for either mythos or logos to generate or accomplish major social changes. In his terms, thought or logos seems to be almost entirely determined by practical realities and goals embedded in the habitus.

As provocative as Bourdieu's language is, he may have gone too far in turning the bias on its head. His position is valuable as a stark corrective to pervasive language habits that presume the priority and transcendence of reason without ever defending it. However, other theorists are working to find language to articulate the importance of praxis or experience in shaping cognition not by assuming the absolute primacy of praxis, but rather by analyzing the connections between logos and praxis. These thinkers are seeking to transcend or revise a false dichotomy or polarity between logos and praxis by exploring the dynamics of their interaction.

The linguist George Lakoff, for example, has tried to ground cognitive processes in experience and action through a close examination of the functions of language and the ways in which the mind generates categories to understand experience. Lakoff's research has sought to combine philosophical, linguistic, and scientific findings into a theory of cognitive functioning. In his 1980 *Metaphors We Live By*, coauthored with philosopher Mark Johnson, Lakoff used traditional philosophical language in a fresh way by talking about culture as a set of pragmatic relations in which individuals are in interaction with nature and with each other; it is those interactions that comprise culture and give rise to cognitive systems. In the view of Lakoff and Johnson, language is rooted in everyday experience. The metaphors and metonymies of language express concrete cultural patterns, such as the spatial orientations and functional relationships (interactional properties, in their language) of human beings to the natural world and to each other.[4] These metaphors and metonymies also enter philosophical language, providing the critical link between everyday experience and larger metaphorical systems. Symbolic systems of action, such as ritual, are metonymous; they are structured to represent a larger whole. Lakoff and Johnson write,

> Religious rituals are typically metaphorical kinds of activities, which usually involve metonymies—real-world objects standing for entities in the world as defined by the conceptual system of the religion. The coherent structure of the ritual is commonly taken as paralleling some aspect of reality as it is seen through the religion. Everyday personal rituals are also experiential gestalts consisting of sequences of actions structured along the natural dimensions of experience—a part-whole structure, stages, causal relationships and a means of accomplishing goals.[5]

Lakoff and Johnson argue that basic cultural metaphors are partially preserved in and propagated by means of ritual, and thus rituals form a crucial part of the experiential foundation for the metaphorical and conceptual systems of the culture.

In the more recent *Women, Fire, and Dangerous Things,* Lakoff seeks to develop the philosophical implications of his earlier research, arguing against the traditional view which he calls "objectivist" in favor of what he calls experientialism. He writes about the need for the shift.

> On the traditional view, reason is abstract and disembodied. On the new view, reason has a bodily basis. The traditional view sees reason as literal, as primarily about propositions that can be objectively either true or false. The new view takes imaginative aspects of reason—metaphor, metonymy, and mental imagery—as central to reason, rather than as a peripheral and inconsequential adjunct to the literal.[6]

He notes that objectivism is often seen as intrinsically linked to realism, but argues that there is a basic realist position that does not subscribe in all particulars to the objectivist view. In his view,

> Basic realism involves at least the following:
> - a commitment to the existence of a real world, both external to human beings and including the reality of human experience
> - a link of some sort between human conceptual systems and other aspects of reality
> - a conception of truth that is not merely based on internal coherence
> - a commitment to the existence of stable knowledge of the external world
> - a rejection of the view that "anything goes"—that any conceptual system is as good as any other.[7]

Experientialism adheres to basic realism but also indicates the notion that cognitive systems are based in physical experience, including the human being's complex physical, functional, and social interactions with the world. Thus physical experience is not merely bodily experience, but the interaction of the human being in all of his or her dimensions with the larger environment.[8]

Lakoff argues that traditional objectivist views are not adequate to help us explain and understand what the result of modern scientific research is telling us about the way the human mind functions linguistically. He believes, further, that it is not merely a matter of adjusting theory to account for data. He writes,

> The classical theory of categories has not evolved in a vacuum. It has developed side by side with some of the most widespread philosophical views in the West. And although it is possible to hold the classical theory of categories without being committed to those philosophical views, the reverse does not seem to be true. The philosophical views which we will be discussing seem to require the classical theory of categories. If the classical theories of categories fall, those philosophical views [i.e., objectivism] fall with it.[9]

An adequate philosophy, in Lakoff's view, has to account for the way the mind actually generates cognitive structures such as language. But Lakoff is not a determinist. He writes, "Philosophy matters. It matters more than most people realize, because philosophical ideas that have developed over the centuries enter our culture in the form of a world view and affect us in thousands of ways."[10] Lakoff's view, then, sees philosophy as embedded in human experience and action but also as a force which shapes, affects, and contributes to culture.

While Lakoff's position is very thought-provoking, particularly about the limitations of "the old view," it does not attempt to describe in any textured way how the generation of cognitive systems of categories is actually embedded in a range of social practices.

On that score, the writings of Charles Taylor are much more helpful. In his *Philosophy and the Human Sciences,* Taylor discusses the intriguing example of the differences between the contractual concept of negotiation in Western European and U.S. cultures versus the notion of consensus in Japanese culture. He argues that the differences between the two cultures are not just differences of language or vocabulary, or even of social realities, but of practices.

> The realities here are practices; and these cannot be identified in abstraction from the language we use to describe them, or invoke them, or carry them out. That the practice of negotiation allows us to distinguish bargaining in good or bad faith, or entering into or break-

ing off negotiations, presupposes that our acts and situation have a certain description for us, for example, that we are distinct parties entering into willed relations. But they cannot have these descriptions for us unless this is somehow expressed in our vocabulary of practice. . . . The situation we have here is one in which the vocabulary of a given social dimension is grounded in the shape of social practice in this dimension; that is, the vocabulary would not make sense, could not be applied sensibly, where this range of practices did not prevail. And yet this range of practices could not exist without the prevalence of this or some related vocabulary.[11]

Taylor sees the practices and language used to describe them as mutually enabling and enforcing and, in some sense, separable. The sense of the language depends on the practices, but the practices are not coherent without the language to describe and transmit it.

At a higher level of generalization, Taylor writes on the relationship between social theory and practice, "a theory is the making explicit of a society's life, that is, a set of institutions and practices. It may shape those practices, but it does not replace them. So even though some feature may find no place in reigning theory, it may still be a constitutive part of living practice."[12] Theory justifies, affects, and contributes to living practice, but it never simply determines it. Practices do not in a simple way determine theory either. However, a theory not related to societal practice fails to express shared goods and quickly loses its ability to shape reality.

Bourdieu, Lakoff, and Taylor demonstrate an emergent strand of Western scholarship exploring language which would ground logos in praxis, or at least describe in a textured manner the close interrelationship between the two. The issues they raise are fundamental since they entail a shift in the way philosophical language is generally used, a shift from the "disembodied" and "abstract" notions of reflection to a more engaged and embedded set of human actions and practices. These new ideas have ramifications not only for the field of philosophy in general but for the direction and possibilities of comparative philosophy.

The issues of the boundaries of philosophy, the functions of philosophy, the practice of philosophy, and the configuration of the "articulacies" which may be considered "philosophical" were central to the project out of which these volumes have emerged. Larry Sullivan, for instance, argued for the "persuasiveness" of behaviors not often considered philosophical in the strict sense. He commented,

I think of drama, for example, that may not be reducible to a structured or discursive argument, although it can be extremely persuasive. Or art in general—for example choreography or visual art—

where demonstration of what is, is made compelling; where what is, what exists, is demonstrated in such a way as to compel some social confirmation or other behavior, or at least the marshalling of ideas or experiences along those configured lines. That then becomes a way of what we referred to earlier as a procedure, as patterned behavior, which here too is reflective. So philosophy then begins to take its place in the company with other behaviors that are not often treated as fully reflexive and yet may have that kind of reflective quality, that ability of stylize experience in such a way that it becomes available for, and a vehicle for, reflection.[13]

The import of Sullivan's comments and the discussion which followed was to blur the clean distinctions between philosophy and other categories of human behavior, to question the distinctiveness of the philosophical.

Other discussions stressed the practical aspects of rationality itself, asking whether any (or at least most) "philosophical" arguments are in fact as disembodied and universalizing as they first appear. In discussion of an Eilberg-Schwartz paper on a distinctive form of Rabbinic argument, Philip Quinn developed the notion of "practical rationality," the *use* rather than the *structure* of logic. If we understand rationality in this way, he argued, it is sometimes easy to understand that a "bad" form of argument (one that violates a tenet of logic) may serve "as a rational means toward an intelligible goal."[14] As Tom Kasulis pointed out, some arguments appeal to universal tenets of logic, some to authorities which are embedded in a particular tradition, and some to rhetorical devices which will work to persuade in a given context. These all use reason, and they all persuade, but they do so in markedly different ways.[15]

Since all of these ideas about the practical uses of philosophy demonstrated that reason and philosophizing were far more complex than the myth of the disembodied and universalizing discourse seemed to suggest, different notions of the activity of philosophizing were offered. Perhaps the most fruitful came from Charles Taylor, who used the Gadamerian notion of "conversation" to paint the practice of philosophy not so much as a form of reasoning that invoked "criteria" to resolve a debate but rather as "a series of 'error-correcting moves,'" where you move from one thesis to a better one, but is impossible to have rational grounds for holding that a position is unprovable. As he put it, 'Even if we could achieve non-distortive understanding, we couldn't know for certain that we had.'"[16]

In these conversations the colloquium built on other philosophical work exploring the relation of philosophy and action and the praxis of philosophy; scholars active in exploring these issues include Stephen Toulmin, Richard Rorty, Jeffrey Stout, and Richard J. Bernstein.[17]

Logos and Praxis: The Case of Chinese Neo-Confucianism

Until quite recently, modern scholars, both Western and Chinese, assumed that modern Western philosophy in its Cartesian, Enlightenment, or analytical modes defined the parameters of "philosophy" for studying China as well as the West. The issues, concepts, and modes of argumentation current in nineteenth- and twentieth-century Western thought had been forged in the crucible of Western intellectual history. Chinese intellectuals of the early twentieth century flocked to Europe and North America to study Western philosophy and brought its methods and issues back to China. Assuming that the product of that historical alchemy was "normative," many scholars—Western and Chinese—wrote about the lack of philosophy, the lack of systematic argumentation, the lack of rationalism, and so on, in Chinese thought in general and many forms of Confucianism in particular.[18]

As reviewed above, some Western theorists have recently begun to reexamine and question long-standing assumptions about the normative nature of the Enlightenment mode of philosophy. The pluralism of the Western philosophical heritage has once more become visible and alive, including those strands that examine philosophy as an enterprise or praxis. Given the lively discussion within Western philosophical circles, it is only natural that scholars of Chinese philosophy would begin to question the presuppositions we have long made about the Chinese "philosophical" enterprise.

This work has already begun, with scholars such as Wei-ming Tu and Peter Bol leading the way; their influence is visible in a new generation of graduate students asking fresh and important questions about Chinese intellectual history.[19] This chapter attempts to build on the efforts of such scholars, and to place their work in a larger context. Historically, the interest in neo-Confucian philosophy was fueled by the presumption that it was the pinnacle of Chinese philosophy, the most "authentically philosophical" strand of Chinese intellectual history. Given recent scholarly developments, it is time to take a hard look at the enterprise and practice of neo-Confucianism, and refine and nuance our heuristic model of "Chinese philosophy" even further.

Every standard history of Chinese philosophy and innumerable courses on Chinese thought and religion contain succinct presentations of the system of neo-Confucian thought. It is certainly possible to give such an account, since neo-Confucian thought is sufficiently "systematic," "coherent," or "rational" to allow it. What most of these presentations, however, fail to note is that no Song, Yuan, Ming, or Qing thinker ever gave such a comprehensive account of the system of neo-Confucianism. Neo-Confucian authors wrote about neo-Confucian understandings of the classics or *Four Books;* they recorded dialogues, interactions, instructions, or thematic lectures of famous teachers; some wrote about the correct lineage of neo-Confucian ideas or discussed the errors of deviant lineages. To be sure, their writings often *assume* a coherent and comprehensive grasp of the Confucian vision, but it is striking that such an overall summary is never presented, even by the great systematizer and synthesizer Zhu Xi. Not even Wing-tsit Chan's classic article on Zhu Xi's "completion" of neo-Confucianism claims that Zhu ever provided such an account.[20] Surely that absence is significant and informative.

Why is it that the neo-Confucians' method of explaining, transmitting, and teaching the tradition differs so centrally from our own? This question points to profound issues in the cross-cultural understanding of philosophy, for what is at stake are assumptions about the nature of philosophy, how it is practiced, and how it is to be grasped, understood, and conveyed to an audience.

The practice of neo-Confucian philosophy does not contribute to contemporary discussions about the relationship of logos to praxis primarily in terms of the generation of cognitive and philosophical systems from praxis; the Chinese, like most traditional thinkers, assumed and asserted that the proper order of things consisted of eternal truths discovered in primordial times, after which human institutions were fashioned.[21] Rather it is in their notions of learning, understanding, and transmitting philosophy that the centrality of praxis to their thinking begins to emerge.

The present discussion of logos and praxis is distinct from, although not entirely unrelated to, the long-discussed issue of the relationship of knowledge (*zhi*) and action (*xing*) within neo-Confucian thought.[22] That is certainly a key philosophical or doctrinal issue for Song and Ming neo-Confucians, but it is all too easy for Western scholars to approach that issue through the Cartesian or existentialist filters of Western philosophy: seeing it is a personal or existential issue for each neo-Confucian to resolve. This discussion explores the relationship of all aspects of philosophy and philosophizing to various dimensions of practice, including the practice of philosophy itself. It is about the nature of the neo-Confucian enterprise and its distinctive characteristics.

This is, of course, a large and complex topic. This chapter can provide only a very brief introduction that will raise issues in three areas: (1) the basic categories or labels used to refer to neo-Confucianism, (2) the genres or modes in which that thought is presented and transmitted in its native setting, and (3) basic conceptual issues (education, cultivation, self, knowledge, mind, and balance) which provide some cognitive basis for the relation of thought and practice.

Cross-cultural Terminology: Understanding Chinese Terms

It has long been noted that there is no exact Chinese equivalent for the English term "neo-Confucianism." This is true on two levels. First, there is no generic equivalent of "neo-Confucian." The Chinese designated these thinkers by a series of narrower school or lineage designations (Chengzhu, School of Mind, Evidential Learning, and so on). Second, none of the traditional Chinese terms contain an equivalent of our "-ism," which suggests a thought system, creed, or ideology. It is in part the English suffix "-ism" which raises expectations that a creed or manifesto is the basis or starting point for neo-Confucianism, which would cast it as an ideology. Modern ideologies such as Marxism are translated into Chinese using the suffix *zhuyi* ("theory," "doctrine"; literally, "the ruling meaning"). However, the Chinese terms suggest other priorities and approaches.

Most basically, the neo-Confucians referred to their commitment to the Way of the Sages (*shengren zhi dao*) or the Sagely Way (*shengdao*). Dao, or Way, has the basic meaning of a "path" or "roadway." By extension it refers to a way of life or a path one follows. It can also, by further extension, refer to the principles that underlie the path, or more precisely underlie the skills or art needed to follow the path. Dao then encompasses both an approach to living and the philosophy that undergirds it; the key notion for present purposes, however, is that the path, the approach, is the basic meaning, and the cognitive dimension is derivative.

The neo-Confucians also referred to the lineage of the Dao (*daotong*), referring to a succession of persons whose lives and teachings had kept the Way of the Sages alive in the world. While most of the members of the lineage were honored for their understanding of and contributions to the understanding of the Dao, they were also honored as representatives of it, i.e., as living exemplars.

Finally, the neo-Confucians referred to each of their schools of thought as a *Xue* (a "study," or "school"); hence, School of Mind (*xinxue*) or Evidential Learning (*shixue*). *Xue* refers overtly to the doctrinal or cognitive content of thought; yet in Chinese, "study" refers not only to doctrinal understanding and argumentation but also to emulation of an ideal mode of behavior. Thus it is not at odds with the idea of a Dao, a way of life. It stresses the Confucian notion that learning is always a matter of character refinement as well as mental discipline.

There is another very basic point: the word *xue* stresses the fact that the "schools" of neo-Confucians were actually practiced in schools; i.e., the transmission of the school was ideally a face-to-face learning process. Private academies and traveling lecturers were crucial factors in the formation and transmission of neo-Confucianism from the Song through the Ming dynasties. In the Qing dynasty the private academies were less effective, and this process of face-to-face interaction seems to have shifted to some extent to the various scholarly projects on which groups collaborated. Although this point merits considerable further study, it is becoming increasingly clear from scholarly work that the neo-Confucian learning and scholarship were not meant to be a solitary, but rather a communal process, an interaction with teachers or fellow scholars.[23] In addition to applying the teachings of neo-Confucianism as a Dao, a way of life, one also literally practiced the learning and development of it through the structured interaction of teacher and pupils, of scholarly colleagues, of friends and correspondents exchanging views and dialoguing about the Way.

Genres

The forms of praxis of neo-Confucians are visible in the corpus of writings which they left as their legacy. We can learn about the processes of neo-Confucian practice and philosophy by examining not only the content of the writings, but their form: the manner and genres that were chosen to communicate thoughts, values, and experiences. Too often modern scholars wade through this rather intimidating corpus in order to cull systematically the comments on a certain theme: in those cases, little attention is paid to the medium; they look only for the message, as if the two were separable.

Perhaps the preeminent neo-Confucian—indeed Confucian—genre is the commentary on the classics or other major intellectual or historical works. The amount of time spent writing and studying commentaries betrays an almost rabbinical rootedness in the classical texts of the tradition. Neo-Confucians perceived themselves as trying to maintain and transmit a correct understanding of these sagely writings through extensive and intensive study and contemplation. They are constantly and consistently in dialogue with the classical past, seeking to apply it to the present. Not only do they write voluminously about the classics; they discuss them as well. The classics were the core of the curriculum, the authoritative proof text for any argument, and the substance of many of the conversations in academies and other centers of neo-Confucian learning. They were not just texts, moreover; these works were repositories of the actions, sayings, and writings of the ancient sages. In the classics neo-Confucians found the supreme and clear models of the Sagely Way. Each generation in the succession of the Way added its wisdom to the evolving commentarial tradition, as they sought to make the eternal truths of the sages speak to the conditions of their generation. Commentary was thus a living genre, practiced by each successive generation of neo-Confucians.

In addition to commentaries, the collected works of neo-Confucians include a broad range of writings that would normally be termed "occasional": letters to friends, poems commemorating various occasions, dedicatory inscriptions, instructions or exhortations to students, prefaces to other people's works, and couplets written for a visit to a temple or mountain or for a famous painting. Because these writings do not look "philosophical," most Western students begin by assuming that they are not where one looks for the "meat" of the author's position. But those who have spent hours and days tracking down allusions to one writer by another have been astonished at how often these allusions lead to just such an occasional writing, especially to poetry. These writings may have been stimulated by the occasion, but they were not viewed by the authors or their audience as "ephemera" or throwaways; that is why they were collected, published, and cited by followers. It was sometimes in such interactions that a key or incisive comment would occur. Neo-Confucian "thought" did not happen only on formal "philosophical" occasions but also in a variety of interactions with colleagues, students, and friends.

Another genre which is prominent in the corpus of many neo-Confucians is the *yulu,* "recorded sayings" or "discourse records." These sometimes voluminous collections of the sayings of a master were collected and recorded by disciples, and then posthumously edited and published as a record of the teachings, often arranged by categories. There is, of course, an ancient foundation for this genre in the famous *Analects* of Confucius; the *Analects,* however, was much more concise and selective than many of the neo-Confucian recorded sayings.

According to the prefaces the *yulu* attempted to do a number things: (1) preserve as complete as possible a record of all of the teachings of a famous master; (2) show the subtle nuances of his responses in different situations and to different interlocutors, especially those beyond the reach of more general audiences; (3) provide a sense of the development of his teachings after his major commentaries and written works were published; (4) make available more broadly the private notes of famous disciples who often scattered to various parts of China after the master's death.[24] However, there is more to it. Zhu Xi defended the reliability of recorded sayings as a source of authentic teachings against Cheng Yi's expressed doubts about such collections:

> When the two masters proclaimed the Way of Confucius and Mencius, it had not been transmitted for a thousand years .... Their followers took their masters' exemplary words and deeds: heard them with

their ears, saw them with their eyes, and recorded them with their
hands. Because they were so intimately involved, one cannot go far
wrong with them.[25]

Neo-Confucian Huang Gan wrote about Zhu Xi's recorded sayings:

> In his teacher-disciple relationships he repeatedly investigated diffi-
> culties; his distinctions became ever finer, his meanings more dis-
> tilled. When you read it is like being in attendance when the master
> was at leisure, receiving the tone of his voice. A thousand years may
> pass, but it is like meeting in the hall, listening with the assembly as
> all the minds return to one. How could the transmission of this book
> be called a small addition?[26]

These statements suggest that the genre is trying to capture the
presence of the master and his human interactions with those around
him. There is something authoritative about the physical experience of
being there, hearing with one's own ears and seeing with one's own
eyes. The genre cannot replicate the first-hand experience, but it aspires
to come as close as possible. Beyond the content of the "teachings" is a
human presence, an embodiment of the Dao, a model, which the editors
are trying to evoke and convey in these texts.[27]

Thus both the Chinese terms used to describe neo-Confucianism
and the genres in which the writings of the great exemplars are recorded
suggest that neo-Confucian philosophy is about living, practice, and human interaction as much as it is about doctrine, argumentation, and
systems of thought. It is an embodied and humanly modeled philosophy.

Issues

It is not only that the labels which neo-Confucians used to refer to
their philosophy and the genres in which they wrote suggest a central
place for practice and the human embodiment of Neo-Confucian ideals;
the content of neo-Confucian thought also witnesses to the centrality of
practice (of human action) in the Way of the Sages. A brief analysis of a
number of key concepts can illustrate the point.

Education

The practice of neo-Confucian education was discussed briefly
above. What was the conceptual framework for Confucian education?
Confucian thinkers from the time of Confucius held a profound faith in
the ability of education to nurture human potential to create civilized
persons who could recover "the deep meaning of human civilization."[28]
The educated person, or perfected person (*zhunzi*), cultivated sagely
and civilized virtues—both intellectual and moral—through the study of

the classics, the emulation of positive moral models, and the practice of the six arts (rituals, music, archery, charioteering, calligraphy, and arithmetic). These disciplines trained body and mind, cultivated moral character, and refined cultural sensitivities; it was a program to educate the whole person. As Wei-ming Tu has written,

> Learning to be human, in this sense, can very well be understood as a process of ritualization that involves submitting oneself to routine exercises, deferring to experienced elders, amulating well-established models, and discovering the most appropriate way of interacting with other human beings.[29]

Clearly, from the beginnings of Confucianism, education was understood as more than the transmittal of information or the sharpening of intellectual tools. It was the refinement of the art of the living, preparation for all of the activities of human life.

The Confucian approach to education was premised on the notion that a human life is vitally connected with other human beings, indeed with the whole human community. Thus the moral and cultural cultivation of education was not merely refining an individual, but a member of family and society, a contributor to civilization, a citizen of the cosmos. As Mencius wrote,

> The people . . . under a true King [or gentleman] move daily towards goodness without realizing who it is that brings this about. A gentleman transforms where he passes, and works wonders where he abides. He is in the same stream as Heaven above and Earth below. Can he be said to bring but small benefit?[30]

Educated persons had cultivated their human nature in order to become transformers of society and moral models for others. They sought as far as possible to emulate the Way of the Sages.

For the early Confucians this was possible in part because sage-kings of antiquity had understood the eternal moral truths of creation and embodied them in the institutions (the "rituals," *li*) of society and recorded them in the classics. The classics were a record, a repository of the wisdom of the sages, but the rituals and institutions of society were their social embodiment. When Confucians studied and submitted themselves to the disciplines and forms of the rituals, they were moving toward participation in those moral truths. As carefully as a ballerina studies the variations handed down by master dancers, the Confucian practiced the rituals as the fine art of civilization.

One could in fact argue that ritual is the base metaphor for Confucian philosophy. What would that mean? For one thing, it would mean that "philosophy" is about human action, and more specifically about human interaction—not just about ethics (as we in the West sometimes translate it) but about normative patterns of human behavior and social interaction. These patterns of human behavior are expressive of fundamental "truths" about life and being, i.e., they constitute a Dao (a way of life, a praxis) that reflects and is the way things are.

Confucius' notion of rituals included not merely formal rituals or sacraments but also the stylized conventions of behavior that constitute the mores and institutions of culture. In using the word "ritual" (*li*), however, he invoked as key to his concept the formal ceremonial sacrifices that had been at the core of Zhou state religion. Zhou rituals, like all rituals, had a metonymic character, in the sense that Lakoff and Johnson discussed: although a specific, concrete action, they were designed to replicate and represent something larger, namely the relationship between Heaven and all social institutions, particularly those related to governance. The rituals expressed and enacted the proper relationship between the ruler and spiritual powers, the ancestors, and the human society that he governed. But they did so in a cultural shorthand, in which symbolic actions were designed to express a much larger whole.

Social rituals, by extension, functioned in an analogous way. In a given social ritual, the individual expressed or enacted his or her specific role in society but also implied and endorsed the entire social order and its normative underpinnings. But social rituals also functioned in Taylor's sense: Confucius' philosophy of ritual was an articulation of the basic values and positions of Chinese society as it was embedded in practices. What he did was make that connection to the practice of social institutions central and defining, putting ethical actions at the very center of "philosophy," and not in a position as derivative from first principles. In practicing the rituals and studying their prototypes in the classics the Confucian was educating himself in "Confucian philosophy" by cultivating the Way of the Sages.

The neo-Confucians built on the Confucian understanding of education, but in the formative years of the movement, there were strong differences over how best to understand that heritage. As Peter Bol has discussed in a recent article, there were three powerful competing notions of how education should seek to recover and implement the Way of the Sages in the eleventh and early twelfth centuries. Wang An-shi was, in Bol's terms, "committed to using the ideas of the sages, kings of antiquity, to transform Sung into an integrated social order."[31] He looked back to the classics and the sages for an understanding of the institutions of the true Confucian order. Su Shi, on the other hand, saw the key to the Way of the Sages as cultural refinement. Bol writes, "Believing that the

sages had composed works that served the common interest because
they learned from the past and drew on their own creativity, Su could
see his approach to cultural accomplishment as the best way for modern
literati to learn how to act as sages themselves."[32] Zhu Xi, however,
argued forcefully that these two approaches were wanting in failing to
see the moral cultivation of the individual as the only base from which
insight about institutional reform or authentic cultural creativity could
emerge. In his mind, Confucian education was centrally and vitally about
the cultivation of moral character.

Cultivation

As Bol's discussion of the Song debates on education emphasizes,
there were indeed multiple strands of cultivation in the Confucian program of education. However, with the triumph of the Chengzhu school
of neo-Confucianism, the primacy and centrality of moral cultivation was
firmly established.

There were still many means and methods of cultivation: the six
arts (particularly calligraphy and ritual) remained important; poetry and
skill in composition were still highly valued; extensive study of classics
and history was vital; the writing of commentaries continued to flourish;
some Confucians practiced forms of quiet sitting to calm their mind and
emotions.

What is key, however, is all of these were understood as means of
cultivating the Way, progress in which always showed itself in the action
of the individual. As Zhu Xi wrote,

> I myself hold that knowing the Way is basic. If one knows the Way
> his learning will be pure. If his learning is pure his mind will be
> correct. It will appear in his conduct of affairs and be expressed in
> his words.[33]

To put it another way, all the arts of cultivation are a means of
practicing the Way, which is fundamentally moral. The realization of
morality, while it may be helped by cognitive understanding, is not solely
a matter of understanding; a purely theoretical understanding of the good
is not even knowledge. Virtue is not something the mind understands or
grasps; it is something that transforms the whole self: attitudes, habits,
and behaviors. In one of Mencius' major statements on moral advance-
ment, cognitive understanding plays no role at all:

The desirable is called "good."
To have it in oneself is called "true."
To possess it fully in oneself is called "beautiful,"
but to shine forth with this full possession is called "great."

To be great and be transformed by this greatness is called "sage"; to be sage and to transcend the understanding is called "divine."[34]

Cultivation, then, is the practice of the skills or arts of the Way. These practices include study and the refinement of intellectual virtues, but it is moral action that is central to the project as defined by Zhu Xi.

Self

Although the quotes cited above make the case that for the Confucians and neo-Confucians both education and moral cultivation are focused upon the behavior of persons, on their interactions with others, it may not be clear why this is so central. After all, some other approaches to education and ethics stress cognition and theoretical reflection without jeopardizing the possibility of practical application after the fact. However, the Confucian understanding of the human self has implications for morality which render theoretical moral knowledge very nearly an oxymoron.

In the Confucian view of the self, the individual is defined in terms of relationships with others; the famous five relationships (*wu-lun*) of classical Confucianism schematize and express this view. The five relationships (ruler-subject; parent-child; husband-wife; elder-younger; friend-friend) are held to be the defining nexus of every human being; all possible relationships are encompassed in this structure and/or grow out of it. As the individual moves through life, he or she moves through most of these relationships, often switching from one side to the other (except in the case of husband-wife). These basic relationships define mutual obligations and responsibilities, reciprocal feelings—basic patterns of human interactions that govern all of life. The self, then, is not an agent entering into relationships; the self is the node of a web of human connections, defined by its location and interaction with other human beings.

Morality is then the appropriate participation in such relationships in which the individual both fulfills and refines his or her role in the various human interactions that comprise the self. If this is the notion of morality, it is no wonder that pure learning will appear in the conduct of affairs and speech; it is in human interaction and relationships that one's knowledge (moral knowledge) is both gained and expressed.

Knowledge

Such a view of self and morality has profound implications for the understanding of knowledge. Knowledge is not an isolated mind speculating on reason or principles but rather an awareness and understanding

of how to be in relation to other human beings, to tradition, to civilization. As Wei-ming Tu has commented,

> If you understand yourself as at center of relationships . . . and not
> as an isolatable individual . . . then thinking is necessarily in that
> context either an actual or imagined conversation . . . . Knowing is a
> transformative act in that connection. . . . What we are trying to do
> becomes an attempt to come up with a kind of communal critical
> self-awareness. It is sociological in nature.[35]

Tu's comment helps clarify why the recorded sayings were so important
a record for the neo-Confucians; they were believed to be a record of
key conversations through which students and disciples of the great neo-
Confucian masters sought through human interaction (conversation) to
achieve that critical communal self-awareness; they were in dialogue
with each other and also with the writings and sayings of the great sages
of the past. Knowledge thus becomes a mode of self-understanding in
which one realizes that all self-understanding can be achieved only
through relationship, only in interaction with other humans.

The humans with whom one interacts may be historical figures or
living persons; the Confucian and neo-Confucian approach to the classics and the histories was to reverence them as records of the thoughts
and actions of exemplars of the past. For instance, in writing history or
studying it, the Confucian saw history as:

> the conscience of collective memory shared by all; the historian's
> responsibility is not only to show what has already been done but to
> suggest, whenever appropriate, what other authentic possibilities may
> have existed and why the failure to realize them has led to disastrous
> consequences. To write history is therefore a political act committed
> in the name of the human community as a whole.[36]

Knowledge, then, is not the property of an individual mind, but participation in the communal critical self-awareness of the Way of the Sages.
Learning to enter into the conversation or discourse, to refine the styles
and genres of writing, to practice the behaviors and mores of the community was part of knowledge, part of participation in the communal
awareness of the *daotong* ("succession of the Way").

Mind

This view of knowledge and of the Dao are supported by a highly
sophisticated view of the mind that affirms, on the one hand, the mind's
rationality and ability to grasp the principles which are the foundation of
the moral universe and, on the other, the complexities of moving from
such a grasping into the action which flows from it.

There are, to be sure, salient debates and differences among the various schools and thinkers within the neo-Confucian movement, but the Chengzhu conception of the human mind became a kind of standard view over against which others proposed variations or refinements. The Chengzhu notion also serves as a kind of balance between extremes of intellectualism and intuitionism (or dynamic activism) and thus seeks to strike a moderate tone on the issue of logos versus praxis.

In Chengzhu neo-Confucianism the human mind-and-heart is poised between the two aspects of the human person.[37] One aspect is the human nature (*xing*), which is defined as "principle" (*li*). The principle of any thing in the world, including a human being, defines the ontological and moral nature of that thing in itself and in relation to the rest of the world. Principles emerge from the Great Ultimate, the One Principle, which also represents the mind of Heaven; from this moral unity all things emerge according to regular and knowable cosmological laws. Principle is rational and knowable; since human nature is itself principle, humans possess an innate capacity to know and understand principle. Since all principles are united in the Great Ultimate, the human mind (in its aspect as human nature) can know and understand its own nature and its interconnections with all principles in the world.

However, the human being and all things in the world are also made up of *qi* (ether or material force). *Qi* is the stuff or vital energy which comprises all things: dispersed, it is the air or ether in the void; condensed, it forms things according to the patterns established by principle. It could be said in this regard to be roughly analogous to the modern notion of molecule, which is comprised of both matter and energy, and which is the "stuff" of the atmosphere, physical objects, and living beings. Although they can be distinguished for the purposes of analysis and discussion, principle and ether never exist except in conjunction. There is no Platonic realm of pure principles nor a chaos of pure ether.

In the human person, ether or material force comprises the physical endowment and characteristics (genes and the like); the habits and dispositions shaped by the environment and the person's responses to them; the intelligence and gifts with which the individual has been endowed.

If the mind as principle is endowed with the ability to reason and understand the way things are and ought to be, it is also affected by its material endowment, habits, and dispositions (ether, material force). To put it too simply, when the mind in an act of understanding or intention simply follows habits and dispositions without recourse to principle, its ether (with its dispositions and ties to the material) becomes even more turbid, and the understanding of innate and external principles becomes that much more difficult. When, however, the mind in an act of understanding or intention focuses on and takes into account principles in the self and in things, the ether becomes less turbid, and the hold of past bad habits or dispositions is weakened. To use another rough analogy, the principle on the mind can be likened to the sun, while the ether can be likened to fog or mist. If the person exercises his or her mind according to principle, the "light" of principle can burn away the "fog" of material force or ether; if however, the person uses the mind as a function of material force, then the fog grows denser and increasingly obscures the "light" of principle.

Because of the interconnectedness of all principles in the moral unity of the Great Ultimate, any act of understanding or intention involves relationships between things and persons in the world. Thus all mental acts are expressions of the individual's grasp of the whole structure of being and society; he or she is always positioning the self in relationship to all principles. The sage mind grasps the unity amid the diversity, the one thread that ties the whole together, the moral coherence amid variety, and thus has a sure and almost intuitive grasp of the principle of any single thing or situation. That grasp is expressed in the concrete words and actions of the individual. Thus the great teacher or the sage is in every action and utterance giving voice to "the whole truth," although a specific action or utterance pertains to a specific topic or person.

The Chengzhu conception of mind clarifies a long-standing Confucian notion that although every human being is potentially perfectible, there are practical reasons why this perfectibility is seldom achieved. As one seeks to express knowledge in one's relationships and actions, the endowment and patterns of material force can block the expression of true human nature unless the person has disciplined and cultivated himself or herself so that behavior is modeled as closely as possible on principle, which includes the natural, moral, and ritual norms of society.[38] It is misdirected or sloppy practice that stands in the way of and muddies the flourishing of knowledge. Study can help to strengthen the clarity of the mind but only if it is linked to moral cultivation. Hence, the practice of philosophy must also be grounded in practice: conversations with other students, studying and writing commentaries, and living out the principles in all of one's interactions.

Balance

The analysis of neo-Confucianism in this chapter has stressed a side often relegated to a second place by long-standing habits of privileging the theoretical and doctrinal. However, it should be both noted and emphasized that Confucianism and neo-Confucianism were deeply committed to the possibilities of human rationality and knowledge for transforming the self. Learning and reflection are central activities, as is intellectual insight. Cheng Yi, for example, studied moral principles in the classics devotedly until he suddenly had a breakthrough and could see the one thread running through it. The neo-Confucians did not privilege practice over theory but rather saw the two as mutually reinforcing, proceeding together as though organically joined. They provide a kind of model for seeing logos and praxis as inseparable aspects of human knowing.

Neo-Confucian Perspectives on Modern Theories of Practice

Among Western philosophers, it is a relatively recent phenomenon to view praxis as primary or equal to theory as part of the enterprise of "making meaning." This essay has suggested that the complementarity of action and thought has had a much longer and deeper history in China. Might it be helpful, then, to ask what the neo-Confucians might say about the modern attempts to integrate practice more centrally into theoretical reflection?

Such a comparative enterprise must negotiate a treacherous gulf between cultures and historical periods. To the extent that the embeddedness of thought in the context of practice is acknowledged, the challenge to such a comparison becomes greater. Yet it can be instructive, in part but not wholly because we so seldom evaluate modern Western theory on the basis of traditional non-Western thought.

In this section, I will endeavor to bring neo-Confucian ideas about the relation of practice and thought to bear on the adequacy of the theories reviewed in the first section of this chapter.

The neo-Confucians would not approve of Bourdieu's approach of discerning the inherent logic of practice, nor of his assumption that human wisdom manipulates rules and ideals to practical ends. The neo-Confucians, to the contrary, held that there was a complex but unified moral and ontological order to reality governed by "principle," which moral will sought to emulate and moral mind to discern. Thus the closest the neo-Confucian might come to Bourdieu's position would be to affirm that moral effort and discernment working in harmony seek to manifest the logic of the functioning (the Way) of the universe.

A neo-Confucian conversation with Lakoff and Johnson would be a complex and subtle task that merits an essay in its own right. To be very brief (and too simple), while certain aspects of neo-Confucian thought might seem to lean toward "a basic realism" (e.g., the idea that each thing and being is constituted in its nature by a "principle" which is part of an ontological order the mind can grasp), the aspects of neo-Confucian writing and teaching explored in this chapter formed a counterweight to the "realist" dynamic and pulled toward a sort of "experientialism."

Moreover, the use of symbols, puns, images, and metaphors in Chinese philosophical writing and teaching and the centrality of ritual as an organizing principle of the moral life resonate strongly with Lakoff's and Johnson's work in *Metaphors We Live By*.

While a neo-Confucian might recognize and affirm much of Lakoff's work, he would argue for a balance of "realism" and "experientialism" because of the interplay of the discerning and intentional aspects of mind in the cultivation of the moral life.

The neo-Confucians would be most comfortable with the position of Charles Taylor, who sees practice and language as mutually enabling and ultimately inseparable. Taylor's example, cited earlier in the essay, that cultural differences about contracts and negotiations are grounded in practice would be understandable to the neo-Confucian, even though the neo-Confucian would have little developed concept of "cultural difference." The neo-Confucian would cast the same point in terms of differences among teachers and philosophies that shaped how their followers understood and embodied basic moral precepts and principles. Disciples debated not only the ideas of their teachers but also their practices, teaching methods, and—most important—their advice for living.

Although neo-Confucian thought, given its premodern historical and cultural context, is not attuned to all of the issues of the linguistic construction of culture that pervade the writing of modern philosophers, they do offer an approach to the relationship of practice and cognitive understanding which can be put into conversation with modern reflections on these issues. Creating such comparative conversations can help to expand the embeddedness of our current discourse and create new questions and perspectives that can be constructively addressed.

Logos and Praxis in Comparative Perspective

One of the factors which has shaped the practice of comparative philosophy and determined both its limits and its limitations is that until quite recently a narrow spectrum of Western philosophy determined the key issues and defined what philosophy was. Since Western philosophy, until recently, has seen the philosophical enterprise as abstract and disembodied reflection, it has seemed possible to abstract philosophical systems from their cultural base, separate out issues, and compare and contrast them with each other. Those who objected to this procedure were branded as cultural relativists arguing for the uniqueness of their cultures, and indeed, the arguments of such scholars were often couched in such terms. Both sides bought into a dichotomy of universalism (a single standard of reason and moral values) and relativism (philosophical positions so contextualized that they have no basis on which to enter into dialogue).

Philosophical approaches that suggest philosophy is naturally embedded in human action and social practices suggest one way out of this dichotomy. For if philosophy makes sense only when seen in the light of the practices in which it is embedded, it is no longer sensible to compare abstract systems of thought but rather ideas or notions as they are embedded in practice. The comparative enterprise itself has become more embodied and more informed by cultural particularities.

This is no simple task, but this chapter suggests that one can go further and explore the very issue of the embeddedness of thought in practice and practice in thought as it is played out in various cultures as one way of beginning to understand the possibilities of comparison. Such an exploration can open up some avenues for coming to understand the "truth" or "authority" of ideas and practices across cultural boundaries.

The practice and understanding of Confucian and neo-Confucian education, when closely examined, has presented a model for seeing the intimate connections between theory and practice as envisioned in another culture. Such studies can help raise issues about the boundaries and configurations of our own cultural constructs and thus help us to see more clearly what issues might be raised in the pursuit of value and truth.

Notes

1. Mircea Eliade's position is most classically stated in *The Sacred and the Profane: The Nature of Religion*, translated by Willard R. Trask (New York: Harcourt, Brace, & World, 1959).

2. The Axial Age problematique was discussed in response to Arthur Adkin's paper at the June 1987 conference. See Francisca Cho Bantly, ed., "Deconstructing/ Reconstructing the Philosophy of Religions," in *Summary Reports from the Con-*

ferences on Religion in Culture and History, 1986–89, The Divinity School, The University of Chicago (Chicago, 1990), 26.

3. Pierre Bourdieu, *Outline of a Theory of Practice,* Cambridge Studies in Social Anthropology, volume 16, translated by Richard Nice (Cambridge: Cambridge University Press, 1977), 109.

4. George Lakoff and Mark Johnson, *Metaphors We Live By* (Chicago: University of Chicago Press, 1980), 118–19.

5. Ibid., 234.

6. George Lakoff, *Women, Fire, and Dangerous Things: What Categories Reveal About the Mind* (Chicago: University of Chicago Press, 1987), xi.

7. Ibid., 158.

8. Ibid., 112.

9. Ibid., 157.

10. Ibid.

11. Charles Taylor, *Philosophy and the Human Sciences: Philosophical Papers,* 2 (Cambridge: Cambridge University Press, 1985), 33–34.

12. Ibid., 100.

13. Larry Sullivan, cited by Sheryl Burkhalter in Bantly, *Summary,* 39 n.2.

14. Philip Quinn, cited in Bantly, *Summary,* 52 n.2.

15 Cited in Bantly, *Summary,* 52–53.

16. Summarized and cited by Laurie Patton in Bantly, *Summary,* 76.

17. For a sustained philosophical discussion of human activity, see e.g., Richard J. Bernstein, *Praxis and Action: Contemporary Philosophies of Human Activity* (Philadelphia: University of Pennsylvania Press, 1971).

18. Hu Shi, for instance, tried to rescue Chinese thought and civilization by applying Western philosophical standards and methods to Chinese philosophy. See *The Development of the Logical Method in Ancient China,* 3rd ed. (Shanghai: The Oriental Book Company, 1928). See also Wing-tsit Chan, "Hu Shih and Chinese Philosophy" *Philosophy East and West* 6(1956):3–12.

19. Wei-ming Tu has been a prolific author. A very nice introduction to the scope of his work is *Humanity and Self-Cultivation: Essays in Confucian Thought* (Berkeley: Asian Humanities Press, 1979). Peter Bol's contributions are perhaps best represented in his dissertation "Culture and the Way in Eleventh-Century

China" (Ph.D. dissertation, Princeton University, 1982) and his forthcoming book, *Man's Culture and Heaven's Way: Transitions in T'ang and Sung China.*

20. Wing-tsit Chan, "Chu Hsi's Completion of Neo-Confucianism," *Études Song, Sung Studies in Memoriam Etienne Balasz,* Series II, part 1 (Paris, 1973), 59–90.

21. Confucius' references to the sage-king founders of Chinese civilization and the Zhou dynasty and even more fundamentally to the patterns "discovered" by the Sage Fuxi in the hexagrams of the *Book of Changes.*

22. For an excellent example by an authority on the subject, see Wei-ming Tu, "The Unity of Knowing and Acting: From a Neo-Confucian Perspective," in *Humanity and Self-Cultivation,* 83–101.

23. See e.g., Wei-ming Tu, "The Sung Confucian Idea of Education: A Background Understanding," in *Neo-Confucian Education: The Formative Stage,* ed. William Theodore de Bary and John W. Chaffee (Berkeley: University of California Press, 1989), 139–50.

24. Based on a study of prefaces and colophons to *yulu* of Zhu Xi, Zhang Zai, Yang Shi, Cheng Yi, and Cheng Hao, all major figures in the formulation of Song neo-Confucianism.

25. Zhu Xi's afterword (*tihou*) to *Ercheng yulu,* 18 ch., *tihou* 1b.

26. Cited in Chien Mu's preface to the modern edition of *Zhuzi yulei,* ed. Li Zhingde (Taiwan: Zheng-zhong shu-jü, 1958).

27. The functions of *yulu* as a neo-Confucian genre will be developed in more detail in an article I am writing on the relation of the oral and the literate in the neo-Confucian tradition.

28. This felicitous phrase is from Wei-ming Tu, in his "Sung Confucian Idea of Education," 145 n.23.

29. Ibid., 143.

30. *Mencius,* 7a:13, translated by D. C. Lau (Middlesex, England: Penguin, 1976), 184.

31. Peter K. Bol, "Chu Hsi's Redefinition of Literati Learning," in *Neo-Confucian Education,* 164 n.23.

32. Bol, "Redefinition," 172.

33. Zhu Xi, "Ta Wang shang-shu," 3:10a; cited in Bol, "Redefinition," 69.

34. *Mencius* 7B:25, cited from Wei-ming Tu, "Sung Confucian Idea of Education," 141.

35.   Cited by Laurie L. Patton in Bantly, *Summary*, 76–77 n.2.

36.   Wei-ming Tu, "Sung Confucian Idea of Education," 144.

37.   In Chinese, the word for heart (*xin*) stands for both the physical heart and the cognitive center of the person (the brain), along with all of the psyche. Strictly speaking, the most accurate translation is mind-and-heart. Because this discussion primarily concerns the role of the cognitive/rational dimension of the mind-and-heart, I will use the shorter "mind" for *xin* for stylistic reasons. The reader should be aware, however, that the term always carries the broader connotations.

38.   On the scope and centrality of ritual norms in the Confucian view of society, see the section on education above.

References

Bantly, Francisca Cho, ed.
    1990 "Deconstructing/Reconstructing the Philosophy of Religions." *Summary Reports from the Conferences on Religion in Culture and History, 1986–89, The Divinity School, The University of Chicago.* Chicago.

Bernstein, Richard J.
    1971 *Praxis in Action: Contemporary Philosophies of Human Activity.* Philadelphia. University of Pennsylvania Press.

Bol, Peter.
    1982 *Culture and the Way in Eleventh-Century China.* Ph.D. Dissertation: Princeton University.

Bourdieu, Pierre.
    1977 *Outline of a Theory of Practice.* Cambridge Studies in Social Anthropology, volume 16. Translated by Richard Nice. Cambridge: Cambridge University Press.

Chan, Wing-tsit.
    1956 "Hu Shih and Chinese Philosophy." *Philosophy East and West.* 6:3–12.

———.
1973 "Chu Hsi's Completion of Neo-Confucianism." *Études Song,* series II, part I, 59–90. Paris.

Eliade, Mircea.
1959 *The Sacred and the Profane: The Nature of Religion.* Translated by Willard R. Trask. New York: Harcourt, Brace, & World.

Hu Shih.
1928 *The Development of the Logical Method in Ancient China,* 3rd ed. Shanghai: The Oriental Book Company.

Lakoff, George.
1987 *Women, Fire and Dangerous Things: What Categories Reveal About the Mind.* Chicago: University of Chicago Press.

Lakoff, George, and Mark Johnson.
1980 *Metaphors We Live By.* Chicago: University of Chicago Press.

Lau, D. C. trans.
1976 *Mencius.* Middlesex, England: Penguin.

Li Zhingde, ed.
1958 *Zhuzi yulei.* Taiwan: Zheng-zhung shujü.

Taylor, Charles.
1985 *Philosophy and the Human Sciences: Philosophical Papers,* 2. Cambridge: University of Cambridge Press.

Tu, Wei-Ming.
1979 *Humanity and Self-Cultivation: Essays in Confucian Thought.* Berkeley: Asian Humanities Press.

———.
1989 "The Sung Confucian Idea of Education: A Background Understanding." In *Neo-Confucian Education: The Formative Stage,* 139–50. Edited by Theodore de Bary and John W. Chaffee. Berkeley: University of California Press.

Section IV

Concluding
Comparative Reflections

The Drama of Interpretation and the Philosophy of Religions: An Essay on Understanding in Comparative Religious Ethics

William Schweiker

The difficulties facing comparative religious studies are legion. Some of them are of particular philosophical concern. What are the conditions that make comparative understanding possible? How, if at all, does such understanding transpire? Moreover, because we seek to undertake the study of religion philosophically, the answers to these question must be found in the interpretation and understanding of religious texts, beliefs, and practices. In a word, comparison forces the philosopher to explore the condition and the shape of understanding entailed in the study of religions.

Faced with this philosophical task concerning comparative study, we must admit a troublesome fact. There is no agreement among thinkers about the character of understanding let alone the relation of philosophic rationality to the substantive concerns of religious studies. The task of this chapter, therefore, is to explore comparative understanding. In order to do so, I will look at the problems and possibilities in a single field of inquiry: religious ethics. My hope is that by attending to the needs of one type of philosophy of religion something about the more general philosophic task of comparison might be illuminated.

Like all theoretical arguments, mine rests on certain guiding assumptions. These cannot be extensively defended here. My basic one is hardly novel. It is that understanding is achieved through interpretation. The attitude and perspective of the interpreter is that of the participant rather than the objectifying perspective of the observer concerned with propositional statements about events or states of affairs. The attitude and perspective of the interpreter clearly bears on the status of the claims that she or he can possibly make. As Jürgen Habermas notes,

> A correct interpretation, therefore, is not true in the sense in which a proposition that reflects an existing state of affairs is true. It would be better to say that a correct interpretation fits, suits, or explicates the meaning of the *interpretandum,* that which the interpreter is to understand.[1]

The problem I face in this essay is that the *interpretandum* is interpretation itself and the form of understanding it enacts. The question then becomes how to construe interpretation.

I join those theorists who see interpretation as dialogical in character. We understand through argument and conversation with others and ourselves. This means that hermeneutical inquiry bears on what someone or something says, the interaction between interpreter and what is said, and that about which the subject matter, the "said," is concerned, its "referent." This requires modifying previous accounts of understanding that took perception as the clue to knowing and as specifying its criteria. Such accounts tended to concentrate philosophic inquiry on the third of the above concerns, that is, the question of reference, while fostering an observer's perspective and attitude on the question of understanding. Hermeneutics contests the epistemological concentration of modern philosophy and its attendant cognitive attitude. This does not mean, as some critics might think, that the interpreter simply constructs the meaning of what is in question. On the contrary, the interpreter "has to explicate the given meaning of objectifications that can only be understood from within the context of the communication process."[2] We are concerned with what calls for interpretation but which requires the participation of the interpreter in order for it to be understood.

The orienting assumption about understanding through dialogic interpretation clearly places my argument within the wider enterprise of phenomenological hermeneutics. My argument is phenomenological in the sense that I hope to specify the structure and intentionality of comparative understanding as a dialectic of translation and insight. It is a hermeneutical inquiry since understanding is reached through the interpretation of meaningful expressions, ones paradigmatically represented by linguistic forms (symbols, texts, and so on) but inclusive of actions and events as well. In this essay I am then considering the activity of comparative interpretation in order to explore its shape and dynamic, what is disclosed in it, and what makes it possible. Hopefully, this will show the plausibility of my guiding assumption and the fruitfulness of this way of thinking about comparative studies.

Granting my agreement with other hermeneutical thinkers, I do forward and defend a particular thesis about comparative understanding. It is certainly a contestable one. I claim that interpretation in comparative religious ethics—and perhaps in the whole of the philosophy of religion as well—is best seen as a performative activity analogous to the ritual and dramatic practices found in religious communities. Other hermeneutical positions are interested in the dynamic of traditions in the attempt to overcome historical alienation (Gadamer), the coordination of social interaction in a differentiated society (Habermas), or the interpretive mediation of self-understanding (Ricoeur). While drawing on these positions, my concern is nevertheless with the reflexive process through which communities and individuals are constituted by the enactment of a world of symbolic meaning.[3] I believe this perspective is most fruitful for exploring the moral and religious beliefs and lives of others.

To offer this account of interpretation I will draw on the resources buried in the concept of mimesis or "imitation." I admit that this sounds odd. Mimesis is usually associated with poetics and aesthetics or, in the Platonic tradition, with epistemology and metaphysics. As we will see, it holds resources for comparative religious studies long neglected by philosophers because of its relation to ritual and drama. Yet because of its ties to epistemology, aesthetics, and even metaphysics, mimesis adds to discourse about such action the means to explore understanding through linguistic forms. To make this claim about mimesis requires retrieving its roots in ritual and dramatic practice, roots long understood by classics scholars but only now bearing historical, philosophical, and theological fruit.[4] Reclaiming those roots enables us to consider the complex relation between discourse and practice in understanding the moral life of others and ourselves.

In order to demonstrate the thesis, I must elucidate it to the point that we can grasp the shape and dynamics of understanding in comparative religious ethics. This elucidation requires that the argument move in several steps while retaining a participant's perspective.

First, I will specify the debates in religious ethics about the shape of comparative understanding. As a way beyond this debate, I want, second, to examine the relation of insight and translation through a phenomenology of comparative understanding. In order to articulate this fully requires, third, retrieving mimesis as a conceptual means for specifying the act which relates translation and insights. This will help us grasp the method, subject matter, conditions, and even criteria for religious ethics. Finally, I can return to comparative religious ethics to specify what my proposal means for work in that discipline. Thus, I begin with what is closest to us—the debate in ethics—and then examine what seems presupposed about understanding in order, finally, to develop a conceptuality capable of moving the debate in a new direction.

Options in Comparative Religious Ethics

Comparative religious ethics finds itself amid a variety of challenges to previous ways of thinking about the moral life, the possibility of understanding others, and the validity of moral claims. Not surprisingly, there is intense debate about the subject matter and method of comparative ethics. From this debate has emerged some basic options about how to proceed in comparative studies. In order to isolate them I want to specify the debate around *what* is in question, *how* thinkers hold we should explore it, and also what they take as the *condition* for comparative understanding. I can do so by drawing a rough typology of positions realizing that this serves heuristic purposes and is not meant as an exhaustive analysis.

At one extreme of our typology are thinkers who seek what Ronald Green calls a "deep structure" to religion.[5] These positions hold that we must understand specific traditions as expressions of universal, or near universal, structures of rationality. The ethics of particular communities are subsumed under a general concept of morality. The pattern of comparative thinking is then formal and transcendental in character. Indeed, these thinkers undertake a metapractical discourse in order to specify the conditions and criteria for the actual practice of comparative ethics. This requires exploring the transcultural conditions of understanding, the origin and justification of obligations to others and human welfare as well as possible responses to moral fault and failure. By examining other traditions we learn the various ways communities have addressed these issues basic to ethics.

In discernible continuity with Kant's moral philosophy, this form of comparative ethics hopes to isolate how the "moral" transcends empirical conditions and cultural variation. *What* one seeks to explore are communities' obligations and rules, as well as their justifications, that demarcate the moral life. By undertaking such inquiry the philosopher hopes to provide the theoretical standpoint for comparative reflection no matter how much that perspective is subsequently enriched by sociological, historical, and anthropological investigation. Indeed, for Green this standpoint is grounded in the *sui generis* character of what he calls "religious reason" and its relation to morality. Such reason "arises because of an important conflict between prudential and moral reason, and it represents reason's effort to bring its own program to a coherent conclusion."[6] Thus reason and the problem it addresses provides the conditions for comparison. I will return to the matter of rational "structure" in comparative understanding later; it is important for the conditions of interpretation and thus of understanding. But initially, we face a rather obvious question concerning this type of ethics: does it adequately acknowledge the diversity of moral communities as well as the historical-linguistic character of its own reflection?

It is this question that has provoked other scholars in comparative ethics to address the relativity of cultural worlds and belief systems. They attend to given forms of life and the discursive practices of traditions without assuming there is a deep structure that makes up morality.[7] In this they signal the turn to language in moral philosophy, a turn shared by hermeneutics. Unlike hermeneutical thinkers, they are less concerned with the ontological question of language and our being-in-the-world. On the contrary, social-linguistic thinkers seek to explore the specificity of moral languages. They are suspicious of what Jeffrey Stout has called "moral Esperanto," that is, a supposedly universal language, like Green's; and perhaps ontological reflection as well, which "rules the deep structure of morality as such."[8] These theorists contest any drive to complete translation of moral vocabularies through the construction of a metalanguage. This does not mean that there is no possibility for insight into the beliefs of others. We are not trapped in our own linguistic communities. The point is that this common ground cannot be specified in some set of moral principles based on the structure of reason.

The common ground or condition needed for understanding others is the simple fact that persons do learn to speak moral languages despite the diversity of those languages. Inasmuch as there is no final moral language, we can expect that encountering the discourse and beliefs of others might enrich our own. As with the formalist concern for rational structures, I will also return to the insights of these social-linguistic thinkers. After all, interpretation is a social, discursive practice. But again we confront a question: is it not the case that the claims of religious communities about how to live are intertwined with other beliefs, ones about the world and the nature of human life? If this is the case, must we not attend to these other ontological and cosmological beliefs precisely in order to carry out the task of comparative ethics? This is a substantive question. It is one some thinkers hold ought to bear on the very method of religious ethics.

This conviction has given rise to yet another approach in comparative ethics. Between the formalists who seek deep structures of reason and the social-linguistic philosophers who explore the diversity of languages are thinkers who argue for a revised form of ethical naturalism.[9] Like social-linguistic thinkers, the new naturalists reject the vision of reason found in ethical formalism. Yet against the concentration on moral language, the naturalist "treats a system of beliefs as a whole and refuses to isolate moral propositions for analysis from propositions about how things are in the world and how they come to be that way."[10] The task, in other words, is to explore beliefs about how persons and communities should live in relation to other convictions concerning the world (its origin, ordering, and end, as well as meaning and value) and the human place in it.

These new naturalists readily grant the particularity and diversity of moral claims. Nevertheless, they insist that all communities have beliefs about the world that contextualize their moral ones. The condition for comparative understanding is therefore neither an analogy of discursive ability nor a deep formal structure of reason. It is based on the dependence of particular propositions on an entire system of beliefs. In exploring the morals of others, the scholar must not begin with theory but with observation and description of a belief system and its import for moral claims.

This form of reflection begins with no a priori set of obligations, aims, or human purposes; it tries to understand how communities address these in light of their convictions about the world. As Lovin and Reynolds note,

> The range of possible connections between norm, fact, and purpose shifts the attention in naturalistic ethics to substantive, rather than formal questions, and suggests that alternative norms must be evaluated in terms of their place in a complete way of life, include a set of beliefs about human persons and the reality in which they must live and may thrive.[11]

These thinkers are concerned with how given construals of the world and existence shape human life in a community or tradition. In the hermeneutic turn I advocate, the relation of the moral life to beliefs about reality will not be lost. However, hermeneutical reflection also holds that understanding always enacts a world of meaning. This radicalizes claims of the new naturalism about the meaning of a moral "world." The condition for understanding others is precisely our way of being in the world, that is, understanding through the act of interpretation.

This sketch of the options in comparative ethics shows that the debate is located along lines that have beset Western moral philosophy over the last few centuries. It pits descriptivist against formalist accounts of moral rationality in asking about *how* comparative work should be conducted; it traverses the range of ethical theories from naturalism to non-naturalism with regard to *what* ethics is all about. The reason for this dispute is perhaps obvious. Each of the positions in our typology explores religious forms of life. But each does so from the perspective of a different account of reasoning and a different idea of the task of ethics. Any move beyond the current debate requires considering the shape of comparative understanding itself. So we must ask a specifically hermeneutical question, what is happening when we understand others?

While a hermeneutical turn is needed in comparative ethics, the current debate does help to specify the demands facing an adequate comparative position. Any contribution to the current discussion must provide some natural construal of moral rationality and detail the relation between moral convictions and the other beliefs that communities hold. It must also specify the very conditions that make comparative understanding possible within its account of *how* we are to approach the beliefs and lives of others. As a step toward answering these issues I want to turn next to consider the dimensions of comparative understanding.

Translation and Insight

It has often been noted that any account of understanding draws on some root metaphor, analogy, activity, or image as a clue for grasping what it means to understand. A central problem in hermeneutical theory is then what image or act is used as the entrance point for examining what it means to understand. And of course there is a paradox in all of this since the activity of understanding is transpiring in the very attempt to comprehend it. The only way to explore the event of understanding is by considering the symbols, images, or pictures we have adopted or invented of it.

In the West, common metaphors taken to be crucial for thinking about understanding have been those of vision and hearing, and this has determined the criteria for truth claims. To understand is to "see" what is the case, to have an insight into what someone or something means.

Truth is, accordingly, a correspondence between precept and concept, thing and representation, reality and mind. Similar claims can be made for metaphors drawn from speaking and listening. We are interested in what persons, texts, beliefs, and events "tell" us about themselves and the world. For these traditional epistemologies, knowing is a synthetic act of seeing or hearing something, an act in which the mind works on what is given it. This means two things. First, knowing has receptive and active dimensions; it receives something (sense perceptions) which it makes sense of through ideas. This means, second, that knowledge is born of the relation of these receptive and active dimensions. The condition of knowledge is not simply sense data or the construction of ideas but the basis of the synthetic act itself. For instance, critical idealism from Kant to Fichte found that condition in the act of the transcendental "I." Hermeneutic reflection, which challenges the immediacy of the "I" to itself, finds this condition in language and the act of dialogic interpretation. It attempts to escape the narrow concerns of epistemology while acknowledging the active and receptive dimensions of understanding.

Given these observations we can ask: what is the construal thinkers have adopted or made to speak about comparative understanding? Ironically, current comparative ethics simply lacks an answer to this question. This is the case even though there is a tacit agreement among scholars that understanding entails analogical insight and is reached through the act of translation. Adopting the participant's perspective, I want to explore what is meant by translation and insight precisely from the vantage point of interpretation. Translation, I contend, is the active even poetic dimension of comparative understanding while insight marks its receptive basically aesthetic dimension. Their relation is found in the practice of interpretation which is by the nature of the case communicative and intersubjective.

Comparison, at least for the West, often arose through travel and adventure, the act of moving between, or "trans-lating," worlds. This historical fact is rich with phenomenological import. Comparative understanding entails some movement; it is an act of translation. This translation is present most simply at the level of linguistic systems, but more profoundly it entails a movement between cultural worlds thanks to the medium of language. Understanding is then the act of making a movement—a translation—between the texts, beliefs, and activities of others and one's own world of meaning. Hans-Georg Gadamer has made this point.

> Reflect for a moment, if you would, on this: what is involved when we translate, when we transpose a dead thing, in a new act of understanding, from what was present as a text only in a foreign

language into our own language? The translation process contains the whole secret of human understanding of the world and of social communication.[12]

This secret of understanding, we must note, takes place by means of what texts, beliefs, and practices of others have to say to us, their subject matter. This is so only because language is the mediating structure of understanding. Thus in translation one finds instantiated a dialectic of linguistic mediation and understanding concerning what something or someone has to say.

Understanding others is then in part translating or carrying over beliefs, practices, texts, and symbols into a language the interpreter can comprehend. Such movement, we should note, is not foreign to religious communities. Through ritual, dramatic action they entail patterns of movement between worlds, between the sacred and the profane, the temporal and eternal, and through various liminal states, as Victor Turner calls them.[13] In these activities the participant is carried over, is translated, from one world to another by means of language and action. The simplicity of this observation ought not to fool us, however. It means that translation is a metaphoric process. To carry over or transfer meaning as a linguistic act is the movement metaphor entails.[14] It is poetically creative of meaning. Comparison is a metaphoric activity in and through translation. This is the active dimension of comparative understanding.

The metaphoricity of translation poses a genuine problem for comparative studies. To what does the translator's claims refer? Do they refer to the community's beliefs that are being translated and/or the meaning created through the clash between the interpreter's linguistic world and those beliefs? If translation is a metaphoric activity, then it would seem impossible to control the creation of meaning and thus achieve any precise knowledge about the actual beliefs of others. This problem is behind the current debate about the need and possibility of a formal metalanguage for comparative studies and the attempt once again to achieve the observer's perspective. Some thinkers argue that complete translation is not possible in any ordinary language fraught with polysemy and metaphoricity. The philosopher must therefore construct an artificial language, a denaturalized discourse as Paul Griffiths calls it, in which to carry out comparison.[15] This discourse would be free of metaphoricity and thus the creation of meaning in its struggle for univocity. Other philosophers despair of this enterprise since we can hardly be certain that any constructed discourse actually accounts for what one is trying to understand. Likewise, it would seem impossible to escape the metaphoric shape of comparative understanding since understanding itself is an activity of translation.

What this dispute shows is that the formal criterion of comparison, which we might put as representing accurately the beliefs and actions of others as they understand them, cannot be justified solely in terms of an analysis of language since the very act of translation is metaphorically charged. The way to meet the problem, and thus to respect the independent status of what one wants to understand, is not to try to escape the metaphoric character of translation, the density of natural discourse, or the participant's attitude. Instead, it is to ask about what transpires in our own activity of translation. This means realizing that translation is dialectically related to another dimension of understanding.

The current debate in comparative ethics is instructive on this point. All contributors to the dispute seem to agree that what arises through comparative work is some analogical insight into the relation between two sets of beliefs and values.[16] And in fact, philosophers have long known that the ability to metaphorize well, to transpose meanings, requires seeing similarities in differences even as metaphoric discourse enables new insight, new discoveries of what was not previously understood. Insight, we might say, is the passive and even aesthetic dimension of comparative understanding that arises within the act of translation. Paul Ricoeur is correct, then, when he notes that to invent (translation) is actually to discover (insight).[17] Just because analogical insight arises within the inventive activity of translation does not mean that we do not discover something true about how others see life.

Translation and insight are the dialectic at the heart of comparative understanding. That we gain insight through comparison shows us both the possibility and the limits of translation as a metaphoric activity. There are similarities enough to enable us to carry over the beliefs and practices of others into our own discourse realizing that this is also productive of new meaning. However, something is also lost or never transported precisely because of the productive character of the metaphoric act of translation. This fact founds the universality of the hermeneutical problem in comparative studies and thus the ongoing task of interpretation for such work.

What I am suggesting is that comparative understanding is an activity of translation within which arises insight into similarities and differences between traditions, communities, and thinkers by means of engaging the symbols, myths, and beliefs they have about human life and the world. This is not a novel suggestion. It coheres with common practice in comparative studies. What has not been addressed in the current discussion is how to conceptualize the dialectic of translation and insight within interpretation. Scholars are in search of a construal of the act of understanding that is the synthesis of these moments, one that

does not simply appeal to a transcendental "I" but is genuinely comparative itself. Mimesis, I contend, helps in this regard. In order to show this I
must explore the way it enables us to consider the range of issues entailed in comparison.

Mimesis and Interpretation

The terminology of mimesis arose in Dionysian cultic worship and
Sicilian mime, in ritual and drama. Only later was it used by Plato and
Aristotle for speaking about art, poetics, moral education, and even metaphysics. Before Plato's reading of it as "imitation," mimesis "meant not
only imitation, but also 'to make like,' 'to bring to presentation,' 'to express,' 'to pre-sent.'"[18] To understand mimesis as a way of thinking about
symbolic action is then to explore representation and the whole field of
human action.

The roots of mimesis in ritual and drama as well as its philosophical
use by Aristotle concerning narrative have all been reclaimed in contemporary thought.[19] There are several reasons why this retrieval of mimesis
is attractive for my argument. First, a turn to performative action means
that the meaning of a text, symbol, or image cannot be understood solely
in terms of its supposed "author" or a "referent" which it seeks to copy.
This challenges classical theories where ideas and works of art imitate
"nature" or eidetic forms. Hence, it has import for *what* the comparativist
studies since it frees him or her to engage the subject matter of the
interpretandum rather than its supposed origin or author. As Ricoeur has
put it, in hermeneutics we are concerned with what is disclosed in front
of the text as a possible way of being in the world.[20] For the ethicist this
disclosure bears on individual and social conduct and character.

Second, reconsidering mimesis says something about *how* understanding takes place. It does so through the activity of interpretation
as itself a form of ritual and dramatic action. This shifts our account
of understanding from perceptual metaphors (seeing/hearing) to that of
a kind of activity or practice which requires the participant's attitude.[21]
As Gadamer and others argue, understanding arises within dialogical interaction. I claim that dialogue itself must be seen as mimetic in
character. What performative mimesis adds to current theories of dialogue is the centrality of practice, and specifically of performative action,
in understanding.[22]

Finally, the turn to mimesis says something about the *conditions*
for understanding: they are found in the relation of language and action
in the activity of interpretation. Mimetic practices, I argue, are the reflex-

ive processes through which a community or individual gains an identity by engaging various construals of life. If I can show that interpretation is the scholar's mimetic praxis, then we will have demonstrated two things. First, we will have isolated the analogical relation between the mimetic activities of religious communities and that of the scholar. This relation is central to the very possibility of understanding. Second, we will also be able to see why moral demands ground other criteria in comparative religious studies. This means that comparative work itself is a kind of moral task, with all of the risk and responsibility that entails. That said, I want now to specify these claims and their importance for interpretation in comparative religious ethics.

The Conditions of Understanding

Any account of understanding must begin with a simple but vexing problem. To understand anything at all requires some pre-given relation to what one is seeking to understand. Without that relation understanding is quite literally impossible, or worse yet, there is the imposition of the interpreter's perspective on the thought and life of others. This is a problem in comparative studies: what is the condition for understanding moral and religious beliefs radically different from one's own? As we have seen, there is virtually no agreement on this point among comparative ethicists. Some look to the deep structure of rationality itself, others hold to the minimal conditions of having the ability to speak a moral language, and still other philosophers construct denaturalized metalanguages as the condition for comparative work.

A turn to performative action, or mimesis, provides a redress to this problem. It suggests that one condition for comparative study is found in the feelings we have of ourselves and of the world that arises in action. As Hans Jonas puts it,

> reality is disclosed in the same act and as one with the disclosure of my own reality—which occurs in self-action: in feeling my own reality by some sort of *effort* I make, I feel the reality of the world. And I make an effort in the encounter with something other than myself.[23]

My task is not to justify this phenomenological claim. At best we can confirm it by elucidating its heuristic import. The point is simply that a condition of understanding is found in human activity. This is because action has an intentional structure that includes the disclosure of a relation between self, the world, and others. And yet, this initial phenomenological observation about action and the disclosure of reality does not completely answer the problem of the conditions for understanding. It does not tell us about a shared horizon within which our actions take place or it assumes that self-action constitutes that horizon. If the latter is the case, how can we be assured that *what* is being understood is not finally the expression of oneself or, more generally, one's cognitive system or even wishes?

Once we conceive of interpretation as a performative action, then we can grasp the temporal/spatial horizon that is the condition for understanding. This horizon is disclosed by the interpreter's action but not constituted by him or her. Again, Jonas puts this well.

> In miming representation (as in speech), the performer's own body in action is the carrier of the symbolism, which remains bound to the transient act itself. Thus the imagery, enacted in the space and time that actor and spectator share, remains merged with the common causal order in which things happen, interact, and pass. As a real event it has its allotted span within the common time, and is no more. It is indeed repeatable, and by this token its eidetic identity defies the uniqueness of real events; but it has to be repeated in order to be present, and it "is" only while being produced.[24]

Any mimetic action inscribes its participants in a common order through the corporeal character of the interaction. Such corporeality is present whether we are speaking of scholars reading texts or participants in a ritual. Thus the participatory character of mimetic action provides a way to consider the conditions that make comparative understanding possible. By undertaking the act of interpretation the scholar enters a shared temporal/spatial order through the effort of that action.

What constitutes the possibility of insight into similarities between beliefs and ways of life is the common order enacted in interpretation. Yet this is also the condition for apprehending differences since what is disclosed in the act is the reality of the other and the interpreter as different. The interpreter feels the reality of the other thanks to the effort of interpretation. In interpretation this "feeling," as Jonas called it, has a cognitive dimension since it is a quality of understanding. We find it, for instance, in the dissonance we sense between the beliefs of others and our own, responses that can range from revulsion to fascination. Such feelings are to moral understanding what sense perceptions are to empirical knowledge.[25] It is hardly surprising, then, that comparativists agree that understanding is characterized by analogical insight. We gain insight into what always remains different even at the level of basic experience.

This also has bearing on ethical reflection. On the one hand, the temporal/spatial horizon presented through the incarnate character of interpretive action is the backing for a naturalist bent in comparative ethics. The moral life takes place within the structure and dynamics of reality, however construed. On the other hand, the irreducibility of oth-

ers and the "feeling" of ourselves in relation to them disclosed in action
requires a hermeneutical approach to ethics. The "world" of moral action
is always an interpreted one, whatever else it might be. In sum, the event
of understanding is not a transcendence of the world; it is a participation
through interaction in the emergence of a common world of meaning in
continuity with a shared causal order of action. However, *what* is being
interpreted? To address this takes us into problems traditionally assigned
to the discourse of mimesis: the status and meaning of representations.

Mimesis and Representation

For much of Western thought, the tactic taken to explore the meaning and truth status of representations was to isolate their cause. This
assumed that "expression is the power of a subject; and expressions
manifest things, and hence essentially refer us to subjects for whom
these things can be manifest."[26] Imitation in classical and even romantic
thought was a way to conceptualize the relation among representation,
its referent, and the representation's cause. The problem the comparativist
faces is that the images, symbols, and myths religious communities use in
interpreting and guiding their lives cannot easily be reduced to the expression of a subject. The aesthetics of expressivism simply fails to account for complex mythic and symbolic systems. How then are we to
explore these? In order to address this we must consider two things: first,
the general problem of symbolic or linguistic expression and, second,
the particular ones scholars explore.

It is the capacity of linguistic and symbolic forms to efface or transform their own cause that is crucial for their semantic effectiveness. A
work escapes the intentions of its author precisely through its inscription
as a text; it takes on a life of its own. What is disclosed is not simply the
intentionality of a human subject. As Charles Taylor notes,

> What comes about through the development of language in the broad-
> est sense is the coming to be of expressive power, the power to
> make things manifest. It is not unambiguously clear that this ought
> to be considered as self-expression/realization. What is made mani-
> fest is not exclusively, nor even mainly, the self, but a world.[27]

Current hermeneutical theory has capitalized on this point since it frees
the interpreter from the search for the ostensive origins of a work. There
is a difficulty in this, however. If we bracket the question of "authorship,"
how do we understand the representation relative to that to which it
refers, to its subject matter?

This question is at the heart of any theory of text, symbol, or action.
To answer it requires that we examine the audience, or subjects, for

whom things can be manifested and also what is being expressed in practices and texts aside from their supposed author. This is to suggest that the "subject matter" of religious ethics must include the lives of those for whom something is manifest in religious practices. Comparison cannot be constricted to the supposed "moral" discourse of a community, as if that discourse could be severed from the world enacted in the discursive and ritual action of a community. As the new naturalists have seen, comparative ethics must consider the relation between beliefs about how humans can and should live with other beliefs about their world.

However, this naturalist argument must be modified by hermeneutical considerations. Comparative philosophy needs to examine the ways persons and communities have a world of meaning as this bears on life and conduct. The ethicist approaches this by interpreting the images of life that communities make and use in shaping character and conduct through their own performative mimetic activities, everything from rituals to methods of interpreting sacred texts to specific ways of life. *What* the comparativist is exploring is the complex practices communities use to symbolize their own lives. The "referent" of these practices is their reception in a specific form of life as well as what they present as possibilities for life. The moral import of this is obvious: a basic ethical question concerns the formation of life and the actual or possible disparity between beliefs about how one ought to live and actual modes of behavior. Exploring the mimetic dynamics of communities is an entry into this problematic. What makes this exploration possible is that the relation of audience, and thus interpreter, to subject matter transpires in language, not simply as a system of signs but as discourse, as the medium of the reciprocal, dialogic action *between* agents. The scholar enters this dialogical space through the unique effort of interpretation. By engaging the symbols, texts, and actions of other communities the comparativist is presenting a new shared world of meaning.

Thus far, I have made two claims and related them to the discourse of mimesis. First, I have argued that the condition of possibility for understanding others is action. The act of interpretation requires and presents a common temporal and spatial order even while it instantiates the difference between interpreter and what is being interpreted. It is analogous to what happens in religious practices and can be thought about by means of the concept of mimesis, especially when we see that mimesis arose out of dramatic and ritual action. Second, I have suggested that whatever it is that comparative ethics wants to study, it is bound up with the images, symbols, and narratives a community employs to inform their life. This means exploring the power of language through interpretive action to present a possible form of life. Put differently, I have briefly addressed the general problem of expression and representation through the metaphoric character of mimetic action. Can mimesis also help us to explore the more particular expressions that comparativists study?

Gadamer has shown that a symbol, image, or work of art is the transformation into figuration of its subject matter: human action in narratives, sacred origins in cosmogonic myths, and so on. In this, the subject matter, whatever it happens to be, achieves a certain ideality beyond its momentary appearance in discourse or specific enactments, ritual or dramatic. The fleeting and fickle shape of human action, for example, enjoys an increase in meaning through its transformation into a drama. Through the transformation into figuration one is concerned not simply with the contingency of a happening but also with its ideality, its character and meaning.

This helps to explain the disappearance of mimesis as a concept in modern reflection on texts, symbols, and works of art. Modern thought entailed a rejection of a stable nature or essence and looked instead to history and the realm of becoming. The criticism of imitation was that "mimesis as a poetic theory demands a very realistic ontology if it is to thrive or to occur at all. The first step in achieving poetic form is contact with form in nature."[28] Aristotelian mimesis, in other words, meant that the interpreter had to grasp the ideality or form found in the nature of human action as it is re-presented by plot. Based on the argument above, this criticism of classical realism need not trouble us. The ideality grasped by interpreting a community's pictures of life is not the form or nature of the human as such, but precisely what that community is struggling to resemble, is using to inform its specific and historically contingent way of life. The ideality of these pictures is how they form and transform ways of being human by presenting a vision of what ought to be. Thus the particular images, symbols, and myths of communities are transformations into figuration of a vision about life as this bears on the ethos and conduct of a community and its members.

By reclaiming the performative roots of mimesis, we are then concerned with the creation and reception of meaning through particular symbolic forms and actions. Unlike modern expressive theories, the pictures that the comparativist interprets manifest a way of life in a world. Attending to the mimetic practices in which those pictures make sense requires that we consider them neither as realistic imitations of nature, brute imaginative creations, nor simple projections of collective or individual consciousness. Rather, they must be explored within symbolic interaction itself. The totality of a community's symbolic world is enacted in mimetic practices while also informing its way of life. Particular figures must then be placed within the whole complex of the interpretive practices of a community.

On reaching this conclusion we return to the vexing problem of the conditions for understanding. Granting the general conditions for understanding noted above, how is it that the interpreter can come to understand the particular images, symbols, and myths of communities? It is here that we must attend to the shift from the active to the receptive character of understanding, from the poetic aspect of mimetic action to its aesthetic dimension. We need to consider the audience and thus the interpreter of religious communities.

Audience and Interpreter

Through the transformation into figuration, the symbols, images, and actions of others break beyond themselves for beholders, to any possible interpreter. Because a way of life has achieved some ideality through figuration, it is presented for someone, for an audience or reader, who thereby can seek to understand what is so presented. The figurations, we might say, have an intentionality; they call for interpreters to complete their meaning. Thus the audience through its interpretative engagement is crucial to the very meaning of symbols, texts, and images. The participant's attitude is basic to the meaning of what one seeks to understand, to the very *interpretandum* in question. It is in the lives of the audience or the interpreter that the symbolic action breaks beyond the confines of a system of signs.

This observation leads us to the passive dimension of understanding. We should recall that the spectator, the *theoros,* was the observer at the ancient rituals. The "theoretical" stance of the interpreter in comparative religious ethics is then not a disengaged viewing, as Plato held. It does not require the observer's attitude as if the claims of the comparativist were strictly reducible to propositional statements about states of affairs. Rather, a theoretic stance is an interaction with others in order to understand what demands interpretation. Understanding begins, as Gadamer has noted, with listening. And he insists that mimesis and "presentation" [*darstellung*] are not merely a copied repetition, but a recognition of the essence. Because they are not merely repetition, but a bringing-forth, the spectator is involved in them."[29]

This recognition, or insight, is a complex phenomenon. As thinkers from Aristotle to Ricoeur attest, amid interpretive interaction there arise various feelings, from pity to fear, that enable the audience to appropriate what is disclosed by symbolic works. We make our own what we interpret in good measure through our affective responses to it. This feeling, as noted before, is cognitive since it arises in the act of interpretation. It is the moral analogue to sense data. Interpretation thereby allows moral self-knowledge linked to the understanding of others precisely through the feeling of one's own activity. This is the import of the phenomenological observation about action made above: self and other are disclosed in the effort and feeling characteristic of action.

The recognition of the relation of self and other is a good internal to the activity of interpretation, as Alasdair MacIntyre might put it.[30] The good of insight is possible because symbols, myths, and rituals intend an audience, beholders, who are taken into the event of understanding. The interpreter is finally not free from what is being interpreted even as *what* is being understood requires interpreters in order to speak. The relation of interpreter to subject matter constituted amid interpretive action accounts for the contemporaneity experienced in the event of understanding. For instance, we understand the claim of ancient texts and we do so now, in the present. This is possible, again as noted before, because of the temporal and spatial conditions of understanding disclosed by action. There is, as Gadamer calls it, a fusion of horizons (*horizontverschmelzung*) definitive of genuine insight. The horizon of meaning of the interpreter, that is, his or her configuration of the temporal/spatial conditions of meaningful action, is transformed and widened by the *interpretandum* even as it is allowed to speak anew through the interpreter's performative act.

The involvement of the audience, and thus the interpreter, in symbolic meaning bears considerable import for comparative ethics. To interpret the figurations of a community is to understand how certain people's lives are taken into specific mimetic practices and come to resemble what is presented in them. By seeking to carry over or translate meanings, the interpreter is taken into an event such that one sees similarities and differences between the sets of beliefs in question. This insight, I am suggesting, is not grounded in the pictures or beliefs so translated since translation is never complete. Insight is an end, a good, of the mimetic action of interpretation; it is how the human good is tied to, if not exhausted by, rational activity. Insight is a form of understanding qualified by affective response born of effort and human encounter. As the good internal to the practices of interpretation, insight emerges from the analogical relation between interpretation and the mimetic activities through which communities form and appropriate construals of how to live.

By using mimesis to explore comparative interpretation, we see that interpretation is the comparative philosopher's mimetic praxis. Insight is its good. This means that the figures of a tradition which inform life are part of *what* comparative religious ethics explores. Doing so is not simply a way of enriching the theoretical task of comparative religious ethics, as Ronald Green and Charles Reynolds suggest.[31] Without engaging these figurations there would be nothing to compare.

Understanding and Responsibility

But what is being understood in specifically ethical terms and how does this relate to the criteria of interpretation? This is the last dimension of mimetic practice of immediate import for our argument. Obviously, what one seeks to study are the beliefs, images, stories, and other figurations of a community about its world and how one should live. And the formal criterion for interpretation is to represent accurately the figures and life of a community as they understand them. This is formal, we must admit, because one would have to specify what counts as an "accurate" representation, how, if at all, we can grasp the way in which a community understands its own beliefs and images, and, finally, whether or not their own self-understanding is helpfully included in judging the adequacy of an interpretation of their religious beliefs and practices.

I cannot address these issues here, nor is it necessary to do so. The reason for this is that we must first specify the grounds internal to interpretation that justify adherence to this formal criterion and its specifications, whatever they are. This justification must be internal to interpretation because, as noted at the outset of this chapter, we are interested in the philosophy of religion and thus a reasoned approach to the study of the religions. So far, I have argued that mimetic interpretation is the shape of reason in comparative ethics. Now I must show that it grounds the demand for adhering to the criterion of valid interpretation. The irony here, from the perspective of some philosophers, is that I am claiming that moral demands form the context for the more narrow epistemic claims of the scholar. The reason for this is actually simple: if understanding requires participation in the communicative activity of interpretation, then demands on participation and action precede the particular criteria for propositional claims.

I want to approach this question about the formal criterion by exploring it once again through the subject matter of comparative ethics. First, we should note that ritual actions in religious communities surround those events in life which are determinative of existence (birth, death, initiation, and so on) and thus are responses to the disruptions and continuities in existence.[32] Mimetic actions are responses to powers—psychological, social, physiological, even cosmic—which persons suffer and enact. Mimetic practices can be seen as patterns of responsibility in a twofold sense: they entail responding to something or someone, and they require being accountable for actions intended, undertaken, and actualized.[33]

What comparative ethics must explore is the texture of responsibility in different communities expressed through mimetic practices. These practices more basically are ways of participating in the enactment of a world of meaning and relations of power. They are a response to the problem of world building and maintenance, as sociologists put it, and thus also basic existential questions such as suffering and death, the problem of evil, and self-understanding.[34] Such problems are profoundly ontological in character: they concern evaluative, affective responses to a world. The question of responsibility, then, touches how persons and communities envision and posture themselves as participants in their world and how this shapes and informs a way of life. It concerns how they take part in the construal of beliefs, symbols, and myths that guide and judge life and also how they appropriate these in a way of life. Given this, responsibility cannot be limited simply to legal demands or to "the amelioration of the human condition by resolving the problem of cooperation."[35]

This does not mean that comparative ethics begins with an a priori concept of natural human aims or with the deep structure of morality. Rather, it explores how the human *need* to participate in its own formation is carried out through mimetic practices that transform personal and social powers by subjecting them to claims of responsibility.[36] Different communities will figure power differently, through ritual and antirituals, myths, prophetic discourse, and so on, and thus entail various patterns of responsibility, different worlds of meaning and ways of being human. What they share, and all that is needed for comparative study, is the dynamic of mimetic activity through which they respond to and participate in a world. Religious traditions fail or die when their mimetic practices no longer donate this sense of active participation.

If this is the case, then we can grasp the justification for adherence to the formal criterion of interpretation. Interpretation is the scholar's mimetic praxis and, as such, serves as a form of responsibility for him or her. In it is enacted a common world, a world that enables and demands response to others and accountability for one's action. The formal criterion of interpretation merely specifies a way to determine this responsiveness and accountability. Scholars ought willingly submit to this criterion because it is grounded in the very shape of their own act of interpretation; it is not heteronomous but an expression of the free exercise of understanding. For the very same reason, the criterion of interpretation is not simply generated from the subjective purposes of interpreters. Again, Habermas is correct when he notes that "a correct interpretation fits, suits, or explicates the meaning of the *interpretandum*."[37] We now see how the demand for a fitting interpretation arises and how it coheres with the common world of understanding enacted in the mimetic act of interpretation.

To conclude, my point has been that the mimetic shape of interpretation helps us understand the justification of the demand to represent accurately the beliefs, symbols, and lives of others. Interpretation is the scholar's mimetic praxis. It is our means of moving between worlds and thus gaining insight into our lives and those of others. Interpretation is also how we respond to and participate in the enactment of a shared world of action and discourse. The condition and the demand of this is found in action itself whose intentionality, I have argued, is the self-other relation it enacts.

A Proposal for Comparative Religious Ethics

That said, I want to return to the debates in comparative ethics in order to show what import this argument has for moral rationality and the point of comparative ethics. Most basically, I have sought to mediate the disputes found in comparative studies while charting different directions for thought. This required isolating the structure of mimetic action in which understanding transpires even though practices and their communities differ. This formal structure is marked by reciprocal action within a shared temporal/spatial order mediated by linguistic, symbolic forms. It is a condition for comparative, descriptive study and also a reason to question radical relativism in normative reflection. Just because cultures and religions enact different "worlds" that define and shape character and conduct does not negate the fact that to be human is to have a world presented through patterns of reciprocal action. It is this shared fact that makes complete moral relativism spurious. The differences between religions are not incommensurable ones. This is because, if my argument holds, comparative interpretation is itself the enactment of a common world of meaning. It is not of course a pre-given moral universe. Yet through interpretation a shared world of meaning allows us to understand what remains different from us and requires respect for that difference.

The approach to understanding I am advocating moves then beyond the formalist/descriptivist debate in comparative ethics. It does so by tracing a common structure to mimetic action while insisting that one must think comparatively by engaging not only that structure but the figurations, symbols, beliefs, and practices that mark a community's moral world. The dialectic of translation and insight characteristic of comparative understanding founds the demand for critical analysis and interpretive engagement in comparative ethics. In other words, the use of reason in comparative ethics is neither purely formal nor simply descriptive; it is interpretive in character.

The position I have sought to chart also circumvents the naturalist/ non-naturalist debate concerning *what* comparative ethics explores. It suggests that comparative ethics is concerned with moral worlds but that the question of a "world" must take seriously the discursive, symbolic forms enacted in communities that give rise to a sense of reality and possible ways of life. This requires examining the relation between basic human needs and beliefs about reality and human life in descriptive and in normative inquiry. Of course, there is no assumption about what *ought* to be the shape of a moral and religious life. Here a comparative religious ethics must carefully engage, interpret, compare, and evaluate traditions. Yet it is to insist that the problem of mimesis—the picturing, making, and forming of a life-world with reference to what is encountered in the effort and feeling of action—is found in all religious traditions. It is to claim that religions can be seen as complex mimetic practices that construe and enact a world and a way of life. For comparative ethics this means taking seriously the naturalist claim about the relationship between moral convictions and other beliefs. Yet it is to understand this within the problem of a moral "world" and thus the narratives, symbols, and practices that shape life.

With this we also see how the turn to performative action helps answer the most disputed point in comparative ethics: the conditions that make possible comparative study. This condition cannot simply be the deep structure of reason or some specified metalanguage. This is because our only access to the structure of rationality is itself an interpretive one and the practice of construing a metalanguage cannot escape the mediation of all human activity by natural linguistic forms. Likewise, the condition for understanding cannot be simply an analogy of discursive ability, as sociolinguistic thinkers seem to hold. This is so because, as noted before, one must also consider that in which linguistic activity takes place, its horizon, if one wants to grasp how it is we can understand what is and must remain different. What is more, the experience of action—the sense of self and other through effort and encounter—shows that language games break beyond themselves just because they are forms of action. Finally, the condition for comparative work cannot simply be the descriptive study of the myth, symbols, and practices communities make and employ in speaking about their world and their lives. These must be interpreted in order to be meaningful and thus are bound to our own act of understanding.

In short, the main options in comparative religious ethics offer deficient accounts of the conditions for their own interpretative activity. By drawing on the conceptual density of mimesis, I have isolated the means to consider the condition for understanding. It is, as we have seen, a shared temporal/spatial order enacted through the interpretive activity of examining the figurations communities make and use to inform their lives. By considering what transpires in interpretation, that is, analogical insight within translation, we have seen that the common world of understanding is a metaphorized world that we invent in order to discover something about others and ourselves. This shared world is enacted in a practice (interpretation) characterized by a movement between worlds (translation) with its own good (insight) and under the moral demand (responsibility) to adhere to the formal criterion of comparison.

The task of comparative religious ethics on this reading is not simply the study of diverse moral traditions, although it is certainly that. More profoundly, the practice of comparative ethics contributes to the enactment of a shared moral universe in which the diverse ways of being human are preserved amid the claims of responsibility. Only by insisting on this do we avoid the tyranny of interpretation, that is, the imposition of the interpreter's perspective on what is under inquiry. To see interpretation as a form of responsibility means that the comparativist must respond to the claim of the other and be accountable for his or her actions. The formal and material criteria for interpretation rest on this moral demand. With this conclusion we reach as well what this argument contributes to the general task of the comparative philosophy of religions. Such work can begin with the simple fact that human beings fashion their lives by engaging various figures that disclose to them something about the meaning, value, and purpose of being human. It reaches its goal when through encountering others in the performative act of interpretation there is some apprehension of the shape, texture, and direction of their lives and our own within a shared space of meaning and responsibility.

Conclusion

Comparative religious ethics seeks to understand other communities and traditions even as it hopes to say something about our moral and religious condition. It would be a mistake, therefore, to think that the argument made in these pages is not itself fundamentally concerned to address the pressing questions that face us. Is it not the case in the West that the images, myths, and symbols we have used or made to guide our lives are now in serious question? Have we not in fact witnessed the decay of mimetic practices that shaped and animated life into repressive and manipulative forms of thought and discourse seen in technological mass culture?

In this situation we lack a measure for responsible existence because the "distinction between life and art, reality and appearance becomes impossible . . . . Life becomes the proto-type of the world of appearances and these the proto-types of life."[38] In response to this situation I have argued that interpretation is our mimetic activity. It is our way of responding to the questions that confront us even as it bears within it the good of understanding that insists on concern for others. In undertaking to engage others, the interpreter struggles to understand how we should live. And this understanding emerges, if at all, within practices that enact the fragile claim of responsibility.[39]

Notes

1. Jürgen Habermas, *Moral Consciousness and Communicative Action,* translated by Christian Lenhardt and Shierry Weber Nicholsen with introduction by Thomas McCarthy (Cambridge, Mass.: The MIT Press, 1990), 27.

2. Ibid., 28.

3. My approach is reflexive in character but this does not mean that I am concerned simply with the act of consciousness and the attempt to grasp the generative power of its act, as in German Idealism. By turning to interpretation as reciprocal action between participants I am suggesting that understanding is always social and linguistic in character. This does not preclude exploring the reciprocal activity constitutive of understanding in a reflexive manner, seeking to understand its dynamic and shape, what is disclosed in it, and even its conditions of possibility. On these issues, see H. Richard Niebuhr, *Faith on Earth: An Inquiry into the Structure of Human Faith,* edited by Richard R. Niebuhr (New Haven, Conn.: Yale University Press, 1989), and Otto Pöggeler, "Die etische-politische Dimension der hermeneutischen Philosophie" in *Probleme der Ethik—zur Diskussiongestellt,* ed. Gerd-Günther Grau (Freiburg/Munich: Karl Alber, 1972), 45–82.

4. This is not to suggest that there is any agreement between thinkers. Else, for instance, contests Koller's claim that mimesis relates dance and music in early Greek thought; Else himself concentrates on drama. Philosophers also disagree. Ricoeur is concerned with narrative mimesis while Morrison takes mimesis to be a way to speak about historical change and reform. Other differences and disputes could be mentioned. What is important is that with the decline of romantic expressivism, mimesis is again considered basic to the task of understanding social existence, historical experience, aesthetic reality, and understanding itself.

For works by classical scholars on mimesis see G. F. Else, "Imitation in the Fifth Century" in *Classical Philology* 53(2, 1958):73–90, Herman Koller, *Die Mimesis in Antike: Nachahmung, Darstellung, Ausdruck* (Bern: A. Francke, 1954), and Göram Sörböm, *Mimesis and Art: Studies in the Origin and Early Development of an Aesthetic Vocabulary* (Stockholm: Bonnier, 1966). For philosophical treatments see Jacques Derrida, "Economimesis," translated by R. Klein, *Diacritics* 11 (1981): 3–25; Hans-Georg Gadamer, *Die Aktualität des Schönen: Kunst als Spiel, Symbol und Fest* (Stuttgart: Philipp Recalm, 1977); René Girard, *Violence and the Sacred,* translated by Patrick Gregory (Baltimore, Md.: The Johns Hopkins University Press, 1977); Karl Morrison, *The Mimetic Tradition of Reform in the West* (Princeton, N.J.: Princeton University Press, 1982); Paul Ricoeur, *Time and Narrative,* volume 1, translated by Kathleen McLaughlin and David Pellauer (Chicago: The University of Chicago Press, 1984); William Schweiker, *Mimetic Reflections: A Study in Hermeneutics, Theology and Ethics* (New York: Fordham University Press, 1990); and Christoph Wulf, "Mimesis" in *Historische Anthopologie: Zum Problem der Humanwissenschaften heute oder Versuch einer Neubegründung,* edited by Gunter Gebauer, et al. (Hamburg: Rowohlt Taschenbuch Verlag, 1989), 83–128.

5.   See Ronald Green, *Religious Reason* (New York: Oxford University Press, 1978), and his *Religion and Moral Reason* (New York: Oxford University Press, 1988). Also see Ronald Green and Charles Reynolds "Cosmogony and the 'Question of Ethics'" in *The Journal of Religious Ethics* 14(1, 1986):139–56; David Little and Sumner B. Twiss, *Comparative Religious Ethics* (New York: Harper and Row, 1978); and John P. Reeder, Jr., *Source, Sanction, and Salvation: Religion and Morality in Christian Traditions* (Englewood Cliffs, N.J.: Prentice Hall, 1988).

6.   Green, *Religious Reason,* 4.

7.   For different examples of this approach, see Charles Larmore, *Patterns of Moral Complexity* (Cambridge: Cambridge University Press, 1987); Jeffrey Stout, *Ethics after Babel: The Languages of Morals and Their Discontents* (Boston: Beacon Press, 1987); and Bernard Williams, *Ethics and the Limits of Philosophy* (Cambridge: Harvard University Press, 1985).

8.   Stout, *After Babel,* 5.

9.   See Francis X. Clooney, "Finding One's Place in the Text: A Look at the Theological Treatment of Caste in Traditional India," *The Journal of Religious Ethics* 17(1, 1989):1–29; Robin W. Lovin and Frank E. Reynolds, "In the Beginning," in *Cosmogony and Ethical Order: New Studies in Comparative Ethics,* edited by Robin W. Lovin and Frank E. Reynolds (Chicago: The University of Chicago Press, 1985), and their "Focus Introduction" in *The Journal of Religious Ethics* 14(1, 1986):48–60.

10.   Lovin and Reynolds, "In the Beginning," 3.

11.   Lovin and Reynolds, "Focus Introduction," 57.

12.   Hans-Georg Gadamer, *Truth and Method,* translated by G. Barden and J. Cumming (New York: Continuum, 1975), 497.

13.   See Victor Turner, *Dramas, Fields, and Metaphors: Symbolic Action in Human Society* (Ithaca, N.Y.: Cornell University Press, 1974).

14.   For helpful discussions of metaphor, see Paul Ricoeur, *The Rule of Metaphor: Multi-Disciplinary Studies in the Creation of Meaning in Language,* translated by Robert Czerny, Kathleen McLaughlin, and John Costello (Toronto: University of Toronto Press, 1977); and Janet Martin Soskice, *Metaphor and Religious Language* (Oxford: Oxford University Press, 1985).

15.   See Paul Griffiths, "Denaturalized Discourse," paper presented for The Colloquium on Religion(s) in History and Culture at the University of Chicago, 1989.

16.   For an example of this claim, see Lee Yearly, *Aquinas and Mencius: Theories of Virtue and Conceptions of Courage* in *Towards a Comparative Philosophy of Religion(s),* edited by David Tracy and Frank E. Reynolds (Albany, N.Y.: State University of New York Press, 1990).

17.   See Paul Ricoeur, *Interpretation Theory: Discourse and the Surplus of Meaning* (Fort Worth, Texas: Texas Christian University, 1976).

18.   Wulf, "Mimesis," 83. For a more extended discussion, see Koller, *Die Mimesis in Antike.*

19.   There are thinkers who have reclaimed the roots of mimesis in ritual. Hans-Georg Gadamer, for instance, draws on mimesis in order to explore the power of texts, symbols, works of art, and thus language to disclose the being of what they figure. René Girard charts how mimetic ritual practices and their linguistic expressions conceal basic social processes, ones marked by violence and appeals to the sacred. There are also philosophers and critics, like Derrida, who draw on the roots of mimesis in mime-drama. They do so in order to deconstruct Western aesthetics and epistemology because of its dependence on the idea of realistic imitation or the priority of speaking over writing. The mime is, after all, a mute signifer. For these theorists language is not a set of ideas, words, and symbols that are imitations of some "referent" transcending them. It is a web of signs productive of meaning through the "play" of those signs when this is activated by an interpreter. Finally, there are theorists such as Paul Ricoeur concerned with narrative. They seek to reclaim Aristotle's insight that plot is the mimesis of human action. Narratives tell us something about human action because they configure action into a meaningful whole, a plot.

20.   See Ricoeur, *Interpretation Theory.*

21.   From my perspective, it is hardly surprising that some religious traditions, like Judaism, have transformed actual ritual practices into textual strategies of interpretation. Historians of religion and anthropologists have also long understood the importance of symbolic action for claims about the world and the human. On this see Turner, *Dramas, Fields and Metaphors* and also Mircea Eliade, *The Sacred and the Profane: The Nature of Religion,* translated by Willard R. Trask (New York: Harcourt, Brace, 1959). Kenneth Burke has explored dramatic action as a way to relate the hexad of terms central to any account of human activity: act, agent, scene, means, purpose, and attitude. See his *On Symbols and Society,* edited with introduction by Joseph R. Gusfield (Chicago: The University of Chicago Press, 1989). What has not been done is to take such action as the clue for exploring understanding within comparative religious ethics. That is the task of this essay.

22.   In saying that interpretation is a form of enactment I am not however restricting the concept of "performative" to speech acts, as J. L. Austin and others have done. I am using it in an anthropological and sociological sense to denote those communal dramatic and ritual activities through which something (a myth, human action, a god) is presented in and for community. See J. L. Austin, *How to Do Things with Words,* 2nd ed., edited by J. O. Urmson and Marina Sbisa (Cambridge: Cambridge University Press, 1975).

23.   Hans Jonas, *The Phenomenon of Life: Toward a Philosophical Biology* (Chicago: The University of Chicago Press, 1982), 148.

24.   Ibid., 163 n.3.

25.   On this see Habermas, *Moral Consciousness and Communicative Action,* 43–115.

26.   Charles Taylor, *Human Agency and Language,* Philosophical Papers I (Cambridge: Cambridge University Press, 1985), 221.

27.   Ibid., 238.

28.   John D. Boyd, *The Function of Mimesis and Its Decline* (Cambridge: Harvard University Press, 1968), 54.

29.   Gadamer, *Truth and Method,* 103.

30.   See Alasdair MacIntyre, *After Virtue: A Study in Moral Theory* (Notre Dame, Ind.: University of Notre Dame Press, 1981).

31.   See Green and Reynolds, "Cosmogony and the 'Question of Ethics,'" 139–45.

32. For the scholar who has tried to develop a theory of mimesis to explore these events, see Girard's *Violence and the Sacred*. Also see William Schweiker, "Sacrifice, Interpretation and the Sacred: The Import of Gadamer and Girard for Religious Studies" in *The Journal of the American Academy of Religion* 55(4, 1987):791–810.

33. For positions that have informed my argument at this point, see H. Richard Niebuhr, *The Responsible Self: An Essay in Christian Moral Philosophy*, with an introduction by James M. Gustafson (New York: Harper and Row, 1963); and Hans Jonas, *The Imperative of Responsibility: In Search of an Ethics for the Technological Age*, translated by Hans Jonas with the collaboration of David Herr (Chicago: The University of Chicago Press, 1984).

34. For example, see Peter L. Berger, *The Sacred Canopy: Elements of a Sociological Theory of Religion* (New York: Doubleday, 1967).

35. Little and Twiss, *Comparative Religious Ethics*, 28.

36. The recent shift in naturalist ethics has been from claims about the natural ends of the human, which seem difficult to sustain in light of the actual diversity of moral communities, to basic human needs. On this see Basil Mitchell, *Morality, Religious and Secular* (Oxford: Clarendon Press, 1980). I am suggesting that one of those needs, and perhaps the crucial one for the human qua human, is the need to picture in order to come to be as a specific person or community. In this essay I cannot explore the implication of this for naturalism in religious ethics.

37. Habermas, *Moral Consciousness and Communicative Action*, 27.

38. Wulf, "Mimesis," 119.

39. I would like to thank Lois Malcolm, Frank E. Reynolds, and Robin Lovin for helpful comments on the argument of this essay.

References

Austin, J. L.
   1975 *How to Do Things with Words*. 2nd ed. Cambridge: Cambridge University Press.

Berger, Peter L.
   1967 *The Sacred Canopy: Elements of a Sociological Theory of Religion*. New York: Doubleday.

Boyd, John D.
1968 *The Function of Mimesis and Its Decline*. Cambridge: Harvard University Press.

Burke, Kenneth.
1989 *On Symbols and Society*. Chicago: The University of Chicago Press.

Clooney, Francis X.
1989 "Finding One's Place in the Text: A Look at the Theological Treatment of Caste in Traditional India," *The Journal of Religious Ethics*. 17:1–29.

Derrida, Jacques.
1981 "Economimesis," trans. by R. Klein *Diacritics* 11, 3–25.

Else, G. F.
1958 "Imitation in the 5th Century," 53:2, *Classical Philology*, 73–90.

Eliade, Mircea
1959 *The Sacred and the Profane: The Nature of Religion*. New York: Harcourt, Brace.

Gadamer, Hans-Georg.
1977 *Die Aktualitat des Schonen: Kunst als Spiel, Symbol und Fest*. Stuttgart: Philip Recalm.

Gadamer, Hans-Georg.
1975 *Truth and Method*. New York: Continuum.

Girard, René.
1977 *Violence and the Sacred*. trans. by Patrick Gregory. Baltimore, Md.: The Johns Hopkins University Press.

Green, Ronald.
1978 *Religious Reason*. New York: Oxford University Press.

Green, Ronald.
1988 *Religion and Moral Reason*. New York: Oxford University Press.

Green, Ronald, and Charles Reynolds.
1986 "Cosmogeny and The 'Question of Ethics,'" *The Journal of Religious Ethics*, 14:1, 139–56.

Griffiths, Paul.
1989 "Denaturalized Discourse," paper presented at the Colloquium on Religion(s) in History and Culture at The University of Chicago.

Habermas, Jürgen
1990 *Moral Consciousness and Communicative Action.* trans. by Christian Lenhardt and Shierry Weber Nicholsen with an introduction by Thomas McCarthy. Cambridge, Mass.: The MIT Press.

Jonas, Hans.
1982 *The Phenomenon of Life: Toward a Philosophical Biology.* Chicago: The University of Chicago Press.

Jonas, Hans.
1984 *The Imperative of Responsibility: In Search of Ethics for the Technological Age,* trans. by Hans Jonas and David Herr. Chicago: The University of Chicago Press.

Koller, Herman.
1954 *Die Mimesis in Antike: Nachahmung, Darstellung, Ausdruck.* Bern: A. Francke.

Larmore, Charles.
1987 *Patterns of Moral Complexity* Cambridge: Cambridge University Press.

Little, David, and Sumner B. Twiss.
1978 *Comparative Religious Ethics.* New York: Harper and Row.

Lovin, Robin W., and Frank E. Reynolds, eds.
1985 *Cosmogony and Ethical Order: New Studies in Comparative Ethics.* Chicago: The University of Chicago Press.

Lovin, Robin W., and Frank E. Reynolds.
1986 "Focus Introduction," *The Journal of Religious Ethics.* 14:1, 48–60.

Morrison, Karl.
1982 *The Mimetic Tradition of Reform in the West.* Princeton, N.J.: Princeton University Press.

MacIntyre, Alasdair.
1981 *After Virtue: A Study in Moral Theology.* Notre Dame, Ind.: University of Notre Dame.

Mitchell, Basil.
1980 *Morality, Religions and Secular.* Oxford: Clarendon Press.

Morrison, Karl.
1982 *The Mimetic Tradition of Reform in the West.* Princeton, N.J.: Princeton University Press.

Niebuhr, H. Richard.
1963 *The Responsible Self: An Essay in Christian Moral Philosophy.*
N.Y.: Harper and Row.

Niebuhr, H. Richard.
1989 *Faith on Earth: An Inquiry into the Structure of Human Faith*, ed. by Richard R. Niebuhr. New Haven, Conn.: Yale University Press.

Pöggeler, Otto.
1972 "Die etische-politische Dimension der hermeneutischen Philosophie," *Probleme der Ethik-zur Diskussion.* ed. by Gerd-Gunther Grau. Freiburg/Munich: Karl Alber.

Reeder, John P., Jr.
1988 *Source, Sanction, and Salvation: Religion and Morality in Christian Traditions.* Englewood Cliffs, N.J.: Prentice Hall.

Ricoeur, Paul.
1976 *Interpretion Theory: Discourse and the Surplus of Meaning.* Fort Worth, Texas: Texas Christian University.

Ricoeur, Paul.
1977 *The Rule of Metaphor: Multi-Disciplinary Studies in the Creation of Meaning in Language.* trans. by Robert Czerny. Toronto: University of Toronto Press.

Ricoeur, Paul.
1984 *Time and Narrative.* Volume 1 trans. by Kathleen McLaughlin and David Pellauer. Chicago: The University of Chicago Press.

Schweiker, William.
1987 "Sacrifice, Interpretation and the Sacred: The Import of Gadamer and Girard for Religious Studies," *The Journal of the American Academy of Religion* 55:4, 791–810.

Schweiker, William.
1990 *Mimetic Reflections: A Study in Hermeneutics, Theology and Ethics.* New York: Forham University Press.

Sorbom, Goram.
1966 *Mimesis and Art: Studies in the Origin and Early Development of an Aesthetic Vocabulary.* Stockholm: Bonnier.

Soskice, Janet Martin.
1985 *Metaphor and Religious Language.* Oxford: Oxford University Press.

Stout, Jeffrey.
1987 *Ethics after Babel: The Language of Morals and Their Discontents.* Boston: Beacon Press.

Taylor, Charles.
1985 *Human Agency and Language,* Philosophical Papers I. Cambridge: Cambridge University Press.

Turner, Victor.
1974 *Dramas, Field, and Metaphors: Symbolic Action in Human Society.* Ithaca, N.Y.: Cornell University Press.

Williams, Bernard.
1985 *Ethics and The Limits of Philosophy.* Cambridge: Harvard University Press.

Wulf, Christoph.
1989 "Mimesis" *Historische Anthopologie: Zum Problem der Humanwissenschaften heute oder Versuch einer Neubegrundung.* ed. by Gunter Gebauer, et al. 83–128. Hamburg: Rowohlt aschenbuch Verlag.

Yearly, Lee.
1990 *Aquinas and Mencius: Theories of Virtue and Conceptions of Courage* in *Towards a Comparative Philosophy of Religion(s).* Albany, N.Y.: State University of New York.

Chapter 10

Reconciliation and Rupture: The Challenge and Threat of Otherness

Richard J. Bernstein

Michael Theunissen begins his classic study, *Der Andere* (*The Other*) by declaring:

> Few issues have exercised as powerful a hold over the thought of this century as that of "the Other." It is difficult to think of a second theme, even one that might be of more substantial significance, that has provoked as widespread an interest as this one; it is difficult to think of a second theme that so sharply marks off the present—admittedly a present growing out of the nineteenth century and reaching back to it—from its historical roots in the tradition. To be sure, the problem of the Other has been thought through in former times and has at times been accorded a prominent place in ethics and anthropology, in legal and political philosophy. But the problem of the Other has certainly never penetrated as deeply as today into the foundations of philosophical thought. It is no longer the simple object of a specific discipline but has already become the topic of first philosophy. The question of the Other cannot be separated from the most primordial questions raised by modern thought.[1]

When Theunissen first made these claims in 1965, he could scarcely have realized how prophetic they would be. Since that time it has become

even more evident that "the question of the Other"—or more accurately
the tangled network of questions—are at the very center of philosophy
and the full range of the cultural disciplines. These questions are at the
heart of the work of Gadamer, Habermas, Ricoeur, Foucault, Derrida,
Levinas, Lyotard, and many others. They are involved in the fascination—one might say the obsession—with incommensurability that has
dominated so much of Anglo-American thought. There is scarcely a cultural discipline today, including the comparative study of religions, that
does not gravitate to the complex of issues concerning alterity and "the
Other."

Even Theunissen's ambitious study of the "social ontology of Husserl,
Heidegger, Sartre, and Buber" now strikes us as quite limited. When
Theunissen characterizes what he means by the Other, he tells us:

> Generally speaking, "the Other" comprehends all those concepts by
> means of which contemporary philosophy has sought to set out the
> structure of being-with, or its original transcendental form. Thus
> among other things, it comprehends the difference between "Thou"
> on the one side and the "alien I"—the alter ego or being-with-the-
> Other—on the other side.[2]

Theunissen's study of the Other focuses primarily on what may be called
the personal other—what the French call *l'autrui*. He does not thematize
the more generic and threatening sense of "the Other" (*l'Autre*) that has
dominated so much recent discussion—when, for example, Foucault
speaks of madness as "the Other of Reason" or when Derrida speaks of
"the Other of philosophy."

Now the question I want to ask is: why? Why have the problems
of the Other penetrated so deeply into the foundations of philosophy;
why is it that these questions are inseparable from "the most primordial
questions raised by modern thought?" Without claiming to give an adequate answer, let me indicate some relevant considerations required for
an answer.

Theunissen provides a clue when he tells us that the concern with
the Other grows out and reaches back to the nineteenth century. We
think immediately of Hegel for whom the question of the Other is at the
heart of his characterization of Spirit (*Geist*) and speculative thinking.
The dialectical logic of *Geist* is a logic of otherness, difference, negativity,
contradiction, and the resolution of contradiction. I do not think there is
another philosopher who so deeply and thoroughly sought to think
through the dialectical power of otherness. I also think that much of the
twentieth-century philosophic concern with alterity can be understood as
a struggle with and against Hegel. Otherness is always breaking out in

the dialectical movement of *Geist*. Any moment that we seize upon contains its *negating* other. Hegel relentlessly pursues the highway of despair where we think we have grasped, mastered, comprehended the other—only to discover our failure and the necessity to move on to comprehend a totality, a whole, a one that is self-grounded and self-differentiating. This is the movement of *aufheben* in which there is affirmation, negation, and sublation. But this is not an endless process of the bad infinite. For it culminates in a grasp of the true infinite where we comprehend a totality that at once self-differentiates itself from itself and is self-identical. There is not only the desire and promise of reconciliation in which all otherness, ruptures, and oppositions are overcome, but the fulfillment of this promise. Hegel is frequently read as if he valorizes totality, sameness, wholeness, the System where—despite his protests to the contrary—otherness and difference are submerged and repressed. But if we read him carefully, he asserts the equiprimordialness of identity and difference. For Hegel is constantly showing us how—like the return of the repressed—otherness and difference rupture our false reconciliations and demand to be encountered.

It is because Hegel can be read as systematically ambiguous, because his "solution" to the problem of the one and the many, identity and difference, the same and the other is so unstable that he is open to so many diverse interpretations and criticisms. Kierkegaard, Heidegger, Sartre, Adorno, Derrida, and Levinas—in radically different ways—challenge and question the very idea of a Hegelian *aufheben* in which identity and difference are reconciled. They can all be read as seeking to show us that what eludes the Hegelian dialectic of sameness and otherness is the otherness of the Other—its singularity that is never quite comprehended by the Concept. From this alleged failure they draw diverse radical consequences. It is as if the Hegelian synthesis has been shattered and fragmented for us—as if "things fall apart, the center cannot hold."

There is another way in which Hegel's long shadow hovers over much of the twentieth-century struggle with otherness. When Spirit (*Geist*) makes its first explicit appearance in the *Phenomenology,* Hegel speaks of "the experience of what Spirit is—this absolute substance which is the unity of the different independent self-consciousnesses which, in their opposition, enjoy perfect freedom and independence: 'I' that is 'We' and 'We' that is 'I.'"[3] He opens his discussion of *Lordship and Bondage* with the powerful and consequential claim that has echoed ever since Hegel: "Self-Consciousness exists in and for itself when, and by the fact that, it exists for another, that it exists only in being acknowledged."[4] But here too there is a fateful ambiguity. Is this "we" a genuine "we"—a *plurality* of independent self-consciousnesses that achieve independence and freedom in and through mutual recognition? Or does this "we" itself turn out to be a monological Absolute Subject in which the several "I's" are properly comprehended as only "moments" within a single Absolute Subject?

Habermas, for example, reads Hegel as still caught within the aporias of the "philosophy of the subject" that has dominated so much of philosophy from Descartes to the present, a "philosophy of the subject" that Habermas argues is now exhausting itself.[5] But ironically, Habermas' own theory of communicative action and his claim that a major paradigm shift has taken place in the linguistic communicative turn of the twentieth century can itself be interpreted as exploiting the dialogical potentials in Hegel's dialectical analysis of mutual recognition. Indeed—in different ways—the pragmatists, especially Peirce, Dewey, and Mead—as well as Buber and Gadamer—break with the philosophy of the Absolute Subject, and give primacy to the dialogue that we are.

Hegel's ambiguous legacy can be approached in still another way—one that brings out the practical implications of what he shows us—practical consequences that have become so poignantly acute for us in the twentieth century. These become all too vivid in Hegel's dialectical examination of Absolute Freedom and Terror. Hegel tells us that "this undivided substance of absolute freedom ascends the throne of the world without any power being able to resist it."[6] Hegel is both incisive and prophetic when he says, "In this absolute freedom . . . all social groups or classes which are the spiritual spheres into which the whole is articulated are abolished; the individual consciousness that belonged to any such sphere, and willed and fulfilled itself in it, has put aside its limitation; its purpose is the general purpose, its language universal law, its work the universal work."[7] This form of absolute freedom and abstract universality, which seeks to destroy all otherness and difference, results in a "fury of destruction."

Hegel understood what has become even more extreme in the twentieth century—how the lust for absolute freedom and abstract universality can seek to destroy all differences, otherness, and plurality. Consequently, it is profoundly ironic that Hegel is frequently caricatured as if he were advocating what he so brilliantly and relentlessly criticized. We can see this in Lyotard's rhetorical ending of his essay, "What is Postmodernism?" where, with direct reference to Hegel, he declares:

> The nineteenth and twentieth centuries have given us as much terror as we can take. We have paid a high enough price for the nostalgia of the whole and the one, for the reconciliation of the concept and the sensible, of the transparent and the communicable experience. Under the general demand for slackening and for appeasement we can hear mutterings of the desire for a return to terror, for the real-

ization of the fantasy to seize reality. The answer is: Let us wage war on totality; let us be witnesses to the unpresentable; let us activate the differences . . . .[8]

"Let us activate the differences"—that might almost be taken as a slogan for the twentieth-century concern with alterity and otherness. Hegel casts his long ambiguous shadow over us because we no longer seem to be able to "hold together" his fragile synthesis. Hegel's Totality and System have been shattered and fragmented. And yet we are still plagued by the questions that he has bequeathed to us. How can we avoid theoretical and practical violence, imperialism, colonization, and invidious marginalization—allowing the "letting be" of differences and otherness? How can we avoid the aporias of excessive nominalism, fragmentation and self-defeating forms of relativism, where we give up any attempt to comprehend and understand otherness and differences, where we stand dumbly silent before otherness? These questions go to the very heart of our everyday lives. It makes eminently good sense that the language of difference and otherness speaks to all those who have experienced the pain and humiliation of being silenced or made invisible because of their own otherness. It also makes sense why there is so much skepticism about appeals to Reason and Universality because these concepts have been used—or rather abused—to suppress and repress otherness and difference. We may no longer be able to "hold together" what Hegel claimed we can and must "hold together." But neither can we forget the lesson Hegel taught us—that when we think through extremes, they have an uncanny way of meeting, of being dependent upon each other.

I do not think it makes much sense to speak of a "solution" to the problems bequeathed to us by the fragmentation of the Hegelian Totality. But I want to show that we can give a reading of the strains and tensions of twentieth-century thought that provides a matrix for thinking about these issues—that we are not simply caught in an endless repetition of aporetic extremes. If I am right, then this also has the important consequences for how we might think about a philosophy of religion that gives a prominent place to the historical and comparative study of religions.

The metaphors that I want to employ to understand our present situation are drawn from Theodor Adorno and Walter Benjamin. They are the metaphors of a "force-field" (*kraftfeld*), and a constellation. By a force-field Adorno means "a relational interplay of attractions and adversions that constitute the dynamic, transmutational structure of a complex phenomenon." By constellation—a metaphor that Adorno borrowed from Benjamin—he means "a juxtaposed rather than integrated cluster of changing elements that resist reduction to a common denominator, essential core, or generative first principle."[9] Both meta-phors highlight the unstable tensed relation of changing elements that resist reduction and unification. The hypothesis that I want to explore is that we now find ourselves in a new force-field and constellation that deeply affects our thinking about otherness—not only in philosophy but in the entire range of the cultural disciplines. In this context I want to focus on the interplay of attractions and adversions between hermeneutics and deconstruction—two juxtaposed, nonreducible elements in this new constellation.

Let me begin with hermeneutics. In our time, hermeneutics is closely associated with Gadamer, although hermeneutic themes have a much broader significance. The most controversial theme in Gadamer is his defense of the ontological significance of the foreknowledge, prejudg-ments and prejudices that are constitutive of our being-in-the-world. Gadamer seeks to expose what he calls the "Enlightenment's prejudice against prejudice." Although Gadamer uses the provocative term "preju-dice," it is evident that he wants to distinguish between blind distorting prejudices and the tacit prejudgments we inherit from the tradition that are *enabling*—that provide the foreknowledge required for all under-standing. Gadamer claims that the prejudgments we inherit from the traditions to which we belong can never become fully transparent. In this respect he challenges the Cartesian claim—echoed throughout the En-lightenment—that by an act of rational self-reflection we can distance ourselves and critically bracket *all* prejudgments that are not based on the authority of Reason itself. Although Gadamer has been deeply influ-enced by Hegel, he also calls into question the very idea of absolute knowledge where all our prejudgments would be grounded in Reason. Gadamer's claims about the constitutive character of our foreknowledge are not unique to hermeneutics. It is a theme that is just as important for understanding the sciences. Peirce himself—in his own critique of Cartesianism—declared in 1868:

> We cannot begin with complete doubt. We must begin with all the prejudices which we actually have when we enter upon the study of philosophy. These prejudices are not to be dispelled by a maxim, for they are things which it does not occur to us *can* be questioned."[10]

We find a similar insistence on the constitutive role of prejudgments in the work of Kuhn, Popper, and Lakatos.[11] But the question that must be faced is how are we to distinguish blind prejudices from enabling preju-dices—what Gadamer calls "legitimate" prejudices. It is here that the encounter with the Other becomes so important for him. For it is only in and through the encounter with the Other than we risk our prejudices and can achieve some critical distance on them. Self-knowledge and self-understanding are always achieved in and through the encounter with the Other.

To understand how this is so we must focus on Gadamer's understanding of our linguistic horizons. As historical beings constituted by changing prejudgments inherited from the traditions to which we belong, our understanding is necessarily limited, finite, and fallible. Nevertheless, our horizons are not closed, they are essentially open and fluid. We can always reach out to understand what is other and different. This does not mean that we escape from our horizons because it is precisely those horizons that enable us to understand what is strange, alien, other. In our dialogical encounters with the Other we aspire to achieve a fusion of horizons. This thesis about the intrinsic openness of our horizons also connects up with motifs that have many other sources in contemporary philosophy. Gadamer is challenging in a hermeneutical context what Karl Popper has challenged in the context of understanding the character of natural scientific inquiry. For Popper criticizes what he calls the "myth of the framework," the myth that "we are prisoners caught in the framework of our theories; our expectations; our past experiences; our language"[12] and that we are so locked into these frameworks that we cannot communicate with those imprisoned in "radically" different frameworks.

Ironically, this is a charge that Popper (and many others) have made against Kuhn. But I think it is an unfair and distortive criticism of Kuhn. Kuhn is actually much closer to Gadamer. The introduction of the notion of incommensurability was not intended to deny that we can compare—indeed, rationally compare—rival paradigms. On the contrary it was intended to clarify what we are doing in such comparison. Kuhn was calling into question in a scientific context what Gadamer calls into question for all understanding, i.e., that there is a neutral, ahistorical, metaframework into which we can adequately translate any language or paradigm and thereby evaluate rival paradigms by an appeal to determinate universal criteria.[13] But neither Kuhn nor Gadamer are calling into question the rationality involved in the comparison of rival paradigms or different horizons. They are challenging what they take to be a misguided and inadequate *theory* of rationality—one committed to clear, determinate, algorithmic decision procedures in evaluating competing claims.

The very metaphor of being prisoners locked into our frameworks, theories, and languages is misguided because it is our inherited fore-knowledge that enables us to reach beyond our limited horizons. But how is this to be accomplished? It is here that Gadamer's understanding and appeal to dialogue becomes so relevant. Gadamer is primarily concerned with our ongoing dialogue with tradition and those classic texts that still have the power to speak to us across temporal distance. But his analysis of the dynamics of dialogue is sufficiently rich to be applicable to whatever we encounter as Other—whether another person, religion, or culture. Beginning with a phenomenological analysis of the to-and-fro movement of play and games where the dynamic structure of play absorbs the player into itself, Gadamer tells us:

> Now I contend that the basic constitution of the game, to be filled with its spirit—the spirit of buoyancy, freedom and the joy of success—and to fulfill him who is playing, is structurally related to the constitution of the dialogue in which language is a reality. When one enters into dialogue with another person and then is carried along further by the dialogue, it is no longer the will of the individual person, holding itself back or exposing itself, that is determinative. Rather, the law of the subject matter [die Sache] is at issue in the dialogue and elicits statement and counter statement and in the end plays them into each other.[14]

For Gadamer, it is always the memory of a living dialogue that informs our dialogue with tradition, texts, and other cultures. We have to learn in this to-and-fro movement what questions are appropriate for what we seek to understand. We have to present the Other in its strongest possible light in order to understand the claim of truth that it makes upon us. This does not mean that we arrive at agreement. In a true conversation or dialogue where we open ourselves to the Other, "truly accepting his point of view as worthy of consideration," we achieve a more discriminating nuanced understanding of *both* our disagreements or conflicts *and* what we share in common.

We see then that for Gadamer all understanding is comparative. And in such a comparison, we not only risk our prejudices and prejudgments, we also need to learn how to imaginatively extend or modify the very categories and genres of our descriptions. This point is perceptively illustrated by Alasdair MacIntyre in the context of anthropology. Speaking of Frazer and John Beattie, MacIntyre tells us:

> To a Frazer, who classified primitive rites as inept technology, we are apt to reply that such rites are not science but, for example, akin of poetry or drama. Thus John Beattie asserts magic is not technology but "the acting out of the expression of desire in symbolic terms." . . . It is, however right to wonder whether, sophisticated as we are, we may not sometimes at least make Fraser's mistake, but in a more subtle way. For when we approach the utterances of an alien culture with well-established classifications of genres in our mind and ask of a given rite or other practice "Is it a piece of applied science? Or a

piece of symbolic and dramatic activity? Or a piece of theology?" we may in fact be asking a set of questions to which any answer may be misleading . . . . For the utterances and practices in question may belong, as it were, to all and to none of the genres that we have in mind . . . . Questions of rationality and irrationality cannot be appropriately posed until in a given culture the relevant utterances are given a decisive interpretation in terms of genres. Myths would then be seen as perhaps potentially science *and* literature *and* theology; but to understand them as myths would be to understand them as actually yet none of these.[15]

We all know how difficult and complex this task can be—that it requires concrete historical knowledge, imagination, and sensitivity to context. This is why abstract discussions about what constitutes philosophy, science, myth, religion, and so on can seem so sterile. We cannot begin any inquiry without drawing upon the repertoire of categories, genres, and modes of description that are available to us—which have complex histories and are far more fluid than we frequently acknowledge. We never escape the danger that, in seeking to understand, we will impose inappropriate genres and thereby distort what we seek to understand. What hermeneutics teaches us is that there is no algorithm or methodological maxim that will protect us from this danger—once and for all. It is a danger and risk constitutive of our hermeneutical situation. But this is precisely why the to-and-fro play of concrete dialogical encounters is so important. Indeed, this is the point of the insistence upon the hermeneutic circle where there is a to-and-fro play of part and whole, concrete detail and global understanding. Clifford Geertz expresses this when he characterizes ethnological work as

> a continuous dialectical tacking between the most local of local detail and the most global of global structure in such a way as to bring both in view simultaneously . . . . Hopping back and forth between the whole conceived through the parts which actualize it and the parts conceived through the whole which motivates them, we seek to turn them, by a sort of intellectual perpetual motion, into explications of one another.[16]

But still there is the nagging and nasty question—how do we know when we have achieved an adequate understanding of the Other. If "adequate" is taken to mean a final complete understanding, then this is impossible—ontologically impossible. The very historicity of our being, with our changing foreknowledge, precludes any such finality. At best we can achieve what David Tracy calls "relative adequacy."[17] But if we grant this, we still want to know what makes an interpretation more or less relatively adequate, how are we to discriminate better and worse,

more perspicuous and less perspicuous interpretations—even if we concede the possibility of a plurality of interpretations. I think that what
hermeneutics teaches us is that there is no way of answering these questions by appealing to *abstract* criteria and standards. Even when we
speak of comprehensiveness, coherence, intelligibility, "making sense,"
and so on we are appealing to what may turn out to be contested plati-
tudes. But this doesn't mean that we cannot evaluate and judge the
appropriateness of specific interpretations—especially when presented
with a conflict of interpretations.

What do we do in cases where a given interpretation is challenged
or contested? We ask for specific evidence and reasons for claiming that
one interpretation is better than another. Willy-nilly, in offering an interpretation, we are always making what Habermas calls validity-claims that
are always open to ongoing criticism. We may and do dispute about
what counts as better and worse reasons in support of our interpretations. Stated in another way, even the relative adequacy of an interpretation is always uncertain—always in principle open to anticipated questioning. But if we give up or modify an interpretation we rightfully expect
that we will be shown why some other interpretation is more adequate—
or perhaps even why there may be conflicting interpretations. This uncertainty is constitutive of hermeneutical understanding. We cannot escape from it. We have to learn to live with it. This is one reason why
hermeneutics so deeply offends those who want more certainty, who
want epistemic algorithms where there can only be *phronesis* (cultivated
practical judgment).

I have attempted to give a sympathetic account of some
hermeneutical motifs. I have sought to do what Gadamer is always urg-
ing us to do—to present what we seek to understand in the strongest
possible light in order to discern the claim to truth that it makes upon us.
But I have also asserted that hermeneutics is only one element in a new
constellation that needs to be juxtaposed with other elements. Or to use
the metaphor of a force-field, we need to grasp the interplay of attractions and adversions with the Other of hermeneutics. For there are many
problems with hermeneutics—problems concerning the meaning of truth,
tradition, and authority; how we are able to relate a hermeneutics of trust
to a hermeneutics of suspicion; problems concerning the ways in which
power relations distort and block dialogical encounters. After all, most of
the situations that Gadamer characterizes as dialogical are not genuine
dialogues—in the sense that there is an independent voice that speaks
for itself. Typically, it is "we" interpreters who represent the "voice of the
other." And of course, there are problems concerning the precise role of
critique in our attempts to understand the Other.[18] But in this context I

want to pursue some of the difficulties that come into sharp relief when we turn to Derrida's deconstructive strategies.

Gadamer's ontological hermeneutics can itself be interpreted as a palimpsest where the layers of his appropriations of Plato, Aristotle, German Romanticism, Hegel, and Heidegger are still visible. What is always foregrounded in Gadamer is the moment of irenic reconciliation. Although Gadamer sometimes characterizes himself as a Hegelian of the "bad infinite" because the hermeneutic experience always opens itself to further experience, and because there can be no finality to hermeneutical understanding, it is the ontological need and demand for reconciliation to which he returns. What is lacking in Gadamer is an equally profound sense of the ruptures, breaks, fissures, gaps—the dis-ruptions that break out in our attempts to fuse horizons. Theoretically and practically, this has become much more manifest and poignant in the twentieth century. It is the irreducible otherness of the Other—its irreducible alterity that tends to be glossed over by Gadamer, and is always in the foreground for Derrida. Frequently, hermeneutics and deconstruction are set over against each other as if they were absolute antitheses—as if they were an exclusive Either/Or. But pursuing the metaphors of constellation and force-field, I want to argue that they stand in a tensed, unstable "relation" of Both/And.

Derrida tells us "deconstruction is, in itself, a positive response to an alterity which necessarily calls, summons or motivates it. Deconstruction is therefore a vocation—a response to a call." Deconstruction is "an openness towards the other."[19] Derrida's response to the Other is itself motivated by ethical-political concerns that pervade all his writings. I know this is not the way in which Derrida has been read and "appropriated" but in another context I have tried to show how an ethical-political horizon is a point of departure for understanding his deconstructive strategies.[20] (Indeed, I think both Gadamer and Derrida lead us back to the primacy of the practical and the ethical). We can witness Derrida's ethical-political concern even in his deconstruction of the metaphysics of presence. For Derrida relentlessly seeks to show us how the tradition of Western metaphysics (and what he sometimes calls "the history of the West") seeks to impose a hierarchical axiology where ethical-ontological distinctions do not merely set up value oppositions but subordinate these values to each other. Furthermore, by returning to or seeking an origin that is taken as prior and is held to be simple, intact, pure, standard, or self-identical, this enterprise then thinks in terms of derivation, exclusion, and marginalization. And Derrida tells us "All metaphysicians, from Plato to Rousseau, Descartes to Husserl, have proceeded in this way, conceiving good to be before evil, the positive before the negative, the simple before the complex, the essential before the accidental, the imitated before the imitation. And thus is not *one* metaphysical gesture among others, it is *the* metaphysical exigency, that has been the most constant, most profound and most potent."[21]

So even here, in Derrida's deconstruction of metaphysics and logocentrism, he is concerned to expose the potent drive toward subordination, marginalization, exile, suppression, and repression of the Other. If we examine much of the philosophy of religion until the present, we can detect vulgar and sophisticated forms of this potent drive. Derrida's language is not that of dialogue, reconciliation, and fusion. It is the language of double readings, double gestures, and double binds. We are always haunted by otherness that never can be completely mastered, domesticated, or contained. And this otherness does not necessarily come from what is "outside." As he tells us, "from the very beginnings of Greek philosophy, the self-identity of the Logos is already fissured and divided."[22] When Derrida tells us that *différance* is a nonconcept or undecidable, he wants to emphasize that "it cannot be defined in terms of oppositional predicates; it is neither *this* nor *that;* but rather this *and* that . . . without being reducible to a dialectical logic."[23] Derrida desperately seeks to break the Hegelian movement from identity to difference to opposition to contradiction to the resolution of contradiction in the "true infinite." For he detects in this movement the drive to "appropriate" the irreducible otherness of *différance* to the dialectical logic of the same and the Other.

But how is this related to hermeneutics? Consider its bearing on the basic hermeneutical motif of dialogue. I do not think Derrida is calling into question the possibility of dialogue. Rather he is showing us the multifarious ways in which it goes wrong and breaks down—that it is an illusion to think that, even in what may seem to be "ideal" conditions of face-to-face spoken communication, we can avoid the danger of supression or repression of the otherness of the Other. And I think Derrida is right that even the gesture of "authentic dialogue" can be complicit with an act of violence—where there is a subtle demand that the Other speak in our language and accept our categories and genres. This is not just an abstract possibility. For it happens all too frequently when there are unequal power relations in the partners of a dialogue. Dialogue itself is threatened by all the traps of logocentrism. There is a constant danger in all comparative analysis that our gestures of openness can betray a subtle and invidious form of ethical-political valorization. What Derrida is showing us is that this is always a danger and a risk. It is an illusion to think we can ever fully escape from it. This is one of the motivations for his language of double binds and double gestures.

So we must be wary of the potential hidden violence in seeking a fusion of horizons. We must be wary that our attempted reconciliations do not mask ruptures, fissures, and *différance* that cannot be reconciled. Derrida tells us:

> We must avoid the temptation of supposing that what occurs today somehow pre-existed in a latent form, merely waiting to be unfolded as an evolutionary development and excludes the crucial notions of rupture and mutation in history. My own conviction is that we must maintain two contradictory affirmations at the same time. On the one hand we affirm the existence of ruptures in history, and on the other we affirm that these ruptures produce gaps or faults (*failles*) in which the most hidden and forgotten archives can emerge and constantly recur and work through history. One must surmount the categorical oppositions of philosophical logic out of fidelity to these conflicting positions of historical discontinuity (rupture) and continuity (repetition) which are neither a pure break with the past nor a pure unfolding or explication of it.[24]

If we return to what I referred to as the shattering of the Hegelian synthesis, we might say that both Gadamer and Derrida are profoundly aware of the double movement of reconciliation and rupture, but Gadamer foregrounds the moment of reconciliation while Derrida foregrounds those ruptures of otherness that are never quite *aufgehoben*.

It would a mistake to think that Derrida is simply celebrating *différance* and otherness—or that he slips into a metaphysical reification of *différance* that is a mirror image of the metaphysics of presence. We can see this in his critical engagement with Levinas.[25] Levinas's formulation of the "problem of the other" is one of the most extreme and radical in the twentieth century. From his perspective the entire tradition of Western philosophy, from Parmenides through Hegel to Husserl and Heidegger, has been ensnared in a dialectic of same and Other where the temptation has always been to encompass or reduce the Other to the same. But this dialectic fails to do justice to what he names the "absolute Other" with its "absolute exteriority." This absolute Other, which he calls the infinite or the metaphysical Other, is an "other with an alterity that is not formal, is not the simple reverse of identity, and is not formed out of resistance to the same, but is prior to every initiative to all imperialism of the same."[26] It is, he says, the stranger (*L'Étranger*) who genuinely disturbs or ruptures the being at home with oneself (*le chez soi*).[27] It is this radically asymmetrical and incommensurable "relation" between the I and the Absolute Other (a "relation" that defies reduction to reciprocal equality) that characterizes what Levinas calls the ethical relation—the face-to-face. Levinas boldly claims the primacy of this ethical "relation" over all ontology.

Derrida questions the very intelligibility of Levinas's notion of the Absolute Other and Absolute Exteriority. He rightly points out how

"Levinas is very close to Hegel, much closer than he admits, and at the very moment when he is apparently opposed to Hegel in the most radical fashion. This is the situation he must share with all anti-Hegelian thinkers."[28] Derrida agrees with Levinas that "the other is the other only if his alterity is absolutely irreducible, that is, infinitely irreducible."[29] But against Levinas, who claims that "to make the other an alter ego . . . is to neutralize its absolute alterity," Derrida argues that "if the other were not recognized as ego, its entire alterity would collapse."[30] The Other, then, "would not be what he is (my fellow man or foreigner) if he were not an alter ego—the other is absolutely other if he is an ego, that is, in a certain way, if he is the same as I."[31] This last claim sounds as if Derrida is siding with Hegel (and Gadamer) against Levinas. But to draw this conclusion would miss the subtlety (and instability) of what Derrida is showing. His "logic" itself, is neither a dialectical logic of reconciliation nor a logic of Either/Or. It is a logic of tensed Both/And—both sameness and radical alterity, both reciprocalness and nonreciprocalness in our "relation" to the Other.

Now the question may be asked—what do these reflections on the otherness of the Other and the double gesture of reconciliation/rupture have to do with a philosophy of religion that is comparative and historical? The constellation of juxtaposed elements that defy integration and the force-field of unstable dynamic attractions and repulsions that I have been sketching provides a matrix for our thinking and praxis. It highlights the double movements and double gestures in any serious comparative work. There is the need to do justice to the otherness and singularity of the Other and the need to seek reconciliation. And both movements have their dangers. For in our desire for reconciliation—in reaching out to understand what is strange, other, and different, we may inadvertently suppress or repress the otherness of the Other. And we may also fall into the trap of claiming that the Other is so absolute, so exterior to our experience, that we undermine the very possibility of understanding and relating ourselves to the Other.

The new constellation and force-field have practical consequences for a philosophy of religion that is comparative and historical. They teach us that we must be self-conscious and self-reflexive about the dangers of slipping into a false essentialism. We cannot describe or understand without using categories and genre concepts. We always begin our inquiries from our own horizons and with the prejudgments that we have inherited from the traditions in which we participate. But we must be vigilant in questioning these genre concepts. We must realize that such concepts as "philosophy," "religion," and "myth" are themselves essentially contested concepts. We must be sensitive to the ways in which we use them if we are not to distort what we are seeking to understand. We must be aware of those imperialistic and colonizing gestures where we judge and evaluate what is other by standards and categories which we take for granted.

Furthermore, both hermeneutics and deconstruction teach us that comparison is intrinsic for any project of understanding. Comparison is not merely a supplement (except in the Derridian sense of a "supplement"). As Gadamer shows us, we can only understand ourselves and our own traditions (including our religious traditions) by risking our prejudgments, and this is to be achieved in and through a hermeneutical encounter with what is Other. And Derrida (as well as Levinas) expose the constant temptation to "reduce" the Other to the same. They teach us how difficult it is to do justice to the singularity and the otherness of the Other. Furthermore, we need to realize just how tentative and fallible we are in seeking to understand our own and other traditions. We must aspire to a fusion of horizons in which we seek to do justice to *both* commonalities and differences, but we can never fully anticipate those ruptures that dis-rupt our projects of reconciliation. There is no way to completely domesticate and contain the threat of otherness.

But still it will be asked, how is this to be done? How are we to practice such a philosophy of religion? What criteria, standards, methods, and procedures are we to employ? It should be clear that there cannot be an univocal answer to these questions. And here we touch upon one of the deepest anxieties that has haunted so much of modern thought and epistemology. In another context I have called this the "Cartesian anxiety."[32] It is the anxiety that unless we can specify a firm foundation for our knowledge claims, unless we can appeal to clear determinate ahistorical criteria for deciding what is true and false, correct and incorrect, then the only alternative is to fall into the abyss of a self-defeating relativism where "anything goes."

But perhaps the most important consequence of the new constellation and force-field is an increasing realization that we must *exorcise* this Cartesian anxiety. We cannot achieve the "metaphysical comfort" of knowing that our knowledge and interpretations rest upon a secure fixed Archemedian point or foundation. There is no escape from uncertainty, ambiguity, and what Derrida calls "undecidability." I am tempted to say— to use an old-fashioned, but not outdated, expression—that this is constitutive of the human condition, of our being-in-the-world. Nevertheless, when our claims to understand and our interpretations are challenged, we must also be prepared to give the best *historical* reasons that we can to support (or to modify) them—with a full awareness that even what "we" take to be good reasons are themselves always open to further challenge and criticism. It makes no sense to think that there is or can be a closure to the open practices of ongoing critique. Instead of focusing on the illusory search for ahistorical permanent criteria, we should focus our attention on the difficult and complex task of sorting out what is right and wrong, adequate and inadequate, in specific instances of competing and conflicting understandings and interpretations.

Although the authors in this volume are extraordinarily diverse in their subject matter and the methods and procedures that they employ, they all exemplify and contribute to the constellation and the force-field that I have been adumbrating. Let me conclude by summarizing some of the motifs that weave in and out of their chapters.

1. They are expressions of what—to use a Heideggerian phrase—is a new *stimmung* ("mood") that affects so much of twentieth-century thought and action. If I were to name it, I would call it radical ontological pluralism in which there is a growing recognition of the irreducible plurality of forms of life—of the spiritual possibilities that can shape our lives. This plurality is ontological because it goes to the heart of our being-in-the-world; it is at once threatening and challenging. It threatens the bias that what is genuinely other can be comprehended or reduced to the same. It is challenging because it is in and through the dialogical encounter with the Other that we achieve a deeper understanding of both ourselves and the Other. This is the way of concretely extending a sense of "we" where plurality and difference are constitutive of the "we."

2. Although there has been an epistemological fascination with the "myth of the framework" and the type of self-defeating enclosed relativism it evokes, I am inclined to say this is something of a red herring—a diversionary side issue. There is virtually no evidence that any of the participants subscribes to this myth. On the contrary all seem to share the hermeneutical principle that our foreknowledge does not imprison us but *enables* us to understand the Other.

3. Although there is always the danger of ethnocentrism (in its pejorative sense) and distortion, and although we can never hope to escape completely from these dangers, it is nevertheless precisely by historical, comparative dialogue that we can achieve critical distance from our prejudices and thereby correct distortions. Distortion takes place *within*

the project of understanding and is corrected within the hermeneutical endeavor to understand. It is fallacious to think that because all understanding presupposes fore-knowledge that it must be necessarily distortive.

4. Perhaps the most difficult task in seeking to understand the otherness of the Other—especially other religious forms of life—is learning how imaginatively to extend, modify, and enrich our categories and genres of classification and description. There is no general method for achieving this. It requires *phronesis* and judgment which are, in principle, always open to criticism.

5. In seeking reconciliations that attempt to do justice to the otherness of the Other, we can never quite anticipate the ruptures, breaks, disruptions that call into question our attempted reconciliations.

6. Finally, pervading all these motifs and the *stimmung* I have sought to characterize is an underlying ethical-political concern. We can witness this in Gadamer when he tells us that hermeneutics is the heir to the older tradition of practical philosophy. And the concern is just as primary for Derrida when he declares that deconstruction is to be characterized by the openness to the Other—and he keeps returning to the questions of response, responsiveness, and responsibility. Although I have indicated some critical reservations about Levinas, I am convinced one of the reasons why he is now receiving so much critical attention is because he so explicitly and sharply links the question of the Other with ethics as first philosophy.

Returning to my original citation from Theunissen, I think that a primary reason why the "problem of the Other" has "penetrated so deeply into the foundations of philosophical thought" and cannot be separated from "the most primordial questions raised by modern thought" is because when we grapple with the challenge of otherness, when we seek a reconciliation with the Other and are aware of ruptures and breaks from which we never fully escape, then the ethical-political problematic that has become so urgent for us today comes into sharp relief. For what David Tracy calls the new founding of a comparative philosophy of religion is itself motivated by, and an expression of, the unstable tensed double gesture of the desire to do justice to the otherness of the Other *and* to seek reconciliation with the Other.

Notes

1. Theunissen, *The Other*, 1.

2. Ibid.

3. Hegel, *The Phenomenology of Spirit*, 110.

4. Hegel, *Phenomenology*, 111.

5. Habermas, *The Philosophic Discourse of Modernity*.

6. Hegel, *Phenomenology*, 357.

7. Ibid.

8. Lyotard, *The Postmodern Condition*, 81–82.

9. Jay, *Adorno*, 14–15.

10. Peirce, *Collected Papers*, 5:265.

11. See Bernstein, *Beyond Objectivism and Relativism*, part 2.

12. Popper, "Normal Science and Its Dangers," 56.

13. See Bernstein, *Beyond Objectivism and Relativism*, 79–92.

14. Gadamer, "Man and Language," 66.

15. MacIntyre, "Rationality and the Explanation of Action," 252–53.

16. Geertz, "From the Native's Point of View," 239.

17. Tracy, *Plurality and Ambiguity*.

18. See Bernstein, *Beyond Objectivism and Relativism*, 150–69.

19. Derrida, "Dialogue with Jacques Derrida," 118.

20. See Bernstein, "Serious Play."

21. Derrida, *Limited Inc.*, 93.

22. Derrida, "Dialogue," 117.

23. Ibid., 113.

24. Ibid.

25. See Derrida, "Violence and Metaphysics."

26. Levinas, *Totality and Infinity*, 38.

27. Ibid., 39.

28. Derrida, "Violence and Metaphysics," 99.

29. Ibid., 104.

30. Ibid., 125.

31. Ibid., 127.

32. See Bernstein, *Beyond Objectivism and Relativism*, 16–25.

References

Bernstein, R. J.
1983 *Beyond Objectivism and Relativism: Science, Hermeneutics, and Praxis*. Philadelphia: University of Pennsylvania Press.

———.
1987 "Serious Play: The Ethical Political Horizon of Jacques Derrida." *Journal of Speculative Philosophy* 1:93–117.

Derrida, J.
1978 "Violence and Metaphysics: An Essay on the Thought of Emmanual Levinas." In *Writing and Difference*, 79–153. Translated by A. Bass. Chicago: University of Chicago Press.

———.
1984 "Dialogue with Jacques Derrida." In *Dialogues with Contemporary Continental Thinkers*, 105–26. Edited by R. Kearney. Manchester, England: Manchester University Press.

———.
1988 *Limited Inc.* Evanston, Ill.: Northwestern University Press.

Gadamer, H. G.
1976 "Man and Language." In *Philosophical Hermeneutics*, 59–68. Translated by D. E. Linge. Berkeley: University of California Press.

Geertz, C.
1979 "From the Native's Point of View: On the Nature of Anthropological Understanding." In *Interpretive Social Science*. Edited by P. Rabinow and W. Sullivan. Berkeley: University of California Press.

Habermas, J.
1987 *The Philosophical Discourse of Modernity*. Translated by F. Lawrence. Cambridge, Mass.: MIT Press.

Hegel, G. W. F.
1977 *The Phenomenology of Spirit*. Translated by A. V. Miller. Oxford: Oxford University Press.

Jay, M.
1989 *Adorno*. Cambridge: Harvard University Press.

Levinas, E.
1969 *Totality and Infinity*. Translated by A. Lingis. Pittsburgh: Duquesne University Press.

Lyotard, J. F.
1984 "Answering the Question: What is Postmodernism." In *The Postmodern Condition: A Report on Knowledge*, 71–82. Translated by G. Bennignton and B. Massumi. Minneapolis: University of Minnesota Press.

MacIntyre, A.
1971 "Rationality and the Explanation of Action." In *Against the Self-Images of the Age*. New York: Schocken Books.

Peirce, C. S.
1931–35 "Some Consequences of Four Incapacities." In *Collected Papers of Charles S. Peirce*. Edited by C. Hartshore and Paul Weiss. Cambridge: Harvard University Press.

Popper, K.
1970 "Normal Science and its Dangers." In *Criticism and the Growth of Knowledge*. Edited by I. Lakatos and A. Misgrave. Cambridge: Cambridge University Press.

Theunissen, M.
1984 *The Other: Studies in the Social Ontology of Husserl, Heidegger, Sartre and Buber*. Translated by C. Macann. Cambridge, Mass.: MIT Press [*Der Andere* was first published in 1965. The second revised German edition appeared in 1977.]

Tracy, D.
1987 *Plurality and Ambiguity: Hermeneutics, Religion, Hope*. San Francisco: Harper and Row.

Index

Academy: modern, 6; neo-Confucian, 244; metapractice of, 101; practice of, 84, 102; Western, 15, 39, 218

Body, 6, 176–177, 189, 192 n.13, 192 n.18, 203, 216

Comparison, 44 n.19, 87; and analysis, 15; anthropological, 14; cross-cultural, 15, 44 n.17, 55, 56, 112, 190; of Durkheim and Xunzi, 215; of Rahner and Kukai, 187–188; structure of, 16
Comparative: philosophy, 239, 255; philosophy of religions, 187, 285, 308, 311; study of religion, 198, 263, 296, 299; understanding, 264, 265, 269–270, 283
Conversation, 8, 55, 240, 251, 255, 264, 302
Cosmogony: Buddhist, 65
Cosmology: of the Bimin-Kuskusmin, 15; Christian, 86, 93, 95

Deconstruction, 8, 56, 127, 197, 300, 305–306, 311
Dialogue, 264, 273, 298, 301–302, 304, 306
Discourse, 2, 40 n.3; and action, 283; community of, 189; denaturalized, 4, 83–84, 101, 271; hierarchy of, 93, 99; metahistorical, 54; metapractical, 6, 266; and practice, 265; and praxis, 98; scientific, 54

Embodiment, 7, 97, 207, 246, 247, 256
Exegesis, 14, 123, 134–135

Hierarchy, 5, 19, 141, 145–148, 210–211, 305; of discourse, 93, 99

Image, 14–15, 22, 33, 269, 277
Imagination, 14–15, 22, 142, 303

Language: and action, 273; discursive, 23; functions of, 236; moral, 267, 274; and myth, 84; philosophical, 236, 239; and positivism, 189; and practice, 239, 255; religious, 189; ritual, 21, 36

Metaphor, 15–16, 23, 39, 44 n.13, 84, 132, 209, 236–237, 255, 269–272
Metaphysics, 6; Bimin-Kuskusmin, 14, 39; Christian, 176; and metapractice, 172–175, 180–182, 188, 184–185; and narrative, 185; and salvation, 100
Metapractice, 2, 3, 5; of the academy, 101; and discourse, 6, 266; and metaphysics, 174–179, 180–182, 188, 184–185
Metapraxis, 2, 5, 174–175
Myth: biblical, 5; of the framework, 301, 310; and history, 16, 32; and interpretation, 14, 23, 25, 27–29, 31–34, 38, 115, 133; and language, 84; of origins, 142, 154; of original equality, 5, 151; of original sin, 71;